FOUL BALL

**MY LIFE AND HARD TIMES
TRYING TO SAVE AN OLD BALLPARK**

Plus **PART II**

JIM
BOUTON

THE LYONS PRESS

Guilford, Connecticut

An imprint of The Globe Pequot Press

www.foulball.com

To buy books in quantity for corporate use
or incentives, call **(800) 962–0973, ext. 4551,**
or e-mail **premiums@GlobePequot.com.**

The Lyons Press is an imprint of The Globe Pequot Press

10 9 8 7 6 5 4 3 2 1

Printed in the United States of America

Designed by Glenn LeDoux

ISBN 1-59228-867-7

Library of Congress Cataloging-in-Publication data is available on file.

For my grandchildren

CONTENTS

"Like me, you could . . . be unfortunate enough to stumble upon a silent war. The trouble is that once you see it, you can't *un*see it. And once you've seen it, keeping quiet, saying nothing, becomes as political an act as speaking out. Either way, you're accountable."

—**Arundhati Roy**

INTRODUCTION

I never intended to write this book. For months I had been throwing notes in a file to write a different book. It was going to be about my 1940s childhood, a *Huckleberry Finn*-type adventure tale of underground forts and tree huts, inventing games and choosing up sides, and being the only ten-year-old in Rochelle Park, New Jersey, with a paper route and an overhand curve that dropped off a table.

Then I got caught up in a more exciting adventure.

You are no doubt familiar with America's most costly hostage crisis, perpetrated by the owners of professional sports teams: "Build us a new stadium," they warn, "or you'll never see your team again." This is intended to spread panic in the streets, or at least in the mayor's office and in the newspapers.

The only people, besides team owners, who want new stadiums are politicians, lawyers, and the media. Politicos like to swagger around a palace—and stadiums are the modern palaces—the bigger the better, especially for mayors suffering from stadium envy. They like to watch games from the owner's box in full view of the TV cameras and hang out in the clubhouse with the players. This is in addition to the usual perks, graft, kickbacks, and patronage that accrue to politicians on big construction projects.

For lawyers, a new stadium offers a virtual buffet. First they get to represent the team against the city, then the city against the people. Then they draft the arguments against a ballot question, and if that doesn't work, they draft the *language* of the ballot question. Then the bond guys come in and collect astronomical fees for underwriting the municipal debt that will pay for the new stadium. Why do they get so much money for doing that? It would take a lawyer to explain it.

The most insidious of the new-stadium supporters are the media, the so-called free press that Thomas Jefferson once said was more important to a democracy than a legislature. Sportswriters, disguised as journalists, pour out the pro-stadium ink, not just because the swankier press boxes make them feel Big League, but because their bosses frequently own part or all of the team. Even "hard news" reporters and "independent" columnists know which side their laptops are buttered on.

Those who don't want new stadiums includes just about everyone else—people who: (1) prefer spending tax dollars on schools and hospitals, (2) don't own adjacent real estate, (3) know how to add and subtract.

We're not just talking about a few million dollars of corporate welfare. The amount of public money spent on sports stadiums over the past fifteen years is estimated to be in excess of *$16 billion*. And that's just what's visible.

Why do so many new stadiums get built if most people don't want them? Because most people don't get to vote on the matter. New-stadium proponents—who also know how to add and subtract—do everything in their collective power to keep the question off the ballot. As Rudolph Giuliani so eloquently put it when asked why New Yorkers should not be allowed to vote on a new stadium, "Because they would vote against it."

The fiercest competition in sports these days is not between teams or leagues but between governments and their own citizens. New stadiums are often guided past the rocky shoals of referendums by lame-duck mayors, friendly courts, and compromised county executives—all supported by dire warnings from the local media that the loss of baseball, or the end of the world as they know it, is at hand.

"If we build it, they will come" has evolved into, "If we don't build it, they will go."

No community, no matter how loyal to its team or financially strapped, is exempt from this shameful tactic. A perennial target is New York City, which faces the theoretical loss of the Yankees to New Jersey—where owner George Steinbrenner has been threatening to move for the past dozen years. It's a bluff, of course—as if Steinbrenner really wants to be a big shot in East Rutherford—but it's a useful excuse for mayors needing a rationale to do something that makes no economic sense whatsoever, at least according to studies done by consultants not on the city payroll.

In spite of the evidence and his understanding of the people's wishes, Yankee fan Rudolph Giuliani, in his last act as mayor, pushed forward plans for *two* new stadiums—one each for the Yankees and Mets, to show what a nonpartisan guy he is—totaling $1.6 billion! The teams themselves would pay a small portion of that sum for cosmetic reasons, but the bulk of the $1.6 billion, plus cost overruns and a minimum of $300 million in transportation upgrades, would fall to the city, landing on its taxpayers.

And this was *after* the terrorist attacks of September 11, 2001, with the city facing a budget gap of $4 billion and a projected debt of $40 billion!

By the way, for you landmark preservationists, one of the proposed sites for a *new* Yankee Stadium, other than the rail yards on the west side of Manhattan, is McCombs Dam Park across from the *old* Yankee Stadium, which would then be demolished to make room for a parking garage. There's no word yet on whether this will be called "The Garage That Ruth Built."

Did anyone from the Yankees or Mets express appreciation to the city for this proposed bonanza? Not exactly. Steinbrenner indicated that he was actually more thrilled for his fellow New Yorkers. "Our fans shouldn't have to wait on line for restrooms and concessions," he said unselfishly on their behalf.

The latest refinement in the owners-holding-teams-hostage game is the threat of eliminating teams altogether via "contraction"—baseball's linguistic equivalent of "collateral damage." This is what faced the Montreal Expos and Minnesota Twins, whose taxpayers have had the temerity to refuse to build new stadiums. In the Twins' case, taxpayers refused to build a *second* new stadium to replace the Metrodome (which opened in 1984), which itself had replaced Metropolitan Stadium where I once pitched against Harmon Killebrew and Tony Oliva. It was only in the negotiations with the Players Association that averted a strike in 2002 that the contraction threat was lifted. But even that is temporary. Part of the deal is that the owners can contract up to two teams after the 2006 season. I wonder if the decision to wait had anything to do with the fact that the most obvious candidate for a 2003 contraction would have been the last-place Milwaukee Brewers—the commissioner's daughter's team.

It's a national epidemic that gets even crazier as you go down the ladder from the majors to the minors. In minor league towns new stadiums are promoted not just as a necessity but as a bargain! Lured by free parking and $2 hot dogs, fans are flocking to multimillion dollar stadiums built with *their* tax dollars. It's as if Joe Sixpack were to help pay for a movie theater in order to get fifty cents off on popcorn.

Unfortunately, there is no vaccine for economic illiteracy. Since 1985, no fewer than 113 minor league baseball stadiums have been built with taxpayer dollars. And the cities let this happen. What's more, they compete with one another to see who can offer the best deal to some team or league—at the expense of their own citizens.

Let them eat hot dogs!

With this in mind, I had followed with some interest the fortunes of Wahconah Park, one of the oldest ballparks in America. Located in Pittsfield, Massachusetts, in the heart of the Berkshire mountains, Wahconah Park has hosted professional baseball since 1892. To attend a game there—with its wooden grandstand, corrugated roof, and plastic owls dangling from the rafters to ward off the pigeons—is to step back in time.

Baseball aficionados, who rank everything from the ballparks to the bratwurst at the concession stands, consistently rate Wahconah Park among the top ten venues in the country. *Money* magazine calls it "the definitive old-time minor league experience" and ranks it in the top five. "Just a little bit of heaven," says *Sports Illustrated*. It leads the league in superlatives. "This rugged Berkshire beauty" has also been called "a great baseball cathedral," "one of the gems in the Northeast," "a throwback to another era," and "Rockwellesque," to name a few.

The place reeks of atmosphere, incorporating the three necessary ingredients for a great ballpark—intimacy, character, and an evocation of the past. This last is the most important, for it is baseball, above all the other sports, that connects the generations. I still remember the day I became a New York Giants fan—at the age of seven. It was 1946. My dad, just back from the war, was digging a dry well in front of our house in Rochelle Park.

"Who's your favorite team, Dad?" I asked.

"The Giants," he said. Simple as that.

From that moment on I rooted for Bobby Thomson and Willie Mays and Whitey Lockman and the rest of the guys. Once or twice every summer my brother Bob and I would go to the Polo Grounds to watch the Giants. We'd go a couple of hours early and sit in the upper deck, above the big Chesterfield pack that hung on the facade, and try to catch balls during batting practice.

The Polo Grounds was especially interesting because it was primarily built for football. Wedging a square baseball field into a rectangular stadium chopped off the foul lines at 280 feet in left, 259 in right, and ballooned out center field to 505 feet. Cheap home runs coexisted with titanic outs.

Not unlike Wahconah Park, whose quirky dimensions offer its own sublime balance. With a grandstand as close to home plate as the pitcher—which is great for fans—there aren't many easy pop fouls, a gift to batters. This is offset by the 434-foot death valley in right center, a gift to pitchers. The park giveth and the park taketh away.

It also hath a history. In 1922 the legendary Jim Thorpe, America's greatest athlete, played center field and went three-for-four for Worcester against the hometown Pittsfield Hillies of the Eastern League. Two years later, a first baseman for the Hartford Senators by the name of Lou Gehrig played three games there, going three-for-nine with a long home run over the center-field fence. In 1925 Casey Stengel, playing for Worcester, was "banished from the park" following a confrontation with "the arbiter" after getting called out on strikes. The park also hosted boxing, featuring greats Willie Pep and Sugar Ray Robinson.

What Wahconah Park may be most noted for, however, is the fact that it was built backwards. As a result, the sun sets over the center field fence and shines in the batters' eyes for ten minutes or so on certain nights. But it's not a tragedy. The umpire suspends play, the players retreat to their dugouts, and the concession stands rake in a few extra bucks. It's a sun delay—Mother Nature's own marketing opportunity.

I once pitched at Wahconah Park back in 1972, when I first toyed with the idea of a comeback, and what was then a Texas Ranger farm team gave me a tryout. I'd been up for a weekend in the Berkshires with my family, staying at a local B&B, and I drove over with my glove and spikes—you never know when a pitcher's mound might become available. I had decent stuff that day, but apparently not enough—for a thirty-three-year-old pariah author.

Now I actually live in the Berkshires, in a town called North Egremont, and Wahconah Park is only a half hour north. But no more tryouts. I just watch the games.

And often reflect on the meaning of a ballpark.

When I was a kid, you started by playing in the backyard—catch, punch ball, running bases. Or you went down to "the field," usually behind a school. Home plate was a bent piece of rubber imbedded in the ground between two scooped-out holes that filled with water when it rained. The pitcher's mound was actually a pit, with a block of wood sticking up that you could break your ankle trying to pitch off. Bases were pieces of paper with rocks on them. Balls were wrapped with black friction tape. Game balls were wrapped with white adhesive tape from your mom's medicine cabinet. Practice balls had yarn flying off them as they sailed through the air.

As you got older you played on fields with grass and team benches, in front of girlfriends who sat on blankets, and old men who watched through a chain-link backstop behind home plate. It was baseball, but it wasn't official. It wasn't a real ballpark, where the big kids played. That would come later—if you were still good enough.

And I was barely good enough at Bloom Township High School in Chicago Heights, Illinois. That's where I transferred in my sophomore year when our family moved to the Midwest. For me, this was a personal disaster of epic proportions. Instead of being a three-sport star at an all-white high school of 500 kids in Ridgewood, New Jersey, I was a pimply-faced bench warmer at a multiethnic sports factory of 3,400 kids on the south side of Chicago.

After my first day of practice for the freshman/sophomore football team—which could have beaten the varsity in Ridgewood—I came home black and blue and discouraged. When my father asked what the problem was, I said, "Dad, these guys are *shaving!*"

As a third-string quarterback, I never got into a game. I never even made the basketball team, and barely made the freshman–sophomore baseball team. This was particularly heartbreaking because my dad had scouted the high schools in the area and had picked Bloom partly because it had such a good sports program.

And a great ballpark! Built in 1926, Heights Park, as it was called, was a beauty. It had a covered wooden grandstand, set back from the field just like in the pros. It was painted dark green and smelled of lime and cement. There was even a concession stand so people could eat hot dogs while watching a game. I just didn't want to be one of the watchers.

But that's what I was. Sitting out in the bullpen, watching games I never got into. That's where I got the nickname Warm Up Bouton, because all I ever did was warm up.

Coach Fred Jacobeit was a nice man but he already had plenty of pitchers, including a guy named Jerry Colangelo who now owns the Arizona Diamondbacks. Jerry and another kid, Miles Zeller, did most of the pitching. They even got to pitch a few games for the varsity. Nothing was worse than sitting in class and watching Colangelo and Zeller leave early for a varsity road game.

That summer, for the first time that I could remember, I did not play baseball. Instead, I worked as a stock boy at the Homewood A&P, stamping "two for thirty-nine cents" on the Contadina tomato paste. The only good thing was the baby food, which was all I could eat because my braces were killing me. I was very depressed. When my old girlfriend from Ridgewood came out to visit, all she could say was, "Jimmy, what's happened to you?"

My junior year wasn't much better. During Careers Week we had to choose a profession and write a report. But I didn't even know who I was, let alone what I wanted to be. The guidance counselor had said we should choose something that suited our personalities. So I did my report on the life of a forest ranger. I'd fit in perfectly with the other squirrels.

Coach Jacobeit let me pitch a few times that year, but it wasn't what I dreamed about. I was still in the bullpen, still Warm Up Bouton.

The summer after my junior year, I decided to give baseball one more chance. I tried out for the Chicago Heights American Legion team, which was basically the same guys from the high school team. I'd have to hitchhike or borrow the car to get there from Homewood.

It had rained on the first day of practice and there were puddles on the field at Heights Park. I arrived early and picked up a rake to help disperse the water. That's when I heard this high-pitched, raspy Italian voice.

"Whatta you doin'?"

A tough-looking guy, about thirty-five, with a black crew cut, bushy eyebrows, and black-rimmed glasses, was standing over by the dugout.

"There's a practice this afternoon," I said. "I'm fixing the field."

"No practice. Too wet," he said, chopping his words off. "I'm Earl DeTella. The manager. What position you play?"

"I'm a pitcher."

"Too small to pitch," he said. "You play second base."

"No!" I said, firmly. "I'm a *pitcher.*"

"Oh yeah?" he said, smiling. "Maybe. We'll see."

After a week of practice, Earl DeTella announced the opening game pitcher: "Jimmy Bouton."

A lot of moans went up. A few teammates, guys like Colangelo who knew Earl from the same neighborhood, told him he was making a mistake, that I was just a bullpen pitcher.

DeTella's eyes got squinty and his chin jutted out.

"You fuckin' guys," he rasped in machine gun bursts. "The day it rained, you stayed home. *He* was raking the field. He wants to play ball. He's my pitcher."

The next day I took the mound at Heights Park and won the ballgame. And then I won my next game. And I won a lot more after that, and before the summer was over I had gone from Warm Up Bouton at Bloom to the ace pitcher for the Post 131 American Legion baseball team.

I was now where I belonged. On the mound. In a real ballpark.

Coach Jacobeit, reading the newspapers that summer like a scout checking the box scores, gave me the ball in my senior year. "You earned it, son," he said, just like the kindly coach in the Chip Hilton sports books. The highlight of the season turned out to be the opening game of the Illinois high school state tournament played in front of a capacity crowd—including a few scouts—at Heights Park.

Once in a while, when I'm down in the basement puttering around, I open an old scrapbook and turn to my favorite page. And I read the first line of a story by the late John E. Meyers, sportswriter for the *Chicago Heights Star.*

> With a bullwhip for a curve and a knuckler squashy as a toma-
> to, Jimmy Bouton pitched the dandiest no-hit, no-run game of
> baseball the Chicago Heights AA Park has contained in 31 years.

Today there's a sign on the fence at Heights Park that says "Jim Bouton Pitched Here." I hope they never tear the place down.

How many players feel the same about Wahconah?

The plight of Wahconah Park began with a process familiar to towns across America. The local team owner, Bill Gladstone, talked the city of Troy, New York, into building him a new stadium. This meant that his Class A New York–Penn League franchise (a Mets farm team from 1988 to 2000 and an Astros farm team in 2001) would be leaving Pittsfield. There is some dispute over whether the New York–Penn League had declared Wahconah Park to be substandard or whether Gladstone just wanted a new stadium; the point was, he'd be leaving for Troy after the 2001 season.

The new stadium in Troy, by the way, is named after Joseph L. Bruno, in recognition of the state senate majority leader's efforts in helping to get it built. It's not known how much consideration, if any, was given to the name Taxpayer Stadium.

It was shortly thereafter that the *Berkshire Eagle*, Pittsfield's only daily newspaper, began lobbying for a new baseball stadium to be built on land it owned at its headquarters in the center of town. A group called Berkshire Sports & Events (BS&E), which consisted of the MediaNews Group of Denver (parent of the *Eagle*), Berkshire Bank, the law firm of Cain Hibbard Myers & Cook, and some local businessmen, was formed to move the project along. BS&E said it was assembling $18.5 million in state grants, revenue bonds, and corporate donations to build the new stadium.

Hello new stadium; goodbye Wahconah Park.

But the people of Pittsfield didn't want to say goodbye to Wahconah Park. In fact they had already voted to renovate their beloved ballpark. Twice. Once in 1997 and again in 1999. And twice their elected officials ignored their votes.

In the summer of 2000, opponents of a new stadium began a petition drive to counter the efforts of BS&E. But once again the City Council, this time ignoring the petition, voted 8 to 3 to ask the state of Massachusetts to authorize the creation of a Civic Authority to build and operate a new stadium. The Authority would also have the right of eminent domain, in case a few people's homes or businesses needed to be demolished to make room for the new stadium that the people didn't want.

Within hours of the Council vote, however, the citizens of Pittsfield took to the streets again. Under Section 44A of the city charter, the "naysayers" (as they were called by the *Eagle*) collected 4,781 signatures, far more than the 3,350 they believed they needed to prevent the creation of a Civic Authority. But once again, they were foiled by city officials and BS&E, who successfully challenged the petition in a municipal hearing.

This time, however, an interesting thing happened. The hearing, now referred to in Pittsfield as "the kangaroo court," was locally televised. And what viewers saw was a McCarthy-like questioning of private citizens, including a seventy-year-old woman named Anne Leaf, a local artist and one of those who stood to lose her home if the new stadium were built. The aptly named Ms. Leaf, a wisp of a woman, looks as if a wind could blow her away. And one almost did.

"Their attorney just chopped me up," said Leaf. "They asked who put me up to it, who else was involved. It was just awful." Observers said most of the dirty work was done by a guy named Mike MacDonald of Cain Hibbard Myers & Cook.

A legal challenge to the hearing fared no better for Ms. Leaf. "The superior court judge, *MIS*-ter Ford, was beholden to the whole damn bunch, the good old boys," she said. "I've never known such a rude man in my life. And he didn't even have the courtesy to tell me the final ruling."

The final ruling was that the anti-Civic Authority group would actually need 4,500 signatures—on a newly worded petition—and all of it within two weeks' time.

The naysayers hit the streets again.

Lashed by the harsh winds of a bitterly cold January, a dedicated band of Wahconah Park lovers, eminent domain targets, and McCarthy-tactic haters, managed to collect—with one day to spare—5,226 signatures. This was more than enough to withstand the challenges, thus overturning the Civic Authority. The matter would now be settled in a special referendum on June 5, 2001.

Every time I would read or hear something about the plight of Wahconah Park, I'd feel a little tug of sadness. How could they abandon a landmark that means so much to the city? As local historian Donna Walto notes, Pittsfield has already "destroyed its most important architecture" and with it, "much of its own history." The lost buildings include Bullfinch Church, built in 1793 and one of only two like it in the world; the old brick Union Station; the Peace Party House; Elm Knoll, where Longfellow got the inspiration for his poem, *The Old Clock on the Stairs*. And those are just a few.

How could that be happening in the Berkshires, famed for its timeless mountains and its ubiquitous antique shops? While Pittsfield is tearing down, the rest of Berkshire County is preserving and renovating. In South County, where I live, the towns of Great Barrington, Stockbridge, and Lenox are all booming, largely because they've maintained the historic character of their downtowns. In North County, the same respect for the past has fueled the growth of Williamstown and North Adams. Sandwiched in between, in the southern part of North County, is Pittsfield, which can't get out of its own way.

Beyond the sadness, there's a certain fear involved in the tearing down of treasured buildings. Tearing down is forgetting. If we can forget so easily, who will remember us?

It's comforting to live in a community that cares about its history. I'm one of those who cringed when the Taliban blew up those ancient Buddhist statues in Afghanistan, and I'm not even a Buddhist. Nor do I care about religion. Baseball is my religion and ballparks are the temples.

I go to Wahconah Park only a few times a year, but I like knowing it's there. Here's a ballpark that gives you a feel for what life might have been like just after World War I. It's like those villages they set up to recreate the past, with the blacksmith and the weavers and the butter churns, only Wahconah is a real working ballpark. I want to be able to take my grandchildren there one day.

Why couldn't Wahconah Park be fixed up? If it no longer met the exacting requirements of major league baseball's affiliated farm teams, maybe it could be home to an independent league team. The Atlantic League, which includes the Long Island Ducks and the Newark Bears, might want to play there. So might the Northern League, whose Albany Diamond Dogs and Glens Falls Lumberjacks would be natural rivals.

What's more, independent league baseball is *better* than the Class A New York–Penn League because the teams are stocked with former AA, AAA, and even major league players.

For the hell of it, I called my friend Chip Elitzer, who I knew had similar feelings about Wahconah Park because we'd gone to games there together. My wife Paula and I would drive up from South County with Chip and his wife Cindy, and their boys, Daniel, Sam, and Jacob. Chip is an investment banker and a smart man. Maybe he could think of something.

So the two of us thought for about five minutes and came up with the answer. *We* could fix up Wahconah Park. We could buy an independent league team to play there. And we could even make some money.

But where would we get the seed money to begin with?

I'm doing pretty well, but I'm far from rich, having lacked the foresight to be born in a time when I could have earned $19,000 per *inning* instead of the $19,000 per *year* that I actually earned as a major leaguer. And while Chip is a successful investment banker, he also has a big house, a seriously ailing father, and three teenagers to put through college.

"Money is not a problem," said Chip. "A good idea can always attract money. We'll contribute the sweat equity."

"Great!" I said. "I know how to sweat."

This could be fun, I thought. Can you imagine? Jim Bouton, baseball team owner. Wouldn't that be a switch? I might finally come to understand the fascination with buying and selling uniformed human beings. Overpaid human beings, to be sure. I'll have to go out and buy some cigars.

And Chip and I would be good partners. How do I know? Hell, we once built a tree house together.

Chip and I have known each other about five years. And two years ago, we built a tree house for his three boys. Okay, maybe it was partly for us, too. It's one of those Swiss Family Robinson–type jobs that belongs in *Architectural Digest*—about twenty-five feet up, with a landing and everything. It would have been fifty feet up but our wives wouldn't let us. Chip and I would be up in the tree, dangling from ropes with hammers and saws, and Paula and Cindy would be hollering at us from down on the ground. "You guys are crazy! Come down out of that tree!" We'd shake our heads and shrug, pretending we couldn't hear what they were saying because we were too high up.

"Whaaat?"

The more Chip and I talked about Wahconah Park, the more we liked it. Pittsfield would get a renovated landmark *and* a professional baseball team, at no cost to the taxpayers. We'd even sell stock to local investors so no one could ever move the team out of town.

If we could build a tree house by ourselves, we could certainly build a minor league baseball team. On second thought, our wives would have *really* hollered at us for that. Maybe we should do a little research. So we called Chip's friend Eric Margenau, who not only owned a few minor league teams but also has a weekend home in nearby Stockbridge. We explained our idea to Eric and asked him about available teams. "There are a number of dormant franchises we could buy," he said. "Once we have a place to play."

We had just acquired a third partner.

Now it was our *other* partners—the ones we lived with—who needed to be on the team. I'm referring to the petite and feisty Cindy Elitzer, Eurasian cutie, loving mother, great cook, expert gardener, and fashion consultant to Chip (who needs all the help he can get); and the tall and feisty Paula Kurman, stunning beauty, great dancer, besotted grandmother, and fashion consultant to Jim (who's only one Peruvian Connection catalog order ahead of Chip).

Paula and Cindy are intelligent, strong-willed, verbally gifted women. The other problem is that they're good friends and often team up together on projects. Like the Jacob's Pillow Dance Festival, the Fairview Hospital Gala, and the betterment of Chip and me.

Saving the oldest minor league ballpark in America would take some time, we admitted in a fit of honesty. Not to mention the lost opportunity costs to a self-employed investment banker and a so-called businessman/writer who tries to spin straw into gold from the comfort of his home.

So, would the women go along with us or not?

The big conference took place around the kitchen table at the Elitzers, after we'd come back from a movie one night. This was going to be a no-nonsense meeting, unlike our other get togethers.

In preparation, Chip and I opened the freezer and scooped ourselves some ice cream.

Cindy gently eased into the subject.

"I think you guys are nuts," she said. "Pittsfield is not going to welcome you. They don't have any vision or leadership."

"That's what *we're* going to bring them," I said. "This is just the kind of idea Pittsfield needs. We could turn that place around."

"That's exactly what I'm afraid of," said Paula.

"Look what happened to the England Brothers department store," Cindy added. "A fabulous old brick building that they tore down and replaced with a very ordinary building. The owner, Cindy Welch, even tried to work with the city to save it, but they just weren't interested. They tore down their beautiful old railroad station, too."

Paula brought up a practical point. "My concern is that Jim doesn't know how to do anything halfway," she said. "And we can't afford to have him spending all his time on something that doesn't produce any income."

Chip nodded. "It's true that we're not going to get any cash back for the first three years," he admitted. "Most of the money we raise will have to go into the ballpark."

"And what are we going to do for money in the meantime?" Paula asked.

By this time Chip and I had polished off the espresso crunch and the dulce de leche and were into the vanilla swiss almond.

"I'm afraid you guys are going to get sucked into a quagmire," Cindy said.

"It could go on indefinitely," added Paula.

"But it'll all be over in a few months," I argued. "Either we get a lease on Wahconah, and a chance to make some money—or we don't, and we go on with our lives."

"And there's always the serendipity factor," Chip pointed out. "This could lead to new sources of income. Jim and I could end up as event promoters. Put on concerts. Who knows? It's not just tilting at windmills."

It went back and forth like this for almost two hours. By then Chip and I were reduced to chocolate chip cookie dough and Phish Food.

Then came the breakthrough. And it was a good thing too, because Chip and I were out of ice cream.

Paula was the one who made the leap. "Well . . . I know the two of you would have fun doing it, and maybe it's worth it just for that."

Cindy agreed. "If you really have to do it, guys, then you really have to do it."

And so it was unanimous.

In the end we had no choice. Here was an opportunity not only to save an old ballpark but to turn The System upside down—a system that extorts taxpayer dollars to build new stadiums for migratory teams. We'd replace the same old threat with a brand new offer: We'll spend *private* dollars to renovate an *existing* ballpark for a *locally* owned team.

The target was irresistible, the right forces were aligned against us, and the impact could be far-reaching. And if our wives might be ambivalent, our bodies were telling us what to do. As Chip said, "If we don't do this, we'll become physically sick."

The situation was absolutely begging us to get involved.

During their "Stadium Yes!" campaign, Berkshire Sports & Events had made three arguments that were repeated endlessly in the *Eagle*:

1. There is no alternative plan.
2. No new stadium, no baseball.
3. It's not about a stadium, it's about "economic development."

This last point was powerfully seductive to a financially strapped city, left largely abandoned in the 1980s by General Electric. Pittsfield's population had declined by 20% to its current 42,000, and the city is so deeply in the red that it had to close a firehouse, cut back on high school sports, and turn out streetlights. Things are so bad that the city's finances are now managed by a state oversight board.

For Pittsfield, whose Fourth of July parade had been regularly featured on national television, it's been a sad comedown. Once the center of Berkshire life, Pittsfield, through bad management, poor vision, and corporate wrongdoing, has ceded its status as an economic hub to nearby towns, with a corresponding loss of tourism. As its population has aged, it struggles to evolve from a manufacturing to a service community.

In short, Pittsfield needs all the help it can get. It does not need the false promise of a new stadium—or the false arguments being made to get it built. That's where Chip and I come in. Because the truth is:

1. We have an alternative plan.
2. We don't need a new stadium to keep baseball in Pittsfield.
3. If it truly is about "economic development," a new stadium makes no sense.

Why spend $18.5 million to build a baseball stadium used for three months a year (and doom a historical landmark!), when the same $18.5 million could be spent on an indoor arena, for example. Simple math tells you that a year-round arena—with professional hockey, arena football, rock concerts, the circus—would draw many more visitors than a summer baseball stadium. And you'd still have Wahconah Park. Even if a new $18.5 million baseball stadium could outdraw Wahconah Park by 50,000 fans, it would be like paying each one $370 to visit Pittsfield!

It was ludicrous.

We figured we'd be doing everybody a favor by pointing this out.

Rather than approach the new stadium opponents, Chip and I decided to meet with Berkshire Sports & Events. Better to work *with* the big boys than against them. Besides, these were businessmen; they'd understand the logic of our plan. Chip could talk the numbers. I'd tell the funny sports stories.

On February 7, 2001, Chip and I met with BS&E at a restaurant in Pittsfield called the North End. A light snow was falling as we arrived. We entered through a back door off the parking lot and stamped the snow off our feet. The smell of beer, cigarettes, and grilled meat greeted us in the hallway. This was a guys' restaurant. It featured heavy wooden beams, a bar, and a giant fish tank. A waitress showed us to a large round table and gave us menus featuring Italian cuisine. We liked the fact that we were the first to arrive. We sat with our backs to the fish and talked strategy.

BS&E had some idea of what we wanted to talk about because Gerry Denmark, a lawyer I knew who had set up the meeting, had given them an overview. They must be intrigued, we figured, or they wouldn't bother. We also knew there'd be egos involved, so Chip and I planned to be team players. We decided to let them take credit for our brilliant idea, which we were calling Plan B. Let *them* hit the home run with *our* bat and ball. We congratulated ourselves on our cleverness.

Our prospective teammates arrived separately and were greeted warmly by the owner, a big guy with a mustache, who seemed to know them. Chip and I stood up to shake their hands. They were Andy Mick, publisher of the *Berkshire Eagle*; Tom Murphy, director of community development for Pittsfield; Mick Callahan, owner of an outdoor sign business; Mike Thiessen, stadium finance consultant; and Jay Pomeroy, Global Communications Manager for GE Plastics. But no one from Berkshire Bank, a key player.

Except for Andy Mick, who looked like he had a case of indigestion even before the meal was served, they all seemed genuinely glad to meet us. This might be easier than we had thought.

And then they started talking—about how a new stadium would be the best thing that ever happened to Pittsfield, that it would spur economic development, that this would be a multi-use stadium that would also host outdoor movies, trade shows, winter ice-skating, flea markets, festivals, bazaars, band concerts, and Boy Scout campouts, and that a new stadium was necessary because they had studies that showed Wahconah Park was falling apart, and that it was a dump, and a money pit, and a lost cause, and decrepit, and crumbling, and past its prime, and beyond repair, and not worth saving, and what's more, new stadiums were the wave of the future.

This was all delivered with great enthusiasm. Murphy did most of the talking, but they all took turns. Callahan gave the local business perspective. Thiessen talked about the finances. Pomeroy, with Amway enthusiasm, took on the role of cheerleader. Meanwhile, Andy Mick, who gave the impression of a bird of prey with his tight mouth and piercing eyes, said very little. For some reason he seemed to be the leader.

It was your basic dog-and-pony show—and Chip and I were just two more guys who had to be won over. What a sell job! Boy Scout *campouts?* Would that be in the outfield? How about a merit badge for retrieving foul balls? For a minute I thought they were going to try and sell us stock.

We waited politely for our chance to speak, nodding at each of them in turn, trying to keep up with the points that would need to be countered.

"What's wrong with Wahconah Park?" we asked finally, the fish tank gurgling behind us.

They laughed and shook their heads. Or rolled their eyes. Andy Mick stared straight ahead at nothing in particular.

"Where do you want to start?" asked a smiling Jay Pomeroy.

Once again they took turns, this time presenting a laundry list of problems: the parking lot floods when it rains, the plumbing is held together with tape and chewing gum, the locker rooms are cramped, there are no exercise facilities, and the sun shines in the batters' eyes, causing "sun delays," which can hold up a game for ten minutes.

Having done our homework, Chip and I matched their enthusiasm: the flooding might be alleviated by lowering a dam downstream from the park, the plumbing could be repaired or replaced, the locker rooms could be expanded, and the "sun delay" could be sold as the quirky feature of a historic ballpark, just as Fenway Park's "Green Monster" turns a short left field into a marketing asset.

They smiled tolerantly at us. Hadn't we been listening?

Chip and I energetically challenged their "economic development" theory. We cited studies that showed there is no economic benefit to having a new minor league baseball stadium. Zero. Zip. Nada. We said we would restore Wahconah Park at no cost to the taxpayers, and that the city could spend the $18.5 million on a completely different reason for people to come to Pittsfield. And furthermore, if they decided to build an arena instead of a stadium, we could provide a hockey team. We explained that our partner Eric Margenau was president of United Sports Ventures, a New York City–based company that owns four minor league hockey teams and a baseball team.

We said that a new stadium was not necessary to keep professional baseball in Pittsfield, that there were two independent leagues that would be happy to play in Wahconah Park. What's more, independent league baseball was better than affiliated baseball, and a properly marketed Wahconah Park would outdraw a new, cookie-cutter stadium. In any case, we were private investors willing to put money into Pittsfield's best known landmark. If we wanted to "waste" our own money on a municipal asset, why not let us do it?

We waited for the applause, but none was forthcoming. In fact, there was a decided lack of interest. They looked like they couldn't wait to start talking again. It was like trying to have a conversation with animated robots at Disney World.

They then launched into a speech about fans wanting to watch New York–Penn League baseball, and about Larry Bossidy, a Pittsfield native son and a former local pitching star, who was looking to buy a team for the new stadium. They added, with a sense of awe bordering on reverence, that Bossidy, former CEO of Allied Signal, was worth about $70 million.

I volunteered that while I was not from Pittsfield and was, at that precise moment, worth something south of $70 million, I had once pitched for the Portland Mavericks, the only independent team in an otherwise affiliated Class A Northwest League. That was in 1977, the year before I made my comeback to the majors with the Atlanta Braves, and we ran away with the league because our players were more experienced. I said we especially enjoyed whomping up on fuzzy-cheeked bonus babies belonging to the San Diego Padres or the Los Angeles Dodgers.

Whenever Chip or I talked, they would smile, and listen, and nod. But they would never engage us on our basic argument. We were like students at rival high schools trying to convince the other side that our school was best. Except that our school *was* best.

Finally, we made the argument that BS&E would have a better chance of winning the Civic Authority referendum on June 5 with our Plan B than with what they were offering. But they said they weren't worried about that. And they returned to their mantra: Wahconah Park was a waste of money, new stadiums were the wave of the future, and Larry Bossidy was worth about $70 million.

Out of curiosity, I asked Jay Pomeroy, Global Communications Manager for GE Plastics, what particular interest *he* had in a new stadium.

"I just love baseball," he said.

Uh-huh.

But it was all very cordial and they even paid the bill. At the end of the evening, we shook hands and agreed to give it more thought. On our way out the door, they said if we wanted to learn more about Wahconah Park, we should call a guy named Phil Scalise. He was an engineer who had done some studies. He would explain about all the problems.

In the car, on the way home, Chip and I tried to make sense of the meeting. We couldn't figure it out. Why were they pushing so hard for a new stadium when it made no sense and the people didn't want it in the first place? Then again, maybe it would take a while for Plan B to sink in. These guys had been living with their new stadium concept for a long time. They certainly weren't going to turn on a dime right in front of us.

But it sure would be interesting, we figured, to see what would happen next. What would become of the slogans "No new stadium, no baseball" and "There is no alternative"? Would Andy Mick rush back to his newsroom and holler, "Stop the presses"? Would he summon his editors and explain that, on the basis of information he had just obtained, it was no longer accurate to repeat those slogans? Would he insist a story be written to clear that up?

Evidently, Andy must have left on a vacation right after our meeting at the North End, because in the days that followed there was no discernible difference in the reporting, the columns, or the editorials of the *Berkshire Eagle*. That's when it occurred to me that it might be a good idea to write Andy Mick a letter, outlining the plan we had presented at the North End.

Sort of a paper trail.

A week later we got an email from Jay Pomeroy, the General Electric Guy Who Just Loves Baseball. Pomeroy said he wasn't giving us an *official* view or anything—only Andy Mick could do that—but that he did want to warn us that "there is a minority in Pittsfield who are against any kind of change and have such a suspicious nature that it is scary!" Pomeroy also wanted us to know it had been nice talking to us, and he looked forward to talking to us again in the near future.

The official view came on March 14, 2001, a little over a month after our meeting at the North End. Andy Mick called Chip to say that he wanted to meet with us, and that he'd be willing to come down to our neck of the woods.

We wondered if Mick's phone call had anything to do with the fact that we had recently shown copies of Plan B to some Berkshire Bank board members, one of whom hadn't heard anything about it and wasn't too happy about that omission. In any case, we agreed to have lunch with Andy at a sushi place in Great Barrington.

When Andy walked in with Mick Callahan, I became optimistic. At our North End meeting, Callahan had been the only one who seemed even halfway open to our plan. Maybe BS&E had decided to run with it. Then again, Andy Mick was looking fiercer than a peregrine falcon. It was hard to tell what might happen. Until the waitress took our order. They chose the cooked fish. And we ordered sushi. Or as Callahan called it, "bait."

Before we had a chance to eat fish or cut bait, Andy Mick gave us the bad news: BS&E was going ahead with its new stadium.

We needed to have lunch to hear this?

Refusing to take no for an answer, which my mother always said was the problem with me, I suggested that BS&E at least do a market test of Plan B by offering it as an alternative. "Give the people a choice," I said. Do it now and BS&E would have almost three months to get a reading before the Civic Authority vote on June 5.

"By making Plan B public *before* the vote," I said, "you can see how the people react, and if that's what they want, you can adopt it. Whereas *after* the vote, if you lose, they might not listen to you on a new alternative."

There was an abrupt silence. Mick Callahan stopped eating in mid-fork.

"We're not going to make it public," said Andy Mick. He did not look pleased.

"Maybe we'll make it public," said Chip, brightly.

Andy Mick's head swiveled in Chip's direction, and his eyes glared, as if he had just spotted a bunny from two hundred feet.

"That's blackmail!" Mick shouted angrily, waggling his finger in Chip's face.

We were stunned. People looked over at us from nearby tables.

Callahan shrugged. "You'll only confuse the voters," he said.

We said we'd think about it. And this time we picked up the tab.

Blackmail. What a notion!

And we would never let such an accusation stop us. But there was a good reason not to go public and it was this: If BS&E were to lose the Civic Authority vote, they wouldn't be able to blame us. Chip and

I just had to hope that BS&E would lose without the voters knowing there was a Plan B, without their knowing that baseball was still possible in Pittsfield, and without their knowing we wanted to restore Wahconah Park.

A few days after being accused of attempted blackmail, Chip wrote to Andy Mick explaining our decision to keep quiet "so as not to confuse the voters." Chip said we would call Andy on June 6, "either to congratulate you, or to suggest serious reconsideration of Plan B."

The funniest thing was that a week later Chip got a note from Andy Mick that read, "Thanks for your support on the stadium issue." And it wasn't a form letter, either; it was a handwritten note. The best part was where Andy said, "Let's get Jim working on a couple of 'Old Timer' baseball games. They could be a big draw in the Berkshires."

What a guy! Maybe I could become director of special events.

Time seemed to slow down over the next few months. Chip and I resumed our squash games. We have these fiercely competitive games where we battle for every point but absolutely refuse to accept a point on a questionable call. We're the anti-McEnroes of the squash court.

Chip learned to play squash at Oxford University, where he spent a year on a Reynolds Fellowship, studying philosophy, politics, and economics. Chip has a boyish preppyness about him, with thick dark hair, warm brown eyes, and an easy smile. When he walks, he leans forward slightly, with his elbows back, taking small quick steps, like a penguin who's late for a meeting. He's fifty-four, but he looks much younger, and sometimes people ask if he's my son. Our games get really competitive after that happens.

I'm more of a racquetball-type guy from Western Michigan University. Old alumni version. I try to stay in shape by pitching batting practice to the local sushi chef, Shige Tanabe, who played ball in Japan. And I like to build things out of stone, like walls and pillars. So I'm in pretty good condition. But at sixty-two, I'm getting a little gray or, as I explain to Paula, ultrablond. When I look in the mirror I see a much younger man than the impostor who shows up in photographs.

The March mud gave way to April mud. Could the May mud be far behind? And what about that Civic Authority referendum up in Pittsfield? Wasn't that coming up soon? Every once in a while, we'd see something in the *Eagle*.

Stadium Supporters Gear Up to Promote Yes Vote

"If it doesn't pass," said Mayor Doyle, "we'll lose the ability to ever attract minor league baseball to the city."

All We Hear from Stadium Opponents Is Negativity

Time to Say Goodbye to Old Ballparks

"Our group believes this is really a 'yes' or 'no' vote for the new stadium," said Jay Pomeroy.

There was our man Pomeroy again, the General Electric guy. Boy, he sure loves baseball—played in a new stadium, if at all possible.

Meanwhile, BS&E was spending a ton of money—some estimates went as high as $250,000, versus less than $1,000 by their opponents—to get its message across. Large, red "Stadium Yes!" signs were plastered all over town—on billboards, store windows, front lawns, and bumper stickers. The Chamber of Commerce, the Berkshire Visitors Bureau, and a group called Downtown Inc. invited Larry Bossidy to speak in favor of the new stadium at an "Economic Development Breakfast." The ticket price was $15 for members, $23 for nonmembers. I assume Bossidy waived his usual fee.

While Larry Bossidy was speaking indoors in support of a new stadium, Joe Guzzo, a city councilman, was marching outdoors against a new stadium. With an American flag sticking out of his backpack, Guzzo, in whose district Wahconah Park is located, went on a twenty-four-hour "sleepless vigil" march at the new stadium site to express his displeasure with the Civic Authority.

Guzzo, Dan Bianchi, and Rick Scapin—known as "The Three Amigos," originally a derisive term, now adopted as a badge of honor by supporters—were the only city councilors to vote against the Civic Authority. The other eight had been solidly in support.

Joe's sleepless vigil was a low-budget approach to an underfinanced campaign. "We don't have any high-dollar backing, like the new stadium proponents do," said Dave Potts, a quality control inspector who had led the petition drives that forced the Civic Authority onto the ballot. "We're just a little grassroots organization, if you want to call us an organization."

Wahconah Park was about to be buried in a landslide.

And then the people voted.

In one of the most stunning election upsets in the history of Berkshire County, the Civic Authority went down to defeat by a 54–45 margin. It was the largest turnout in memory, with 50.6% of the city's 28,495 registered voters having had their say. A huge victory for the naysayers.

Now they were the *yay!* sayers.

"This is for the people of Pittsfield," said a happy Anne Leaf, "God love 'em."

It was a remarkable turn of events. Chip and I never believed the Civic Authority would be defeated. The BS&E guys we met were pretty confident, plus they had all that muscle behind them. They seemed impressive, if somewhat single-minded. And we had never met any of the opponents, who were just names in the newspaper.

This was also exciting. And very odd. Here we were, back in the game, as the result of a Herculean effort from total strangers who had no idea what was around the corner. What would they think of Plan B? Would they be against it because they really are naysayers?

And what must Andy Mick be thinking right now?

It didn't take long to find out. In back-to-back editorials, the *Berkshire Eagle* angrily castigated its own readers:

> A crippling blow . . . voters have doomed a piece of downtown real estate to continued decay . . . the unforgivable abusive treatment of Larry Bossidy . . . we should demand action from the naysayers . . . we await proposals from David Potts, Eugene Nadeau and the rest of Anne Leaf's "modern Minutemen." Ms. Leaf's analogy is a smear on the Minutemen who were not simply a destructive force of fear-mongers but were in fact nation builders . . . it is now time to stop hiding behind the flag and do something difficult—offer a recipe for positive change.

According to the *Eagle*, Pittsfield voters should now give up their day jobs and assume the function of city officials—who would presumably be available to give them a hand. The strangest comment was the one about the voters having "doomed a piece of downtown real estate to continued decay." That real estate was owned by the *Eagle*! They could turn it into a park if they wanted to.

As part of its message that the voters stink, the *Eagle* quoted a few dejected new-stadium supporters.

Larry Bossidy, who has lived in Ridgefield, Connecticut, for the past thirty-two years, said of his former home, "I thought this town was ready to say yes to something."

Mayor Doyle said, "It's depressing that you could have people come into this community and offer to donate money and then have the city reject their offer. Not to be bitter or anything, but I'll be interested to see what their plan is now to keep professional baseball."

Stadium Yes! chairman Edward O'Keefe said, "We eagerly await the plan our opponents have to revitalize Pittsfield. We are all ears."

Okay. Listen up.

While Chip and I are not the opponents referred to above, it just so happens that we *do* have a plan "to keep professional baseball," that would "revitalize Pittsfield," and that the town might be "ready to say yes to."

It's called Plan B.

The day after the election, as promised, Chip called Andy Mick to talk about our plan. When Andy didn't call back, Chip left another message. Still no response. Maybe Andy was on vacation again.

Time to play hardball.

In an open letter to the Pittsfield City Council and Berkshire Sports & Events, we outlined our plan, making the following points:

1. **Economic development:** Pittsfield is better served by putting the $18.5 million earmarked for a new baseball stadium toward an indoor arena, and letting us preserve Wahconah Park at no cost to the taxpayers.
2. **Marketing:** We'll make improvements to Wahconah Park and create a "must see" entertainment experience at a nationally promoted historic ballpark that will attract fans from all over the Berkshires and beyond.
3. **Long-term lease:** We'll bring an independent league team to Pittsfield in time for the 2002 season.
4. **Independent league:** The AA-level Northern and Atlantic Leagues play a better brand of baseball than the Class A New York–Penn League.

5. **Local ownership:** We'll sell stock to local residents, providing team continuity and stability, instead of musical chairs.
6. **Hockey:** If money earmarked for a new stadium is spent instead on an indoor arena, we'll provide a professional hockey team.
7. **Credentials:** Our all-Berkshire partnership provides a strong set of managerial, promotional, and financial skills.

We also sent copies to the local media, which consist of three Pittsfield radio stations, one public radio station in nearby Albany, New York, two weekly newspapers, and the *Berkshire Eagle*.

That was on June 11. On June 12 Andy Mick called Chip.

He sounded irritated.

"What's this?" he asked, referring to our open letter.

"Time for Plan B," said Chip. "I told you we'd be calling. So what do you think of our proposal? We'd like your support."

There was a pause.

"It's not my decision," said Andy Mick, very matter of fact. "The guy you have to convince is my boss in Denver."

"Dean Singleton?" asked Chip, who had already looked him up. Singleton is the CEO of MediaNews Group.

"Yeah," said Andy Mick, casually. "I'll see what he wants to do. I'll be traveling on business. I'll call you back and we'll talk again."

It must have been a long business trip, because Andy never called back. We thought of sending out a search party.

And strangely enough, the *Eagle* did not print Plan B—our revolutionary plan to change the balance of power between a city and its baseball team.

A historic ballpark soon to be abandoned, a government that ignores its citizens, a newspaper at war with its readers, the curious involvement of General Electric, and the shots are being called by a guy in Denver?

It was about this time that I began taking notes.

o o o

26

PART I
SUMMER 2001

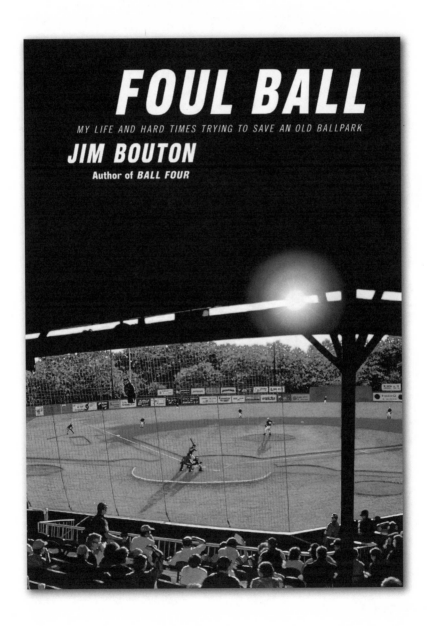

FOUL BALL

MY LIFE AND HARD TIMES TRYING TO SAVE AN OLD BALLPARK

JIM BOUTON

Author of BALL FOUR

CHAPTER 1

"Fuckyouski!"

JUNE 13
WEDNESDAY

Today we got Andy Mick's response to Plan B. It appeared in an editorial in the *Berkshire Eagle*. Chip called me up to read it to me. The unsigned editorial read as follows:

> When you scoop away the whip [sic] cream from a South County partnership's sundae of proposed athletic venues for Pittsfield, you won't find much substantive confection. The trio, including former Yankees pitcher Jim Bouton of Egremont, pledge to bring an as yet to be organized independent Northern League team to Wahconah Park—for which they will do "modest" renovations—and an as yet undetermined minor league hockey team to a proposed $22 million indoor arena—on the site of the rejected $18.5 million downtown baseball stadium—which they expect someone else to build. The partners concede that Wahconah is not up to being home to a New York–Penn League affiliate; they're counting on dilapidated charm. Does this sound like a recipe for success?

Chip and I had to laugh. For months the *Eagle* has been saying there's no alternative to a new stadium. Now our Plan B comes along—hasn't even been out there twenty-four hours—and already they don't like it. And this is the paper that accused the new stadium opponents of being "naysayers."

I'm sure I've met David Scribner, the editor-in-chief of the *Eagle*, but I don't remember him. It might have been at a party at my friend Alan Chartock's house. Alan is the executive director of WAMC, Northeast Public Radio, based in Albany. Scribner is a frequent guest on WAMC, reading the morning news in exchange for an *Eagle* plug and appearing on a program that Alan hosts called the *Media Project*, which examines how that industry does or doesn't do its job.

Now there's an idea! How about a joint appearance with Scribner and me on the *Media Project* or WAMC's *Vox Pop* call-in show? We could debate the merits of our plan for Wahconah Park, or examine the *Eagle's* conflict of interest with the new stadium. Either topic would be of interest to Berkshire residents, if not the entire listening area.

Alan is always fighting against conflicts of interest and corporate attempts to buy off the media. It's the main message of his WAMC fund drives, which mix humor, fear, and outright begging to raise the thousands of dollars necessary . . . "to keep this beacon lit, and I'm not kidding you, folks, this is it. If we don't have twenty callers in the next five minutes, this public radio station and everything it stands for will be gone forever. Gone, do you hear me? We can't let that happen . . . because we're all in this together . . . this is *our* radio station. Why aren't those phones ringing? Not a single phone! Listen to me. This is Kafkaesque. We gotta do it *now!* Dive, dive, dive . . . Whatever you can give . . . because . . . and I'm deadly serious right now . . . because let me tell you about what happens when the corporate big shots come around with their money. One day, not too long ago, three men came into my office . . . "

And he's not afraid to talk tough to the big boys. One time the NBC Nightly News asked him to comment on General Electric's continual legal battle to avoid cleaning up the PCBs it dumped into the Hudson River.

"I looked right into the camera," said Chartock, "and I said, 'Jack Welch, clean up your mess!' Of course, they never used it because NBC is owned by General Electric."

When he's not fulminating about media malfeasance, Dr. Chartock, or "that little pain in the ass" as he's known by his carefully cultivated enemies, teaches political communication at the State University of New York at Albany, offers commentaries on the NBC-TV affiliate, recently hosted a *Me & Mario* radio show with former Governor Cuomo, and writes a weekly column for the *Eagle*.

Alan is a legend in the Berkshires. And WAMC is his living room where people are invited over to learn about what's happening in the neighborhood and the world at large. You drive up from New York City, tune into WAMC, and you know you're home.

I told Chip that WAMC could be the necessary balance to the *Berkshire Eagle*—the area's most powerful radio station versus Pittsfield's only daily newspaper. Wait until Chartock finds out what's really going on with Wahconah Park, I said. This will be a whole different ball game.

Chip and I then called Chartock at his office in Albany; Chip is good at patching people in on conference calls. We told Alan about the *Eagle's* editorial, briefed him on our plan for Wahconah Park, and filled him in on our problems with the *Eagle*.

"So," said Chartock, in a neutral tone of voice. "They won't give a sucker an even break."

An even break? What happened to "the flaunting of corporate power, the dereliction of journalistic responsibility, and the unbridled tyranny of a one-paper town?"

Undeterred, I pressed on.

"What about a *Media Project* with me and Scribner?" I said. "We could debate the very things you talk about on that program, with one of your regular guests, about a perfect example right here in our community! Scribner and I, *mano a mano*. I could ask Scribner if that was his real name or did he have it changed to match his job. The listeners would love it."

"Scribner hasn't been on for months," said Chartock evenly. "And we've done programs in the past about the *Eagle's* conflict of interest. Why don't you write a letter to the editor? More people read the letters than the editorials."

This was not exactly what I expected to hear. But we thanked Alan for his time and hung up. Maybe Alan wasn't feeling well today. Or maybe he was ambivalent.

Back in May, Alan had written about the new stadium in his "I, Publius" column in the *Eagle*.

> I think that once again the people of Pittsfield have a real opportunity to turn their city around. A new minor league stadium will bring people into a largely deserted business district that needs help big time. . . .
> I have a theory that many of the people who are left in Pittsfield actually want to live in a dying city. They want a North Street in which once thriving storefronts are filled with governmental/social service agencies. . . .

Now it would appear that a goodly number of folks in town are prepared to cut their own throats once again.

Alan, who has a good crap detector and gets to the core of most issues faster than anyone else, hadn't gotten deep enough on this one. So when Paula and I ran into him at the movies a few days after that column appeared, I briefed Alan on the sad history of teams and leagues that force cities to build new stadiums by threatening to leave. I also told him I was working on an alternative plan for Pittsfield—which I couldn't reveal at that moment—and that he might just possibly be on the wrong side of this one.

A rueful grin appeared on Alan's face, and his eyes rolled up, behind his glasses.

"Uh-oh," he said, stroking his beard.

But after today's phone call, maybe it's Chip and I who should be saying "Uh-oh."

JUNE 14
THURSDAY

Along with the voters of Pittsfield.

Because it suddenly appears that a new stadium is not dead after all. The front-page headline in today's *Berkshire Eagle* reads REVISED STADIUM CONCEPT DRAWS TENTATIVE SUPPORT. According to the story, Mayor Doyle "has asked for and received tentative support" from the City Council and Berkshire Sports & Events for the same new stadium in the same downtown location—but without a Civic Authority. It turns out it was the Civic Authority that people were voting against, not a new stadium.

A "new stadium" question would presumably require another special referendum.

This evening Chip and I drove up to the Bousquet Ski Area, a few miles southwest of downtown Pittsfield, where a "brainstorming session" would be held to consider various proposals for local sports arenas. As new players in this sports facility game, Chip and I figured we'd better show up.

The meeting had been organized by George Jervas, Bousquet's owner, who thinks the best location for a new stadium is across the street from his ski area. It's not the first time he's made this proposal. Apparently, when he had suggested it last year—as an alternative to the downtown site owned by the *Eagle*—Mayor Doyle had called him into his office and read him the riot act, and he backed off.

The Bousquet meeting was held in a large, post-and-beam room with windows that overlooked the slopes. A few people checked us out as we walked in—the new boys in town. Chip and I sat at a table in the back with a box containing four hundred copies of our proposal—about three hundred more than we needed.

We were joined by Eric Lincoln, who had spotted us from across the room. Eric is a reporter for the *Record*, a weekly newspaper based in Great Barrington. I remembered Eric from my days as a TV sportscaster in New York, when he was a sports writer with the *New York Times*. Eric is a big guy, a former blocking back for Columbia who likes to quote Dan Dierdorf's line: "I started out six-foot-three and when I retired I was five-foot-eight." Eric, who always seems like he's just climbed a flight of stairs, is partial to baseball caps, logo shirts, clogs, and dress slacks—at the same time.

Eric pointed out some of the heavy hitters in attendance. Standing over near the door—maybe so they could exit quickly—were Mayor Doyle, State Senator Andy Nuciforo, City Council President Tom Hickey, city councilors Gary Grunin and Gerald Lee, and two of the Three Amigos—Dan Bianchi and Rick Scapin.

Good thing Chip and I came.

The meeting was hosted by a lawyer for the Bousquet Ski Area. He said he hoped the meeting could be "the beginning of the end of all the negativity." Since it wasn't our party, Chip and I planned to wait until near the end before saying anything.

After half an hour of suggestions from various residents—which included a new downtown baseball stadium, a renovated Wahconah Park, and an ice rink—Mayor Doyle stepped forward and said, "Why not do all three?" This got a small round of applause from the crowd.

Two speakers later, a woman stood up and said, "What about this new proposal for Wahconah Park I've heard about? Does anyone know anything about that?"

Recognizing a cue when we heard it, Chip and I sprang into action. As Chip moved to the microphone, I handed out copies of our proposal. Chip, who has the uncanny ability to speak in complete paragraphs without notes, delivered the logic of our plan to save Wahconah Park. I followed him at the microphone with the passion part—an emotional pitch that conjured up soft summer nights and the enchanting fragrance of hot dogs and mustard.

And we got a standing ovation!

Except from the mayor, who walked out while Chip was talking.

JUNE 15
FRIDAY

Today I got a call from a guy named Hunter Golden who said he was a reporter for the *Eagle* and did I have few minutes to answer some questions. I said sure.

"What guarantee would Pittsfield have," asked Golden, "that the United Hockey League would stay in town more than just a few years, in view of struggling UHL franchises?" Why would he ask a question like that, I wondered. A United Hockey League team was merely a sidebar to our plan for Wahconah Park. Why Golden wanted to focus on hockey instead of on the larger question of a new stadium versus Wahconah Park became clear with his second question.

"What kind of players are we likely to get in view of recent violence in the UHL?" he asked. "Players brought up on charges of high-sticking, et cetera."

This was not a reporter. This was a man on a mission.

"What guarantees did Pittsfield get from the Red Sox, Senators, Rangers, Brewers, Cubs, Mets, and Astros baseball teams over the past thirty years?" I asked him. "And as far as hockey violence is concerned," I said, just getting warmed up, "we'll do psychological testing of all players, get letters of recommendation from their teachers, and require two years of Boy Scout participation."

Maybe I was a tad sarcastic.

The investigative journalist thanked me for my time and hung up. I never saw what he wrote, if anything.

It reminded me of my days as a McGovern delegate at the Democratic Convention in Miami in 1972—a time of hippies, free love, and pot smoking, often simultaneously. As the vice chairman of the New Jersey delegation, I was asked by a reporter what I planned to do about rumors that certain people in our group were smoking pot. I said anyone found smoking pot who refused to share it with the others would be sent home.

I never saw anything written about that either.

Chip got a call from Mayor Doyle's secretary today. The mayor wants to meet with us at City Hall on Monday morning at 8:30. What the hell does that mean? Has he changed his mind on a new stadium? Does he want to hear more about our proposal? Is he going to ask us to butt out?

Maybe he's going to ask me to organize a Mayors' Old Timer baseball game.

JUNE 16
SATURDAY

Suddenly the field is getting crowded. "College League May Be On Deck," reads a headline in today's *Eagle*. The story talks about a proposal from the New England Collegiate Baseball League to play in Wahconah Park in 2002, to replace the departing Pittsfield Astros. And who likes this idea right away? The mayor. "I'm very impressed," said Gerald S. Doyle, Jr. "It fits right in with our goal, which is to have some kind of structured baseball at Wahconah Park, as we've said all along."

"Structured baseball?" When I hear nonsense, I get nervous.

We had a great time tonight at the Jacob's Pillow Gala, the annual fund-raiser for the famous dance festival. Lawns, tents, candles, the whole thing. Paula and Cindy are on the Gala Committee, which means they get to stuff envelopes and write little notes on the invitations that say "Hope to see you there" and "Will you be needing another table for ten this year?" And buy new outfits. Chip and I had responsibilities, too. Our job, besides wearing assigned clothing, was to meet and greet, and dance with our wives for the entire evening—without ever mentioning the words Wahconah or Park.

So the first guy we ran into asked us how things were going up there in Pittsfield.

JUNE 17
SUNDAY

Well, what do you know? Maybe there's hope for the *Eagle* after all. In his "City Limits" column, in which he calls us an "intriguing trial balloon," Dan Valenti writes, "It's early going with much to be said and specified, but with that footnote, I'm throwing my early support behind [Jim Bouton's] plan."

Valenti also happens to be Pittsfield's most popular morning radio talk show host. It figures that he would look like a hippie, at least according to the picture that appears with his column. Right on, brother!

JUNE 18
MONDAY

Big meeting with Mayor Doyle this morning. I picked up Chip at 7:30 at his home in Great Barrington, about thirteen minutes from my house in North Egremont. When you make the same trip over and over, you get to know precisely how long it takes. Like our drives to Pittsfield when we used to play squash at the YMCA: thirty-six minutes from Chip's house on a nice day, in the off season, mid-morning. We'd take a slightly different route each time to see how many seconds we could shave off. We always took the back roads, past woods and streams and old barns. On some routes we'd let beauty trump efficiency until we ended up with the perfect drive.

One time we saw a fox in front of his den and since then we never fail to look for the fox, no matter what else we have on our minds.

And we have plenty on our minds—like politics and world affairs, none of which we agree on. Another time we rescued a box turtle from the middle of the road and transported it to a swampy area behind Chip's house. Were we nature lovers doing the right thing, or misguided "do-gooders" taking a turtle away from its eggs? Just the kind of topic to eat up thirty-six minutes.

On the drive up to Pittsfield today we talked about the mayor's show of support for the New England Collegiate Baseball League.

"We can't share Wahconah Park with a college league team," I said. "That would mean baseball every night of the summer. It's too much of a drain on the facility. You need the road trips to get the field back in shape, clean the locker room, make repairs, stuff like that."

"Plus," said Chip, "a nonprofit collegiate team would draw too many fans away from us—the ones paying the expenses."

"The mayor probably knows that already," I said. "But most people wouldn't."

"We're going to look mean-spirited if we decline to share the ballpark," said Chip.

"Maybe that's the idea," I said.

"The other thing the college league does," said Chip, "is fill Wahconah Park until a new stadium can be built. That's what the Mayor has said he still wants to do."

"Why is he still talking about a new stadium?" I said. "He'll never get reelected on that. What do you think the benefits are for him?"

"Maybe it's the legacy thing," said Chip. "Mayor Doyle Stadium."

"Maybe they're going to let him play third base," I said.

"What we have to do," said Chip, "is to win him over and let him take credit for the idea. Same thing we offered to Berkshire Sports & Events."

"If the meeting doesn't go well today," I said. "I'd like to try something a little offbeat. Get close to the bone. Ask how he'd like to be remembered by his grandchildren. Does he want to be remembered as a politician who just served his time? Or as a man who stood up to power?"

"That sounds like a good idea," said Chip. "If you can find the right time to say it."

We parked next to City Hall in a one-hour spot. We figured the meeting shouldn't take much longer than that since the mayor's secretary had said he had meetings all morning long. We let her know we had arrived, and we waited in an outer office where we examined an assortment of plaques on the wall that paid tribute to Mayor Doyle. Several of them commemorated the 1998 settlement agreement with General Electric, in which GE has to compensate Pittsfield for decades of dumping PCBs.

After about five minutes of plaque viewing, we were ushered through a small anteroom into "the corner office," as Dan Valenti likes to call it. This is a not-very-large, high-ceilinged room with wood paneling, tall windows, and a dusty-rose carpet. A large, framed photograph on the wall features Charles Hibbard, the first mayor of Pittsfield. The date reads 1891.

Mayor Gerald S. Doyle, Jr., son of a former Pittsfield commissioner of public works, rose from his desk to shake hands. Also greeting us was Tom Murphy, the director of community development, whom we remembered from the North End restaurant, and who we've learned is the mayor's cousin. A regular family dynasty. There was a hearty hello all around—four guys looking to work things out.

Doyle, tanned and fleshy with a balding dome, settled into his swivel chair, looking somehow retired. His style, as exhibited this morning and at the Bousquet meeting last week, is a combination of regular-guy affability and unjustly accused fury, creating the overall impression of a pugnacious maitre d'.

Murphy, a tall, puffy-faced man with thinning blond hair, is a second-banana type of guy. A right-hand man who sat to the right of the mayor with a pad of paper on his lap.

Murphy started it off with small talk about some problems they were having with the newspapers and the police officers' union. Then things veered to the Bousquet Ski Area where George Jervas had apparently violated some building codes by laying water pipes close to electrical lines, but the city had given him a break, and he would never be a problem.

I wondered what Murphy meant by that.

After about half an hour, with Chip and me smiling and nodding, the mayor finally said, "Let's talk about Wahconah Park," and lit a cigarette. Instinct told me not to ask him to refrain from smoking.

"First of all," said the mayor, "you sent your open letter to the wrong guys. The City Council doesn't run this town, I do. The people you need to see are the park commissioners—who make recommendations to me. And on Wahconah Park, it's not a lease, it's a license agreement that *I* negotiate. All it needs is *my* signature and I don't have to get anybody's approval."

It's good to be the king.

Chip and I, as humble servants, then delivered our pitch, the highlight of which was that the mayor could be a hero. "The people want our plan for Wahconah Park," we said, "and that issue alone could get you reelected."

The mayor and Murphy seemed to be attentive as Chip and I spoke, the mayor puffing on his cigarette and gazing into the distance, as if the logic of our plan was somehow sinking in. We had already been there for over an hour and there was no effort to discourage us, as there had been at the North End restaurant.

At one point the phone rang, and the mayor's eyes rolled up. Grabbing the receiver, he listened for about three seconds and shouted, "That fuckin' asshole's a waste of time!"

Greatly irritated, the mayor punched a button on the phone, listened for a second and said, "Very." Then, after about five seconds of highly annoyed listening, he said, "Fine." Then he hung up.

Sometimes it's *not* good to be the king.

But our meeting was going well. So well, in fact, that I had no need to deliver the "close to the bone" speech I had suggested on the drive up. It would have been out of place with a mayor who seemed to be considering what we had to say. And we couldn't believe how much time he was giving us. What had happened to all his meetings? Chip joked that we were probably going to get a parking ticket.

"Don't worry about it," said the mayor. "If you get a ticket, just send it to me. I'll take care of it."

It's good to *know* the king.

With nothing decided, but nothing rejected either, the meeting ended. And as Chip and I walked out the door, we offered the mayor one more shot at the legacy thing.

"You could be known as the mayor who saved Wahconah Park," I said. "I can see you throwing out the first pitch on Opening Day."

Doyle and Murphy both smiled at the thought. Murphy probably figuring he could be the ball boy.

And when we got to my car there was no ticket on the windshield—possibly because of a job action by the police officers' union.

Following our meeting with the mayor, we looked for a place to eat. It had to be someplace local because we had promised to meet a writer from the *Pittsfield Gazette*, a small weekly newspaper, at the Pittsfield Astros Media Day at Wahconah this afternoon. The season is about to start in the New York–Penn League, which plays from now until the end of August.

After driving up and down North Street, we settled on the Lantern, a dimly lit joint with neon beer signs and curtains in the window. The place had "great burgers" written all over it—the kind of place we could never take our wives, due to the conspicuous absence of free-range mesclun greens and roasted-vegetable gallettes drizzled with a housemade coulis of hoisin sauce and double-crusted fennel seeds.

Chip and I ordered burgers and talked about Mayor Doyle.

We agreed that if he *really* wanted to be reelected, he'd back our plan for Wahconah Park—unless he's already accepted his reward for supporting a new stadium. On the other hand, he had seemed to be open-minded, even asking for a letter describing how we plan to proceed. We were optimistic. And the burgers were great.

"Did you notice that he looks like Tony Soprano?" said Chip.

"Let's hope he's not armed," I said.

Media Day is where reporters wander around the field with cameras, notepads, and tape recorders asking players and coaches, and a manager (called "the skipper") how the ballclub is shaping up and what kind of year they're going to have. The correct answers are "Good hustling ball club" and "We're going to surprise a few people." This actually gets written down and recorded, and then everybody eats lunch consisting of cold cuts and potato salad.

Today the Pittsfield Astros—last year known as the Pittsfield Mets until the major league Mets ended their working agreement with owner Bill Gladstone, who then hooked on with the Houston Astros, and who next year will be moving to a new stadium in Troy, New York—said hello and goodbye to Pittsfield.

Media Day was scheduled for ten-thirty in the morning, so it figured to be mostly over by the time Chip and I got there. We didn't want to steal any thunder from the Pittsfield Astros, who will need all the noise they can get, so we just skirted around the periphery of the ballpark.

After speaking to the guy from the *Gazette,* we were spotted by Dan Valenti, who came over to say hello. I could tell it was Dan because he looked like his picture and he was wearing jeans and a flowered shirt to complete the ensemble. Dan is a skinny little guy, with glasses and shoulder-length hair streaked with gray. He looks like a wasted guitarist from a '60s rock band.

We thanked Dan for his support yesterday and complimented him on his independence. Considering the position of his bosses at the *Eagle*, was he ever worried about losing his column? "If it happens, it happens," he said. "That's the small stuff. Besides, my column is good for their credibility. And I don't need it."

Freedom is never having to say "I need it."

The next thing we did was check out the possibilities for two ideas for revitalizing Wahconah Park. First was our "Taste of the Berkshires" food court—a collection of booths featuring specialties from local restaurants that would augment the hot dogs and beer. The second was our "Not-So-Luxury Boxes"—a retro version of corporate suites that would go up on the roof, if it can take the load.

That's when we ran into Rick Murphy, the general manager of the Pittsfield Astros. Rick, who's in his mid-thirties but looks like a kid, is the cousin of the mayor's right hand man, Tom Murphy, who, of course, is also a cousin of the mayor. Anybody who is anybody in Pittsfield is related to somebody who is not just anybody.

"What is this, Appalachia?" said Chip.

We introduced ourselves and asked Rick if he had a moment, but he acted as if we had asked him for his wallet. He cocked his head at a funny angle, took six steps backward, and began squinting at us. Since he was now out of range for civilized conversation, Chip and I took a few steps forward. Rick took a few steps back. Forward, back. Forward, back. It was like at a cocktail party where some overbearing guy with bad breath and no respect for personal space marches you across the room—only we were the guys with the bad breath.

Finally accepting Rick Murphy's six feet of personal space, we asked why he seemed reluctant to speak with us. With his mouth twisted in what looked like pain, which I first thought might be from the braces on his teeth, Rick let on that he didn't appreciate what we had said about him.

This came as a surprise to Chip and me since neither of us had ever heard of him before. What had we said?

"I'd rather not talk about it right now," said Rick Murphy, squinting and puckering his lips as if he were sucking on a lemon.

After a halting discussion about why "right now" might or might not be the best time to talk, Rick finally allowed as how he was offended that our marketing plan called for a more aggressive promotion of Wahconah Park—as if he'd been sitting on his hands for three years. In spite of the fact that we had never mentioned Rick Murphy's name or his marketing program, being gentlemen, Chip and I apologized for any negative inferences that might have been made. Then we asked him if he had any thoughts about working with us in a possible transition.

Murphy, still cocking, squinting, puckering, and backing off, now folded his arms.

"We might consider selling you our mailing list," he said.

JUNE 19
TUESDAY

At about five o'clock this morning I heard a noise coming from my office, which is right next to our bedroom. "What's that?" murmured Paula, lying next to me in a full spoon. "Sounds like the fax machine," I said. Paula buried her head in the pillow. "I told you we shouldn't have put your office next to the bedroom," she said. I promised to redesign the house after lunch and got up to close the door.

But before I closed it, I took a peek to see what Chip had faxed me—because I knew it was from him. Chip, whose office happens to be next to *his* bedroom, now has Wahconah Park on the brain, and he can't sleep if he's got a brilliant idea, or if a letter has to be drafted. Cindy, who is less articulate than Paula at five o'clock in the morning, just groans before she rolls over. Chip says Cindy expresses her thoughts to him later in the day.

Today's fax is Chip's response to Mayor Doyle's request that we describe how we plan to proceed. I added my two sentences, and Chip faxed it to the mayor, who is probably not sleeping at City Hall.

Chip's detailed letter described four steps:

1. Acquire a long-term lease from the city.
2. Buy an independent league franchise.
3. Sell stock to local citizens.
4. Improve Wahconah Park.

The first step is getting the lease. This is the asset that will allow us to get the best deal for Pittsfield. Unlike team owners who use their league franchise to play one city against another, *we'll use Wahconah Park to play one franchise against another. They* will be the ones who need *us*, instead of the other way around. Pittsfield will control its own baseball destiny. That's the key to our plan.

And right now, we'll be able to bargain with franchises from two leagues—the Atlantic and the Northern. But we can't buy the team first. Because we're dedicated solely to Wahconah Park, it would be folly to buy a team—or pay for an option we might not be able to exercise—on the mere hope of getting a lease on Wahconah Park.

However, with a lease in hand and a buyer's market—there are three dormant franchises in the Northern League and an expansion franchise possibility in the unbalanced seven-team Atlantic League—we could easily negotiate the purchase of a franchise within a few weeks. And we wouldn't need to sell stock just to buy a franchise that will probably cost less than $500,000.

We can take our time selling stock—to cover whatever we don't put in ourselves—while we field bids to improve Wahconah Park. Chip, who has raised millions of dollars for all kinds of deals, has good reason to believe we'd be oversubscribed.

Immediate improvements to Wahconah would include bigger and better restrooms, our Taste of the Berkshires food court and Not-So-Luxury Boxes, and exterior painting. Longer term, we envision expanded locker rooms, a walkway museum, and a Hall of Fame.

In his letter, Chip also reminded the mayor that he and Eric Margenau and I come with substantial credentials: "Our partnership brings over fifteen years of experience in building and running successful minor league sports teams. Of the fourteen professional teams currently or previously owned (eight of them baseball), twelve are enduring assets in their original cities. The other two are thriving in new homes after being forced to relocate by affiliated minor league stadium requirements."

But it all starts with the lease, and the sooner we get it the better. "Although we could wait until Labor Day and probably still make the 2002 season," Chip wrote, "we would benefit greatly from a decision while most of the 2001 season remains to be played."

He closed with "Thank you for your support."

That sounds like Andy Mick thanking us for *our* support.

Meanwhile, the *Berkshire Eagle* continued to promulgate its own sad view of the world. Today's editorial—THROWING OUT THE LAST PITCH—is also misleading:

> Opening day today in Pittsfield . . . is a melancholy one, as it heralds the all but certain end to Pittsfield's long and proud connection with minor league baseball . . .
> A proposal to put a Northern League team in [Wahconah Park] has been floated . . . and should the city embrace this idea it would once again be selling itself short. . . .
> In short, the park's advocates have no plan for it.

No plan? What about Plan B? The plan for which the mayor has asked for a timetable. The plan Andy Mick said he'd pass along to Dean Singleton for his consideration.

That plan.

So here we have Plan B, which the *Eagle* suppressed before the June 5 referendum, "so as not to confuse the voters," still being suppressed after it's been made public.

When is a plan a plan? When the *Berkshire Eagle* has printed it, and not before.

And that's not all.

Even our visit to Media Day did not pass without comment. David Scribner added this jab to his weekly column:

> Fresh from a two-hour meeting with Mayor Doyle, former
> Yankee pitcher Jim Bouton . . . crashed the Pittsfield Astros
> media showcase at Wahconah Park yesterday and strutted about
> as if he owned the joint. Maybe he thinks he does. What did the
> Mayor promise him?

What's with the hostility? Chip and I didn't lose the Civic Authority vote. We're just a couple of businessmen looking to invest private money in a city-owned facility. Why aren't we welcomed with open arms?

More important is the question of what constitutes a fair response by the city's only daily newspaper to a well-intended proposal. A proposal that has yet to be reviewed by interested parties like the Chamber of Commerce, the Rotary Club, or the local Tourism Board, not to mention city officials. You would think that the *Berkshire Eagle*—with a financial stake in the outcome of a new stadium versus Wahconah Park—would bend over backward to at least give the appearance of fairness.

But you would be wrong.

"It's like having *Pravda* against you in Russia," said Chip.

"And we don't have Radio Free Europe," I said, "with WAMC doing a hands-off at this point. What we need is our own web site."

"Samizdat!" said Chip. "That's Russian for self-publish. That's what the Russian people had to do."

Starting tomorrow, like freedom-loving Russians, we're going on the Internet with Plan B, as outlined in our open letter to Berkshire Sports & Events and the City Council.

Fuckyouski!

o o o

CHAPTER 2

"A good plan without money is
better than a bad plan with money"

JUNE 20
WEDNESDAY

Before flying to Chicago to give a motivational talk, I called Chip from the airport. He told me that the Parks Commission was meeting next Monday night and that we should both be there. I agreed. Chip said he's also going to try to speak with each of the City Council members before then. He figures if he can convince the councilors, the parks commissioners may follow along.

So far, he's not off to the best start. Today he spoke with Tom Hickey, who's president of the City Council, and James Massery.

"Hickey said he still hasn't seen our open letter," said Chip, "even though we sent it ten days ago. And when I tried to explain our plan to him he said, 'It's going to cost you too much money, and you don't know what you're getting into.'"

"It's true we don't know what we're getting into," I said. "But whatever it is, we'll probably have to wipe it off our shoes."

"And Massery said he hadn't seen our letter either," said Chip.

"I wonder if the councilors' mail is being screened by the mayor?" I said.

"You mean Tony?" said Chip.

We both laughed at this reference to Tony Soprano.

"What did Massery have to say?" I asked.

"He blames Dan Bianchi for the defeat of the Civic Authority," said Chip. "He said Bianchi is 'the brains behind the other two'— meaning Guzzo and Scapin."

Then Massery revealed something interesting about the relationship between BS&E and the city councilors.

Chip said Massery told him, "I can't just walk away from this—unless Andy Mick *releases* us."

"Releases us?" I said.

"It looks like the city councilors are waiting for instructions from Andy Mick," said Chip.

"And Andy Mick is waiting for instructions from Dean Singleton," I said. "Mr. Big behind the curtain."

"It's like a political convention," said Chip, "where delegates will be loyal to their favorite son until he releases them."

"Except in this case," I said, "the favorite son is beholden to a power broker from a different state."

Then Massery brought things back to the local level.

"I've got some scores to settle," he told Chip.

"I guess that's what passes for democracy in Pittsfield," I said.

JUNE 21
THURSDAY—CHICAGO, IL

"There's got to be money involved," said Paula, speculating on the motives of our opponents. "*Big* money."

I had called home to get an update on Wahconah Park.

"It's not just a lack of vision," said Paula, who by now is a little deeper into Wahconah Park than she'd like to be. "There's more to it than that. You can tell from their anger."

We speculated on what it might be. Real estate is the most obvious. It's a pretty good bet that the value of the *Eagle's* headquarters property would increase by an amount exceeding the $2 million they claim the donated parcel is worth. Plus they'd probably get naming rights—Eagle Stadium—which by itself is worth more than $2 million. Chip had said Berkshire Bank would make money on the bonds and construction loans. And Cain Hibbard Myers & Cook would clean up on the legal fees. Those are the big fish.

Then there are the pilot fish that swim nearby and pick the shark's teeth. Like Robert Smith, the parks commissioner and drinking buddy of the mayor, who owns a bar called the Brewery across the street from the new stadium site. It turns out Smith also owns the North End restaurant where the BS&E guys were so warmly greeted. Smitty, as he's known around town, might be a tough vote for us to get.

Ego is another possibility. Eric Lincoln had said that Dean Singleton once tried to buy the Oakland Athletics. He was also unsuccessful in his bid for naming rights to the Denver Broncos' new stadium, which is now called Invesco Field at Mile High. Would "Singleton Field" in Pittsfield be enough for such a guy? Not likely.

"I keep wondering what General Electric gets out of all this," said Paula.

"It would give Jay Pomeroy something to do," I said. "Get him out of the office."

"I still think it's money," said Paula.

"Couldn't be that much money," I said. "The entire downtown of Pittsfield isn't worth more than a few million dollars."

There was a long pause on the phone. And then it came to me, like a bolt of garbage. It *is* about real estate—not its potential for increased value but rather its potential for unlimited liability!

"I know what it might be," I said, the light bulb blinking furiously above my head.

"Money," said Paula.

"How about tens of millions," I said. "Maybe even hundreds of millions."

"Now you're talking."

"What if the new stadium site is a toxic waste dump?" I said. "Center field would make a very good Band-Aid. A Band-Aid over a tumor."

"Omigod," said Paula, "that makes sense. And it could very well explain why GE is involved."

"Maybe that's why they didn't like our arena idea, which would require going deep into the ground for a foundation," I said. "Whereas a stadium would sit on top of the problem and not expose it. Maybe that's why they didn't build a mall there, even though the people had voted for it."

"If that's what it is," said Paula, "you and Chip don't stand a chance. And now I'm *really* worried because with that kind of money involved, those guys could get seriously nasty."

"All the more reason to keep going," I said. "If what we're thinking is true, people should know about it."

"I feel like I'm in the middle of a movie," said Paula. "What's the name of that . . . ?"

"*Erin Brockovich*."

"Right," said Paula. "And the tobacco one with Russell Crowe."

"*The Insider*."

"Right. And they did everything they could to ruin those people," she said. "It's not like going up against the baseball establishment."

Paula still remembers the fallout from *Ball Four,* even though I met her seven years after the book came out.

"If I write a book," I said, "maybe Jack Welch would try to ban it. He could take on the role of Bowie Kuhn."

"Don't be funny," said Paula. "You know what I mean."

"I'd better have *you* start the car in the morning," I said.

"Uh-huh," said Paula. "Fly home safely, Babe."

JUNE 22
FRIDAY

Chip spoke on the phone today with Miles Wolff, the commissioner of the Northern League. Miles lives in Quebec City during the baseball season, where he owns one of the teams in his league. Chip told Miles about our plans for Wahconah Park and our interest in possibly buying a franchise. Miles said he knew about me, and that he and Eric Margenau went way back as fellow baseball entrepreneurs.

Chip asked him about the cost of a team. Miles said that the floor is set by a new franchise price of $500,000, but that they won't sell a new franchise until their dormant franchises are placed. He said they currently have three dormant franchises: one owned by Jonathan Fleisig that has been inactive for two years, another owned by Bob Wirz that has been inactive for one year, and one owned by Van Schley that will probably move to a new stadium in Brockton, Massachusetts, next year. A fourth team that's been struggling might also be available.

Miles also advised Chip that independent league teams have to pay 100% of their expenses—umpires, travel, player salaries, uniforms, equipment, et cetera—and are more expensive to run than affiliated league teams whose expenses are mostly paid by major league baseball.

This matches what Eric Margenau had told us. Right now, it looks like we'll need about $1.5 million: $500,000 to purchase a franchise, $500,000 of operating expenses before any money comes in, $250,000 for immediate upgrades to Wahconah Park, and another $250,000 in reserve.

Back in January, Chip constructed a financial model that allowed us to play "what if" games with independent variables such as attendance, fan revenue, number of games, and so on. Then he created spreadsheets that showed cash flows and return on investment over five, ten, and twenty years.

Eric had said it costs about $1 million per year to run an independent league baseball team. Based on that, Chip's numbers showed that we could "break even" with an average attendance of 2,500 per game as follows: 2,500 fans per game $\times$ $10 revenue per fan ($5 ticket + $5 for souvenirs and food) = $25,000 revenue per game $\times$ 40 home games = $1,000,000.

Improvements to Wahconah Park and dividends to stockholders could raise the required attendance to 3,000 fans per game. This would seem to be quite a challenge, given that the Pittsfield Mets averaged 2,000 fans per game in recent years. But the potential is there, with current seating for 4,000 and room to add another 1,000 seats. And if we could increase the attendance to 3,500 per game, we'd make a nice profit.

Our plan to increase attendance, which we had detailed in our Plan B, revolves around improving the fan experience at the games and marketing Wahconah Park—locally and nationally—as a historic landmark.

But first we have to get a lease on that historic landmark.

JUNE 23
SATURDAY

This morning I went down to pick up the newspaper at the Old Country Store in the bustling metropolis of North Egremont. The entire downtown consists of four corners that feature, in addition to the store, a restaurant, a B&B, and a barn. A cast of characters wearing camouflage hunting gear, or baseball caps with tractor company logos on the front, is always on hand to sip coffee, buy worms, check lottery tickets, and offer commentaries on the news of the day.

After eight years of my living here, the guys at the store have finally come to understand that I do not have any inside information about why the Red Sox can't seem to win when it counts. Because of my ignorance about these and other important matters, I have been properly downgraded from "Yankee big shot" to "the guy who lives on the hill"—or Bouton Mountain as they call it.

Sometimes, on my way to pick up the paper in the winter, I'll stop by Prospect Lake where some of these same guys are ice fishing—or rather drinking beer and eating venison sausage grilled over a log fire. I like to go out on the ice and see if they caught anything. The sausage tastes great. Maybe we should sell it at Wahconah Park.

"I see you're in the paper again," said Craig Elliot, owner of the store and the unofficial mayor of North Egremont.

Craig was referring to my opinion piece in the *Record*, which hit the stands today. I wrote that Wahconah Park was "our own Field of Dreams right here in the Berkshires," and that it needed nothing more than "loving improvements, phased in over a period of years." Most important, I said we needed an answer from the city "as soon as possible, in order to be ready for the 2002 season."

"Better be careful up there in Pittsfield," said Craig.

It's a warning I get a lot these days.

I picked up the mail from our post office box in the back of the store, paid for my *New York Times,* the *Record,* and of course the *Eagle*—so I could see what our opponents had to say today—and headed back up the hill.

JUNE 24
SUNDAY

Eric Lincoln called this afternoon. He likes to keep us up to date with what's happening behind the scenes. Today's subject was the City Council, as Chip and I will be going to the next meeting on Tuesday night.

"Every one of them has been 'touched' on this new stadium issue," said Eric.

"Touched?"

"You know," said Eric. "Bribed. Offered a payoff."

"How do you know that?" I asked.

"Dan Bianchi," said Eric. "He told me how it's done."

Then he reported a conversation he'd had with Bianchi, who, in addition to his work as a city councilor, happens to own an energy consulting company.

"Bianchi said he got a phone call one day from Dean Singleton out in Denver. Singleton told him he was involved with the California energy crisis and that they might need a consultant. He asked Bianchi if he wanted 'to come out and chat.' Singleton offered to send the company plane. Bianchi said he knew exactly what it meant."

"What about the other councilors?" I asked.

"Bianchi said they've all been approached, or are in somebody's pocket. He said it's a sad story."

I asked Eric what he thought the payoffs were to the others.

"I don't know about Pittsfield," said Eric, "but in Lowell, Massachusetts, the mayor and the councilmen got free luxury boxes, and their kids got jobs at the stadium."

Lowell?

"They had the same situation there," said Eric. "With the *Lowell Sun* backing a new stadium built by the taxpayers."

"Who owns the *Lowell Sun?*" I asked.

"Dean Singleton," said Eric.

Eric would make a great spy, except he's not so easy to hide.

JUNE 25
MONDAY

Got a call this morning from Peter Arlos, who is the county treasurer and a former Pittsfield city councilor. The seventy-five-year-old Arlos, who is also known as the Aging Greek God among other nicknames, is a famous local character. What *kind* of character depends on when you happen to catch him. In a pin-striped suit, the six-foot-three Arlos looks like a state senator; in his sweatpants and bedroom slippers, he looks, as Eric Lincoln says, "like a guy from Bay Ridge going out for the morning paper."

Arlos's favorite mode is that of a tall Columbo in plaid shirt and khakis. "You'll have to excuse me," he'll say, scratching his head and shuffling his papers, "but I'm just a dyslexic guy trying to understand." This enables him to get away with almost anything. Like the time in 1971 when he petitioned the Pittsfield City Council to demand the removal of troops from Vietnam.

Born of immigrant parents in Pittsfield, where he played high school baseball and football, The Greek—as he's called by some, or The Clown as he's referred to by the *Eagle*—has been thrilling constituents and annoying the insiders for over forty years. It was Arlos, for example, who arranged for Andrew Zimbalist, the noted sports economist, to come and speak against the new stadium three days before the Civic Authority vote.

The reason Arlos called today was to give us some advice about the park commissioners' meeting tonight. Even though we're not on the agenda, we felt maybe we should at least introduce ourselves to the commissioners, since they'll be the ones making the decision on Wahconah Park.

"If you go to that meeting tonight," said Arlos, "just sit quietly in the back of the room and listen. They don't like it when people get in their face, if you know what I mean."

We promised to sit in the back and behave ourselves.

Once in Pittsfield, we stopped at the Lantern for burgers—and pea soup because we needed something green—and assessed our situation. Which we think is pretty good, considering that we just started two weeks ago. Except for the *Eagle* and BS&E—which Eric Lincoln says are one and the same—whoever has seen our plan seems to like it or at least, like the mayor, is willing to listen.

Chip and I figure that once we make our pitch in public in front of the City Council tomorrow night, we're "in." Not only do we have the best plan for Wahconah Park, we have the *only* plan. Nothing has come of the mayor's statement ten days ago that he still wants a new stadium, and a college league can't afford to pay the upkeep at Wahconah Park.

My only concern is that Berkshire Sports & Events will try to head us off by putting its own team into Wahconah Park—run by somebody like Jay Pomeroy—with the intention of moving into a new stadium as soon as they can get one built. To keep its new stadium hopes alive, BS&E needs to block us from getting a lease on Wahconah. The next few weeks are crucial. We need to get approved by the park commissioners before BS&E comes up with a team.

The commissioners meet in a place called Springside House, which looks like an old inn or a college president's house gone to seed. The meeting room is about twenty by thirty feet, with beat-up linoleum floors, and a pair of fat columns, toward the front, that seem to have no purpose except to partially obstruct the view of the audience. The commissioners sit behind a wood-grained, formica table that faces about forty cafeteria-style chairs, divided by a makeshift aisle. A Coke machine sits in the stairwell just outside. It does not look like a place where momentous decisions are made.

Before the meeting, Chip and I introduced ourselves to the four commissioners in attendance: Jim Conant, Cliff Nilan, Anthony Massimiano, and the chairman, Bob Smith, aka Smitty, the mayor's drinking buddy. The fifth commissioner, Sue Colker, was absent.

Following Arlos's advice, we sat in the back by a radiator.

There were fewer than a dozen people in the room, each petitioning for one thing or another. Arlos himself was there with three petitions of his own, covering everything from park fees to carnival usage to preserving Wahconah Park—a light evening for him. Councilor Joe Guzzo made "yet another request" to have Wahconah Park submitted as a candidate for the Massachusetts Historical Register. The commissioners promised that this time they would follow up, and Joe returned to his seat, rolling his eyes.

Following a guy who wanted to add a three-piece band to his parade permit, Chip and I were startled to hear our names called, under "new business." Okay. It's not what we expected, but we'll wing it.

Moving to the front of the room, we made an impromptu pitch for a 30-year lease on Wahconah Park that would enable us to do two important things: secure a team on the best terms for Pittsfield, and give us time to recoup our upfront investments in the ballpark. We also emphasized that we needed a decision as soon as possible to put us in the best bargaining position for getting a team.

The commissioners nodded and didn't say much. Evidently they were so impressed they were speechless. The only question came from Cliff Nilan as Chip and I were on our way back to our seats.

"How does Bouton stay so skinny?" he wondered aloud.

It looked like Arlos was right about us sitting in the back. He doesn't call himself The Oracle of Delphi for nothing.

On the drive home, we felt confident. We were surprised that the reception was as good as it was—no negative vibes from anyone. Chip said he thinks BS&E will just suddenly quit on a new stadium, pick up the cause of the arena, and ask for our support. Chip is the only person I know who is more optimistic than I am—and Paula calls *me* a pathological optimist.

"You represent a new force in town," said Chip as we wound our way home over the increasingly familiar back roads. "A gravitational pull, knocking their planets out of alignment."

This led to a discussion about the moon, looming in the sky ahead. I told Chip I could never figure out whether it was waxing or waning. He said, "It's simple. All you have to remember is the code: Wane-right—a play on the word wainwright, you know . . . ."

"Carpenter," I said.

"Right," said Chip. "A builder of wagons."

"I've heard the expression," I said, "but I can never remember what's supposed be on the right—the light or the shadow?"

"The shadow," said Chip.

"But there's nothing in the code that says that," I said. "So what good is it?"

"That's true," said Chip. "You *do* have to remember something."

"So why isn't the code: wane-*shadow*-right?"

"There's no such word," said Chip.

"It would soon become a word," I said, "more useful than wain-wright. Who makes wagons anymore?"

"A lot of people use the wainwright code," said Chip.

"Might as well fix the wax and wane problem, too," I said, "for folks who don't know what those words mean."

"Are you suggesting *decline*-shadow-right?" said Chip.

"Shadow-right-*decline* would be a more logical progression," I said. "We could coin a new term."

"Let's get the lease on Wahconah Park first," said Chip.

JUNE 26
TUESDAY

The *Eagle* has landed on us again.

An editorial headlined BALLPARK PLAN HITS SOME BAD HOPS accuses us of "Orwellian semantics," saying our plan to sell stock to local people "shouldn't disguise the indication that the group doesn't have the financial wherewithal to make the bid on its own . . . in sharp contrast to Larry Bossidy, the deep-pocketed former Pittsfield resident."

Now how did Scribner arrive at this? Is he running credit reports on us? Paula and I have several accounts and a construction loan at Berkshire Bank. Is the *Eagle* checking our balances with its BS&E partner? I don't know what Chip's finances look like, but Eric Margenau's firm, United Sports Ventures, Inc., already owns five successful minor league teams, and that's available on the Internet. But the larger question is this: how can Scribner print something like that without speaking to us first? In fact, he has yet to talk with any of us about anything.

Of course we don't have the $1.5 million we'll need, any more than BS&E had the *$18.5* million it needed for a new stadium. Larry Bossidy, the $70 million man, was only going to spring for a team.

And our proposal would use 100% private financing, whereas BS&E would have used mostly public money to finance a new stadium. The point is, we've got a much better shot at raising our money than BS&E had.

Hell, we've already had guys handing us their business cards, wanting to get in. These are substantial people who would love nothing more than to be part of this project. At the Jacob's Pillow Gala alone, Chip and I collected half a dozen cards. Imagine if our wives had allowed us to say the words Wahconah or Park.

In any case, as Chip says, "a good plan without money is better than a bad plan with money." Just look what happened to the Civic Authority.

But we're dealing with perceptions, and a lot of people are awed by money. Especially $70 million. So, for the *Eagle,* still pushing a new stadium, it's a cheap and easy argument to make—and impossible to refute without putting a stack of bills on the table.

Let's see, where can we get a stack of bills?

We called Eric Margenau at his office in New York City. Margenau is the money guy—our plan calls for him to put up $500,000 seed money, and for Chip and me to sell $1.5 million worth of stock and then give him back his $500,000. That's assuming we get Wahconah Park, of course. If we don't get it, Chip and I would be the only losers—some out-of-pocket dollars, and a few months of wasted time. We figured that made us all equal partners.

Margenau laughed when we told him about the *Eagle's* editorial.

"It's a joke," he said. "I could write a check for a million and a half tomorrow."

That's a decent stack of bills.

With $1.5 million practically in our back pocket, Chip and I got in the car and headed back up to Pittsfield and our first City Council meeting.

We were juiced. Tonight we would be introducing ourselves to the people of Pittsfield. The city council meetings are televised and everyone watches them, either live or on one of the repeats. We hadn't thought fast enough to get on tonight's agenda, but we can make a quick pitch during the "open mike" session, which is what everyone tunes in for.

The Pittsfield City Council chamber looks like all the council chambers you've ever seen, as if local municipalities ordered from the Council Chamber Catalog. A curved, laminated wood dais, with chairs, microphones, and name plates, sits on a platform facing eighty seats, in a room decorated with flags and framed prints of the Constitution, the Declaration of Independence, and the Bill of Rights. Catalog item C, without drapes.

Chip and I arrived a half hour early for the 7:30 meeting and parked in our lucky spot outside City Hall. Once inside, we collated our handouts which we had color coded for easier identification: white for our original Plan B, blue for Chip's letter to the mayor explaining how we plan to proceed, and beige for my piece in the *Record* where I called Wahconah Park "our own Field of Dreams."

We put collated sets at the place of each city councilor, at the table where the mayor sits just below the dais, and on every chair in the room. We added our names to the open mike sign-up sheet in slots seven and eight—not first, but not last either. We introduced ourselves to the people as they filed in. We were so organized it would make your head spin.

And we met some folks we had known only from the newspapers—the famous "naysayers" who had made our bid for Wahconah Park possible: Anne Leaf, Dave Potts, and Gene Nadeau, plus a lot of their friends and neighbors. They were smiling and seemed happy to meet us. They sure didn't act like naysayers.

Unfortunately, our first public appearance was all over in a matter of minutes.

Six minutes to be exact. For the first time in anyone's memory, the Council voted 8 to 3—with Bianchi, Guzzo, and Scapin dissenting— to enforce a three-minute rule during the open mike session. Prior to tonight, people had been allowed to ramble on until they were finished. But tonight—for some strange reason—the gavel would fall sharply after three minutes.

Chip went first, explaining the logic of our plan to folks unaccustomed to the concept of local control. "Think of us as a ballpark shopping for a team," said Chip, "rather than the other way around." He then addressed the money issue raised by today's *Eagle*. "If no one is willing to invest," said Chip, our partnership is prepared to do it "all by ourselves."

Of course, Chip and I believed that we'd never have to take Margenau up on his boast that he could "write a check for $1.5 million," but it allowed us to justify saying we could do it "all by ourselves." And what would Chip and I do if it turned out we couldn't sell any stock? Simple. We'd sit down with Margenau and have a long talk about how the two of us could help him run *his* ball club.

Following Chip at the microphone, I used my three minutes to extol the virtues of independent Northern League or Atlantic League baseball over the Class A New York–Penn League. And I explained why we needed a speedy decision—by the Fourth of July if possible. Evidently the people in the audience had no trouble understanding the brilliance of our plan, because we got the most vigorous and only sustained applause of the evening.

As with most political events, the best stuff happened afterwards in the hallway. The people who had just applauded us inside were now crowded around us in a stairwell outside. Could these be the same people that Jay Pomeroy had warned us about, that "minority in Pittsfield who have such a suspicious nature it is scary"?

Hardly. The funny thing was, it felt like a reunion of long-lost relatives. Comrades in arms. Regiments from allied armies bumping into each other in Paris. *They* had won the war—and *we* had the reconstruction plan.

At that moment, a familiar figure walked by and conspicuously refused to say hello to either Chip or me. It was Mayor Doyle. The very same mayor who had invited us to his office just last week—the one who offered to take care of our parking ticket.

Not a good sign.

We turned back to our new friends in the hallway and tried to answer their questions. Did we know why Berkshire Sports & Events is so fixated on a new stadium? Why do they keep pushing something the people don't want? Why won't they listen to other ideas?

That's when I floated my pollution theory.

"Is it possible," I said, "that the new stadium site is a toxic waste dump? That PCBs have migrated from General Electric property?"

"It's funny you should say that," said Dave Potts. "There were some test borings done there in 1994 that have never been made public. The recent borings that showed that a baseball stadium was okay were done by a guy who is part of Berkshire Sports & Events."

"Phil Scalise?" I said, remembering the guy we'd been referred to by BS&E at the North End restaurant back in February.

"That's the one," someone said.

"I'll send you some EPA stuff from Tim Gray," said Potts. "He's with the Housatonic River Initiative. He may know something about those test borings. And he can tell you about the GE settlement where the city got half of what it should have gotten."

On the drive home, Chip and I reviewed our roller-coaster ride.

"Number one," said Chip, "the mayor is not our friend. It's clear he and Murphy were just pumping us for information last week."

"It was like asking the opposing team for a copy of its game plan," I said.

But it really doesn't matter, because we aren't keeping any secrets. All candor all the time is our strategy. Or as Chip says—quoting Woodrow Wilson's 1918 prescription for avoiding wars—"Open agreements, openly arrived at."

So where are we now? The *Eagle* is against us. The City Council is waiting to hear from Andy Mick. And the mayor is ignoring us. Can his hand-picked park commissioners be far behind? It seems our only friends are the people who were against a new stadium.

The battle lines are drawn.

And it's time to shoot back.

Starting tomorrow we are adding a few items to our web site— namely our February and March letters to Andy Mick, which reveal that, contrary to what the *Eagle* and BS&E had been saying prior to the Civic Authority vote, there *was* an alternative plan to keep professional baseball in Pittsfield and what's more, *they had asked us not to make it public.*

"Might as well let everyone know what we're dealing with here," I said.

There was a long silence in the car. I asked Chip what he thought our chances were.

"Fifty-fifty," he said.

And we drove on, into the darkness.

JUNE 27
WEDNESDAY

Chip and I talked on the phone today with Eric Margenau, who told us about his conversation with Jonathan Fleisig, the New York City commodities trader who owns one of the dormant Northern League franchises. Margenau said he had invited Fleisig to join forces with us but that Fleisig declined.

"I have the front position in terms of the Northern League," Fleisig told him, "and the front position in terms of Wahconah Park."

This means that Fleisig believes he already has a deal—or at least an understanding—with somebody in Pittsfield, most likely the mayor. If that's true, we not only have to get a lease on Wahconah Park, we now have to wrest it away from someone else.

Of course, nobody in Pittsfield would ever know if a back-room deal already exists with Fleisig—except for the mayor and BS&E.

And they're not exactly famous for "open agreements openly arrived at."

JUNE 28
THURSDAY

Turns out we're battling not only Jonathan Fleisig but also the commissioner of the Northern League. Eric Lincoln said Miles Wolff had told him that "Fleisig has first refusal on Wahconah Park because he's been dormant for two years," and that any dormant franchises "are ahead of the Bouton group."

When Eric asked Wolff if that made him "the king-maker," Wolff said, very matter of factly, "Yes, I'm the king-maker."

This, of course, is how the game is played: a league or team dictates to a city exactly who will play in that city's ballpark. Or *not* play if the city refuses to renovate or replace that ballpark on demand.

But it would be a whole new ball game if we got the lease on Wahconah Park, because then we'd have choices—not just among teams but among leagues—as follows: (1) we could buy one of the dormant Northern League franchises, (2) we could buy the struggling Northern League franchise in Glens Falls, New York, or (3) we could buy an Atlantic League expansion franchise, which would balance their current seven-team lineup, thus solving a major scheduling problem for them.

Let Pittsfield be the king-maker.

A bit of good news: Bob Mellace, the parks director who serves as an administrator for the park commissioners, told Chip that he wants an "open discussion in public" before granting a lease. Chip told Mellace that we would welcome that.

More good news: Peter Arlos says he's been hearing from people that Chip and I came across very well at the televised city council meeting. "It's all highly positive," said Arlos.

It can't be just our good looks.

JUNE 29
FRIDAY

Pittsfield won't have Mayor Doyle to kick around anymore.

At least not after 2001. Today he announced that he will not run for a third term in November. Coincidentally, it was revealed that the state attorney general is investigating the management practices of the Doyle administration. Or, as Chip says, "having a sit-down with Tony." Maybe this is what the mayor was thinking about while he was puffing on that cigarette during our meeting eleven days ago.

So, is this good for Wahconah Park, or bad for Wahconah Park?

Possible clue: The same afternoon that Doyle was announcing he wouldn't run again, his press secretary, Curt Preisser, was announcing that the mayor was still "entertaining the idea of a new stadium."

What's worse than a lame-duck mayor with a chip on his shoulder? A lame-duck mayor with a chip on his shoulder who needs powerful friends.

o o o

CHAPTER 3

"Salting the earth"

JULY 1
SUNDAY

Chip spoke with Dan Bianchi today. He asked Dan what he thought of our idea to have the City Council vote on recommending our plan to the park commissioners. "Don't ask for a vote of confidence," said Dan, "because you won't get it. There's still a lot of quiet support here for a new stadium."

Chip asked Dan outright if any of the councilors had been bribed. Dan mentioned the phone call from Singleton, when he'd been offered consulting work in the energy field. "It smelled to me," said Dan. "Clearly meant to be an offer."

What about the other councilors? "Soft payoffs," said Bianchi. "For example, Massery had an old building that was about to be condemned, but the city bailed him out by buying it for top dollar. And Barry, who's a lawyer, has probably been offered new business. Things like that."

They talked about the lack of leadership—councilors who admit they're waiting for instructions from BS&E, and a mayor who's on the way out.

"There's a power vacuum in Pittsfield," said Bianchi. "We not only have a lame-duck mayor, but one who'll be hiding from the attorney general."

Chip and I agreed we have to move into that power vacuum. And we have to make our case not just to the people but to the business community—the part not tied to BS&E. There must be *some* business leaders in town for whom logic still applies. They need to stand up and be counted.

Maybe we can help them to their feet. Chip and I have been invited to write an opinion piece for the weekly *Pittsfield Gazette*, and the Rotary Club has invited me to be their luncheon speaker on July 5. Onward we go into the vacuum.

Or the vacuum cleaner.

JULY 2
MONDAY

The word now comes down that the parks commissioners will *not* be meeting as scheduled next Monday, on July 9. Not only will we not get a decision, as we had originally hoped, but we won't even be having the "open discussion in public" that Bob Mellace had said would be required before a lease could be granted. Since the commissioners meet every other Monday, on the night before the City Council meetings, the next meeting won't be until July 23.

What does this mean? Well, it's summertime. Fish are jumping. Maybe they're taking a vacation.

Or maybe not.

According to Paula, "They're going to do everything in their power to make sure you don't have a shot at it."

At the Old Country Store this morning, I was talking to owner Craig Elliot about Wahconah Park, and a retired doctor who lives in the neighborhood asked what was in it for me.

"Save an old ballpark, make some money, have fun," I said.

"Hey, this is me you're talking to," said the doctor, scoffing at my answer. "What's the *real* reason?"

"All right then," I said. "Same reason I wrote *Ball Four*: cynicism, blood money, revenge."

"And speaking of your book," said the doctor. "My wife's best friend named her son Mickey after Mickey Mantle, and when she heard you were going to be our neighbor she thought that was terrible. That you were the worst guy in the world."

I looked at Craig. He shrugged sympathetically.

"It's a tough crowd," he said.

JULY 3
TUESDAY

Following Dave Potts's suggestion, I spoke with environmentalist Tim Gray of the Housatonic River Initiative about my pollution theory: that a new baseball stadium might be used to cover a toxic waste problem on the *Eagle* property. Unlike a Civic Center or an indoor arena, which would require deep footings and a lot of digging, an above-ground grandstand and a large outfield could mask a multitude of subterranean sins. I asked Tim if he knew about some test borings in 1994 that were never made public.

"I don't know anything about them," he said, "but I can check with the DEP (Department of Environmental Protection) in Springfield, the next time I'm down there."

"Do you think the stadium site could be polluted?" I asked.

"I know there used to be junk yards down there," said Gray. "Junk and scrap yards were notorious PCB dumps. For decades, General Electric was filling every little hole it could find. And the *Eagle* might have deposited some nasty chemicals of its own."

"How does anyone know who's responsible?" I said.

"If it's PCBs," said Gray, "GE is responsible. Any new PCBs found in Pittsfield belong to them. They're already identified as the principal party; it's their fingerprint. Anything else is the property owner's responsibility."

"If there's pollution down there," I said, "how much would it cost to clean it up?"

"Hard to tell," said Gray. "It could be in the millions. If they have to remove contaminated soil, the question is, how far down do they go? Twenty feet? Forty feet? Or more. It's an unknown liability."

"Could a baseball field cover that up?" I asked.

"Probably would," said Gray. "The EPA likes to cap stuff. Three years ago we got information that when Gerry Doyle, Senior, was the commissioner of public works, the roads had been sprayed with oil to keep the dust down—but it was laden with PCBs. The day after we turned in our report, all of a sudden the roads are being paved. A paved road is considered 'blessed.'"

"Who had the roads paved?" I asked.

"Gerry Doyle, Junior," said Gray.

JULY 4
WEDNESDAY

What better thing is there to do on our nation's birthday in Great Barrington, Massachusetts, than pitch batting practice to a sushi chef? Also his kitchen helpers, a carpenter, a lawyer, a bunch of kids, and a college guy who has the ability to turn pro one day.

The ol' knuckler was dancing pretty good, too, especially against the carpenter and the lawyer. The kids and the kitchen help got straight stuff. The college guy got the old, beat-up balls so the outfielders wouldn't have to bother searching for them in the woods. And Shige Tanabe, who was a very good amateur player in Japan, got medium-speed fastballs, which he blasted all over the field. A happy sushi chef is a good sushi chef.

After about an hour of pitching, with a few towel breaks, I sat down and told Paula the knuckler was really jumping.

"Oh, is that so?" said Paula with her best mock-adoring look, as she patted the sweat off the tip of my nose. "Tell me how wonderful you were, sweetheart."

JULY 5
THURSDAY

Chip and I fired back with both barrels today.

The opinion piece that we wrote for the *Pittsfield Gazette*—which hit the stands this morning—became the subject of my talk at the Rotary Club lunch this afternoon. I made copies on pink paper—to distinguish it from our other handouts—and put a stack on the table where people checked in.

About eighty people, an equal mix of men and women, grazed at a buffet and sat down at round tables in a mini-ballroom. I was introduced as "the former Yankee now trying to play ball here in Pittsfield."

"We need the business community to help save Wahconah Park," I said, challenging their presumed support for a new stadium. "You have to change horses and ride fast."

I told them about our plan and why we needed a lease as soon as possible. I said the problem was that the mayor and most of the city councilors say they won't support us until Berkshire Sports & Events folds its tent, and that BS&E says it can't do anything until *it* hears from Dean Singleton.

"Think about it," I said, pausing for effect. "The heart of your city is in the hands of some guy in Denver."

The glasses had stopped clinking by this time.

"This political game we're engaged in right now," I said, "is not a spectator sport. The people have already spoken. Now it's up to *you*, the business community, to stand up and be counted."

The room got even quieter.

"How many people here today," I said, asking for a show of hands, "are in favor of our proposal to keep professional baseball in Wahconah Park?"

A roomful of hands went up. I counted them out loud. Seventy-nine. Then I asked who still favored a new stadium. Just one.

I thanked them for the chance to speak, accepted a Rotary paper weight, and returned to my seat. Someone asked if I knew the guy who had raised his hand for the new stadium. I said I didn't.

"Phil Massery," he said. "James Massery's brother."

JULY 6
FRIDAY

Got a call today from David Colby, president of the Pittsfield Chamber of Commerce, whom I had met at the Rotary Club luncheon yesterday. Colby explained that the Chamber had previously endorsed the new-stadium plan, but that he liked what I had to say and wanted to hear more.

"Could Chip and I speak at your next meeting?" I asked.

"I don't want to commit political suicide," he said. "I'll have to check with Berkshire Sports & Events. We have some overlapping board members."

Raising your hand is one thing. Extending your neck is quite another.

The Rotary Club response was gratifying but not surprising. I believe we would have gotten the same result from any group—even if our opponents had been given equal time. That's how much of a no-brainer our plan is. We just need to get our message out.

This is now a public relations battle. If we can get the people behind us, we can put the councilors and the commissioners on the spot. Make them declare where they stand. Right now—except for councilors Bianchi, Guzzo, and Scapin—they're all holding back.

Not one public official, except for Mayor Doyle, has come forward and said, "I still favor a new stadium." *That* would be political suicide. Such a losing proposition could be espoused only by a lame-duck mayor, or someone like Scribner who can hide behind his unsigned, no-discussion, no-accountability editorials.

This allows the new-stadium guys to hide in the grass. "A lot of silent support," as Dan Bianchi says. We make our case, but our opponents don't respond.

"We're punching, and they're just leaning back," said Chip. "It's the rope-a-dope strategy."

JULY 7
SATURDAY

Bill Carey, a staff writer for the *Eagle*, telephoned Chip to ask a few questions and Chip patched me into the conversation. It was quite a long interview. We'll see what happens with that.

Tonight I packed for a five-day trip to the West Coast. I have a couple of talks to give, and some book signings, and a meeting with the Seattle Mariners about the possibility of their hosting a Pilots Old Timers' Day in 2002. The Pilots are the team I wrote about in *Ball Four* that played only one year in Seattle, 1969, before they were abruptly pulled away—a week before the next season began—and moved to Milwaukee where they were renamed the Brewers. The Pilots have never had an Old Timers' Day and it would be fun to get everybody together—well, almost everybody—just one last time, for a nice hello and a proper goodbye.

JULY 8
SUNDAY

Well, whadda ya know? The *Berkshire Eagle* ran a front-page story by Bill Carey. And it was fair!

Under the headline BALLPARK SUITORS WANT ACTION, Carey made the key points that time was of the essence and that our plan was being delayed by city officials who have told us that they're waiting to hear from Berkshire Sports & Events. He quoted me saying, "The clock is running out on our proposal," and Chip saying, "The future of professional baseball in Pittsfield is waiting for a signal from a man in Denver."

I wonder how much longer Carey will be working at the *Eagle*.

This afternoon I got ready to leave for the airport. I packed my cell phone, my laptop, and my Palm Pilot and confirmed that Chip had my itinerary with the hotel phones and fax numbers. I told him I'd be calling in to get the latest Wahconah update.

"I'll just call Chip, to see how you're doing," said Paula.

I gave her a big hug, and told her I'd miss *her*, too.

JULY 9
MONDAY—SEATTLE, WA

It's always great to wake up in Seattle. The smell of the ocean. The sounds of the waterfront. The seagulls. It reminds me of that summer with the Pilots, and the boat trips with the kids to Whidbey Island and the Olympic Peninsula. And of course, manager Joe Schultz and the players.

Now here I am again, thirty-two years later, keeping notes for a different kind of adventure with its own cast of curious characters. One of them is my partner Chip, who called with the latest news.

"I thanked Bill Carey for his courage in running yesterday's story," said Chip. "He said his editor wasn't very happy with him because he hadn't run it by Berkshire Sports & Events first."

"I guess Eric Lincoln was right when he said Berkshire Sports & Events and the *Eagle* are one and the same," I said.

"Then there was an item in today's *Eagle*," said Chip, "about the closing of the North End Restaurant. It quoted Smitty saying that the closing was 'voluntary and had nothing to do with taxes.'"

"Never would have crossed my mind," I said, laughing.

"I wonder if the mayor ate and drank him into insolvency," said Chip. The story also said that Smith had originally purchased the building in 1999 for $230,000—with a mortgage of *$260,000* from Berkshire Bank.

"As a park commissioner," I said, joking, "maybe Smitty wanted to divest himself of a conflict of interest with the bank."

"I doubt it," said Chip. "The story also said that the Brewery, and Smitty's food service contract with GE Plastics, remain in place."

"GE Plastics?" I said. "Because Jay Pomeroy just luuuves Smitty's cooking."

"I also sent Bob Mellace an email," said Chip, "suggesting that the July 23 Parks Commission meeting be advertised in advance, and that it be held at a larger venue for the public discussion that he had called for."

"I can't wait for that public discussion," I said. "We'll get the same show of hands there that I got at the Rotary luncheon. Times ten."

"I also made the case for why we needed a thirty-year lease," said Chip, "and added a few more details to our plan, like the $25,000 in annual capital improvements and being responsible for all maintenance at Wahconah Park, including major structural repairs."

"How much do you think we're really going to spend in the first year?" I asked.

"About $250,000."

"Then why don't we say that?"

"It's too early," said Chip. "We'll save it for later. We don't want to show all our cards right now."

I wished Chip well at the open mike, and we hung up.

The Wahconah Warriors never rest.

Tonight I had dinner at Mike Fuller's house. I had met Mike a few years ago, on his web site—www.seattlepilots.com—which is so comprehensive you can hear the hot water not running in the clubhouse.

There's also a link to a page where fans can vote on whether or not they would attend a Pilots Old Timers' Day in 2002.

Joining us at dinner was Charles Kapner, the world's leading collector of Pilots memorabilia. Charles has a room in his house that's lined with official Pilots mugs, pennants, bumper stickers, hair bonnets, baby bibs, demitasse spoons, cuff link sets, wind breakers, swizzle sticks, bar coasters, plastic radio baseballs, and a very catchy "Go, Go, You Pilots" 45 rpm record. This is in addition to the usual tickets, posters, and yearbooks. Hell, we had more items than wins! Charles is still looking for an official Pilots *usher's* jacket, if anyone happens to come across one.

Both Mike and Charles are pushing for a Pilots Old Timers' Day.

I asked Mike how many "hits" he's had on his Pilots web site.

"According to the guy who hosts my site," said Mike, "it gets more than any other site he has, including the Catholic Archdiocese of Los Angeles."

The Seattle Pilots more popular than Jesus?

JULY 10
TUESDAY—SEATTLE, WA

How many guys would rather eat a room service dinner at a hotel in Seattle than have hot dogs and beer at the All-Star Game at Safeco Field? With a free ticket, no less. Count me in that demented group. And why? Very simple. I was waiting for Chip's call with an update on tonight's City Council meeting back in Pittsfield.

I hated to miss our second council appearance even if it was just three minutes' worth. The televised open mike is one of the best ways to get our message across. I was imagining Chip at the mike when he called.

"Are you sitting down?" he asked, with a smile in his voice.

Then he read me today's *Eagle* editorial.

> Neither MediaNews Group CEO Dean Singleton nor Berkshire Sports & Events . . . is impeding proposals to keep baseball at Wahconah Park . . . as a South County trio has charged . . . in a blatant attempt to manipulate city councilors with misinformation.

We laughed at this obvious projection from Scribner, Mr. Misinformation himself.

"The guy is desperate," said Chip.

"That means we're having an impact," I said.

"The best evidence of that," said Chip, "was the open mike, where three mayoral candidates, Dave Potts, Peter McHugh, and Ed Baptiste, and a city council candidate, Jonathan Lothrop, spoke in favor of our plan for Wahconah Park. And no one spoke against."

"There is no better barometer of public sentiment," I said, "than a candidate running for office."

Or *not* running. Along with the mayor, four of the eight new-stadium councilors have decided not to seek reelection, and the Three Amigos—Bianchi, Guzzo, and Scapin—are running unopposed.

"The stadium issue has become the third rail of Pittsfield politics," said Chip.

"Tell me about your open mike," I said.

"I used the first minute to refute Scribner's editorial," said Chip, "quoting Andy Mick saying that it's not his decision—'The guy you have to convince is my boss in Denver'—and quoting an unnamed councilor saying, 'We can't just walk away from this unless Andy Mick releases us.'"

"You should have named Massery directly," I said.

"I didn't want to embarrass him too much," said Chip. "He was sitting right there."

I said it was too bad that Massery didn't jump up and shout, "I never said that!"

We laughed at the thought. Then Chip got serious.

"Wait 'til you hear this," he said. "I had to use the rest of my open mike to address a front-page story in today's *Eagle* headlined MEDIANEWS IS STILL OFFERING $2 MILLION FOR A NEW STADIUM. Dean Singleton is quoted as saying that a new stadium 'would work just as well in South Berkshire County or even in North Adams, and we own newspapers in both places.'"

"And then he's going to steal Christmas," I said.

"I told them that since the county can support only one team, Pittsfield's punishment for not backing a new stadium would be to lose professional baseball forever. The city's natural monopoly—which has blocked other teams from coming into the Berkshires for eighty-two years—would be *given to another city by its own home-town newspaper.*"

"It's so transparent," I said. "You'd think they would be ashamed or embarrassed."

"This really pisses me off," said Chip. "It's like what the Romans used to do whenever another city challenged the empire. They would salt the earth so the people could never grow crops again."

"Caligula was a new-coliseum backer as I recall," I said.

"Here's the cute part," said Chip. "The story said that the $2 million available for a new stadium 'must contribute to downtown economic development.' Nothing against Pittsfield, you understand, the *Eagle* just wants to improve a downtown. Any downtown."

"And only with a new baseball stadium," I said.

"The article ends," said Chip, "by saying that the proposed stadium site is now for sale. It quotes Andy Mick saying, 'We can't just sit there on a vacant piece of property forever.' And rumor has it that a drugstore is interested."

"Eagle Drugs," I said. "The newspaper's gift to the city."

"At the end of my open mike," said Chip, "I asked for a show of hands like you did at the Rotary, and 90% of the audience of about forty people were in favor of our proposal, including Bianchi and Guzzo. Scapin was absent, and the other eight councilors just sat there. When I asked who still supported a new stadium, guess who conspicuously raised his fat hand?"

"The mayor," I said.

"Right," said Chip. "Tony."

Before he hung up, Chip said he was writing an opinion piece entitled "Salting the Earth" that will address the latest threat from Singleton. Chip said he's going to offer it to the *Eagle.*

Now there's optimism for you.

The irony here is that if Singleton is serious about helping build a new stadium somewhere else in the Berkshires, Pittsfield's best defense would be to give us a lease on Wahconah Park so we can get a team established and block out everyone else.

Of course, the *Eagle* never suggested *that* solution.

It's just a bluff, of course. The *Eagle* would never actually help fund a new stadium anywhere but Pittsfield. It would make a terrible national story. I can just see the headline—MEDIANEWS GROUP TO LOCAL BASEBALL FANS: DROP DEAD!

How can the *Eagle* get away with even threatening such a thing? A couple of reasons. First, it has no competition. As the only daily paper, it's the only game in town. Small circulation weeklies, like the *Gazette* and the *Record*, can't compete—and not so much for readers as for those all important advertisers and community leaders who need to stay on good terms with what amounts to a state-run (or in this case, insider-run) propaganda machine.

Another reason is the very nature of a newspaper. It's disposable. Today's outrageous editorial is tomorrow's trash. There's no accountability. No peer review. No bill to pay. No body of work that must stand scrutiny. Editorials are snapshots—very often distorted ones—that never make it into a photo album. And balance is minimal. Critical op-ed pieces don't appear for days, if at all. Letters to the editor can be weeks behind the point they're challenging.

Editorials are blobs of thought, easily reshaped to cover one's tracks, back off previous mistakes, fudge prior opinions—without acknowledgment or apology. And always there are the misdirection plays, the fake hand-offs, as when the *Eagle* will occasionally complain about the "good old boys," ignoring the fact that its top executives *are* the "good old boys."

No lie is too obvious; no contradiction is too blatant. Before the Civic Authority vote, possessing information to the contrary, the *Eagle* continued to proclaim "no stadium, no baseball" and "there's no alternative." After the vote, Scribner blamed the mayor and his aides —"a political regime thoroughly out of touch with reality"—which is like a football coach blaming his linemen for a faulty game plan.

The process is insidious, like water torture, where no single drop seems that bad. Like getting pecked to death by magpies. It's relentless, creating an aura of inevitability, and ultimately debilitating. The end result is a dispiriting sense that although something isn't right, it can't be changed, and so what else is new?

"Pretty rough up there in Pittsfield," friends will say to Chip or me, with a vague notion that something rotten is going on.

But for the people of Pittsfield who know what the hell is going on, it's pretty damn clear. The *Eagle*'s threat to help build a baseball stadium in a nearby town is just one more kick in the balls.

When I called Paula tonight and told her what was happening, she got very agitated.

"I get so angry" she said. "I don't know how you keep going with those idiots taking cheap shots at you every day."

"At this point," I said, "it's *because* of the cheap shots. The game has changed. Now it's a challenge. It's us against them. It's actually more fun."

And we're not going away.

JULY 11
WEDNESDAY—SEATTLE, WA / SAN FRANCISCO, CA

Met this morning with Gregg Green, promotions director for the Seattle Mariners. Green is a young guy with close-cropped, rust-colored hair and glasses. He said he had read *Ball Four* as a kid and that he liked it. I told him about my idea for a Pilots Old Timers' Day at Safeco Field in 2002.

"You could bill it as the Original Mariners and the One and Only Pilots," I said.

"That's the Mariners' twenty-fifth anniversary," said Green. "We're already planning lots of events. What's the significance of 2002 for the Pilots?"

"Without the Pilots you wouldn't have the Mariners," I said.

I recounted the history of the two teams. How when the Pilots were moved to Milwaukee after their only season in Seattle, the city sued major league baseball, and as part of the settlement Seattle was promised an expansion franchise, which became the Mariners.

"The Mariners were born in 1977, but they were *conceived* in 1969," I said. "It was only a one-season stand, but it was still love."

Green smiled courteously. "Too bad the Pilots don't have their own anniversary," he said.

"It's too late for the Pilots' twenty-fifth anniversary," I said. "And the thirtieth. If we wait for the thirty-fifth in 2004, who knows how many of us will still be left? We've already lost Joe Schultz, Sal Maglie, Ray Oyler, George Brunet, and Gene Brabender. And Gary Bell says he isn't feeling that well."

Green laughed.

"Maybe Budweiser would sponsor a 'Pound a Bud' weekend, in honor of Joe Schultz," I said. "The old Pilots could arrive in the harbor, in a tall ship, like the Flying Dutchman, sailing the seas since '69."

Green scribbled on his pad.

"We won't be making any decisions until after the World Series, in October," he said.

"I'd like to move faster than that, if possible," I said. "So we can plan a nice weekend. Tie it in with a local charity. The Arc of King County, which provides services to the disabled, is interested in hosting a luncheon and a golf tournament."

"I'll get back to you in a couple of weeks," said Green.

I thanked Green for his time and left him with a *Sports Illustrated* article endorsing a Pilots Old Timers' Game, and a stack of emails to Mike Fuller's web site from people who said they would go.

It isn't easy being a marketing genius.

On my flight from Seattle to San Francisco, where I was scheduled to speak at a convention of mortgage bankers, I saw a familiar face sitting in front of me. It was Jerry Colangelo, my old high school pitching rival and now owner of the Arizona Diamondbacks. Colangelo was in the last row of first class and I was in the first row of coach. So we pulled the curtain aside and talked.

Colangelo had Yogi Berra's book, *If You Come to a Fork in the Road, Take It.* We laughed over a photo of Yogi and Joe Garagiola as kids. I told Colangelo about the telegram Garagiola sent when they opened the Yogi Berra Museum in New Jersey: "When we were kids, growing up on The Hill in St. Louis," Garagiola wrote, "the subject of having a museum named after one of us never came up."

We laughed about that and then I remembered a story that Big Pete Sheehy, the Yankee clubhouse man, told me about the day Yogi joined the Yankees. Yogi had come straight from the training base in Maryland and was still in his Navy blues.

"My name is Yogi Berra," he said to Big Pete. "I don't look like a ballplayer in this sailor suit, but I am."

Big Pete said, "You don't even look like a sailor."

Colangelo and I get along fine these days. The last time Paula and I were in Phoenix, he was a very gracious host, giving us a personal tour of the new Bank One Ballpark and inviting us to sit in his family box next to the dugout.

We never talk about our old rivalry except to joke about it. When I was inducted into the Bloom Hall of Fame in 1990 (five years after Colangelo), I said I looked back on my high school days with the same fondness that veterans have for World War II. And at our high school centennial last year, I told a field house full of people that it was harder to make the frosh–soph baseball team at Bloom than the New York Yankees. Jerry gets a big kick out of that story.

Then Colangelo said he had some bad news.

"You know Earl DeTella died," he said.

"Oh no," I said. "No. Not Earl."

"Two weeks ago," said Jerry. "Heart attack. He was seventy-five."

I felt a sad flutter in my stomach. Earl was one of the main people in my life. He was always on the edge of my thoughts about baseball, and how it happened that I ended up in the big leagues.

"We're getting to that age when these things happen," said Colangelo.

"Geez, I thought Earl would live to be in his nineties," I said. "He was always so strong. Still working with his hands. I just saw him last year."

I told Jerry I could still hear Earl's voice, hollering at me as I raked the field, that first day I met him at Heights Park.

"Hey! Whatta you doin'?" I said, imitating DeTella's familiar high-pitched rasp.

Jerry smiled and nodded.

We wished each other well. And Colangelo went back to reading Yogi's book.

I closed out the day in San Francisco with a call to Chip to find out what was happening.

"The news is not good," he said.

Then he read a story in the *Eagle* headlined BOARD TO TAKE TIME ON WAHCONAH, which quoted new Parks Commission Chairman Cliff Nilan saying, "I'm not sure we're going to rush in and make a decision on this too quickly."

We figured this was Nilan's response to Chip's email suggesting the July 23 Parks Commission meeting be advertised in advance and held at a large venue.

"The next meeting," Nilan told the *Eagle,* "will be in August."

The best guess seems to be August 13, which is the the first Monday in August that precedes a Tuesday City Council meeting.

This makes two Parks Commission meetings that have been canceled since our off-the-cuff presentation on June 25—a presentation in which we clearly stated a need for timely action in the best interests of Pittsfield. It can't be a coincidence.

"They're trying to run out the clock on us," I said.

"That's why," said Chip, "when anyone asks what our deadline is, we shouldn't give them a date."

"What they're really asking," I said, "is how many bullets we have left."

"The other reason they're stalling," said Chip, "is that they're probably negotiating with Fleisig. He knows about our proposal. He's not going to come up here and tangle with us unless he's got some kind of deal."

"I still think BS&E is trying to get a New York–Penn League team," I said. "Purchased by GE and run by Jay Pomeroy."

"Because Pomeroy just . . . what?" asked Chip.

"Luuuuves baseball," I said.

JULY 12
THURSDAY—SAN FRANCISCO, CA

The roller coaster is on its way back up.

Chip called to say he had spoken with David Colby, the president of the Chamber of Commerce, who heard me at the Rotary luncheon last week.

"We're invited to address an ad hoc meeting at nine o'clock tomorrow morning. When are you getting back?"

"Not until the afternoon," I said, "unless I take the red-eye."

"You don't have to do that," said Chip. "I can take care of it."

"I know you can," I said. "But I'd like to be there. I'll fly stand-by tonight, go right from the airport, and meet you for breakfast in Pittsfield."

Then Chip read me some of his "Salting the Earth" piece, which appeared in this week's *Pittsfield Gazette:*

> In ancient times, the Romans reserved a special punishment for cities that dared rise up against the Empire. They salted the earth, so that the people could never grow crops on their once-fertile fields. Mr. Singleton is offended that the citizens of Pittsfield rejected his offer to help build a new stadium for them. They will pay the price.
>
> Or will they? The business community and individual citizens could rise up with strong voices and demand that their elected officials and the park commissioners respond to our proposal to bring professional baseball permanently to Wahconah Park.
>
> Mayor Doyle and many of the current city councilors . . . are not running for re-election. But they were elected to serve to the best of their abilities through their entire term, which doesn't end until December 31st.
>
> By Labor Day, many of our promising opportunities to acquire a baseball franchise will have passed . . . and if we don't get action on our proposal until January 2002, it will be far, far too late to save the 2002 season, and maybe—if the earth has been salted—to save any future baseball season for Pittsfield.

"That's great," I said, "make copies and bring them to the meeting tomorrow morning."

"I'll put it on gray paper," said Chip. "We're already using white, blue, beige, and pink."

"They're trying to get us to run out of colors," I said.

Meanwhile, in a parallel universe, the *Eagle* continued with its own version of reality. Today's editorial, as read by Chip, was entitled No Hurry on Wahconah Park Plan.

> The Parks Commission wisely will not be rushed into accepting . . . a proposed 30-year deal to lease Wahconah Park to a trio of South County entrepreneurs who promise to maintain the crumbling facility . . . [a deal] that would exclude a collegiate team . . . [by] a group perilously light on financing. . . . Aging Wahconah

Park cannot be reconstructed into a modern facility acceptable to the minor leagues. . . . There is, however, still a possibility that an affiliated team could find a home in the Berkshires if a new stadium were to be constructed in North Adams, a city that would no doubt welcome . . .

Chip said he's already writing a rebuttal for the *Eagle* op-ed page that he hopes to have finished by tonight. And, just to see what happens, he said he also Fed-Ex'ed a letter to Dean Singleton explaining how Singleton's "new stadium anywhere" proposal makes him look like a spoiler.

Chip said he's also still married to Cindy.

Then we talked about Councilman Gary Grunin, who recently announced that he is running for mayor. His only problems are that he's been a staunch new-stadium supporter, he's a close friend of Mayor Doyle, he may have conflict-of-interest problems because his companies did $55,947 worth of business with the city, and he was vice president of the Council and a member of the finance committee while Pittsfield was running up a $9 million deficit.

Other than that he's clear.

"You can't buy opponents like this," said Chip.

Grunin is a trim, well-dressed fellow, about five-foot-eight, with dark eyes and a mustache. Among pro-Wahconah folks, he has a reputation for being shifty. His body language doesn't help. With his head inclined forward, as if he were looking through his eyebrows, and his dark eyes darting around the room, it seems like he's pulling a fast one.

"He looks like a rat," I said to Chip, "guarding a piece of cheese."

Grunin was recently quoted in the *Eagle* defending city officials who want to delay action on Wahconah Park. "We shouldn't jump at the first proposal," he said. "We sort of rushed into the Civic Authority, and look where that got us."

It'll be interesting to see what Grunin has to say at the meeting tomorrow morning. He's also vice president of the Chamber of Commerce. The guy is everywhere, like kudzu.

In my speech tonight, I told the California mortgage bankers that they were just the people I wanted to speak to because, what with interest rates going down and all, Paula and I were looking to refinance and what's more, a house in Massachusetts would give them some needed geographical diversity. They laughed, in a fiduciary kind of way.

Then I headed for the airport.

JULY 13
FRIDAY

The plane was early and I arrived in Pittsfield before the coffee shop where Chip and I had agreed to meet was even open. So I sat on my luggage and waited.

When he finally showed up, I told him I had actually arrived last night and that I had slept in the hallway. For a moment he believed me—such is our fanaticism for this enterprise.

"If we can get the Chamber of Commerce to endorse us," said Chip, downing a blueberry muffin, "that will send a strong message."

The meeting was held in a small conference room at the chamber headquarters on North Street. Seated around the table were about twenty people, including chamber president David Colby and Gary Grunin. Chip and I handed out copies from our growing stack of color-coded documents.

The first words, surprisingly, were spoken by Gary Grunin.

"I thought it would be a good idea to invite you here," said Grunin, as if it had been his idea to have us come and speak.

Chip and I took turns making our pitch, focusing on the need for the business community to break ranks and get behind our proposal. Unlike at the Parks Commission meeting, we got lots of questions, the answers to which were contained in the documents before them, which we quoted as they followed along, in "the blue one" or "the beige one."

It *seemed* that we were getting through but who can tell in this town whose leaders are always looking over their shoulders? Or through their eyebrows.

On the drive home from Pittsfield, Chip told me about his new email correspondent, Bill Everhart—the editorial page editor of the *Eagle*. The relationship began when Chip emailed his "Salting the Earth" piece to Scribner and Everhart answered it. And he was none too happy.

"As the author of the majority of the *Eagle*'s editorials on ballpark issues over the past few years I am angered, though certainly not surprised, by the snide assertion that our editorials are 'following a political agenda,'" Everhart wrote. "Andy Mick? I never consult with Mr. Mick on editorials. Dean Singleton? I doubt if Mr. Singleton knows me from Adam. . . . Your letter, which cannot run for obvious reasons, suggests you have contracted a case of Pittsfield paranoia. . . . You have a right to make your case to the city. So make it! No one is stopping you."

This was interesting because we had always assumed—like most people in the Berkshires—that Scribner, who is listed as editor in chief, writes the editorials. Especially since Scribner's column is indistinguishable from the editorials. We wondered if Scribner just approved Everhart's editorials, or were they so philosophically entwined that it didn't matter who wrote and who edited?

"So what did you write back?" I asked Chip.

"I said I welcomed the dialogue," said Chip, "and I asked him for a reasoned rebuttal to our proposal for Wahconah Park."

"Did he do that?"

"No," said Chip. "But he did give me some background on the new-stadium concept. He said it had originated with the editorial department and that when Andy Mick arrived they sold it to him, and he sold it to Singleton."

"No wonder it doesn't make sense financially," I said. "It was dreamed up by writers."

"Everhart's expertise is that he claims to have visited every minor league ballpark in the Northeast," said Chip. "He says he's talked with fans, and team officials, and ballplayers, and community leaders, who all think new stadiums are a great idea."

"Did he say he'd spoken to any taxpayers," I asked. "Someone who might rather have more school supplies or a fire truck?"

"No," said Chip. "But he did admit that there was room for only one minor-league franchise, and that if Singleton's new-stadium advocacy could be seen as blocking our proposal for Wahconah Park, then our proposal could be seen as blocking a new stadium."

"Precisely!" I said. "The difference is that the people have voted for Wahconah Park three different times. Not once for a new stadium."

"That's what I told him in my follow-up email," said Chip. "I also said that we're prepared to answer anybody's questions and concerns at length, and do it publicly, and that the *Eagle* should sponsor a debate."

"What did he say to that?"

"He never responded to the debate idea," said Chip.

"They don't want to debate," I said, "because they know they'd lose. They're chicken-shit. They'd rather just lob a few grenades and then run."

By this time, we had pulled into my driveway and I was home at last, after five days on the road.

"It's so good to have you back," said Paula, as we wrapped our arms around each other. "Even though Chip got to hug you first."

"But I never get the two of you mixed up," I said. "I know you're the curvy one."

JULY 14
SATURDAY

Chip is amazing. At precisely 3:07 this morning, he sends an email to Bill Everhart, in response to a Letter to the Editor in yesterday's *Eagle* from someone named Frank Bonnevie. I don't know if Chip stayed up late last night or woke up early this morning. Or if he simply doesn't sleep at all.

In any case, this guy Bonnevie had written a letter that touched on nearly every issue raised to date about a new stadium versus our proposal for Wahconah Park, as follows:

> *I cannot believe the nerve . . . this group wants a lease on Wahconah Park and it doesn't have a baseball team . . . they wanted the citizens . . . to help them buy a team.*

Is there still a hockey team coming? Who is going to build the 6,000-seat hockey arena? Why can't Elitzer, Bouton and Margenau share Wahconah Park with a collegiate league team?

The citizens . . . voted down the Civic Authority because they didn't like the powers it had. But by moving the ballpark around, the ballfield will fit in between the people that want to sell the land and the people that don't. There is no need for eminent domain. . . . This is the only project that has a chance of being built.

It's a very brief letter, so carefully crafted it's almost like Haiku. A little *too* carefully crafted, we thought—and a little too angry—for just a regular citizen.

So Chip is on the hunt for one Frank Bonnevie. Or his alter ego.

"Dear Bill," Chip's 3:07 a.m. email to Everhart begins. "After reading the letter by Frank Bonnevie, I am struck once again by how difficult it is to correct *Eagle*-fostered misinformation. Any chance you could publish my July 12 letter responding to your editorial of that same date as an op-ed piece?" Then Chip adds a P.S. "I would also appreciate your assistance in contacting Mr. Bonnevie to supply him directly with this same information. I can't find his name in the phone book. Thanks, Chip."

At 9:18 a.m., after I wake up but before I brush my teeth, I send Chip this email:

> They should call YOU the Bulldog.

At 2:52 p.m., Everhart emails Chip:

> Dear Chip: Mr. Bonnevie has a right to his
> opinion and has an unlisted number, which he
> doesn't want divulged. A letter from you
> making your case for Wahconah Park is welcome,
> but not one that offers speculation about the
> motives of Mr. Singleton that you can't
> support with evidence. Bill.

At 3:44 p.m., Chip emails Everhart:

> Dear Bill, I'm attaching the email letter I had
> previously sent that I was asking you to publish.
> It is the dispassionate and information-
> packed one, not the "conspiracy theory" one.
> I do think it would be helpful to your
> readership, including folks like Mr. Bonnevie,
> if you would print it as an op-ed piece.

Then he adds this bit:

> Verizon does not have any person with the
> last name Bonnevie with an unlisted number.
> (They don't divulge such numbers, but they do
> say whether or not they have them.) Do you
> know for a fact that "Frank Bonnevie" is
> using his real name and that he resides in
> Pittsfield? Everyone is entitled to his own
> opinion in a letter to the editor but he also
> has an obligation to identify himself
> correctly. Thanks, Chip.

At 4:26 p.m., I send Chip another email:

> I'm laughing out loud right now about your
> wonderful tenaciousness. In a very polite
> way, you simply will not let go of Everhart's
> leg. I have never seen anything like it.

At 7:06 p.m., Everhart emails Chip:

> Frank Bonnevie is a veteran letter writer
> from Pittsfield. And our computer system is
> not set up to read attachments. Please send
> your letter/op-ed piece in a different format.
> Thanks, Bill.

At 6:35 *the next morning*—a Sunday morning—Chip sends the letter/op-ed piece in a different format, with instructions about which parts should be underlined and asking whether or not they plan to run it and when.

Whew!

Chip is one of those guys you would want to have with you in a foxhole.

Which is where the two of us might be living shortly.

JULY 15
SUNDAY

Our friend, Alex Bloomstein, an attorney and dance choreographer (I'm not kidding) who is part of a family of friends that Paula and I hang out with, told us something weird today. He said he was driving in his car last week, listening to WAMC, and he heard David Scribner tell Alan Chartock that Chip and I were "carpetbaggers."

"I couldn't believe it," said Alex. "I almost drove off the road."

Alex is a neighbor of Chartock's.

"Did Alan ever call you about that?" he asked.

"Not yet," I said.

Given WAMC's reputation for journalistic integrity—equal time and all that—maybe Chip and I will be invited to discuss the subject that Scribner was referring to with his "carpetbagger" remark. Especially since Chip had just sent Alan a copy of his "Salting the Earth" article with a note that said, "Might it be timely to have a *Vox Pop* debate?"

Not timely enough. Chip said he bumped into Alan this morning at the Farmer's Market in Great Barrington.

"He didn't want to talk about it," said Chip.

Meanwhile, it's important to understand that Scribner's carpetbagger accusation has less to do with geography than it does with class, as in class warfare.

There are three distinct sections of Berkshire County—a vertical rectangle that covers the westernmost eighth of Massachusetts.

The South County part—defined by Lenox, Stockbridge, and Great Barrington—is the rapidly expanding, artsy-craftsy, weekender, big-city transplant, celebrity-sighting, sushi-eating area.

North County has two different sections: The northernmost tip—consisting of Williamstown and North Adams—is the theater festival, MASS MoCA (Museum of Contemporary Art)-attending, ski weekend, college-town area. The rest of North County—the heart of which is Pittsfield—is the declining, industrial, blue-collar, county government, hill country section.

To understand how these areas relate, just follow the traffic pattern, which flows north and south, between South County and the northernmost tip of North County, through and around—preferably around—Pittsfield.

Given these cultural and geographic divides, and the New Englander's legendary reputation for xenophobia, you might expect that the natives and the transplants do not get along. But this is not the case. For some reason, maybe because it's been "discovered" slowly over the years, Berkshire County works pretty well as a community. Million-dollar houses sit right next door to $100,000 fixer-uppers or working farms. This makes it tough to get a mortgage—appraisers have trouble finding comparable sales in the immediate neighborhood because there are few comparable homes.

Your wealthiest neighbor might be driving a pick-up truck, and it's not a fashion statement. In fact, fashion is out. Even among transplants, there is a definite disdain for "chic." When Paula and I first moved up here from New Jersey, she noticed women going out to restaurants with naked faces and undyed hair. What stands out to us now is the make-up and the dyed hair of the tourists, which looks artificial and out of place. They don't call the Berkshires "the un-Hamptons" for nothing.

Accordingly, the term South County, as used in Scribner's column or in the *Eagle*'s editorials, can be a double-edged sword. It's either one of the "enlightened communities" to which Pittsfield has "foolishly surrendered," or it's the home of "carpetbaggers" who have no business being in Pittsfield.

Both are perfect for wrapping fish.

JULY 16
MONDAY

Today is Media Day for the South County duo. First up, a program called *Perspectives* on Pittsfield Community Television, hosted by Councilor Joe Guzzo, one of the famous Three Amigos.

Joe looks like a character from a children's story book. He's short and round with a scruffy beard, a bulbous nose, crinkly eyes, and a mouth that looks like it's saying, "heh heh heh." In short, Joe looks like a gnome, a lawn ornament come to life. This morning, in Bermudas and flip-flops, he looked as if he had just stepped out of someone's flower garden.

Chip and I were wearing sports coats and slacks with open-necked dress shirts—casual cool. We brought a list of questions for Joe to ask us in case he needed any help. Tough questions, the ones our opponents are asking in the media and behind our backs in a way that implies there are no answers. The ones they would ask us in person if they wanted to fight fair.

Questions like this:

- You want a thirty-year lease on Wahconah Park. Why such a long time?
- You've been accused of not having the money to pull this off. What do you say to that?
- Why can't you share Wahconah with a collegiate league team?
- Why should you get a lease if you don't have a team?

And then a few softball questions:

- What plans do you have for fixing up the park?
- How does independent league baseball compare to the New York–Penn League?

We gave the sound-bite answers required for television. Chip tackled the financial questions. I took the baseball ones. And Joe handled it all like a pro—which came as no surprise, since Joe for many years had his own radio show. Until it was censored, that is.

On May 1 of this year, Joe quit his radio show, *City Talk*, after WBEC's management ordered him to stop talking about the Civic Authority. WBEC, which once stood for Berkshire Eagle Communications and used to be owned by the *Eagle*, still uses that paper for its news gathering. Clarence Fanto, managing editor of the *Eagle*, reads the news on WBEC just as David Scribner does on WAMC.

The day after Joe walked out, WBEC replaced him with a more impartial commentator. A fair, open-minded individual. Fellow by the name of Doyle. Gerry Doyle. The mayor. Or "Tony," if you will.

I defy anyone to dream up stuff like this.

And what did Joe Guzzo think about it? "I think it was a planned thing," he said.

From the Joe Guzzo TV show, we drove over to the Larry Kratka radio show at WUPE. Larry seems to be one of our supporters—at least until he gets replaced—and we had a good hour chatting and taking calls. Too bad the mayor didn't show up. Larry had invited him to share the mike with us, but he declined.

After the show was over, Chip and I stopped by the office of Larry's boss, station owner Phil Weiner, who said he had heard of our proposal for Wahconah Park. We told him about the problems we were up against and asked for his help.

"What we'd like to have," said Chip, "is for some reputable group or organization to sponsor a debate, open to the public, where we can take on any and all questions, and where we in turn can question our opponents."

"Maybe WUPE could do it," I said, "in cooperation with another radio station, or Pittsfield Community Television, or even the *Eagle*. It could be held in a small theater or a school auditorium."

Weiner, an agreeable-looking man who appeared to be in his late fifties, listened carefully and nodded as we spoke.

"I have to call a few people," he said, finally.

In Pittsfield, we're discovering, everyone has to check with someone else, so they know what to think.

"Well, that might be good," I said, on our way to the car.

"Not if he's calling Andy Mick," said Chip.

Here's how far gone we are. Chip went on the Internet to search for Frank Bonnevie and came up with a guy by that name who either owns or runs a karate and kickboxing school in Pittsfield. We had the address of the school. Why not stop by and see if he's there?

We rang the doorbell at a seedy-looking, one-story building along a highway. A rugged-looking, square-jawed guy of about forty, wearing jeans and a tee shirt, answered the door.

"Frank Bonnevie?" asked Chip.

"Yeah, what can I do for you?" he said, eyeing us warily.

We introduced ourselves, said we had seen the letter in the *Eagle*, and wondered if he had a few minutes to talk. A look came over his face that said, "I don't get it, but I'm curious," and he invited us in.

Frank Bonnevie looks like a guy who has a black belt in *something*. A strong silent type who seems less like a letter writer than a mouth puncher. Needless to say, we were very polite. You don't mess with a fellow who can wipe out a horde of barbarians with a few well-placed kicks.

As if it were perfectly normal that two guys would seek out a total stranger who happened to write a letter to the newspaper, Chip and I—very politely—clarified a few things about our proposal. Not the type to roll over for a couple of smart-asses in sports coats, Bonnevie aggressively defended his belief in a new stadium.

"Well, I think we should keep Wahconah Park," announced a woman who had just walked into the room. She appeared to be in her mid-twenties and was carrying some cleaning supplies.

Bonnevie gave her a pained look. The topic did not seem to be a new one between them. And pretty soon it was three against one, with Bonnevie refusing to yield, and us trying to change his mind as if he were the Chairman of the House Ways and Means Committee.

At this point it was all just sport. We had already confirmed that there was, in fact, a Frank Bonnevie, and that he was certainly articulate enough to have written that letter to the editor. I'm not sure Bonnevie understood just who we were—two nuts on a mission, with time to kill in Pittsfield.

And that was just the morning.

After a quick lunch at the Lantern, we suddenly had a great idea. As long as we're in town, why not drop into the *Eagle*'s nest? See if anybody's around. Maybe Chip can meet his new pen pal, Bill Everhart. Find out if and when he plans to run Chip's letter/op-ed piece.

Photo by Chip Elitzer

Photo by Eric Lincoln

The *Eagle's* headquarters is a massive, factory-like brick building with an impressive clock tower rising above the five-story structure. We pulled into the parking lot and headed for the entrance.

"This is like walking behind enemy lines," said Chip.

"Watch for a muzzle flash from the upper windows," I said.

At the reception desk, we asked for Bill Carey because we figured he'd at least say hello to us. Maybe Carey could arrange for us to meet Everhart. To our surprise, we got more than that. Carey, a big man with a full head of healthy-looking hair combed straight back, invited us into the newsroom. There, he introduced us to Everhart and Clarence Fanto, who led us to a small conference room where we were eventually joined by David Scribner and a photographer.

It was almost as if they had expected us.

The conversation began with Carey asking us questions while he took notes on a pad of paper. Chip and I reviewed the brief history of our quest for Wahconah Park and conveyed our disappointment that the *Eagle,* which had criticized the naysayers for not having a plan, was now criticizing us for having one. Carey nodded, in apparent understanding.

"Now *we're* the naysayers," Carey said.

As we spoke with Carey, Everhart edited Chip's letter/op-ed piece by crossing things out with a ballpoint pen, while Scribner wandered in and out of the room.

Everhart and Scribner make quite a pair. Everhart, about six-foot-two, with watery eyes and a drooping mustache, is a dour fellow with a somewhat startled look behind his glasses. Scribner, or "the little twerp in the cowboy hat" as he's called by a few of his colleagues, is five-foot-six with wavy brown hair and a squinty-eyed smirk on his face. Today he was hatless, but he was wearing cowboy boots.

The only contentious moment came when Scribner challenged our view that BS&E and the *Eagle* were hindering our efforts.

"BS&E is finished," said Scribner. "You've seen the For Sale sign on the property. What do you think that means? There isn't going to be a new stadium."

"That doesn't prevent the *Eagle* from campaigning against our proposal for Wahconah Park," I said.

"That's ridiculous," said Scribner. "Go make your case! No one is stopping you."

As Scribner talked he walked around, waving one hand for emphasis and playing with his hair with the other. At one point he looked at us and said, "I'm suspicious of you guys."

"Suspicious of what?" I asked.

"Yeah," said Chip. "How do we stand to enrich ourselves at the expense of the city?"

"I don't know," said Scribner, touching his hair again. "I'm just suspicious."

Well, there it was. Finally, we had found one of those people whom Jay Pomeroy had been talking about—that "minority in Pittsfield who have such a suspicious nature that it is scary."

On the way home in the car, we tried to figure it all out. It looked like the *Eagle* was going to run Chip's letter, and probably do a story about our visit. But that didn't mean we had changed anyone's mind or that we were going to start getting a fair shake.

"They have too much invested, emotionally and financially," said Chip, "even if they believed we had the best deal for Pittsfield."

"Why can't they see it?" I said. "These are newspaper guys. They're supposed to be the ones with the shit detectors."

"It's a metaphysical problem," said Chip. He then launched into a discussion about post-deconstructionist philosophy, which postulates that there is no objective truth—that events only make sense by the way we interpret them, adding meaning to what's happening.

It was all very abstract, and the more Chip talked the slower the car went, because he can't think and drive at the same time. I know he's digging deep when we're going forty mph in a fifty mph zone, where he normally goes sixty.

Here we were doing twenty mph in a forty.

"It's like play-by-play announcers," said Chip, "making sense out of what might otherwise be seen as an incomprehensible free-for-all."

"So does that mean their view is just as valid as ours?" I asked.

"Theoretically," said Chip.

"Then how do we know our view is correct?"

Chip pulled the car over to the side so he could think harder. This was in lieu of stopping altogether in the middle of the road.

"We don't," said Chip, "in any absolute sense. Ideally, everyone should be intellectually honest enough to admit the possibility that they're wrong. The people who scare me are the ones who know for sure what truth is."

"Like religious fanatics," I said.

"Yes," said Chip, "but it's not limited to religion. Any uncompromising belief system will do. Look at the Communists."

"Do the new-stadium guys believe their view is correct?"

"I'm sure they've convinced themselves," said Chip, "but our arrival on the scene makes it harder for them to hold onto that, and to convince others."

"That's why they're pissed," I said.

"One of the indicators of the correctness of a particular view in our culture," said Chip, "is the extent to which the behavior of the participants matches the principles of a free, democratic society."

"We score well on that," I said.

"Their refusal to debate," said Chip, "or engage in rational discussion, or involve the public in any meaningful way, doesn't jibe with their stated goal of contributing to the public good."

"You convinced me," I said. "Where do I sign?"

Chip put the car in gear and pulled back onto the highway. But that didn't mean he was finished thinking.

"Remember in the meeting when Scribner said, 'Go make your case! Nobody's stopping you,'" said Chip.

"Right," I said. "What about it?"

"That's the same thing Everhart said in one of his emails."

"So maybe they collaborate on the editorials," I said.

"You know, we never did find out," said Chip, "which one did the writing and which one did the editing."

"Maybe they want to keep it a secret," I said, "so people don't know who to snub at cocktail parties."

"That's not fair," said Chip. "They should have to face the music together."

"They're like Siamese twins," I said, "joined at the spleen."

"And they share a bile duct," Chip added.

"They should have a single name," I said. "Like Ever-Scrib."

"Right," said Chip. "People could say, 'Did you see what that idiot, Ever-Scrib, said today?'"

o o o

CHAPTER 4

"We're like the U.S. Marshals"

JULY 17
TUESDAY

I picked up Chip at 7:30 this morning for the trip to Pittsfield and our meeting with Mike Daly, a vice president at Berkshire Bank, and Gerry Denmark, the bank's lawyer. We wanted to find out where the bank stood with respect to Berkshire Sports & Events and explain how that relationship might be hurting all of us.

It figured to be an interesting meeting. Daly had given Paula and me our first mortgage when we built our home here nine years ago. And Denmark was representing the bank. Denmark has a good sense of humor and we had almost become social friends, but we could never fit a dinner into our busy schedules.

A secretary brought Chip and me to the mandatory wood-paneled conference room. Daly and Denmark entered a few minutes later. They smiled and shook hands, but there was an undercurrent of tension. They were not happy about something.

"You called the meeting," said Daly. "What's up?"

"There's a high risk that Pittsfield could be without baseball," said Chip. "Berkshire Sports & Events is threatening to build a new stadium anywhere in the Berkshires, possibly North Adams, which could make the bank look bad."

"And," I said, "city officials won't take action on our proposal for Wahconah Park until they're released by BS&E."

"We're not doing anything," said Daly.

"You're part of BS&E," I said.

"Don't put us in a box," said Daly.

"We're not putting you in a box," said Chip. "Everybody else is. We're just reporting to you how you are being perceived."

"There is no BS&E anymore," said Denmark. "We're in the process of dissolving it."

"The public perception," said Chip, "is that it still exists."

"You see that For Sale sign?" asked Daly, pointing out the window toward the new stadium site. "That's all that means, a public declaration. That's as public as you can get. But I have to tell you that we'd support a new stadium, if it was in Bousquet or anywhere else."

"Why would you do such a thing after the people voted against it?" I asked.

"The Civic Authority went down for a lot of other reasons," said Denmark. "It wasn't baseball, it was the firemen who didn't have a contract, the teachers . . ."

It went back and forth like that, and every once in a while it seemed like they were starting to get it. But as soon as Daly would say, "We'll take another look at this," in the next breath he'd add, "but we'd still support a new stadium if anyone wanted to build it."

Timing our exit, Chip and I rose to shake hands immediately after Daly's next "We'll take another look at this."

But Denmark had the last word as Chip and I went out the door.

"You won't be able to point to Berkshire Sports & Events as the reason for failing to save baseball for Pittsfield," he said. "It's your ball game to win or lose."

We came back home right after the meeting because Paula and I had to catch the twelve-thirty ferry in Bridgeport, Connecticut, for a few days in the Hamptons with Paula's family.

I drove so Chip could think.

"The bank and the *Eagle* have interests outside Pittsfield," said Chip. "They can dodge responsibility. But the elected officials can't."

"That's right," I said. "The city officials are stupidly following Berkshire Sports & Events' new-stadium agenda—which has simply moved underground."

"Did you see how Daly pointed to the For Sale sign?" said Chip. "Just like Scribner did yesterday?"

"Look over *here* at this sign!" I said, doing my wizard imitation. "Pay no attention to what's happening behind the curtain."

"By Daly's own words to us," said Chip, "he basically confirmed what we're saying. If that meeting were played on TV, what lesson would the public take from it?"

"That nobody gives a shit what the public thinks," I said. "Write that down."

JULY 18
WEDNESDAY—WATERMILL, NY

While I relaxed in the Hamptons, my partner was holding the fort in Massachusetts.

"Did we get the lease yet?" I joked into my cell phone.

"No," said Chip. "But we got a letter from Phil Weiner, the WUPE guy, who writes, 'Evidently there are others, in addition to your group, interested in providing baseball at Wahconah Park.'"

"Sounds like he has inside information," I said.

"He's definitely part of the old-boy network," said Chip. "The ones who know what's best for everyone else. Weiner says things like, '*Those* that will make the decision' and 'what *they* decide is best for the city.'"

"What did he say about sponsoring a debate?" I asked.

"He said, 'It doesn't seem that a public forum now would serve any purpose.'"

"Not their purpose, anyway," I said. "Is there anything positive in the letter?"

"He wishes us 'the best of luck,'" said Chip.

"At least Weiner got back to us," I said. "That's better than the rest of them."

"I'm going to write him a nice letter back," said Chip, "saying that no matter what 'others' may be interested—a collegiate team, New York–Penn League team, an independent league team connected to BS&E—we are the only ones making a long-term commitment to Wahconah Park."

"You think we're being too pushy?" I asked.

"Pushy?" said Chip. "What do they expect? We write letters, get no reply. Emails go unanswered. Phone calls aren't returned."

"You're right," I said. "If we backed off, they would just think we quit. That's what they want us to do. Potsy had said what they try to do is wear you down. Hope you get discouraged and go away. And Dan Valenti had said the same thing."

"We just have to keep moving forward," said Chip, "with sweet reasonableness."

The most recent sweetly reasonable thing Chip did was to write another open letter, addressed to Mayor Doyle, City Council President Tom Hickey, and Parks Commission Chairman Cliff Nilan, asking for prompt consideration of our proposal. And to counter the reasons previously given by city officials for not taking action—"we can't do anything until BS&E says it has given up on building a new stadium, or until BS&E folds its tent"—Chip reported our recent visits to the *Eagle* and Berkshire Bank.

"The editor of the *Eagle*," wrote Chip, "pointed to the For Sale sign on the stadium property as a clear signal that 'there isn't going to be a new stadium,' and a senior representative of the bank told us that 'BS&E was being dissolved.'"

In other words, no more excuses. Act on our proposal.

Chip made one more pitch to have the July 23 Parks Commission meeting rescheduled and "held at a school auditorium, where a large number of citizens can attend, and where TV and radio stations can broadcast the proceedings. We would be prepared to present and defend our proposal in all reasonable detail, and we welcome the opportunity to share the stage with any representatives of competing proposals in a real give-and-take format."

So reasonable it brings tears to my eyes.

JULY 19
THURSDAY—WATERMILL, NY

Speaking of tears, I was on the phone with Tim Gray and we got to talking about the Housatonic River Initiative (HRI) and how he learned about the pollution in Pittsfield.

"Basically, from GE employees," said Gray. "They would come and tell us where the barrels were buried, and about the midnight dumping. GE was even trucking in PCBs from outside Pittsfield."

"Did city officials know about that?"

"The rumors were that the city was somehow involved," said Gray. "We went to the EPA, but they wouldn't do anything. For two years they were telling us there was no pollution. Then the bulldozers hit the barrels—867 barrels full of toxic stuff. And that was just one site."

"It doesn't sound like the EPA is anxious to find problems," I said.

"The EPA is a creation of Congress," said Gray. "And polluters like GE have close ties to the political establishment. For a year, Kennedy and Kerry had canoed the river with us. Then they stopped returning our calls and got on the settlement bandwagon."

I told Gray about a framed newspaper article Chip and I had seen in the mayor's office, showing Doyle signing the settlement agreement.

"It was all done in Boston, behind closed doors," said Gray, "with Doyle and Hickey representing Pittsfield. Which was a joke, because it was Doyle and Hickey who had been against our efforts to uncover the pollution. They essentially just sat there while GE fought with the EPA. We had all the facts, we could have made a much stronger case, but GE refused to negotiate if HRI was involved."

"Who chose Doyle and Hickey?" I asked.

"The EPA," said Gray. "And the contaminated property owners were going berserk. HRI went to Boston to challenge the consent decree in court. I never saw more lawyers in my life. Then we saw pictures of Clinton playing golf with Jack Welch, in the local newspaper. We spent nine months on our brief, and everything was dismissed. By a judge appointed by Kennedy."

"So, was that the end of it?" I asked.

"No," said Gray. "Afterwards, the EPA announced they were going to clean the river and then gave Doyle credit for it."

"What's your feeling about the settlement?" I asked.

"It could have been a lot better," said Gray. "Newell Street was never properly cleaned up, a lot of sites were left out, pollution from the river is getting dumped right across the street from a school, dumps are continuing to rise surrounded by people's wells. If they tried to do that in any other town, they'd never get away with it."

JULY 20
FRIDAY—NEW YORK, NY

Tomorrow is Old Timers' Day at Yankee Stadium, and I've been invited back again. I'm becoming a regular. This will be my fourth in a row since my first one in 1998—after a twenty-eight-year banishment for having written *Ball Four*.

Today's *Wall Street Journal* had a few things to say about Wrigley Field, home of the Chicago Cubs and the second-oldest ballpark in the major leagues—built in 1914, just two years after Fenway Park in Boston. In its "Review & Outlook" column, the *Journal* congratulated the Cubs' owner, the Tribune Company, for spending its own money—a modest $11 million—to upgrade the ballpark:

> When ordinary people want to fix up their homes, they generally don't knock them down and build from scratch. But when taxpayers foot the bill, ambitions become more Neroesque. Earlier this year the Pittsburgh Pirates razed a Three Rivers Stadium that was only 30 years old in favor of a far grander new stadium also funded by the public—and despite a public referendum that had rejected it.

Pittsburgh. Pittsfield. See any similarities?

On this topic, the argument used by Berkshire Sports & Events to justify a new stadium—that most of the $18.5 million cost would come from state money, not Pittsfield money—is very misleading. Aside from the question of why state taxpayers should have to finance distant stadiums, there is the matter of the hidden cost to the cities that use those state funds to build stadiums. States don't have "stadium" money. They have "economic development" or "regional tourism" funds available for certain projects. If a city chooses to build a stadium with its share of that money, then it can't build something else. It can't go back to the state and say, "Thanks for the 'stadium' money, now we'd like some 'concert hall' money."

Chip called this afternoon.

"I took a friend to watch a game at Wahconah Park last night," he said "and I went up to the press box to say hello."

"How was the view?" I asked, wondering what it would look like from our Not-So-Luxury Boxes on the roof.

"Fantastic," said Chip. "We could sell twelve to fourteen season boxes at $5,000 each—if the structure can support them."

"The key thing," I said, "is to build them from the same materials as the rest of the stadium, with open-air sides and backs, so they're perfectly compatible—to keep the landmark designation."

"We'll have engineers and preservationists check it out," said Chip. "As soon as we get the lease."

"What's happening on that front?" I asked. "Did the *Eagle* run your op-ed piece?"

"Yes they did," said Chip.

"It's a good thing," I said. "Because your open letters and letters to Weiner and op-ed pieces were getting backed up like airplanes on a runway."

"Or worse," said Chip, "circling the airport waiting to land, and running out of fuel."

"So what do you think our chances are right now?" I asked.

"Fifty-fifty," said Chip.

JULY 21
SATURDAY—NEW YORK, NY

Old Timers' Day.

At Yankee Stadium. I still get a kick out of walking in there. "I once pitched here," I say to myself, almost in disbelief. How the hell did I do that? It seems so impossible now.

But then the fans remind you, in the most pleasant of ways.

"Heyy Bullldogg!" they holler as you get off the bus with the other players. A few old guys still remember some night that you fanned eight, walked two, and won 3–1. Nights *I* can't even remember.

And then there's the clubhouse, with the old timers sharing lockers with the current players, who are all six-foot-three. Moose Skowron, one of my favorite Yankees, believes the old timers were better. Still wearing his 1950s crew cut, he's a little perturbed at me for thinking otherwise.

"Some of the guys are upset with you," he says, sitting there in his baseball underwear, sipping a cup of coffee. "You shouldn't be saying today's players are better."

"Who's upset?" I ask.

"I'm not saying," says Moose. "Just some of the guys."

"It's only one opinion, Moose. I'm sure I'm outnumbered."

"You shouldn't say it even if you think it," says Moose.

Out on the field, the day explodes—reporters, cameras, fans, friends waving, people hollering. Keith Olbermann, my favorite TV sports guy, comes over with a prized treasure—a 1969 Seattle Pilots autographed baseball. I smile as I recognize the names, identifying one he couldn't figure out. And I think to myself that I am holding a baseball that once sat in a box of a dozen, on a table in the tiny clubhouse at old Sicks Stadium. Four dozen balls a day that we never saw again.

"Where'd you get it?" I ask.

"eBay," says Olbermann.

"What did you pay for it?"

"Nine hundred and fifty dollars," he says. "A bargain."

"If only we had known," I say.

Before the game I warmed up with Rick Cerone, a Yankee catcher from the '80s, who also happens to own the Newark Bears of the Atlantic League. I briefed Rick on our plans for Wahconah Park and told him we wanted to buy a franchise.

"It's the right time," he said. "We need another team."

"When does the league have to know by?" I asked.

"September's not too late."

"I hope we know before then," I said.

On Old Timers' Day, the game itself is anticlimactic. If you're a pitcher, what you try to do is not give up a home run, which is what everyone tends to remember. The problem is that the one thing the old timers can still do is swing a bat. What they can't do is make a nice running catch in the outfield with the bases loaded when you need it. Hitting is what everybody wants to watch anyway.

Well, almost everybody.

Fortunately, my knuckleball was jumping, if you can believe that. Who knew that a pitch I learned when I was twelve years old would still be working fifty years later—at Yankee Stadium? But then how many pitchers my age have a sushi chef they can pitch batting practice to?

What happened in the game? Let the record show that the old right-hander pitched *two* scoreless innings, six up and six down. As a result, I may never get invited back again.

JULY 22
SUNDAY

Speaking of old timers, Alan Chartock turned sixty today. Paula and I drove up late from the city last night so we could attend the party today at his house in Great Barrington. As my gift to Alan, I didn't say a word about Wahconah Park.

When I finally checked my phone messages, there was one from Gerry Denmark of Berkshire Bank.

"I just want you to know," said Gerry. "That a letter went out to Andy Mick saying, 'Thank you, but we're going to dissolve BS&E. But we would support a new stadium if it went ahead.' I hope that gets the ball rolling. I wish you luck."

That was good of Gerry. It looks like the bank, at least, does not want to be seen as standing in our way. That's a good sign.

JULY 23
MONDAY

Another good sign is the response we're getting from the people of Pittsfield. Folks are starting to make phone calls, write letters, and lobby on our behalf. A local CPA named Sandra Herkowitz, for example, recently wrote to City Council President Tom Hickey asking how he could say that he *hadn't* received our proposal yet, when in fact "on July 10 a proposal was faxed to Mr. Nilan, Mr. Doyle and to you." She then wrote to Cliff Nilan, urging him to "expeditiously meet with the Bouton group."

A fellow named Ken Ramsdell is making Wahconah Park a top priority for his Voter Vigilance Committee. And in addition to Dave Potts, Gene Nadeau, and Anne Leaf—the anti-Civic Authority activists who are solidly behind us—we have people showing up at council meetings to applaud and lend support. Chip and I now have a mailing list, a fax list, and an email list of the rapidly expanding group we call our "Wahconah Yes! Team."

It seems like the whole town is behind us.

This morning, Chip and I were in-studio guests on the *Dan Valenti Show* and the lines were jammed with callers, all of them in favor of our plan for Wahconah Park. In fact, except for Frank Bonnevie, we have yet to find anyone except the mayor who's publicly opposed, and that includes public officials, candidates for office, and anyone who stops us on the street. Which is happening a lot since we had our picture in the newspaper.

"Please don't give up," people say to us in some variation or another. "We're behind you."

"We are not going away," we tell them, which is how we signed off this morning on Valenti's show.

"We're like the U.S. Marshals," I said to Chip. "Riding into town to save the people from the corrupt sheriff."

"And his low-down, good-for-nothing deputies," said Chip.

Late in the day, the news came down from Pittsfield. It arrived in a press release that someone had faxed to Chip. Jonathan Fleisig, owner of the Massachusetts Mad Dogs, the dormant Northern League franchise, had been welcomed this afternoon at City Hall by Mayor Doyle.

"Now we know why the park commissioners canceled their July 9 and July 23 meetings," said Chip. "They were waiting for Fleisig."

"And Fleisig was waiting until he had his deal worked out with the mayor," I said.

The official announcement—FOR IMMEDIATE RELEASE!—on City of Pittsfield, Massachusetts, stationery quotes the mayor as saying, "I was very encouraged by what Mr. Fleisig had to say about his ball club and his desire to explore the option of moving to Pittsfield. . . . We will evaluate his detailed and complete proposal along with any others we may receive."

That same press release also quotes Fleisig: "The Mayor made it clear that he is open to all proposals for professional baseball at Wahconah Park and that if the Massachusetts Mad Dogs were to move here we would have to come up with the best proposal." Attached to the press release is a letter from Miles Wolff, which says,

> *I have been following the story of Wahconah Park in your local paper in recent weeks. With regards to the proposal from the Bouton and Margenau group, I have never spoken with these men on the possibility of purchasing a franchise. I would like to make this statement as clear as possible. The Northern League does not have at this time an expansion franchise for sale, nor am I aware of any franchise negotiating with this group. Furthermore, sale of a franchise would need the approval of the Northern League board of directors. We would . . . encourage the Bouton group or other local interests to work with [Jonathan Fleisig], not against [him].*
>
> *For the long-term success of professional baseball in Pittsfield, we all believe a new stadium is necessary in the future. However, in the short term the Northern League can operate in Wahconah Park until plans for a new stadium are finalized.*

Well.

Between Doyle and Fleisig and Wolff, it's hard to know where to begin. There are so many marvelously revealing comments.

Like all that business about *proposals*. The Mayor calls Fleisig's proposal "detailed and complete," but he says that it will still be evaluated with any other proposals "we may receive." And Fleisig says that "the Mayor is clear that he is open to all proposals," and that "to move here we would have to come up with the best proposal." Is there some doubt about proposals being fairly evaluated?

It's so transparent—like what a four-year-old might volunteer without being asked: "I didn't take any cookies out of the cookie jar." Oh, really? Let's go take a look. Except you probably wouldn't do that for fear you'd embarrass the child.

Which is how I feel about Miles Wolff. I'm embarrassed for the guy. I know him as a man who loves baseball, who once owned the Durham Bulls AA baseball team in the Carolina League, and who once wrote a fine novel about that experience called *Season of the Owl*. Now, here he is, pressured into creative writing of the worst kind: lying by omission. Specifically, the omission of Chip Elitzer from the "Bouton and Margenau group," who Miles claims to have "never spoken with . . . on the possibility of purchasing a franchise."

The "Bouton and Margenau group"?

Now I've seen our three-man partnership referred to—in shorthand—as "The Bouton group," or the "Bouton and Elitzer group" (because Chip and I are carrying the ball at this point), but never as the "Bouton and Margenau group." What stories in our "local paper" has Miles "been following"?

Why might Miles have excluded Chip Elitzer? Maybe because on June 22, Miles and Chip had an extended phone conversation about our plans for Wahconah Park and the possibility of our group buying a Northern League franchise. To include Chip he'd have to lie outright about having "never spoken" with us. Of course then he wouldn't have been able to cast doubt on our credibility in favor of his man Fleisig, which was the point of his letter.

"Miles Wolff's statement that he never spoke with us is absolutely Clintonesque," said Chip, using one of his favorite terms of endearment.

You do have to give Wolff credit for one bit of honesty, however, no matter how unintended the consequences. His comments that "we all believe a new stadium is necessary in the future," and that "in the short term the Northern League can operate in Wahconah Park until plans for a new stadium are finalized," couldn't be more clear about his and Fleisig's intentions. I guess we can now add *them* to the list of people publicly supporting a new stadium in Pittsfield—a list that consists of a lame-duck mayor, a karate school owner, and a fellow named Ever-Scrib.

The good news is that since we knew Fleisig was coming, I had already started drafting a response. All it needed was some editing, which in my case means I would be working on it for several hours. Or as Paula says, "However many hours you have."

By 11:00 p.m., I still wasn't finished.

"I'm getting ready for bed," said Paula.

"It's only 11:00, Babe," I said. "I'll be there in a half hour."

At 11:20, I went to print it out and my computer froze, losing the entire letter. The entire goddamned letter. Now I know there are people who in this circumstance simply push the shift key, the escape key, and the tab key, while simultaneously holding down the control key with their big toe and poking a small triangle thing on the side of the computer with the end of a paper clip, and the letter magically reappears on the screen, but I'm not one of them.

Fortunately, I had saved some of it to my desktop and I was able to reconstruct it. At half past midnight, I went on the Internet to email it to Chip, but before I could hit the send button I received an instant message.

```
Chip: Is that you Jim?
 Jim: Yep. I'm finished.
Chip: Don't fax it, you'll wake up Cindy.
 Jim: I wasn't going to. I'm emailing it. Fax me
      your suggestions in the morning. Good night.
Chip: Good night.
```

At 4:50 a.m. I hear the fax machine. I quietly get out of bed, close the door to my office so as not to wake Paula, and look at Chip's edits. I like them. I don't want to wake up Cindy so I go onto the Internet. Before I can hit the send button, an instant message comes on the screen.

```
Chip: I'm pissed. What we need is a truth squad.
 Jim: I like our rapid response strategy.
Chip: We have to beat the story to market. Help
      people interpret the news.
 Jim: Which needs a lot of interpreting.
Chip: We should add one more paragraph calling for
      an open debate.
 Jim: Good idea. Then I'll email it back to you.
Chip: I'll send it to our fax list. You send it to
      our email list.
 Jim: Talk to you later.
```

JULY 24
TUESDAY

At breakfast this morning I was bragging to Paula about how Chip and I would be quoted on the *Dan Valenti Show* today at nine o'clock about a story that won't hit the streets until ten.

"It's a slugfest," I said. "They throw a left and before it lands, we smash them in the mouth with a right."

"The mayor is going to think you stayed up all night writing that," said Paula.

In my response to the mayor's welcoming of Fleisig, I had asked, "What are the options for Wahconah Park?" And I listed five alternatives to our proposal:

1. Collegiate League team that cannot afford to pay for repairs.
2. New York–Penn League team that would require a temporary waiver from the league to play in a substandard facility.
3. Independent league team owned by outsiders looking to play in a new stadium—such as Fleisig.
4. Any team whose owners are connected to BS&E.
5. Do nothing, which would run out the clock on our plan.

"All of the above options," I wrote, "have the same common denominator: no long-term commitment to Wahconah Park, which therefore makes them acceptable to the Mayor and the new stadium die-hards.

"Only our proposal," I concluded, "offers the commitment to Wahconah Park desired by the vast majority of citizens. We call on the candidates to state their position on our proposal as a clear signal to voters and current elected officials that they understand and respect the wishes of the people."

Not the most stirring prose, but clear enough.

What did the *Eagle* do with the Fleisig story?

On the front page, under the headline FRANCHISE OWNER STEPS UP WITH WAHCONAH PARK PLAN, there was a story by Dusty Bahlman and a picture of Fleisig holding a ball. Bahlman had not challenged

Miles Wolff's lie by omission that he had "never spoken" to "the Bouton and Margenau" group. In fact, Bahlman quoted it. But he also quoted Chip as saying that we *had* spoken to Miles Wolff, without addressing the contradiction.

Bahlman also quoted Chip's description of the Fleisig proposal "as a means to keep the cause of a new stadium in Pittsfield connected to political life support systems."

The only deception was a subheading that quoted Mayor Doyle saying, "Mr. Fleisig brings to the table an established ballclub." In fact, Fleisig has a dormant franchise, not an established ballclub. His Massachusetts Mad Dogs played only two years in Lynn—1998 and 1999—before he left town rather than pay for ballpark repairs.

It appears that Fleisig will do anything to get off on the right foot in Pittsfield. He said he'd be willing to share Wahconah Park with the Collegiate League.

A few messages were waiting for me when I got home tonight.

Email from Dan Valenti:

```
>  Got Jim's fax in time to mention main points
>  on the air today. The response to our show
>  yesterday was enormous -- both on and off the
>  air. Folks agree with what Jim is saying in
>  his letter. I was encouraged by Jim's state-
>  ment: "We promise you we are not going away,"
>  because success can only be had here through
>  near-fanatical persistence.
```

How about *actual* fanatical persistence?

Email from Chip to Dave Potts:

```
>  I am concerned that the Mayor's hand-picked park
>  commissioners will sign a lease with Fleisig and
>  and have it approved by his city council majority.
>  That would be reminiscent of what they did with
>  with the Civic Authority only to have it thwarted
>  by your famous petition drive. Is it time to
>  go back to the people?
```

Email from Dave Potts to us:

```
>  I have to start marketing myself as a mayoral
>  candidate not a crusader of causes or I'll
>  blow my opportunity to be Mayor... And I just
>  heard from my new-found friend, Gary Grunin.
>  The sleaze bag thinks he can win me over to
>  his side by including me in on the latest
>  information regarding Wahconah Park. He told
>  me not to say anything (which means they want
>  me to leak it to you) but Doyle is talking with
>  someone from the Atlantic League.
```

Faxed copy of Chamber of Commerce memo to Cliff Nilan:

<u>Swift action is necessary on any and all proposals to keep professional baseball in Pittsfield!</u>

The underlining and exclamation are *not* mine.

JULY 25
WEDNESDAY

Paula and I went to Jacob's Pillow tonight. During the drive to Becket, in the hill country east of Pittsfield, we talked.

"It's one of the few times," said Paula, "that I have your undivided attention these days."

"That's how I work, Babe," I said. "You know that."

"I don't take it personally," she said. "Over the years, I've come to understand. But it takes something to live with someone like that."

"Like what?" I asked.

"Families of people on a mission or a cause," said Paula, "have a great deal of adjusting to do, picking up the slack. It's not always convenient."

"That's why I clean up after the meals," I said. "So I feel like I'm doing my share."

"And it's not always romantic, either," said Paula.

"Sorry about that," I said.

"It's *intellectually* sexy," said Paula. "It's one of the things that made me fall for you in the first place. You were as focused on me as you are on this project."

"If I were still that focused on you," I said, "we'd be exhausted."

"I'm very proud of you," said Paula. "And that's certainly sexy and romantic. So it has its ups and downs."

"You'd just like a few more ups," I said.

We drove on, through the village of Monterey, past the general store where they sell these great sticky buns.

"You know," I said. "This is the most alive I have felt since Laurie died."

"I know that," said Paula. "And believe me, I'm glad to see that back again. So I'm not complaining."

There was a silent pause, as there always is when we're reminded of the daughter we lost four years ago, in an automobile accident, at the age of thirty-one.

"I almost forgot what it feels like," I said finally, "to have this kind of energy."

"And I'm enjoying watching you and Chip," said Paula. "You work well together. The way certain couples dance well together."

"What do you mean?"

"You anticipate each other's moves," said Paula. "You don't get in each other's way. No ego. Happy to be part of a team. And you share a sense of adventure, and a sense of humor."

"You know we're getting married in August," I said.

"Well," said Paula, "you make a lovely couple."

o o o

CHAPTER 5

"I like our fifty-fifty chances better today than I did yesterday"

JULY 26
THURSDAY

My partner woke up pissed this morning. Fortunately, it was the one who lives in Great Barrington.

"I woke up at five-thirty," said Chip. "Staggered out of bed, went to the web site, checked out the *Eagle,* and as soon as I saw the editorial I got pissed."

In a commentary about how the Parks Commission should decide among the three competing proposals, Ever-Scrib had written:

> Interestingly, Mr. Wolff claims he knows nothing of the franchise proposed by a trio of South County entrepreneurs . . . who had claimed to have been negotiating with the Northern League.
>
> Mr. Wolff's revelation prompted a resumption of Mr. Elitzer's stance that any competing idea is a conspiracy to reactivate the defunct downtown stadium project and led to his astonishingly absurd assertion that Pittsfield voters have endorsed his contingent . . .
>
> Let objective criteria, publicly discussed, prevail in the decision, rather than political vendettas or hysterical rhetoric.

"By this time," said Chip, "my grogginess had left, and I spent the next two hours writing a response."

In two succinct pages, Chip exposed Miles Wolff's deception, explained how the competing proposals keep the possibility of a new stadium alive, and why we believe the public is behind us. Chip wrote that the only line of Ever-Scrib's editorial that he agreed with was the final one. And since the *Eagle* is not likely to print Chip's response, we posted it on our web site. After emailing and faxing it to everyone else, of course.

Later this morning, Chip and I got a call from Eric Margenau, who said that Jay Acton had called him. I knew Acton as a part-time literary agent who dabbles in business ventures. Eric said that he and Acton and Miles Wolff go back to the days when they owned a minor league team together in Utica, New York.

"I hear you're looking for a Northern League team," Acton told Eric. "And I have one for you. I can get the Wirz franchise if you want it."

This was exciting news. Bob Wirz owns The Spirit, the dormant Northern League franchise that last played in Waterbury, Connecticut, in 2000. One of Acton's business ventures is brokering the sale and purchase of minor league baseball franchises.

"Acton said he talks with Miles Wolff all the time," said Eric, "and that Miles had said he 'sent Fleisig up to Pittsfield to do that press conference for whatever it accomplished'—and not because Fleisig is really interested in being there."

"Why is Fleisig not interested in Pittsfield?" I asked, surprised.

"He's looking for a new stadium," said Eric. "Acton said Miles could care less whether Pittsfield gets Fleisig or Wirz, either situation is fine with him. And candidly, Miles would prefer to get the Wirz situation solved."

"How much does Wirz want for his franchise?" Chip asked.

"According to Acton," said Eric, "the price is $450,000."

"I bet it's $350,000," said Chip.

"Maybe we could get an option to buy," I said. "That would put us in a good bargaining position."

"Game over," said Chip, smelling blood.

After talking with Eric, Chip and I called Acton and set up a meeting for tomorrow at his office in New York City.

No sooner had we hung up with Acton than we got a call from Frank Boulton, the owner of the Long Island Ducks and the commissioner of the Atlantic League, the other independent league operating in the northeast.

The Atlantic League is a "full season" league that plays about 140 games per year, and the Northern League is a "short season" league that plays about 90 games per year, the number of games depending on the number of teams in the league in a given year. And while the two leagues overlap somewhat geographically and compete for available baseball talent, they do not compete for fans because the cities are far enough apart and the leagues, for survival purposes, respect each other's territories.

The Northern League, with its shorter season, is better suited to the Berkshire summers. However, Pittsfield has supported full-season baseball in the past, when for many years it was home to an affiliated AA Eastern League team. There has also been talk of the Atlantic League adding a "short season" division in the near future.

Chip had left a message with Frank Boulton that we wanted to talk about buying a franchise.

"I've got an idea," said Boulton, speaking from his office at the newly built EAB Park in Huntington, Long Island. "Why don't you lease a team for the year?"

The team Boulton wants us to lease is the Lehigh Valley Diamonds, which Frank calls the Road Warriors because they play all their games on the road. This is because the league only has homes for seven teams while it waits for a new stadium to be completed in Lehigh Valley, Pennsylvania, in time for the 2003 season. Until then, the league has had to fund a perpetually traveling eighth team to provide a balanced schedule.

Chip and I could solve this problem by leasing a franchise for 2002, with an option to buy for 2003 and beyond. This would accomplish two things: the Atlantic League could bring those poor guys off the road, and we could prove the viability of Wahconah Park—to ourselves and others.

A successful 2002 season in Wahconah would then give us the enviable choice of (1) exercising our option with the Atlantic League, especially if they add a short season division, or (2) buying a Northern League franchise.

"We would lease with an option to buy," Chip told Boulton. "If things work out as we expect, we could exercise our option for 2003 and beyond."

"Why don't the two of you come down to Long Island," said Boulton. "You'll watch the Ducks play, and we'll talk."

Chip and I checked our calendars and said that we could be there next Tuesday. The roller coaster is on the way up again.

"Wouldn't it be great," I said, "if we could have possibilities in *both* leagues? Then we could deal with Fleisig."

"We'll see your team, and raise you one," said Chip.

Negotiating with two different teams from two different leagues; this is *exactly* what we had envisioned from the beginning! Our revolutionary plan to get the best deal for Pittsfield.

If only Pittsfield will let us.

At dinner, Chip and I updated Cindy and Paula.

"That was quick," said Paula, about the two meetings that Chip and I had arranged.

"Chip is very tenacious," I said.

"Like somebody else I know," said Paula.

"I may be the bulldog," I said, "but Chip is a pit bull."

"What's Eric?" asked Chip.

"He's a bloodhound," I said. "He sniffs things out. He can't chase or bite, but he knows where to sniff."

"And he knows where the bones are buried," said Cindy.

"We're a well-rounded canine team," I said.

JULY 27
FRIDAY—NEW YORK, NY

For our meeting in New York today with Jay Acton and our Northern League front, we took the train rather than go by car. Partly because we like trains, but mostly because we were in a hurry. If we could wrap up the meeting quickly, and catch the three forty-five train home, Chip could still make dinner and a show tonight with Cindy and their friends Steve and Nansi. Very important.

On the ride down I asked Chip how he was even allowed to come to New York today in the first place. What had Cindy said? Then I answered my own question with my Cindy imitation.

"Ohhhh *Chip!*" I said. "How *could* you? You can't *do* this! We've had these tickets for *three months*. We haven't spent *any* time with Steve and Nansi . . . you're a *stranger* to your kids . . . you have *no* time for me . . ."

Chip had a sheepish grin on his face.

"You've been listening," he said.

The other reason for taking the train was that we had a lot of thinking to do—twenty-five-miles-per-hour-type thinking.

"Unless the Atlantic League adds a short-season division," said Chip, as the train rumbled along, "we probably wouldn't exercise the option to buy. But we'd need it to avoid being held up by the Northern League."

"Right," I said. "Miles Wolff wouldn't want to lose Pittsfield."

"Just the fact that we're talking with the Atlantic League," said Chip, "should set off the alarm bells."

"Why do you think Wirz is suddenly in the picture?" I asked.

"Maybe Miles is having a change of heart about giving Fleisig an exclusive," said Chip.

"You could be right," I said. "Eric Lincoln, who was working on a story for the *Record,* said he told Miles that he had backed the wrong horse with the mayor."

"Maybe Miles wants to have *two* horses in the race," said Chip.

"May the best horse win," I said.

We met with Jay Acton and his partner, Jim Goldsmith, at an office in lower Manhattan. Acton is about six-foot-three with a Kennedyesque mop of gray hair that makes him look younger than a guy in his sixties. Goldsmith is trim, dark-haired, about forty-five, who looks like the former Hofstra quarterback that he is.

The conversation began with the trials and tribulations of owning a minor league baseball team. Acton talked about the time a bus driver didn't show up and the manager had to drive the bus.

"Next thing you know," said Acton, "we get a call from the manager. He's in a ravine off some highway we can't find on a map."

Then there were the wacky promotions for which the minor leagues are famous. Not the harmless, family-style promotions they have today, but the slightly dangerous stuff they used to do.

"How about Bladder Buster Night?" said Acton. "The beer is free until somebody goes to the bathroom. And whoever leaves their seat gets booed. They always get a full house for Bladder Buster."

"My favorite was Diving for Dollars," I said. "This was back in the '60s, when I played in the Carolina League. They'd scatter a thousand one-dollar bills around the field and yell, 'Charge!' People would pour out of the stands to try and gather up as many as they could. Of course, there were a lot of collisions out there, which is why the players would be standing on the top step of the dugout, cheering them on."

After the funny stories, we got down to business. Chip and I talked about our plans for Wahconah Park, the opposition we faced in Pittsfield, our confidence that we were the people's choice, and why it would be good to have us in the league.

Then we talked numbers. We started at $350,000, they started at $600,000, and after a while, we ended up at $450,000.

"The sale would be conditional," said Chip, "upon our getting a lease."

"So it's an option to buy," said Goldsmith. "What are you going to pay for the option?"

"Nothing," said Chip. "We're not asking for an exclusive. If Wirz gets a better offer in the meantime, he can take it."

"He's got nothing to lose," I said. "There's no guarantee we're going to get Wahconah, but at least it gives Wirz an *opportunity* to sell. If we don't get Wahconah, he's no worse off then he is now."

"When does the league need to know by?" asked Chip.

"Schedules are drawn up in September," said Acton.

"We could make it September 15," said Goldsmith.

"And we'll need a letter from the league," I said, "stating that our ownership group is approved."

"No problem," said Acton. "I'll see if I can reach Miles later this afternoon."

"This has to be done within twenty-four hours," said Chip. "We don't want our offer getting shopped around."

"We'll confirm it in a fax," said Goldsmith.

We sealed the deal at the Cedar Tavern, the legendary bar where Kerouac and Ginsberg used to hang out. For me, it recalled the Lion's Head in Greenwich Village, another historic literary bar where Pete

Hamill and the new breed of sportswriters, Lenny Shecter, Vic Ziegel, and Larry Merchant used to go in the '60s. The burgers were better at Cedar Tavern, but the fries were no match for the burnt potatoes at the Lion's Head. Especially the ones served by Jessica Lange, before she became a famous actress.

During the train ride home we discussed the possibilities.

"They could do the deal as is," said Chip, "they could ask for another $50,000, or they could sell to another group and knock us out of the box."

"But I got the feeling they liked us and wouldn't do that," I said.

"We can only go so far on our good looks," said Chip.

"Aaaaand," I said, drawing it out for dramatic effect, "if we get *this* deal done, we go down to Bristol and make our pitch to ESPN."

This is a subject Chip and I have avoided talking about. It's an idea I've had for many years but haven't been able to sell to a television network. The idea, which I call *Bus League,* is to follow a minor league team—on and off the field—with video cameras. Shoot it like a documentary and edit it like a soap opera. The star of the show could be a utility infielder or the clubhouse man.

It was an idea I had proposed to Ted Turner, back in 1978, long before these so-called "reality shows" even existed. Ted passed me off to his programming guy at the time, Bob Wussler, who passed the idea back to me, saying television wasn't ready for it. Of course, TV has long since bypassed *Bus League,* with phony set-ups that have nothing to do with reality. Now I'm waiting until the current shows become so absurd—we may be there now—that *real* reality is the refreshing breakthrough.

I even made a *Bus League* pilot with my friend, Marty Goldensohn. We spent two weeks video taping the Birmingham Barons, the Chicago White Sox AA franchise in the Southern League. Last year, we pitched it as the "noncontrived" reality show where the struggle to make a team, win games, and have a shot at the big leagues represents true "survival." And now there's Wahconah Park. The show could be called *Desperadoes—The last chance for twenty-five young ballplayers and one old ballbark.*

The reason Chip and I haven't talked about this is because we didn't want it to complicate our effort for Wahconah Park. We're not in this to sell a television show. If we get Wahconah Park and the TV thing happens, great. If not, that's okay too. The television show is just a bonus.

We do not, under any circumstances, want to even mention the TV possibility to anyone. The *Berkshire Eagle,* which has already blasted us for not building an indoor arena we never promised, would have a field day. I can see the headlines:

SOUTH COUNTY TRIO BANKING ON TV LONGSHOT
NATIONAL EXPOSURE TO BRING TV GAWKERS
TRIO SHOULD GUARANTEE TV SHOW FIRST
TV SHOW PROMISE BROKEN

"If we get an option on the Wirz franchise," I told Chip, "that might clinch it for ESPN, which almost bought *Bus League* a few years ago."

"With ESPN in our pocket," said Chip. "We could make a helluva presentation to the parks commissioners on August 13."

"Can you imagine what that would do for Pittsfield?" I said.

"Put them on the map," said Chip.

"Look how many people go to Dyersville, Iowa, every year," I said, "just to see the cornfield where they filmed *Field of Dreams.*"

"And that was ten years ago," said Chip.

"We could have spring training in Orlando at Champions Park, which is owned by Disney, which owns ESPN," I said. "The first episode could be a one-hour special about who makes the team."

"We'd have to add another thousand seats at Wahconah Park," said Chip.

"No trouble raising money for that," I said.

"I think we sell forty units at $50,000 a unit," said Chip, already thinking about how much stock we could sell.

"With two million," I said, "We could turn Wahconah Park into a showplace. A historic showplace."

There was a long pause as we dreamed about the possibilities.

"So what do you think our chances are now?" I said.

"Still fifty-fifty," said Chip.

I called Paula on my cell phone to give her the good news about our meeting with Acton and Goldsmith. She said she heard a piece this morning on WAMC about Fleisig and the Northern League.

"Doesn't matter," I said. "We just leapfrogged over them."

As the train pulled into the station, I insisted on driving home.

"You've still got a long night ahead of you," I said.

"I can always sleep during the show," said Chip.

JULY 28
SATURDAY

I'm flying out to California this afternoon because tomorrow I'm going to be inducted into the Hall of Fame. The *people's* Hall of Fame, that is.

A Pasadena-based non-profit organization "dedicated to fostering an appreciation of American art and culture through baseball history" has set up its own Hall of Fame called "The Baseball Reliquary—The Shrine of the Eternals." It bills itself as being "similar in concept to the National Baseball Hall of Fame" located in Cooperstown, New York, but differs philosophically in that "statistical accomplishment is not a criterion for election."

The Reliquary is said to honor "rebels, radicals, and reprobates," which gave me three shots at it. Officially, the way you get voted in—by fans, not sportswriters—is to be one of those individuals, "from the obscure to the well known, who have impacted the baseball landscape." I guess they figure *Ball Four* left a few craters.

I'm being inducted in only the third year of the Reliquary's existence, along with Satchel Paige and Jimmy Piersall. Previous inductees, all of whom have had books written by or about them, include Moe Berg, Dock Ellis, Curt Flood, Bill Lee, Pam Postema, and Bill Veeck. Pretty distinguished company. We might not win too many ballgames—unless Satchel were pitching—but we could certainly out-spy, out-talk, out-think, out-wit, out-write, out-promote, and out-hallucinate any nine guys from the *regular* Hall of Fame.

Before I left for the airport, I got a fax from Chip. It's a letter from Jim Goldsmith saying that our proposal to buy the Wirz franchise "cannot be evaluated within twenty-four hours." Goldsmith said a more realistic time frame would be next Friday, August 3, since our proposal "requires input from Bob Wirz, Miles Wolff, and Jonathan Fleisig."

Input from Fleisig? That doesn't sound good. And from whom might Fleisig seek input?

JULY 29
SUNDAY—PASADENA, CA

I called Chip this morning to get an update. He read a few paragraphs from Friday's *Eagle,* which we had missed during our trip to New York. A story quotes Tom Murphy, the mayor's water boy, saying, "We feel comfortable that everything that could come forward in the way of a proposal for next season is now before us."

"Coming from Murphy," I said, "that can mean only one thing. Another proposal is in the works."

"That sounds paranoid," said Chip.

"Not if I'm right," I said. "It makes me clairvoyant. In fact, I want to go on record right now as saying that a surprise is coming."

"Send me an email to that effect," said Chip. "It'll be dated, and we'll have proof that you're not paranoid. Or that you are."

So I sent him the email.

And then I got inducted. Which is not the same as indicted. Which I had been, a long time ago. Which is why I'm now being inducted, if you get my drift.

The Baseball Reliquary, which has no official home, holds its induction ceremonies at the Pasadena Central Library, in a small auditorium off the main reading room. Another room features the official Reliquary artifacts, billed as "a traveling museum of baseball curiosities and wonderments" and looking very much like a Ripley's Believe It or Not carnival exhibit.

Available for your viewing pleasure are the "Mordecai Brown Finger" (the missing digit belonging to that three-fingered pitcher from the early 1900s), the "Babe Ruth Cigar" (partially smoked and "believed to have been retrieved from Rose Hick's brothel in Philadelphia on April 27, 1924"), and the "Eddie Gaedel Athletic

Supporter" (sweat-stained "souvenir" from the dwarf who once pinch-hit for the St. Louis Browns).

Now isn't that vastly superior to the more commercialized Hall of Fame in Cooperstown, with its video imagery and cases of balls and bats? As the Reliquary's resident historian, Albert Kilchesty says, "While the Hall of Fame uses exhibits to trigger the imagination, the Reliquary uses the imagination to trigger the artifact."

Are the artifacts authentic? In some cases yes, but you have to guess which ones—that's part of the fun. As Reliquary founder Terry Cannon explains, "An artifact is just an artifact. What's important are the stories. If we don't bring them back, they'll be lost."

The other part of the fun is spoofing the regular Hall of Fame, which has its own—completely bogus—history. That story, vigorously supported by the citizens of Cooperstown, not to mention the Chamber of Commerce, has baseball being invented by a local guy named Abner Doubleday. It even comes with "the Doubleday ball," found in a dust-covered attic trunk.

In a game of dueling legends, a prominently featured Reliquary artifact is a mid-nineteenth-century "Soil Sample" taken from the legendary Elysian Fields in Hoboken, New Jersey, where, most historians agree, the first game of baseball was played, in 1846.

The auditorium at the Pasadena Central Library was filled with about three hundred fans wearing a motley collection of baseball jerseys and hats. The ceremonies began with the clanging of a cow bell in honor of Hilda Chester, the legendary Brooklyn Dodger fan who used that bell and a drill-sergeant voice to motivate her beloved "Bums." The new Hilda Award, which recognizes the contributions of fans, was then awarded to seventy-seven-year-old Rea Wilson who, after the death of her husband, visited all thirty major league ballparks, traveling 58,000 miles in her van.

The musical "keynote" address was delivered by four-time Grammy award nominee, pianist/composer David Frishberg. This was a big treat for me, especially when Frishberg played my favorite baseball song, the nostalgic "Van Lingle Mungo," which is simply the names of players from the '30s and '40s sung to a haunting refrain. I had first heard the tune in the early '70s when I was a TV sportscaster, and I rounded up baseball cards of all the players in the song, shot film of them being shuffled by a kid, and edited the film to match the song. I always played that piece on Opening Day of the baseball season. Of course, I'd sent Frishberg a copy. And it was wonderful to see him after all these years.

Frishberg told a funny story about an appearance he had made on the Dick Cavett show with Van Lingle Mungo himself, shortly after the song came out. The hulking former Dodger pitcher said to him, "So, when am I going to start seeing some money from this, anyway?" Frishberg told Mungo that to make money, *he'd* have to write a song about Frishberg. Frishberg, a skinny fellow, said he was lucky he wasn't decked by the big right-hander.

First to be inducted was Satchel Paige, who was represented in the audience by nearly a dozen relatives, including a grandson who accepted the award on his behalf—and who looked like he could throw a decent "hurry-up ball" himself. Satchel, the self-proclaimed "World's Greatest Pitcher," was just as memorable for his mouth as for his arm. His rules for life included "Keep the juices flowing by jangling around gently as you move" and "Don't look back; something might be gaining on you."

Next up was Jimmy Piersall, who overcame mental illness to play seventeen years in the big leagues, and whose book *Fear Strikes Out* was made into a major motion picture. Unable to attend because of a scheduling conflict, Piersall was represented by his stepson, Robert Jones. Piersall, whose greatest contribution to baseball may have been his insistence that the game should be fun to play, celebrated his 100th career home run by running around the bases backwards, to the dismay of his manager.

Then it was my turn. After an introduction by Mr. Kilchesty that was longer than my career, I thanked some people who had helped me along the way: my dad and brothers for fending off countless knuckleballs in all those games of catch; my American Legion coach Earl DeTella for knowing what it means to rake a field; my high school coach Fred Jacobeit for being a good man; my college coach Fred Stevens for giving a shot to a non-scholarship walk-on; my Yankee pitching coach Johnny Sain who told me not to be afraid to "climb those golden stairs"; my Yankee teammates, Mickey, Whitey, Yogi, and Elston, who helped me win twenty games and took me up on the roof of the Shoreham Hotel in Washington, D.C., to drink beer and look in windows; my Seattle Pilot teammates, who were the greatest collection of castoffs ever to play the game; my Seattle Pilot manager Joe Schultz, who taught us how to "Pound the old Budweiser"; and my *Ball Four* editor Lenny Shecter, who used to say that "a guy could make a living just telling the truth."

Then I took the truth and stretched it a little bit. In a rambling tirade on "The Future of Baseball," I said the game was doomed because American kids were no longer playing sandlot ball, having been taught in Little League that you needed parents and uniforms in order to play. The only hope was prison.

"That's right," I said. "With more kids living below the poverty line and younger kids being tried as adults, our prisons will become the new sandlots—if we build 'em, they will come. With tax dollars going for new stadiums at the expense of our schools, parents will try to get their kids into a good prison. I can see the bumper stickers: My kid plays left field for Sing Sing.

"Once again, American kids will be choosing up sides, playing with taped bats and balls, using rocks for bases. Playing for the love of the game. One day, some French guy might come here and write, 'Whoever wants to know the heart and mind of America had better learn about prison baseball.'"

I like to close on a positive note.

JULY 30
MONDAY

Having taken the red-eye back from California, I slept until noon.

When I awoke, I telephoned Chip to get an update.

"A lot is happening," he said. "First of all, the *Eagle* ran a story today by Dusty Bahlman saying that a thirty-year lease would require a special act of the state legislature."

"But we don't need a thirty-year lease," I said.

"And Dusty quotes me to that effect," said Chip, "saying we don't care whether it's a lease or a renewable license; we just want to ensure that, if we assume responsibility for all maintenance, repairs, and improvements, the city is not going to come in at the ten- or fifteen-year mark and say 'Thanks for everything. Goodbye.'"

"It still won't prevent them from beating us over the head with the thirty-year lease," I said.

"Right," said Chip. "Dusty quotes Tom Murphy as saying that 'a short term license is the best possible scenario at this time.'"

"It's so nice of Murphy," I said, "to offer such a helpful suggestion to the park commissioners."

"Then," said Chip, "Dusty ends his story by going after Miles Wolff's misleading statement that he hadn't spoken with me about buying a Northern League franchise. Dusty wrote that, 'Wolff did not dispute Elitzer's account when it was read to him by a reporter.'"

"That was nice of Dusty to follow up," I said.

"I called Dusty to thank him," said Chip, "and his comment about Miles was, 'I hate it when people do that shit.'"

"Too bad Dusty and Bill Carey aren't running the paper," I said.

"And get this," said Chip. "Guess who's partners with James Ryan, the collegiate league guy who wants to play in Wahconah?"

"Yasser Arafat," I said.

"Jim Goldsmith," said Chip. "The same guy who's trying to sell us the Wirz franchise!"

"You'd think Goldsmith would have said something," I said.

"I discovered it by accident," said Chip, "when I happened to be rereading the original article in the *Eagle*, where the mayor said the New England Collegiate League could provide 'structured baseball' for Wahconah."

"Would you say that was Clintonesque of Goldsmith?" I said.

"Yes, I would," said Chip. "So then I called Goldsmith and gave him an opportunity to say that he was partners with Ryan, but he never did. Until I asked him directly, and then he acknowledged it."

"We have to keep an eye on him," I said.

"Agreed," said Chip. "Anyway, I told Goldsmith that we still needed the letter from Miles, approving us and Wahconah Park for the long term, so we can be on an equal footing with Fleisig."

"What did he say?" I asked.

"He hemmed and hawed," said Chip, "saying he's working on it."

"Based on this," I said, "I don't believe we're going to get Wahconah Park."

"But I'm still fifty-fifty," said Chip, "because the Northern League doesn't want to risk not having a team in Pittsfield."

"Unless they've been told by the mayor," I said, "that they're going to get Wahconah Park, no matter what we do."

"You mean a done deal?" said Chip.

"Yeah," I said.

"Funny you should say that," said Chip, "because today I got an email from Gene Nadeau entitled 'Another Done Deal?'"

"Listening to the mayor on the radio Sunday morning," wrote Nadeau, "sounded like we've got another done deal. There's no doubt that Fleisig is his man. The mayor said 'show me the money . . . show me the team,' when he knows darn right well that Miles Wolff will make certain that Chip and Jim and Eric are frozen out from purchasing a team."

"It's amazing," I said, "Nadeau doesn't even know Fleisig or Wolff and yet he understands the dynamics."

"Maybe better than we do," said Chip.

"Now here's the laugh of the day," said Chip. "Right after my call to Goldsmith, I get a call from Ryan. And guess what he wants?"

"Peace in the Middle East," I said.

"Something just as likely," said Chip. "Ryan asked if we wanted to join forces and buy a New York–Penn League team! Of course, I declined."

"How can that possibly be?" I asked. "Don't Ryan and Goldsmith talk to each other?"

"Evidently not," said Chip.

Before hitting the sack tonight, I was answering some email and an instant message popped onto my screen.

```
JG: Jim, this is Jim Goldsmith.
JB: What's happening?
JG: Can you explain something to me? What is the
    fascination with Pittsfield? I can understand
    it from your perspective but why are guys like
    Jonathan Fleisig and Frank Boulton fight-
    ing to get in there? It was a marginal draw at
    best for Gladstone who can't wait to get out
    of town. These guys are falling all over them-
    selves like it is Yankee Stadium.
```

JB: I think Fleisig is being used by the mayor to
    block us because he still harbors dreams of
    a new stadium. A commitment to Wahconah ends
    that. But the mayor is a lame duck, soon to be
    replaced by one of the pro-Wahconah candidates
    running for mayor.

JG: I spoke to Fleisig today and it seems he is
    gearing up for a fight in Pittsfield.

JB: Fleisig is not a good fit for Pittsfield
    because he wants a new stadium, which was
    soundly defeated in the June referendum—and
    that was when the pro-Wahconah folks had no
    alternative. Now they have us.

JG: He is a bit desperate though with no place to
    play and the clock ticking on his franchise.

JB: What does Fleisig win if he prevails? If
    Pittsfield doesn't build him a stadium he'll be
    unhappy and the Northern League will be looking
    to put him somewhere else.

JG: Yeah but the league can't have both Fleisig and
    Wirz sitting out. And then tomorrow you guys
    meet with Frank Boulton [Atlantic League] and
    he gets in the mix.

JB: Fleisig's new stadium scenario is a long shot for
    the Northern League. Bob Wirz's sale to us is a
    better fit. The league could back both of us and
    see who wins, but why take a chance when we're a
    sure thing with Wirz's franchise? Boulton's only
    in the mix if you guys aren't with us.

JG: As to the Northern League you are correct.
    Why not back both Wirz and Fleisig and let the
    chips fall where they may?

JB: The league's downside there is that if Fleisig
    wins it's only temporary and they'll still have
    two teams in limbo.

JG: I agree. And what if Bossidy resurfaces?

JB: Bossidy is a new-stadium proponent and lacks
    Wahconah credibility.

JG: Remember Miles is not only a commissioner he is
    also a multiple team owner. He would not have
    gotten involved if he did not have an agenda
    that he could see to the end.

JB: The fact is that the people of Pittsfield love
    their old ballpark and any owner not committed to
    that can't make it in this market. Won't Fleisig
    see that for the good of the league?

JG: Fleisig is most interested in Fleisig. And even if he's not real he'll gear up to fight just for the leverage... which can be a lot of different things—an extension of time, or money, or...

JB: The more time that passes the stronger we get because a new administration will be for Wahconah Park and we're the only ones committed to that. Anything else is just games and won't look good in the long run.

JG: If the longer it goes the better, why not shoot out the lights in '02 and propose for '03?

JB: We're committed to Wahconah however long that takes. Eventually it should end up with us because we have the people behind us. Power to the people.

JG: Right on.

JB: Why does the Northern League want to screw around with an uncertain future?

JG: I don't think they do. Just trying to understand where everybody else is coming from. I think the city thinks it has options and most of them are not real.

JB: I don't know where everybody else is coming from but Chip and I have been up front from the beginning. There is nobody who doesn't understand who we are and what we want.

And that's how it went. Hidden agendas—the mayor, Fleisig, Wolff, Goldsmith, Bossidy. We're playing poker with a gang of hustlers and sharps, and all our cards are face-up on the table. We're not the U.S. Marshals. We're a couple of greenhorns, in suits and ties, just off the train.

JULY 31
TUESDAY—ISLIP, NY

Let's hope Frank Boulton deals straight.

I enjoyed showing Chip how to get to Long Island via the ferry. He's always looking for a novel route to get someplace. We parked down below and walked up to the top deck to feel the ocean air.

"What did you think of Goldsmith's comment last night about Bossidy?" I asked. "Do you think he's still in the game?"

"It's possible," said Chip, "but I don't trust anything Goldsmith says. I sure wouldn't want to be his partner."

"He and Tom Murphy would get along great," I said. "It was Murphy's comment about there being no other proposals that convinces me there *will* be. Because if Bossidy *is* involved, Murphy would certainly know it."

"The park commissioners meet in two weeks," said Chip. "We'll know who was bullshitting us by then."

EAB Park in Central Islip is another one of those well-appointed, cookie-cutter stadiums they want to build in Pittsfield. The 6,000-seat facility cost $22 million and is part of the Atlantic League constellation of stadiums, built or under construction—largely with public funds—since the league began play in 1998. Other new stadiums are located in Atlantic City, Newark, and Somerset County, New Jersey; Aberdeen, Maryland; Bridgeport, Connecticut; and the one being built in Lehigh Valley, Pennsylvania. Only Nashua, New Hampshire, boasts its existing "historic" Holman Stadium, where Dodger legends Roy Campanella and Don Newcombe once played.

"We'll sell Frank on the historic value of our ballpark," said Chip, as we pulled into the parking lot a little after three o'clock.

"Wahconah Park can be the Wrigley Field or the Fenway Park of the Atlantic League," I said.

Frank Boulton is a big guy, about fifty, with a helmet of blond hair and a boyish face. First thing he did was give us a tour of the facility, which he insists is "a ballpark, not a stadium. I associate a stadium with football, or something big and cold." We accepted Frank's homey definition. EAB Park is home to the Long Island Ducks, which Frank owns and operates in addition to his duties as league commissioner.

Then we were escorted into Frank's office, where we were joined by Bud Harrelson, the former Mets player and manager who is now the president of the Atlantic League, and Joe Klein, former major league general manager with the Rangers, Indians, and Tigers, who is now the league's executive director.

Joe was the manager of the Texas Ranger farm team in Pittsfield when I had that tryout at Wahconah Park back in 1972.

"I don't know why the hell you didn't sign me up that day," I said to Joe. "Nobody even reached the warning track off me."

"Right after you left," he said, grinning, "we released the six guys you pitched to."

Last week, at our meeting with Acton and Goldsmith in New York, Goldsmith had said that Miles Wolff and Frank Boulton don't like each other personally. So it was somewhat of a surprise that Frank had nice things to say about Miles.

"I like Miles," said Frank. "He's a good operator. But the Northern League is going to fold; they're not going to make it. Miles wants my help. We've talked about having us absorb a few teams from the Northern League. Maybe create a short-season division."

"We'd be one of the stronger franchises in that division," I said.

"You have to understand," said Frank, "we're a new stadium league—except for Nashua, where we're doing a major upgrade."

"We're planning a major upgrade for Wahconah Park," said Chip. "New concessions stands, bigger bathrooms, extra seating, expanded locker rooms."

"Wahconah Park could be the Fenway Park or the Wrigley Field of the Atlantic League," I said.

"Our 140-game season might be too long for the Berkshires," said Frank. "We start the first week in May and go to the middle of September, with another two weeks for playoffs."

"Pittsfield used to have a 140-game schedule," I said, "when Joe was there with the Rangers, in the Eastern League."

"It can get pretty cold and wet up there," said Joe.

"Here's what we can do for 2002," said Frank. "You play forty-nine games at Wahconah and ninety-one on the road. The home teams would pick up your travel for the additional road games because they'd have the extra gate revenue."

"We'd play with an option to buy," said Chip. "If we're as successful as we think we're going to be, we can exercise our option and join your league. If we're not successful, we'll just grab our balls and go home."

"We'd probably also exercise our option," I said, "if the Atlantic League has that short-season division."

"But it would be *your* option," said Frank, "not the league's. What if you're not successful and we're stuck with you? Or you are successful and join the Northern League?"

"If we're not successful," said Chip, "it would be foolish of us to throw good money after bad. We wouldn't do it."

"And if we join the Northern League," I said, "we at least solve your scheduling problem for 2002."

"It sounds like it might work," said Frank. "Let me talk to the board and I'll get back to you."

"We'd need a letter," said Chip, "confirming whatever understanding we have."

"Draft what you want and send it to me," said Frank. "I'll take a look at it."

"When is the latest you need to know that we've got Wahconah Park?" I asked.

"We normally make up the schedule right after Labor Day," said Frank. "We could probably put it off until the middle of September. But that's the cutoff. When are you going to know by?"

"We should know something by the end of August," said Chip.

Now we could relax and enjoy the ballgame.

But not before Frank made sure that we were stocked up with Long Island Ducks souvenir programs, hats, T-shirts, water bottles, and the most coveted item in the stadium—excuse me, ballpark— official bobble-head doll replicas of Ducks mascot Quackerjack. Plus two Quackerjack mouth-horn quacker things.

Ever the congenial host, Frank invited us to watch the game from his box seats next to the dugout. And, as if that weren't enough, I was invited onto the field to throw out the first pitch, for which I received a nice ovation from the capacity crowd, the twenty-sixth consecutive sell-out and thirty-fifth so far this season, according to the official Ducks news bulletin.

The only thing better would have been a capacity crowd at historic Wahconah Park.

"The cool of the evening."

That's how my old Yankee pitching coach, Johnny Sain, described the feeling a starting pitcher has after winning a tough ballgame. You sit back and relax, knowing you've accomplished something and don't have to go back out there again for a few more days. That's how it felt to Chip and me on our ferry boat ride back to Bridgeport, standing on the deck with the night air in our faces and the stars and the city lights in the distance.

"I like these guys," said Chip.

"Me, too," I said, "Especially Frank. He's direct and straightforward, and he seems honest."

"It felt like we were being welcomed into the fraternity of baseball owners," said Chip.

"It's not that chummy a club," I said. "You probably wouldn't like most of the brothers. And I'd get blackballed, for sure."

"But I got the feeling we can work with the Atlantic League," said Chip. "I never had that with the Northern League. We've never met them, but we certainly didn't get honesty or respect over the phone, or in the newspaper quotes."

"I bet Miles felt uncomfortable about it," I said. "My vague memory is that he's a good guy. He probably got pressured into it by the scumbags in Pittsfield."

"Tony leaned on him a little," said Chip.

The moonlight was glancing off the water. The moon almost always makes me think of Laurie. The night she died, Paula and I had a driver take us to the hospital in New Jersey because neither of us was in any shape to drive. It was a three-hour trip under a full moon. I try not to associate the moon with Laurie, because I don't want to feel sad all the time, but sometimes I'm not successful.

"You know I put a big stone in the backyard," I said. "I had picked it out to use as a headstone for her grave in New Jersey but the cemetery wouldn't accept a natural stone. I set it in a grove of trees, and I can see it from the windows. Sometimes I go out and touch it or stand next to it. It helps me connect to Laurie."

"We never knew Laurie," said Chip. "But Cindy and I really wish we had. And I'm sorry you never got a chance to know my dad before *his* accident."

Almost exactly a year before Laurie died, Chip's dad suffered a broken neck after falling backwards trying to fix a light bulb. Ever since, he's been confined to a wheelchair and on a respirator. He's living at home in East Greenbush, New York, about an hour's drive from Chip.

"How *is* your Dad?" I asked.

"The same," said Chip. "Some days are better than others. I don't know how my mother does it."

"I like the fact that you bring him to all the family functions," I said. "It must be a great comfort to have his grandchildren around."

"I think it is," said Chip. "But then I think about what he's missed these past five years, watching the boys grow up. You know, he was a good skier, a very active man. We could have had some great times."

"I can't imagine Laurie like that," I said. "Spending two thirds of her life, damaged and helpless. She was a dynamo, like your dad."

There was a long silence as we leaned on the rail, looking out at the moon.

"So is it waxing or waning?" asked Chip.

"Using my special code, 'shadow-right-decline,'" I said, "I see that it's waxing."

"Very good," said Chip.

"In view of our meeting with the Atlantic League today," I said in the car on the way home, "what do you think our chances are now?"

"Fifty-fifty," said Chip. "But I like our fifty-fifty chances better today than I did yesterday."

o o o

CHAPTER 6

"Frankly, I don't give a shit, I'm only in this for the money"

AUGUST 1
WEDNESDAY

Here's the latest from the Northern League, in a message left on Chip's answering machine:

"Hey Chip, this is Jim Goldsmith . . . uh, just reporting in. I don't really have any . . . uh . . . good news to report . . . uh . . . Bob Wirz and . . . uh, has not really, uh . . . warmed up to your position . . . um, he is, uh . . . sort of made a decision that he's going to continue his effort in Lynn . . . uh . . . and, and uh, and that uh . . . that's the situation as it stands . . . stands is not, you know is not something that's entertaining for him to try and do . . . uh . . . I . . . I'm traveling throughout the week, and uh . . . I will try to speak to you soon."

"Sounds like dissembling to me," said Chip.

"Or, he could have been eating taffy," I said. "With dentures."

Today I pitched batting practice to Shige Tanabe and assorted friends. One of the new additions is home-builder Jeff Polidoro, who backed Shige in the sushi restaurant they own in Great Barrington.

"The thing I like about Shige," said Jeff, "is his work ethic. He came to my work site and asked if he could help. I had him carve the openings for the door locks. I couldn't believe how quick and how perfect he was. He'd finish what I gave him and come back and ask, 'What more work?' And I'd give him another dozen locks to do. So now I've got a homeowner with sushi-grade door locks."

Chip and I plan to give Shige a booth at our "Taste of the Berkshires" food court. But we haven't told him yet because he'd probably start planning the menu.

AUGUST 2
THURSDAY

Paula and I were looking out the window at our unfinished patio, which I haven't had time to do anything about. My plan is to build a multilevel stone terrace with steps leading down to the backyard. But even if I had time, we still couldn't afford to do it right now.

Paula worries about the patchwork way we make a living—from my motivational speaking, some freelance writing, sporadic royalties from *Ball Four*, her radio commentaries, and sales of books, baseballs, and photos from my web site.

"What if the economy turns bad?" said Paula. "And companies can't afford motivational speakers anymore?"

She usually says something like this at three o'clock in the morning when she can't sleep. Paula says she's a light sleeper because I'm not, and somebody has to worry about things.

"If the economy goes bad," I mumbled, "companies will need even more motivation and I'll make a fortune."

"But we're getting older," said Paula, "and who wants to listen to old people?"

"I'll be a *wise* old people," I said. "Now let's get some sleep."

"And you're spending too much time on Wahconah Park," said Paula. "It's such a long shot."

"My whole life is a long shot," I said, irritated.

"I'm serious, Jim," said Paula. "What if we can't pay our mortgage and they come to take away our beautiful home?"

"We'll spend our last fifty dollars on an AK-47," I said, and I went back to sleep.

AUGUST 3
FRIDAY

Chip and I may need an AK-47 to get a lease on Wahconah Park.

Chip got a call this morning from Frank Boulton, who said he could lease us an Atlantic League franchise for 2002, but he couldn't give us the option to buy. Chip explained that we couldn't spend money on Wahconah Park without knowing whether we've got an Atlantic or a Northern League franchise beyond 2002. Frank said he was going to call Miles Wolff to see what could be done about getting us a Northern League franchise.

Lotsa luck.

This is a big downer for us. We were counting on Frank to give us that option to buy, which we could exercise for 2003 and beyond or, more likely, use it to pry a Northern League franchise loose from Miles Wolff. And we wanted to have something from one of the two leagues for a "show and tell" at the next park commissioners' meeting, whenever they have it.

"It looks like we're going to need some help on this," I said. "Maybe it's time to meet with Steve Picheny."

Steve Picheny is a big mover and shaker in the Berkshires. He and his wife Helice are involved in all kinds of civic and charitable endeavors. Picheny is a very smart businessman. Our only hesitation with Steve is that if he likes the idea he may want to get involved, which we're afraid might mean "take over." And we're having too much fun doing it by ourselves.

"Steve's aware of what's happening," said Chip. "Whenever I see him, he always wants to know if he can be helpful. Did you know that his lawyer is Jeff Cook of Cain Hibbard Myers & Cook?"

"That's what Steve told me yesterday," I said. "And today he left a message on my answering machine saying, 'I told Jeff you guys were terrific and that your hearts were in the right place.'"

By 11:00 this morning, Chip and I and our well-placed hearts were on our way to Picheny's office in Great Barrington. It's at the end of Railroad Street, above the new steak house he had just opened called Pearl's.

"Now remember," said Chip, as we parked the car, "don't open your kimono."

"Okay," I said. "And I'll keep my legs crossed, too."

Steve Picheny is a good-looking guy, about sixty, who smiles a lot and always seems like he's about to go play tennis. With his perpetual tan and compact body, he could pass for a personal fitness trainer. A Mercedes-convertible-coupe-driving personal fitness trainer.

"I see where you're having some problems up there in Pittsfield," said Picheny, smiling broadly.

"We made them an offer they can't refuse," I said. "And they're refusing it."

"That's Pittsfield," said Picheny. "They never have done the right thing, historically."

Chip and I told Picheny how and why we got involved, Picheny asked us a few questions, and before we knew it our kimonos were wide open.

"So, you're in a catch-22," said Picheny, quickly sizing up the situation. "You can't get a lease without a team, and you can't get a team without a lease."

"The people of Pittsfield understand why we don't have a team and how that works to their benefit," I said, "but our opponents—the new-stadium die-hards—are using it against us, pretending not to understand."

"The mayor says 'show me the team,'" said Chip, "while he conspires with the Northern League to make sure we don't get one."

"You need to work with somebody behind the scenes," said Picheny.

"We don't know anybody behind the scenes," said Chip. "That's one of our problems; we have no alliances. Nobody owes us any favors and we don't owe any favors—that's why they don't trust us."

"I've got an idea for you, Steve," I said, half joking. "Why don't *you* get behind the indoor arena—Picheny Arena—and we'll take Wahconah Park."

"That's all I need," said Picheny, laughing.

"Whatever benefits the mayor and the city councilors might be getting on the stadium," I said, "they could still get on the arena."

When I said the word *benefits*, Picheny held up his hand and rubbed his fingers together in the classic money gesture.

"I told you I called Jeff Cook," said Picheny, "but he's got a conflict because one of his partners represents Fleisig. But I'm going to give him another call. He might want to do something."

We thanked Picheny for his time and headed for the car.

"How about Cain Hibbard representing Fleisig?" said Chip.

"What a coincidence," I said, sarcastically. "The same law firm that represents Berkshire Sports & Events represents Fleisig."

"I wonder who's paying the bill?" said Chip.

"You have such a suspicious nature that it is scary," I said.

When we got back to Chip's house, we discovered an unexpected email from Jim Goldsmith.

"I heard from Wirz last night," Goldsmith wrote. "I believe his position is shifting and he would like to get back into discussions with your group. Are you still interested???"

"That's really strange," I said to Chip. "Why is Wirz interested today and not last week? And why wasn't he *always* interested, since he has nothing to lose with our offer?"

"And why is Goldsmith contacting us," said Chip, "when he knows we first need the league approval from Miles Wolff?"

"It's all bogus," I said. "The Northern League is going through the *motions* of negotiating to avoid charges of freezing us out."

"They can't possibly believe we would buy Wirz's franchise before we signed a lease on Wahconah," said Chip.

"They're going to appear to bargain, but not come to terms," I said. "And I guarantee you we're never going to get that letter from Miles Wolff."

"Do you think they need to protect themselves?" asked Chip.

"It looks like they think they do," I said. "And they know better than anybody what's being done behind the scenes to block us out."

At the end of the day we called Eric Margenau with an update. We told him about the mayor saying "show me the team" at the same time that Miles Wolff was refusing to give us a letter of approval and that Goldsmith was playing games with the Wirz franchise.

"They're fucking outlaws," Margenau shouted into the phone. "They're scurrilous. They can take that league and stick it up their ass. We're a lot better deal for them than Fleisig and that mayor and his merry band of bandits."

So to speak.

AUGUST 4
SATURDAY

Chip has a fiendishly good idea.

"Let's take a phone poll immediately after our presentation to the park commissioners on the 13th," said Chip. "We can ask the viewers at home to vote for one of three proposals—ours, Fleisig's, or the collegiate league's—by calling one of three phone numbers. You leave the lines open for about three minutes, a computer registers all the calls, and you get an instant result that we can announce on the spot."

"It's like the show of hands at that Rotary luncheon," I said, "only bigger."

"Right," said Chip. "And it can be verified on a computer printout if anyone wants to check."

"But we shouldn't tell anybody ahead of time," I said, "otherwise the merry band of bandits will jam the lines or use a speed dial."

"No," said Chip. "We should announce it ahead of time, and get everybody talking about it, so more people will tune in to vote."

"It's a great idea if it works," I said. "But it makes me nervous."

And that's how it was that Chip emailed AT&T this morning to see how one would go about pulling off such a stunt.

Today there was a pool party at the home of our neighbors over the hill on the north side of Bouton Mountain. While Paula and Cindy mingled with friends, Chip and I lurked near the seafood bar, attacking the oysters as they were being shucked, like a couple of starving sea lions.

"Guess who Maureen Hannon knows?" said Chip, referring to a guest at the party. Maureen works for the National Trust for Historic Preservation and is very active in the Berkshire community.

"I'll bite. Who?" I said.

"Dean Singleton," said Chip. "The salter of the earth."

With that, Chip and I left our post at the seafood bar and walked over to have a word or three with Ms. Hannon.

"Sure, I know Dean," said Maureen. "I've been teaching him how to ski. He's a very nice guy."

"Have you been following our progress, or lack of it, on Wahconah Park?" I asked.

142

"Of course," said Maureen. "I think it's great what you're trying to do. I'm all for saving Wahconah Park."

"I sent Mr. Singleton a letter back in July," said Chip, "telling him he could run with our plan for Wahconah Park and that we would back him to the hilt. I never got a response."

"He might not have seen the letter," said Maureen. "His sister opens his mail and maybe she didn't think it was important. But I think Dean would like you guys."

"Maybe you can tell him," said Chip, "that he's being badly served by his local people at the *Eagle*."

"We don't have deep discussions," said Maureen. "He's very shy and he doesn't say much. We talk on the ski lifts once in a while."

"He must be a baseball fan," I said. "How about if I sent him a copy of *Ball Four*, as a way of introduction?"

"I think he'd like that," said Maureen. "In fact, why don't you give it to me and I'll see that he gets it. I'll be seeing him in a few weeks."

Before I had another oyster, I went back to the house and autographed a copy of *Ball Four*, as follows: "Dean, It might be fun to play on the same team. Best wishes, Jim Bouton." And I left it with Maureen.

"Turtle on a fence post," said Chip.

"What does that mean?" I asked.

"Divine intervention," said Chip. "A turtle can't climb a fence post by himself. Someone or some force had to put it there. That's what having Maureen at the party is for us."

Turtle on a fence post.

AUGUST 5
SUNDAY

The *Eagle* sportswriter Howard Herman wrote an article today that supports our plan for Wahconah Park.

Sort of.

A local ownership group is superior to an out-of-town group, which is why the South County trio has my support.

> But . . . if they can't run down a team, all the loving words
> about Wahconah Park won't amount to anything.

The reporters at the *Eagle* are covering the "what" part of the story—that we don't have a team. What they're not covering is the "how" and "why"—*how* our not having a team might benefit the city, and *why* certain people might want to keep us from getting one.

Why haven't reporters tried to investigate whether or not there is a "done deal," as some have speculated? If the mayor does already have a deal with Fleisig, for example, or is conspiring with Miles Wolff to deny us a shot at the Wirz franchise, that could be against the law.

Dusty Bahlman made a brief stab when he challenged Miles Wolff's statement that he had "never spoken with . . . the Bouton and Margenau group" about buying a franchise. But he never followed up. Why would Miles make such a misleading statement in the first place, for example? And who, if anyone, might benefit from it? Besides Fleisig.

Think about it. Several groups are bidding for the opportunity to lease or license a public facility. Are proper procedures being followed? Is there a level playing field? And what does this say about the credibility or legitimacy of other government contracts? Like the GE settlement, for example. Most reporters would jump all over this. Where are the local Woodwards and Bernsteins?

Or Theo Steins.

Theo Stein, many in Pittsfield will recall, was the prize-winning *Eagle* journalist in the late 1990s who covered the illegal dumping of PCBs by General Electric. According to Tim Gray, "It was Stein's reporting that forced the EPA and GE to even consider doing something about the problem."

Where is Theo Stein today? "He was offered a college fellowship," said Gray, "and he's now working for the *Denver Post*, another MediaNews Group paper." Did Stein's fellowship opportunity, which pulled him off the GE story at the height of the controversy, raise questions among environmentalists? It did for Gray. "We lost the most knowledgeable man in the field," he said. "And his replacement—a guy named Jack Dew—has been terrible."

It hasn't always been this way. For most of its 110-year history, the *Berkshire Eagle* has had an excellent reputation, with a Pulitzer and other prizes to its credit, under the leadership of publisher and editor Lawrence K. "Pete" Miller. But poor business decisions by the third generation of Millers led in 1995 to the forced sale of the *Eagle* and its companion newspapers to Dean Singleton, described by the *Columbia Journalism Review* as a "slash-and-burn publisher . . . who pocketed a bundle by shutting down the *Houston Post*."

The transition, supervised by David Scribner (who had recently arrived from the *Middletown Press* in Connecticut), was "as efficient as it was gut-wrenching" according to the *Columbia Journalism Review*. "People were told whether they had a job or not. If they did, Scribner handed them a piece of paper that described the basic terms. They were expected to put their initials in a box marked 'accept' or 'reject' on the spot. There were no negotiations."

The editorial style of the new regime was established the following day when there was not a single story in the *Eagle* about the staff reductions or the manner in which they were achieved, even though it was being reported by other media. "There's a gag order," said editorial writer Elizabeth Field, "and we can no longer report in the *Berkshire Eagle* any activities going on here."

On the second day after the sale, there was a story that gave the details of the transaction, but as the *Review* reports, "it was accompanied by a self-serving sidebar with questions and answers compiled by Singleton's management team. The first two answers (the ones which appeared on the front page) stressed that there were no layoffs or pay cuts at the *Eagle* since everyone was now a new employee of a different company."

Talk about Orwellian semantics.

AUGUST 6
MONDAY

Right now, we're in a countdown to the park commissioners' meeting, which could be next week. We're putting together a very comprehensive proposal that will have eight sections: principals, marketing plan, facilities plan, license agreement, ownership structure, financial plan, league negotiations, and next steps. And one new item that we're adding to our proposal—as a last-minute surprise—is a commitment to invest at least $250,000 in capital improvements by opening day 2002.

I'm writing the marketing plan. Chip is writing everything else. Chip is our technical, financial, and strategic-planning writer. I'm the sentimental bullshit, baseball credential, marketing guy. Chip is the steak, I'm the sizzle. Right now, for example, I'm planning a response to Howard Herman's column in yesterday's *Eagle,* in which he said we needed to have a team before we could get a lease. I'll be frying up a batch of words this afternoon.

This morning, I got a disturbing phone call from Eric Lincoln. He said Peter Arlos told him that Cliff Nilan was saying, "I'm going to have that lease signed by that other fella, Fleisig. At least I know he's got a franchise."

Nilan's going to have it signed? What about the other commissioners? Does Nilan speak for all of them? And how can he say this a week before the presentations? Has a decision already been made?

AUGUST 7
TUESDAY

Today's *Eagle* features a letter to the editor from Mayor Doyle, head-lined "Fix" Speculation is Insult to Commission:

> The Pittsfield Parks Commission, just like numerous other commissions and committees, is made up of good, caring people who donate their time . . .
> To insinuate that a "fix is in" for or against any proposal for baseball at Wahconah Park is ridiculous . . .
> Making these baseless accusations is not only insulting to members of the Parks Commission, it is embarrassing for Pittsfield.

I agree with the mayor. Speculation about a "fix" *is* embarrassing to Pittsfield. And someone should speak to Cliff Nilan about that.

And someone should speak to Jonathan Fleisig about the bad publicity he's getting on the Internet.

Just for the hell of it, Chip typed "Jonathan Fleisig" into the Google search engine and came up with some interesting material. Evidently Fleisig is none too popular in Topeka, Kansas. Earlier this year, according to the *Topeka Capital-Journal*, Fleisig's Central Hockey League team—the Topeka ScareCrows—had been booted out of the league for a variety of reasons. Only a temporary restraining order has allowed Fleisig to resume playing.

"The league wanted to end its contract with the ScareCrows," CHL Commissioner Thomas Berry is quoted as saying, "because Fleisig hadn't paid league fees totaling $90,000 this year, because the ScareCrows don't have a required letter of credit for $100,000, and because of reports that the team was going to leave the CHL with two years left on its contract."

This is separate from Fleisig's abandonment of Lynn, Massachusetts, two years ago, when he walked out with his Mad Dogs rather than pay for repairs at the town's aging ballpark.

But that's not the best part. The number one entry in a Google search for Jonathan Fleisig is something called "A Tribute to Jonathan Fleisig." I guess you could call it a fan site. A disgruntled fan.

What it is, boys and girls, is a photo of a horse's ass that suddenly springs to life with an animated action that is nothing short of astonishing. A cut-out picture of Fleisig's head—inside a red circle with the diagonal red stripe—is expelled from the horse's ass and plops onto the ground where it steams for a few seconds. Steam comes off it. I'm not kidding.

That's not all. At the same time that Fleisig's head is being disgorged from the horse's posterior orifice, a voice is saying, "Frankly, I don't give a shit, I'm only in this for the money. Frankly, I don't give a shit, I'm only in this for the money." Over and over again. It's a deep, rich voice—as befits the subject matter—and I'm wondering whom it belongs to. It's probably not Fleisig, because it sounds too professional—like a radio personality.

By way of explanation, at the bottom of the web page, there's a quote from Oklahoma City Blazers general manager, Brad Lund, on the prospect of the ScareCrows leaving the Central Hockey League. "It's a blessing in disguise to have Fleisig out of the league. He's been nothing but problems."

Then the horse and the voice do their thing all over again. And again. And again. I don't know how often it repeats. I only watched it about thirty-six times and then I had to run some errands.

"What do you think we should do with this information?" I asked Chip, regarding Fleisig's newly discovered connection to the horsey set.

"I think we hold back on it," he said. "Wait for the right moment. We don't want to blow him up too soon. They might try to find a replacement."

"And we'll end up bidding against Berkshire Sports & Events for the Wirz franchise," I said.

AUGUST 8
WEDNESDAY

Today's *Eagle* contained a good news/bad news story about Wahconah Park. The good news is that the Parks Commission has finally confirmed it will hold a public meeting on August 13, at which petitioners can make their presentations and the public will be allowed to comment. And it's being held in the City Council chamber, where it can be televised. The other good news is that a decision will be announced on August 20.

The bad news is that the park commissioners have listed eight "minimum conditions" that should be addressed by the petitioners, as follows:

1. Written contractual ownership of a professional baseball team or a binding agreement for the purchase of a team.
2. Provide articles of incorporation for the ownership entity.
3. Three years of documented financial disclosure (personal income tax returns) for each owner of the entity that owns or proposes to own a franchise.
4. Proposal for a minimum two-season license (with option to renew) that includes a minimum of $25,000 annual fee payable to the city.

5. Provide an annual letter of credit for amount due to the city for the remainder of the license agreement.
6. Provide a letter of reference from the franchise's [league commissioner] stating that all parties involved in ownership will not be in conflict of any territorial or ownership rules or regulations of any organization or league.
7. Letter from league's presiding authority endorsing the proposal.
8. Petitioner will assume all costs associated with maintenance and repairs to Wahconah Park.

"Well, I wonder who *that* was directed at," I said to Chip. "Especially items 1, 4, 6, and 7."

"Looks like something Curt Preisser wrote," said Chip, referring to Mayor Doyle's press secretary, who many now believe is the defacto mayor of Pittsfield.

"I think I'll prepare an *alternate* list of minimum conditions," I said, "that we can send out to the media."

Under my own heading, "Response to Park Commission's Minimum Conditions," I wrote that while "the eight criteria suggested by the commission effectively knock us out of the box," they "fail to address a number of important conditions we believe the citizens of Pittsfield will want to consider." Then I listed our "alternate minimum conditions" as follows:

1. Document the depth of your interest in preserving and restoring Wahconah Park. Include any position papers or statements previously made on the subject.
2. Amount of money you plan to invest, just in capital improvements, at Wahconah Park before Opening Day 2002 (suggested minimum: $250,000).
3. Percent of total maintenance costs, ordinarily paid by the city of Pittsfield—in addition to baseball-related maintenance and repairs—that you are willing to absorb. As a guide, use the amount actually spent over past five years—$500,000, or an annual average of $100,000 (suggested: 100%).
4. If you intend to make a significant investment in Wahconah Park, attendance will need to rise above its recent per-game

average of 2,000. Provide a detailed marketing plan that explains how you will achieve this.

5. Percent of local ownership of your franchise.

6. Describe the type of lease or license agreement you would expect to sign and why. Include length, renewal terms and any restrictions. If you are seeking a short-term lease or license, explain what protections you are willing to offer the city in case you leave town after a few years.

7. Document your experience operating professional sports teams. Include the number of teams you have owned and operated, the number of teams still playing, and the number of towns you have abandoned, if any.

8. Provide a letter from your league commissioner accepting Wahconah Park as a permanent home for your team (extra credit: pledge to refrain from lobbying for new stadium).

In the interest of fairness, I did not include a requirement to reveal the existence of any lawsuits that may have been filed or examples of negative publicity (including web sites) in connection with the petitioner's ownership of a professional sports team.

Before taking Cindy and Paula out to dinner tonight, Chip and I took a dip in the Elitzer pool. Treading water in the deep end, we reminisced about how the two of us ended up so involved with Wahconah Park. With a decision coming on August 20th, we felt the end drawing near.

"In the beginning it was just for fun," said Chip. "Then it became a campaign. And now I actually think we could make some money."

"Frankly, I don't give a shit, I'm only in this for the money," I said in my best baritone voice. "Frankly, I don't give a shit, I'm only in this . . ."

"That would make a great theme song," said Chip. "Who do you think will play us in the movie?"

"I'll take Al Pacino," I said.

"You don't look anything like Pacino," said Chip.

"I know," I said, "but he's a good actor."

"You should be played by Robert Redford," said Chip.

"And who's going to play you?" I asked.

"Dustin Hoffman," said Chip.

150

"You're better looking than Dustin Hoffman," I said. "But not by much."

In the parking lot outside Gon San, where Paula and I would be meeting Chip and Cindy for dinner, we ran into Steve and Helice Picheny, who had just pulled up in their convertible.

"I spoke to Jeff," said Picheny, referring to Jeff Cook of Cain Hibbard Myers & Cook. "It's too late to do anything. You didn't do it the right way. You needed to get somebody that was politically connected on your side."

"We tried that," I said. "We went to Andy Mick and BS&E. How much more connected can you get? We said here's an idea, run with it. We tried to play ball with these guys. We didn't want anything for ourselves. That came later, after they opposed us."

"Well, they're not going to let you have it," said Picheny. "And it's too late for me to help. Sorry. It's very political up there. "

At dinner, I related that conversation to Chip and Cindy.

"It's more confirmation of a 'done deal,'" said Chip.

"If it's a done deal," said Paula, "why do you guys continue?"

"It's a challenge," said Chip. "And anything is still possible. We're not finished yet."

"I'm curious to see how far they'll go," I said.

"It's interesting to watch what's happening," said Chip. "The more reasonable we get, the more bizarre they get."

"We're plumbing the depths of their unreasonableness," I said.

AUGUST 9
THURSDAY

At least someone is trying to be reasonable. Here are the highlights of Jonathan Levine's editorial in this week's *Pittsfield Gazette*:

> The conditions seem crafted to further thwart the Jim Bouton group looking to bring an independent team to Wahconah Park.
> But they don't have a team yet. They're trying to create something from scratch, something with local identity and permanence, something that will save Wahconah from the wrecking ball.

The parks commission's first suggested 'minimum condition' is a proof of ownership of a team, followed by letters of reference from league authorities. Notably, Larry Bossidy was never asked to provide any of these proofs when the city granted him a succession of 'exclusive' windows to get a team for the proposed Eagle stadium. [The *Gazette*'s pet name for the new stadium.]

Indeed the entire way the commission operates these days has been troubling, prompting the *Gazette* to make inquiries this summer to the district attorney regarding overall commission procedures.

Commissioners may have legitimate concerns about the Bouton group. But their recent history—and the way they have acted on the proposal thus far—suggests that, yes, the fix may be on.

One of those who is not surprised at the way we're being treated by the boys up in Pittsfield is Tim Gray. Seems that he and the Housatonic River Initiative have had a similar experience.

"What they're doing to you is so parallel to what they did to us," he said. "When I saw that first article about you and Chip in the *Berkshire Eagle*, I said these guys are going to get slammed. The *Eagle* wrote editorials bashing our group, too. They called me an eco-Nazi. There was a massive agenda to discredit us."

"Let me guess," I said, "they distorted your proposals, too."

"All the time," said Gray. "The *Eagle* said, 'HRI Out to Destroy Consent Decree'—that was the Doyle sweetheart deal. But our agenda was not to kill the settlement. We were just trying to point out the deficiencies. The *Eagle* called us the 'radical South County environmentalists.'"

"That's their xenophobic game plan," I said. "They call us the 'under-financed South County trio.' Scribner actually called me a carpetbagger."

"Scribner called me a 'gadfly from Lee, who shouldn't be involved in Pittsfield business,'" said Gray.

"But that's absurd," I said. "The Housatonic flows through Lenox and Lee and Great Barrington."

"And all the way down to Long Island Sound," said Gray. "PCBs are heavier than water and they settle wherever there's a dam. The dam in Lenox holds most of the PCBs. There are more at the Rising Pond dam in Housatonic. They were left out of the settlement because HRI was shut out of the negotiations."

"I see people fishing in the Housatonic," I said.

"Yes," said Gray. "But they're not supposed to eat them."

"Are you still finding pollution?"

"It's ongoing," said Gray. "We're turning in site after site. Back when Gerry Doyle called me 'the worst thing that ever happened to Pittsfield,' we only knew about twenty homes. Now we're up to two-hundred and sixty. Then there's Vicon [now Energy Answers], next to Wal-Mart, emitting dioxins into the air for ten to fifteen years. Still pumping today. GE workers said barrels have been sent to Vicon."

"I don't think most people are aware of that," I said. "And I've never even heard of Vicon."

"After the settlement, the *Berkshire Eagle* stopped printing stories about still finding PCBs," said Gray. "They want people to think it's over. Ever since Theo [Stein] left, they are not turning up anything. Jack Dew was told about the city dump, but he does nothing about it. We're fighting a paper *and* GE. It's sad for the Berkshires because the *Eagle* is our main source."

AUGUST 10
FRIDAY

The *Eagle* isn't all bad. In today's Letters to the Editor they ran my response to Howard Herman's Sunday column, in which he had offered his tentative support to our proposal—*if* we can get a team.

Under the headline A TEAM THAT WILL TRULY BE PITTSFIELD'S, I wrote the following:

> The reason we should be supported is precisely because we do not already have a team. If we already had a team, and for some reason were not able to obtain a lease for Wahconah Park, we'd have to go shopping for a place to play, like Mr. Fleisig has been doing for the past two years. . . .
>
> Mr. Fleisig has no allegiance to a particular city, let alone a particular ballpark within that city. In fact, Mr. Fleisig has been trying to get a variety of cities to build him a new stadium. . . .
>
> Our local partnership, on the other hand, is committed not only to Pittsfield, but specifically to Wahconah Park. . . . The reality is that Pittsfield and the Berkshires represent a scarce and

potentially valuable opportunity: a proven market with a long tradition of professional baseball in a historic ballpark that fans are passionate about. On the other hand, what these two leagues have to offer—franchises—are currently quite plentiful, Mr. Fleisig being just one example. . . .

We propose to take advantage of that reality, rather than let Pittsfield be a pawn in the traditional league/owner power-play scenario. . . . If our proposal . . . is accepted by the Parks Commission . . . then Pittsfield will have changed the traditional balance of power between cities and team owners in its favor.

This will be Pittsfield's team, not Mr. Fleisig's or anyone else bearing a franchise in need of a home.

Too bad you can't hear violins playing in a newspaper.

Chip got an email from Jim Goldsmith today. Goldsmith said Bob Wirz has been unavailable, and that we would not be getting a letter of approval from Miles Wolff.

"They've decided to back Fleisig exclusively," said Chip. "Which is no surprise."

"I'd like to write a letter to Miles Wolff," I said, "and predict that Bossidy will come waltzing in at the last minute with a Red Sox farm team, and win the vote of the parks commissioners because his only competition is an easily defeated Fleisig who was merely being used by the mayor to block the real competition, which is us. Therefore, the Northern League, in its own best interest, should approve us and allow a fair fight with Fleisig."

"It won't work," said Chip. "The Parks Commission's vote is just a replay of the Civic Authority vote. The Northern League was content to be a back-up to Bossidy in that situation, too. To call Wolff and cry wolf won't work with Wolff. Our only leverage is to get the lease."

o o o

CHAPTER 7

"Hey, anybody can have a bad day, OK?"

AUGUST 11
SATURDAY

"We're all ready to go with 7 West Communications," said Chip.

This is the telemarketing company we hired to execute our surprise "viewer preference" poll immediately after our presentation to the Parks Commission on Monday night.

"Run it by me again one more time," I said.

"After our presentation, but before we leave the podium," said Chip, "I'm going to announce that the viewers watching at home on television can vote for one of the three proposals they just saw—Bouton, Fleisig, or collegiate—by calling one of three 800 numbers on their TV screens."

"But we're only going to have a few minutes," I said. "Then the commissioners are going to tell us to go sit down."

"Three minutes is all we need," said Chip. "That's plenty of time for anyone to get up, walk across the room, and dial the number."

"What if 7 West gets ten thousand calls in three minutes?" I said. "From what I understand, half of Pittsfield watches these programs."

"It's computerized," said Chip. "7 West has assured me they can handle any number of calls."

"I'm still worried about a technical glitch," I said. "If our point is that we're the people's choice, and we don't win our own poll, the game's over."

"I did a dry run this morning," said Chip. "After each call, a recorded message says, 'Thank you. Your preference for the Bouton—or Fleisig or Collegiate—proposal has been recorded.'"

"Even before you announce the poll on Monday night," I said, "I should be on my cell phone with 7 West to make sure everything's set. Then I'll stay on the line during the poll until we get the results."

"For the people sitting in the council chamber," said Chip, "I'll fill up the three minutes by explaining exactly how these polls are designed to work."

"If Fleisig wins," I said, "I can just say I was disconnected."

"Right," said Chip, with a nervous laugh.

AUGUST 12
SUNDAY

As part of our presentation to the parks commissioners tomorrow night, Chip and I had hoped to include letters from both the Atlantic and Northern leagues, as evidence of our ability to negotiate for a franchise in either league. But the Northern League is blocking us out, and all we've got from the Atlantic League is Chip's letter to Frank Boulton—a letter which says we agree to "lease" a team for 2002, but which includes an "option to buy" that the league is still thinking about.

"I spoke with Frank this morning," said Chip. "He said we could use the letter I had sent him, but he still couldn't get the rest of his people to agree to the $1 million buyout price."

The asking price for a new Atlantic League franchise is $2 million (four times the quoted price of a new Northern League franchise), but Chip and I had suggested that we be allowed to buy a "crippled franchise" that could be based only in Pittsfield. Our logic was that a franchise that can't be shopped around had half as much value. And this would be fine with us since we're committed to Pittsfield.

"I asked Frank," said Chip, "if we get Wahconah, can we come back and make a pitch to the key people in the league for a 'Pittsfield only' franchise? And Frank said he could arrange that."

"This is actually better than a full commitment from Frank," I said, "because it means we don't have to be committed to him beyond 2002. We can still negotiate with either league after we get the lease. We could end up paying less than $1 million for a crippled franchise, or less than $450,000 for the Wirz franchise."

"That's right," said Chip. "And Frank is going to wish he had given us a full commitment."

"And so will Miles Wolff," I said. "Chip, you're the greatest."

"I'm having fun, Jim," he said.

AUGUST 13
MONDAY

Chip and I stopped at Kwik Print and picked up 100 bound copies of our proposal and drove up to Pittsfield early for a pre-game meal at the Lantern. Eric Margenau, who was coming to be introduced and to be available for questions, would meet us in the City Council chamber. Paula would also be meeting us there, and Cindy wasn't able to come. Over a double order of bacon cheeseburgers—for energy—Chip and I reviewed our game plan.

"Remember," said Chip, "we need to go last in the program so we can hit them with our telephone poll."

"We should get last bats," I said, "since we're the home team."

After a swing by Wahconah Park for luck, Chip and I headed for City Hall, where we were the first to arrive. This gave us time to meet with the guys from Pittsfield Community Television, explain how our phone poll would work, and give them the sheet of paper with the names and numbers.

As the chamber filled up, Chip and I welcomed arrivals as if we were maitre d's at a restaurant. It was good to see so many of our supporters filing in. There were Dave and Grace Potts, who look like two of The Four Freedoms in the Norman Rockwell series. Based on looks alone, Potsy should be elected mayor—Mr. Smith goes to Washington.

Then there was Gene Nadeau, and Anne Leaf, and Sandra Herkowitz, and Elaine Soldato, and Katy Roucher, and a bleacher full of supporters, and it gave us a good feeling. This was our team—the Wahconah Yes! team—showing up for the big game.

"The public comment portion of tonight's meeting should be quite interesting," said Chip.

"We're all set if a fight breaks out," I said.

Soon Paula arrived in her famous lime green jacket, the one she wears to Old Timers' Games at Yankee Stadium so I can pick her out of the crowd from down on the field. It felt like a bouquet of flowers had just been delivered to the Council chamber.

The audience seemed to be composed of three groups: petitioners, politicians, and our supporters. The only anti-Wahconah person not part of a presenting team was our man Frank Bonnevie, standing over against the wall, karate arms folded across his chest, surveying the scene.

Maybe I was wrong about our chances in a fight.

As the room filled up, Chip and I sought out Cliff Nilan to see if he'd buy our home team argument and let us bat last. Nilan is a fit-looking fifty-four, with a gray brush cut and a Roy Rogers face. His youthful appearance, small stature, and serious manner combine to give the impression of a junior high school student-council president. Nilan also leads the league in tics and mannerisms, especially when he's nervous.

Nilan listened to our request with a look of studied indifference. "Whatever you want," he said. Then he tugged on his ear and ran a finger inside his collar.

Come to think of it, Nilan would make a good third base coach.

As Chip and I returned to our seats, Fleisig entered the room.

"Who's that?" asked Paula.

"Fleisig," I said. I recognized him from his picture in the paper.

Fleisig was accompanied by a small entourage, which included three men and a young, blonde woman. Fleisig is about six-foot-two, nice looking, about thirty-seven, with close-cropped curly brown hair. He looks like he could have been the president of his college fraternity, or a poster boy for the Young Republicans Club.

"Uh-oh," said Paula.

"What do you mean, uh-oh?" I said.

"He's got a beautiful speaking voice," said Paula. "Deep and resonant, like a radio voice. And it really carries. Make sure that you speak up."

It *was* a beautiful voice. And familiar, too. Seemed like I'd heard it just recently. On a web site, maybe. Something to do with a horse.

Of course, the first thing Fleisig did was go up and speak to Cliff Nilan. That can't be good, we figured. And we were right. After few twitches and a neck crane, Nilan was signaling for Chip and me to come back up.

"Fleisig wants to go last," said Nilan, reaching into his pocket. "So I'm going to flip a coin."

Rather than risk losing our phone poll, Chip and I thought fast and proposed a compromise: we'd let Fleisig go last if we could each have a three-minute follow-up to the other's presentation.

"What's this going to be," said Fleisig, "a debate?"

"Not at all," said Chip.

"In any case," I said, "you'd still have the last three minutes."

Fleisig thought it over.

"I guess it's okay," he said, annoyed, even though he was getting what he wanted. "Let's just get started."

"Whatever you want," said Nilan.

Satisfied that neither side had gotten an advantage, the Bouton and Fleisig teams returned to their seats.

"Look at Fleisig," said Paula, giving me a nudge and nodding toward Fleisig, who was seated a few rows ahead and across the aisle. "A jacket, a tie, and no socks. Pure Hamptons."

Finally, at 7:00 p.m., the long-awaited Parks Commission public meeting to entertain proposals for the use of Wahconah Park was called to order with an announcement by Chairman Cliff Nilan.

"The Commission has decided," said Nilan, running a finger under his nose and stroking the full length of his tie, "that we would not have public input this evening and would just listen to the presenters presenting their proposals."

So much for a public meeting.

Nilan's announcement was accepted by the audience with a rolling of eyes and an exchange of glances and whispers. There were no raised voices, no shouts about democracy or power to the people. Just a resigned silence.

After thanking Councilor Gary Grunin and his Orders & Rules Committee for "letting us use this room," Nilan introduced Councilor Matt Kerwood, who, Nilan said, "has a wonderful idea." Kerwood's wonderful idea turned out to be an Adopt-a-Park program for the city's parks, modeled after the familiar Adopt-an-Ugly-Highway-Sign program where a company or organization gets its name on a billboard for cleaning a section of highway—or, more likely, pays cash for a billboard and lets the highway department do the cleaning. Next thing we're going to see is Adopt-a-Canyon, or Adopt-a-Redwood Forest. Unfortunately, my Adopt-a-Driveway program still has no takers.

With that important business out of the way, Nilan introduced team owner James Ryan and commissioner Tom Hutton from the New England Collegiate League. This was the preliminary bout preceding the heavyweight fight. In summary, a Collegiate League team plays twenty games, and since it's nonprofit, it can pay only part of the maintenance expense. Their presentation took about twenty minutes, but it seemed like forty. As a courtesy, the commissioners asked a few questions and the audience applauded politely.

The room grew still for the main event.

"Before Mr. Elitzer and Mr. Bouton come up," said Nilan, "I want to recognize several councilors in the audience—Councilor Bianchi and Councilor Lee, President Hickey, Councilor Scapin, and Councilor Kerwood, and Councilor Grunin are here. And I think the city bodes well by these councilors showing an interest in this matter. Okay, Mr. Elitzer and Mr. Bouton."

Chip, batting in the lead-off spot, moved to the podium. Facing the commissioners, with his back to the audience, he began by tossing thank yous around like bags of peanuts. He thanked the commissioners "as volunteers who often have a thankless task." He thanked them for taking on the responsibility of caring for thirty parks, "something for which you are not often publicly thanked." He thanked them for "taking upon yourselves the task of having to choose the best proposal." He even thanked them for "giving us the opportunity" to speak in the first place.

Chip is nothing if not polite.

After introducing Eric and me from the audience, Chip brought up the list of eight "minimum criteria" that had been suggested by the Parks Commission. Chip said our proposal addressed not only those eight but "other important areas the commission may want to consider in evaluating not only us but the other people who are presenting tonight."

Beginning with management.

"You've heard it said that the three most important things in real estate are location, location, and location," said Chip. "In the same way, venture capitalists say the three most important things in business are management, management, and management.

"In Jim Bouton we have a former baseball player who's also a writer, and in Eric Margenau we have a successful sports entrepreneur," said Chip. "I'm the interchangeable piece—investment bankers are a dime a dozen.

"And since a partnership takes on all the attributes of its partners, we can say that our partnership has won twenty games for the Yankees, won several World Series games, and written a best-selling book. We can say that we have successfully owned and operated fourteen minor league sports teams, and that we were involved in taking Federal Express public."

This reminded me of Bob Uecker's line after his Milwaukee Braves roommate, home run slugger Eddie Mathews, had hit his 399th home run. Uecker, then a back-up catcher, went around saying, "Me and my roomie have 400 home runs between us."

"You'll find all this in the proposal we have submitted to you," said Chip. "But you should rely not just on what we tell you about ourselves, but on what you can also learn independently."

At this point, I had to stifle a smile because I knew what was next. Chip was taking a slight detour from the proposal.

"Here it comes," I whispered to Paula.

"The Internet, for example, can be a source of information," said Chip. "Go to one of the search engines, like Google. Type in the name Jim Bouton. Type in Eric Margenau, Chip Elitzer. Learn about the other presenters, too. Type in Jonathan Fleisig."

Sometimes Chip can be cruel.

Then it was my turn for the marketing and facilities portion of our proposal.

"Knock 'em dead," whispered Paula, as I stood up to take my turn at the podium. For a guy who does motivational speaking for a living, I have to admit I was a little nervous.

"Our goal is to double attendance," I began, "by marketing three underappreciated assets to local, regional, and national consumers.

"One, a locally owned team that will be a source of pride and stability, and a new reason to go to the games.

"Two, a legendary ballpark with its own logo and historic identity, whose quirky charms are as interesting as the game itself.

"Three, Independent League baseball, which offers superior play, more local players, and returning favorites.

"Our marketing strategy," I said, "is based on 'share of customer' rather than 'share of market.' We want to capture for Pittsfield some of the tourists who are already flocking to Tanglewood, the Norman Rockwell Museum, Shakespeare & Company, MASS MoCA, the Williamstown Theater Festival, and the numerous restaurants throughout the county.

"Besides," I said, "you can only eat so much sushi. Then you need to have a hot dog." This got a laugh from the audience and a smile from the commissioners.

"Imagine Wahconah Park as a town square," I said. "Where people come early to hang out, grab a bite to eat in our 'Taste of the Berkshires' food court, visit with neighbors. Imagine Pittsfield and Wahconah Park with their own jackets, hats, and T-shirts. Imagine a Walkway Museum and Hall of Fame with photos and artifacts going back to the late 1800s.

"Our plan calls for local, regional, and national marketing," I said, "with placement of brochures in local B&Bs, cross-promotions with cultural organizations, and the inclusion of Wahconah Park on national historic site maps—the ballpark that refused to die."

"As far as publicity," I said, "reporters from around the country often call to ask what I'm doing these days. I tell them about everything *except* Wahconah Park—because I want to save that story until we're ready. But I can open that tap at any time."

As I was saying this last bit, the commissioners looked uncomfortable. Especially Nilan, who played with his pencil and pretended to look at some papers. The others looked down, or at each other.

"As year-round custodians of an irreplaceable asset owned by the city," I said, launching into the facilities part of our plan, "we plan to invest *no less than $250,000* in capital improvements before Opening Day 2002."

This was our big surprise and I paused to let it sink in.

"A quarter of a million!" I said. "Invested right here in Wahconah Park. Something no team owner has ever done before."

The only reaction to this from the commissioners was a decided non-reaction. It was as if I had said we were going to add an extra water fountain.

"In addition to the $250,000," I said, "our partnership will pay for all maintenance and repairs to Wahconah Park, on a year-round basis. Repairs that have cost the city of Pittsfield more than $500,000 over the past five years. That $500,000 could pay for a lot of street lights. Or a fire truck. Or high school sports."

I talked about improvements that would be phased in over the years. How we could alleviate flooding in the parking lot. How we'd enlarge the locker rooms and restrooms. How moving the concessions from under the wooden grandstand would reduce the risk of fire. How an $80,000 paint job with an undercoat and rust protection would be better than the usual quick spray-paint. How our Not-So-Luxury Boxes would be compatible with the style of the stadium.

"We are going to do things right," I said. "Long-term. And permanent."

Then, like a tag-team match, I turned it back over to Chip.

"As far as a long-term lease or license is concerned," said Chip, "we believe Pittsfield is best served by granting us a time frame that enables us to plan projects and commitments from the perspective of an owner, not a renter. This contract could be canceled by the city immediately upon our failure to provide any one of the following:

"One, professional baseball.

"Two, a minimum of $250,000 invested by opening day 2002.

"Three, a minimum of $25,000 annually in capital investments.

"Four, year-round maintenance and repairs.

"Five, reasonable use of Wahconah Park for other events."

At this point, I began to notice a certain stillness in the room. The only movement—except for Nilan's mannerisms, and the relentless vibrating of Matt Kerwood's left foot, which looked like it had a motor in it—was the synchronized nodding of heads.

"This is not a 'take it or leave it' proposal," said Chip, as if it needed to be sweetened any further. "We are willing to talk about any and all ideas the Commission may have to achieve the same ends."

While the commissioners contemplated the ramifications of actually talking with us, Chip moved on to the ownership structure.

"By November of this year," said Chip, "we will be making an offer to sell 51% of the team to a broad base of Berkshire businesses and individuals, with a preference for the citizens of Pittsfield. We will do it not because we need to do it, as has been suggested in some quarters, but for marketing and political reasons. Local owner-ship will provide a sense of fan loyalty to bring fans to the ballpark, and it will make it difficult, if not impossible, for anyone to move Pittsfield's own ball team to another city."

This earned a few positive grunts from old-timers in the audience who have seen at least seven different franchises come and go through Pittsfield over the past thirty years.

"Now I want to move on to the topic of league negotiations," said Chip. "While we may seem to be at a disadvantage because we do not already own a team, the reverse is true. As my partner Jim Bouton wrote recently in a letter to the *Berkshire Eagle,* 'If we already owned a team, we'd be shopping around for a place to play,' just as our opponents tonight are doing."

Chip reviewed the familiar scenario where cities woo teams to come or stay with expensive new stadiums or upgrades, at taxpayer expense, only to have them leave if the city doesn't do more. He explained that to change that balance of power in favor of Pittsfield, we needed a lever—an exclusive lease or license for Wahconah Park—that would enable us to negotiate the best deal possible between the Atlantic and Northern leagues.

"We propose to take advantage of a reality," said Chip. "Which is that it is Pittsfield that has the scarce asset—a proven market for professional baseball in a historic ballpark that fans are passionate about. And we are asking you, on behalf of Pittsfield, to *back our play*—and change the balance of power between cities and teams."

That was my cue to join Chip at the microphone for the grand finale. After asking the Commission to "recommend our proposal and exclude all other proposals," I made one last humble appeal—in the name of common decency and for the good of mankind.

"I would like to direct my final pitch," I said, "to Mayor Doyle, who has said that he has an open mind. If the mayor will choose our proposal, we will invite him to come back from his retirement and throw out the first pitch on opening day. Thank you."

Thunderous and sustained applause—plus a few whoops and hollers—emanated from our sixty or so supporters filling the last four rows of seats and lining the walls in the back of the room.

And it went on.

And on.

"Any, any uh..." said Cliff Nilan, trying to make himself heard. But the applause continued. This was well beyond the usual polite "smattering" or the hearty "hear, hear" applause.

"Any questions from the Commission?" implored Nilan, as the applause extended past the "pay attention, we're trying to make a point" level, and veered perilously close to "you idiots better listen to these guys."

"Commissioner Conant?" said Nilan, grateful to see a raised hand, as the applause continued.

Then finally the applause stopped, but it wasn't happy about it.

"I want to compliment you," said Conant, "on a well-done and thorough presentation."

"We worked all day on it," I said. A few people laughed.

"You worked more than a day, I'm sure," said Conant. "The point I wanted to make was, there was continuous reference to a contract, but I haven't seen any copy of it. And I'm not going to vote for any proposal if I don't see a contract."

"We don't have a signable contract," said Chip. "But what we have is a written and bound proposal, which lays out the principal terms, that Jim will be handing to you now."

With a bunch of our spiffy-looking proposals in hand, I walked along the front of the dais and dealt them out like playing cards to the commissioners.

"We felt it would be presumptuous for us to draw up a contract and say, 'Here, sign it,'" said Chip. "Normal business practice is that before you start the lawyers' clocks ticking, you like to know that there is substantial agreement. What really counts is, Do you like our proposal? And are the principal terms we've outlined acceptable? And if so, either our lawyer or your lawyer can take the first cut at drafting a contract—and that can be done in a matter of days."

For the next twenty minutes, the questions and answers generated a barrage of verbiage between us and the parks commissioners best summarized as follows:

Massimiano: I just want to say that I have serious concerns about essentially turning over Wahconah Park to you, almost on an ownership basis, for a period of what you describe as thirty years.

Bouton: The only way to get anyone to invest the kind of money we're talking about is to give them enough time to earn it back. Otherwise, you're going to continue with Wahconah Park the way you have been—with a cheap coat of spray paint, rags wrapped around the pipes, and the place coming down around your ears.

Massimiano: Your statements that you would be the ultimate arbiters of who could use the park and that you would keep the fees for the use of the park—high school football and baseball use those fees to support themselves. I find that troubling.

Bouton: Events that have historically taken place at Wahconah Park can continue. And we have no intention of taking fees from high school sports. The fees we were talking about were for things like rock concerts or other events, some of which *we* might be able to attract.

Elitzer: The presumption has to be that any use of the park must be entertained, and if our denial is shown to be unreasonable, then we'd be in default of the lease and you could terminate us.

Smith: Correct me if I'm wrong, but don't we have to get permission from the Astros during the season if we want to do anything with the park?

Nilan: No! We can do it.

Smith: Well, we've sat down with them when we talked about doing a concert or something . . .

Nilan: All we have to check is if the gate's open and they're not playing. That's it!

Massimiano: And then they give us the keys back when their season is over.

Bouton: We'd be happy to give you the keys back, although you might want to give them right back to us so we can open up and make the repairs that the city was normally making.

This generated a knowing laugh from the back of the room and a sour look from Massimiano. Ba-*dum*-bump.

With no further questions and the laughter dissolving into applause, Chip and I returned to our seats. Nilan called for a five-minute break.

"Great job," said Paula, "And the audience loved it."

"I've got to go outside and call 7 West," I said. "Give them a heads up on an approximate time for the phone poll."

"You don't need the poll," said Paula. "The people are clearly on your side."

"We want to reach the thousands at home, watching on television," said Chip. "They'll just brush off this crowd here."

Outside City Hall, I wandered around in the dark with my cell phone, looking for a place to call where I wouldn't be seen by the smokers milling around by the door. Ducking behind a small spruce tree, I reached 7 West, who said they were all set. I just needed to call them about five minutes before we were ready.

Back inside, Cliff Nilan called on Jonathan Fleisig. This was Pittsfield's first glimpse of the mayor's choice for Wahconah Park, and all eyes followed him to the podium. Speaking from notes, Fleisig then gave a presentation that is hard to describe, although the word "rambling" would be a good start. But there was more to it than that—a particular quality that can only be captured with Fleisig's own words. Herewith, some verbatim passages:

Mr. Chairman. Commission. Thank you for having me. It's been a while, and by that I don't necessarily mean tonight, but it's been literally a year since we were fortunate enough to have the mayor and his contingent come down to the Northern League All-Star game over a year ago and tell us a little about Pittsfield and about the new stadium you guys are proposing. And since then I've been the, I'd say bridesmaid of sorts, saying that if the new stadium doesn't get built, or even if it does get built, hey, I'd love to be in Pittsfield. So I guess in that little contest of who was talking first, I might actually win this one. Heh, heh.

I'm actually thrilled to be here. You know, I spent my camp years here, et cetera, et cetera. My goal tonight is a), to hopefully get us all to Wahconah Park by the ninth inning so we can finish the end of the game. All right? But you asked me to do certain things and that's what I've done. You asked for a handful of answers to questions that you had, so I've prepared those answers for you.

At one point, Fleisig introduced his general manager, Mike Kardemas, who was sitting in the audience. Then he introduced Miles Wolff, who got up and spoke for a few minutes. As Wolff was speaking, I looked at Paula for her reaction to Fleisig. With a quizzical look on her face, she shrugged, as if to say "What was that?" Then Fleisig was back at the podium.

Usually, I'm told that I like to talk a lot about myself. I'll try to calm that down for tonight. But just to give you a little background on myself . . . basically I'm just a baseball wannabe. I wanted to play major league baseball but I just didn't have the capabilities, it's that simple. So what I've done for the last eighteen years or so was, hopefully, to give myself an opportunity to somehow get back in it. And from my adventure into baseball in '95/'96, I proceeded to go out and—because the same marketing techniques that's used—I went to Bakersfield, California, and bought a hockey team, and went to Topeka, Kansas, and bought another hockey team. I wish in one way that I had a chance to be Jim Bouton, OK, and be a baseball player. In another sense I wanna be Mike Kardemas and be general manager. I'm stuck now trying to be the owner. If I had my choice I'd rather *play* in Wahconah Park than own a team in Wahconah Park, to be honest with you.

New England Collegiate Baseball League? I love baseball, OK. If we can get another twenty games in there, OK? and Mr. Ryan and I can work it out some way, then let's do it, OK. If I have to work a little harder on the grounds crew, so be it. I love baseball, that's what it's all about, OK.

One thing that we'll get to later on is . . . you know . . . I'm all about community and charity. I usually judge my teams by the three Cs, I call them—community, charity and championships. I may not have won any championships so far in my hockey . . . I think I've done pretty well in community and charity. And Pittsfield's going to be no different.

What I'd like to do, is basically set up a presence here in Pittsfield, OK, and most of the charity work that I do for . . . say in Bakersfield right now? . . . what I would like to do is make that a focus of my charity . . . make Pittsfield high school athletics my primary charity focus.

I know that there are some tough times going on with high school sports nowadays. I raise a *lot* of money with my sports teams, OK? This is my way of giving back. So, you know what? I'd like nothing better than to host all the high school baseball games. If I can raise the money to buy them new bats, new uniforms, and everything else, so be it.

OK. A lot of things are said . . . uh . . . I agree with Chip in one essence that you should really do your due diligence about everything. And I'm real proud of everything I've done. OK, in sports.

I leaned over to Chip and said, "He agrees with you in one essence." Chip nodded and smiled. Paula was slowly shaking her head, the grammarian in her soul mourning the demise of the English language.

I guess the buzzword is local, local, local. I just didn't have the opportunity to be born in the Berkshires, OK? Once again, I'm a wannabe. It's that simple. All right? I don't wanna get on airplanes, OK? If I had my druthers, I don't wish to have a baseball team go out there in California. I'd like to sell all my assets if I could, and just come back and concentrate on baseball in the Northeast. I love it with a passion. OK? And what I do there? In charity? Just imagine what I can do here. All right? And I'd really love it if you'd go over a bunch of this stuff.

I'd like to become a member of this community, OK? Michael would like to become a member of this community, OK? And we'd like to join in this community and do it *together*. OK? It's very simple. If I'm fortunate enough, and you people are able to grant me—OK—use of Wahconah Park, the first thing I'm gonna do is go out and ask, "Hey! Who wants to be part of this?" OK?

It's not about ego, it's not about me, it's not about Mr. Elitzer or Mr. Bouton, either. It's about baseball, OK? And if other people want to share in my dream, hey, that's great. As long as we're winning and the fans are doing good, OK, and it's comfortable in Wahconah Park, and everyone's having fun, then let's do it together. I'm not about fighting, OK? I'm about the community and the charity and making things work. OK?

Chip sat there looking at his watch. Paula looked dumbfounded, her mouth slightly open. I wanted to go up and put my hand on Fleisig's shoulder, and tell him he could stop now, and that everything would be all right.

At the end of this, there's a bunch of paraphernalia, everything from CD ROMs that I use, to programs, to a bunch of other stuff that I produce, because you know what? I draw 6,000 people in Bakersfield when it's 110 degrees to a *hockey* game! And my team isn't any good, I'll tell you that, too. All right. All right? Not yet. Cause I don't cheat. I don't cheat on the salary cap, all right, but I work hard. I have, like to think are some brilliant marketing techniques. OK.

I did not bring a big marketing plan because I wasn't asked to. I'm not going to go through all the things I'm gonna do at Wahconah because I wasn't asked to, OK? But I will tell you this: no one will try harder than Mike, myself, and Miles and everybody that stands with us, OK? And we'll give it everything we have, and I wouldn't be here if I didn't think I could be successful, so . . . I hope you chew on it, and if you have any questions I'll be glad to answer them.

While the commissioners conferred among themselves, Paula urged us not to do our phone poll. "It would be overkill," she said. "It would look like piling on, and you might actually create some sympathy for him."

Chip and I trust Paula's instincts on stuff like this, so I went outside and called 7 West to tell them we were canceling for the evening. Then the commissioners were ready with their questions for Fleisig, the answers to which were as follows:

You can throw away, really, all the numbers that I put out, OK? I'm in a business, OK? I have to produce revenue. If I have to spend more expenses in order to create that revenue, then so be it, I'll do it. I spent a million dollars for ice in Topeka, Kansas. OK? It was a good investment. If I have to spend more . . . ? I mean I love the luxury box ideas and some of the things that Mr. Bouton came up with. I think it's great. I have some other ideas of my own as well, OK? If it produces revenue and pays for itself, then you do it. So, there's no, necessarily, cap on it. It's, you know what? What's prudent, what makes good business sense, OK?

We're not here to burn money, we're here to put on baseball games and have everyone have fun, OK? Do we want to paint it? What kind of paint *do* we want to put on it? Personally, I like the idea of having murals painted, you know, little baseball things, by maybe local high school students. OK? Or some little kids.

I mean the bottom line is you're in a business, and if people aren't going to come to Wahconah Park because it's unsafe—the way it was in Lynn—then I don't have a business anymore. I mean I'm trying to be a realist here, OK? I want to be here, OK? I love it here, it's beautiful. I had a great weekend here. I mean it's nice.

What I want is, I want you to tell me, "Jonathan, you know what? it's a good idea." You know what? you wanna have a bar-becue fest, bring one in. Hey, you want to bring in major league lacrosse for one or two games to see if people like it, bring it in. You know, if I can make more money and have revenue from some idea that you guys come up with, great, all right?

As far as high school games go, I mean, one of the things Mr. Ryan and I discussed is, you know, I'd like to have double head-ers. I'd like to have, you know, at four o'clock we have maybe a high school game or Mr. Ryan's games or something like that, and at seven o'clock you bring on a pro team. Let everybody get in for one price. You know, I want to be imaginative.

Nobody has ever asked me these questions. I mean, people are making assumptions because certain things are written in the newspaper that aren't true at all, OK? I love baseball. I wanna be here, OK? You want me to give you my word? You want me to sign something off? I'll do it. As long as this Wahconah Park, OK, as long as I can make money, OK, and I mean, you know, it's not going to make a *lot* of money, but as long as I can do a good job business-wise, why would I ever leave? I live in the Northeast, this is where I want to be, OK? It's that simple.

I hope you like me, because if you give it to me, you're stuck with me. I'm not going anywhere, OK? It's that simple.

There was a smattering of applause as Fleisig returned to his corner, but for all intents and purposes it was all over. He had lost on a self-inflicted TKO. Not only did we not need the phone poll, but we decided not to use the three-minute follow-up we had been promised. Which is just as well, because as soon as Fleisig was done speaking, Nilan adjourned the meeting without so much as a glance in our direction.

But Chip and I were sky high. We moved about the Council chamber with a quiet confidence, gracious in victory, awaiting only the judges' decision just a week away. Like magnanimous boxers who've been pummeling their opponents for fifteen rounds, Chip and I went over and touched gloves with the Fleisig team. That's when Chip had a memorable exchange with Fleisig's attorney, Mike MacDonald, of Cain Hibbard Myers & Cook.

"Do you work for Jeff Cook?" asked Chip, dropping the name of Steve Picheny's attorney.

"Actually it's the other way around," said MacDonald, a little put out. "Jeff Cook works for *me*."

"Was he kidding?" I asked Chip later.

"No, he was serious," said Chip. "He seemed annoyed that I didn't know the pecking order."

Out in the hall, Chip and I chatted with some of our Wahconah Yes! teammates—folks like Potsy and Nadeau and Soldato and Roucher, and others whose faces we're starting to put with names, like Sue Gordon and Jim Moran and Tim Zwingelstein. All agreed it had been no contest, but there was a noticeable lack of euphoria.

"It's not over yet" was a common expression. So was "don't count on anything with these guys" and "you better keep your eyes open." Chip and I felt like we'd just won the World Series and our teammates were acting like we'd only won a regular season game. We were into "cool of the evening," and they were into "yes, but." It was a little disconcerting.

But it didn't spoil our fun.

The first thing Chip said to Paula, once the three of us were outside the building, was, "I can't wait to hear your observations."

And we couldn't wait to get back and tell Cindy all about it.

"So, how did it go?" she asked, as we came through the door.

And the four of us cozied up around the same kitchen table where our adventure had begun.

"Our guys were great, the college league isn't even in the running, and Fleisig was pathetic," said my totally unbiased wife.

"What was Fleisig like?" asked Cindy, automatically moving containers of food from the refrigerator to the table.

"He's a nice-looking man with a beautiful speaking voice," said Paula, "and then he spoils it all by speaking."

"I actually felt sorry for him," said Chip, digging into the Indonesian-style chicken.

"'Hey, you know what?'" said Paula, imitating Fleisig. "'I wanna be Jim Bouton. I'm a baseball wannabe, OK? And you know what? I'm not telling you my, you know, plans for Wahconah Park, all right, because, guess what, I wasn't asked to, OK? It's that simple. Hey, I love baseball, OK? OK?'"

"Nooooo," said Cindy, not quite believing.

"She's not kidding," I said. "It was painful. Like watching a train wreck in slow motion."

By this time, the chicken was history and it was time for ice cream. And some of Jacob Elitzer's leftover birthday cake.

"What did they think of your proposal?" asked Cindy.

"Their big concern was the thirty years," said Chip. "Even when I said they could cancel us if we didn't perform, they were still worried. They were more worried about what they might lose than what they'd surely get."

"It almost sounded as if they were afraid we *would* be successful," I said.

"How did they *look?*" said Cindy, "And I'm asking you, Paula, because I trust your judgment more than Jim and Chip. At least you've got your feet on the ground."

Chip and I can endure almost any insult while eating ice cream.

"With Fleisig," said Paula, checking her notes, "they leaned forward and looked directly at him, called him by his first name, and were openly friendly and encouraging. With Jim and Chip they were deliberately noncommittal. A bit nervous. Careful to look respectfully attentive, but not fully engaged. Except when Jim talked about reporters calling him and asking what he's doing these days. When he said that, a few of them were literally rocked back—a physical reaction. The guy on the left blinked hard a few times."

"That was Massimiano," said Chip.

"Why would they be afraid of publicity?" asked Cindy.

"There seems to be a deeply rooted fear of outsiders in Pittsfield," said Paula, "which others have already commented on. Because outsiders mean change and change is what they fear the most. It threatens their tightly held power structure. Power is more important to them than money, more *real* to them. Money belongs to others, to rich people, a breed apart; but power is something they can taste, and they're addicted to it. And so long as membership is restricted, they can run everything."

"The last thing they want," I said, "is for two guys from South County showing them how it's done."

"Because that will neuter them," said Paula. "And their little insiders' club, where they trade favors and peddle influence, will become irrelevant."

"So why would they want Fleisig?" asked Cindy. "He's from New York."

"Fleisig is controllable," said Paula. "They sense that he has no personal strength and that he will play the game and our guys won't. They don't trust anybody who isn't beholden."

"The irony," said Chip, "is that we want the ballpark more than Fleisig does."

"Their great joy," said Paula, "will be in refusing to let you have it *because* you want it so badly. That's the fix for them, the high, the proof of their power. And the better your proposal, the bigger the thrill they'll get in rejecting it."

"Then we might as well throw in the towel right now," I said, just kidding.

"But you won't," said Paula, "because the two of you are motivated by a game that's stacked against you. And because they don't want you to have it, you're even more determined to get it."

174

"But we really believe in what we're doing," said Chip. "It's not just an exercise. We'll actually do what we say we're going to do."

"A lot of good things get done because of people's characteristics," said Paula. "Look at Churchill."

"We're the right guys at the right moment for Pittsfield," I said.

"If I didn't believe that," said Paula, "I wouldn't have been behind you."

There was a long pause.

"For what it's worth," said Chip, "after the meeting Smitty came over and shook my hand warmly, looked me in the eye, and said, 'You did a really good job. Excellent presentation.'"

"I'm not sure that means anything," Paula said.

"Maybe we made them an offer they can't refuse," said Chip.

"The only thing I would do over," I said, "is my comment to Massimiano about getting the keys back so we could go in and make repairs to Wahconah Park. It was too sarcastic. I should have put it in the form of a teaching fable—about a king who loses his castle because he won't give anyone the keys to help him defend it."

"I like that," said Paula.

"Personally," said Chip, "I liked Jim's sarcasm better."

"I still don't understand how they can go against you guys," said Cindy. "Especially now that everyone's seen Fleisig up close."

"They can always find a reason," said Paula.

"Because, hey, you know what?" I said. "Anybody can have a bad day, OK?"

o o o

CHAPTER 8

"An unbelievable amount of shit"

AUGUST 14
TUESDAY

I woke up with a brainstorm today: we should have an artist draw a picture of our proposed improvements to Wahconah Park. And the artist's name should be James Akers. The other day, Akers was having copies made at Kwik Print and saw our bound proposals sitting on the counter. Because he's a baseball fan and had been following our adventure up in Pittsfield, he left a note for me at Kwik Print, asking if he could be of any help.

And so it was that Chip and I ended up having lunch today at Gon San with Jamie Akers. Between rounds of Shige's special sushi, we explained what we hoped to do at Wahconah Park and showed Jamie the pictures we had pulled off the Internet. As Chip and I talked, Jamie's pencil raced over the paper tablecloth. In a few strokes our Taste of the Berkshires food court and our Not-So-Luxury Boxes came to life.

"That's actually better than we imagined," said Chip, marveling at the power of a few lines on a piece of paper.

"This is just a sketch," said Jamie. "It would help if I had a few more pictures to work from. Any chance that you'll be going to Wahconah Park?"

"Not until tonight," I said. "And we wouldn't be able to have the prints ready for you until first thing in the morning."

We laughed. And then we told Jamie we were on a tight budget.

"No problem," he said. "Let this be my contribution to saving the ballpark."

This is like walking down the street and finding an artist holding a sign that says *Will Sketch For Tickets.*

I picked up Chip at six o'clock for the drive to Pittsfield. Our plan was to have me do the open mike, giving Chip a well-deserved night off, and then go to Wahconah Park to take pictures and watch the game.

In the car we talked about what I'd say during the open mike. Even though the City Council would not be making the decision on Wahconah Park, the open mike was a good way to publicly address the Parks Commission, and to reinforce our proposal.

"One of the points you need to make," said Chip, "is that everything in our proposal is negotiable. That requires them to at least sit down with us and try to work something out."

"I've already got that covered," I said. "And then I'm going to deal with the 'not-owning-a-team' business again. We need to pound home why that's an advantage for Pittsfield."

"Then you deal with the lease," said Chip, "and you've got it."

"Then I have a surprise at the end," I said, "that I'm not going to tell you about."

"Uh-oh," said Chip.

It was fun walking into the Council chamber tonight. Like returning to the stadium where you pitched a great game the night before—it sort of feels like you own the joint. And our Wahconah Yes! teammates—Potsy and the crew—were already beginning to settle into the last few rows.

Once again, the festivities started off with a bang. Tonight's surprise was a motion to move the open mike session from its customary first place on the agenda to much later in the evening. Supposedly, this was necessary because the clock was ticking on some highly paid consultants who had been invited to make a presentation. The vote to delay the open mike passed 8–3. The "no" votes belonged to the Three Amigos.

Announcement of the delay produced a groan from the back of the room. That's because most people come for the open mike and then take off. Now they'd have to wait through an hour or two of boring council business.

"This was done on purpose," said Chip. "They wanted to take us out of prime time. The open mike is a thorn in their side."

"You're right," I said. "There'll be a lot fewer people watching TV at nine o'clock than at seven."

"It's like when they enforced the 'three-minute rule,'" said Chip. "And it was by the same 8–3 vote."

"Since I'm taking care of the open mike tonight," I said, "you go to the game and I'll meet you there afterwards."

"No," said Chip. "I'll stay here in case you need me."

"That doesn't make any sense," I said. "*Go* to the game, take the pictures we need while it's still light out, and I'll meet you at the ballpark. If I'm not there when the game's over, you come back here."

"No, I'll stay here," said Chip.

"That's stupid!" I said. "No sense both of us sitting around. You're not going to say anything anyway."

"I'm staying," said Chip.

"Okay, goddamn it," I said, "we'll both go to the game. And I'll come back about eight thirty, in time for the open mike."

"All right, let's go," said Chip. "But I'm coming back with you."

It's like we're married, for crissakes.

So off we went to Wahconah Park. And right after our sausage and peppers at the concession stand, we went on a photo shoot. We shot every possible view from every conceivable angle. While Chip was shooting the grandstand from the field, I was shooting the roof from the bleachers. We looked like detectives gathering evidence at a crime scene.

Meanwhile the stands were filling up. "Good luck with Wahconah Park," people would say to us. Or, "Aren't you the baseball guys?"

"Would you mind if I took a picture of you taking a picture of my girlfriend?" one guy said to me.

Then there were the autograph people. Of course I said yes. I always say yes to autographs. It'll be a sad day when nobody asks.

But I've noticed that autograph seekers generally do not care if you are involved in doing something at the moment. I've had people ask for my autograph while I was standing at a urinal. No kidding. One day I'm going to be dying on the street and some guy is going to ask for my autograph. "Can't you see I'm dying?" I'll tell him. "I just want *one*," he'll say.

Suddenly it was 8:30 and I knew the open mike would be starting, and I didn't want to miss it. Now where the hell was Chip? And how was I going to find him in that crowd? I couldn't just holler his name. Then people would really know we were nuts.

So I did the only thing I could do; I headed for the car. I figured Chip would know where I was, and he could either stay at Wahconah and wait for me or have someone drop him off at City Hall.

Then I heard a voice from above.

"Wait for me!" said Chip, "I'll be right down."

There he was, on the roof of Wahconah Park, with a camera dangling from his neck. I hadn't seen him that high up since we built the tree house.

We arrived at the Council chamber in time for me to deliver my open mike remarks, which I had written out in advance.

"My partner Chip Elitzer and I have six minutes between us," I said. "How about I take up four minutes and Chip takes the night off? We just saved you two minutes."

There was a moment of hesitation as the councilors weighed the two-minute benefit of *less* Bouton/Elitzer versus whatever four-minute trick I might have up my sleeve. But the two-minute savings won out, and Council President Tom Hickey nodded his acceptance.

"I want to address three points with respect to our proposal last night before the Parks Commission," I said. Then I went over the things that Chip and I had talked about in the car: how Wahconah Park would be available for high school sports, how any long-term investment would require a long-term lease, and how willing we are to negotiate.

With a minute to go, I came to my favorite part—the hearts and flowers moment.

"Now I *should* say the rest of this on bended knee," I began, as a few councilors got quizzical looks. "Wahconah Park, we love you. We don't want to just use you for a few years like all the others." Then I paused for effect. "We want to *marry* you. If you turn us down you'll break our hearts, and the hearts of the people of Pittsfield."

At this point, all hell broke loose on the councilors' faces. The Three Amigos loved it. Dan Bianchi, leaning forward on his elbows, hands clasped, was absolutely beaming. Joe Guzzo was doing his "heh, heh, heh" laugh and nodding in appreciation. Rick Scapin was grinning broadly and looking around, checking everybody else's reaction.

The other councilors, however, were not so thrilled, although Tom Hickey was sort of smiling. Gerald Lee and Paul Dowd sat there stone-faced. Bill Barry smiled weakly, looking for help. James Massery and Jim Brassard appeared to be smirking. Matt Kerwood was clearly searching for a clue as to how to react. And Gary Grunin looked absolutely alarmed. He looked as if armed bandits—or maybe a large cat—had just entered the chamber.

Meanwhile, the back of the room got a big kick out of the whole thing. During their sustained applause routine—which the Wahconah Yes! team has down pat by now—I could see the men were laughing and the women were all mushy. If it registered the same way with the viewers at home, we'll be in good shape.

After the open mike, Chip and I went out in the hallway to say goodnight to our teammates.

"You guys are winning people over," said Potsy, still laughing about my marriage proposal. "The whole town is with you."

"Wouldn't it be fun," I said, "if they gave it to Fleisig next week and we got to see what the public was capable of?"

"Pitchforks and torches," someone said.

"Barrel of tar and some feathers," said Potsy.

On that note, Chip and I headed back to Wahconah to catch the end of the ballgame. Unfortunately, the concession stands were closed and there was nothing to eat.

"When *we* get Wahconah Park," I said, "we'll make sure at least one food stall stays open until the last out."

"It's a wonder we don't get fat," said Chip, "the way we eat."

"That's because we're constantly moving," I said. "Like sharks, who have to keep swimming or die."

We went right to the press box because Chip wanted me to see the view from up there. And it was spectacular. If you want to know what the poets are talking about when they get dreamy about base-ball, just go up to the press box at a minor league ballgame on an August night.

"Can you imagine our Not-So-Luxury Boxes up here?" said Chip, looking out over the field.

I had always appreciated minor league ballparks from the perspective of a player. The tiny dugouts—cozy or cramped, depending on whether you were winning or losing. The funky locker rooms. The bullpen sanctuaries, beyond the prying eyes of managers and coaches, where we'd trade insults with male fans and acquire the phone numbers of female fans.

But the view from the press box at night is a whole different thing. From there you can see the entire experience, a self-contained world in which the game is incidental. Your eye pulls back from the players, to the wider panorama—beholding an activity of some sort, that appears to be glowing in the dark. Like a votive candle. Or an astronaut's view of earth.

The sensation is magnified at Wahconah Park, with its cozy grandstand, old-fashioned lights, and modest scoreboard. It's like looking at the stars from a country lane as opposed to a city street.

My fear is that Wahconah will disappear, replaced by the noise and hoopla of programmed fun and sponsor messages. Or worse, ruined with a cheap upgrade—like plaid slipcovers on a Louis XIV chair. That's why our Not-So-Luxury Boxes must be done with the greatest of care—in Early-Wahconah style, with a corrugated roof, wood bench seats, and open on all sides.

"Wahconah Park should be a working museum," I said. "The Museum of Minor League Memories."

AUGUST 15
WEDNESDAY

This afternoon, I stopped at Chip's after running some errands in Great Barrington. Usually I pull into his circular drive, check for signs of life, and if no one's home I keep going. Today there was the usual gang of teenagers milling around, friends of the Elitzer boys, planning to do something that seemed to involve bathing suits and a board game.

Chip handed me the paper with the latest *Eagle* droppings.

Under the headline CLINGING TO BASEBALL IN PITTSFIELD, Ever-Scrib had written:

> From the rubble of a June 5 vote in which Pittsfield voters squandered a golden opportunity to build a new stadium ... three proposals have emerged to keep baseball alive at aging Wahconah Park. All three were aired before the Parks Commission Monday night, but the process produced more questions than answers.
>
> Two proposals ... would bring independent pro baseball to the city. The proposals for rehabilitating the ballpark and marketing the team offered by Mr. Elitzer and Mr. Bouton were admirable in their detail, particularly in contrast to the vague outlines provided by Mr. Fleisig. The grim reality, however, is that these gentlemen don't have a team, and despite their tortured rationalizations that this is in some way a selling point, it is a serious deficiency.
>
> It is clear that neither of the independent league proposals are the answers to the Berkshires long-term interest in protecting its proud minor league heritage. ... Wahconah Park is already two decades out of date and won't last forever. ... Someday the Berkshires will need to build a new ballpark, perhaps in North Adams, Lanesboro or Great Barrington if not in Pittsfield, and until that day, Pittsfield will struggle to make do while regretting its missed opportunities.

"Can you imagine?" I said sarcastically, "People wanting to preserve their history?"

"Yeah," said Chip. "Who do they think they are?"

"That fucking paper will not give up," I said.

"Neither will Goldsmith," said Chip. "He called this morning and said Wirz is willing to go against the league. He's offering to sell his franchise to us before Monday night."

"Hmmmm, Monday night," I said. "What a coincidence. The same night as the decision."

We both laughed.

"It's absurd," I said. "What does Goldsmith think we're going to do? Give Wirz a deposit and then try to go get an approval from Miles Wolff?"

"I told him the approval has to come first," said Chip.

"But he knows that," I said. "So what's he bothering us for?"

"And listen to the price," said Chip. "It's $550,000. I just laughed and told him now it would have to be for something south of $450,000."

"For some strange reason the value of Wirz's franchise just jumped by $100,000," I said, "and by Monday afternoon, it'll be up to $650,000."

"I wonder if Wirz even knows what's going on," said Chip.

"Wait until Wirz finds out how much Goldsmith, Fleisig, and Wolff have cost him," I said.

"Guess who else called?" said Chip. "Gary Grunin. He wants to meet with us. He said it's important because he's 'going to be the next mayor.'"

"The tide is turning!" I said. "The rats are deserting the ship."

"And I think we should meet with him," said Chip, "even though he wants to use us for his own political advantage."

"Why help him?" I said. "You know he's going to work against us behind our backs."

"He might," said Chip. "But it can't hurt us to meet with him. We're not going to pose for pictures with the guy. We're not appearing with him."

"That's why Grunin looked stricken last night," I said. "He realized he has to get on our bandwagon. Otherwise he has no chance."

"He wants to meet us for breakfast tomorrow in Pittsfield," said Chip. "He doesn't have the time to come down here."

"Tell him we'll meet him at Carol's in Lenox," I said. "That's half way and they serve a great breakfast. We can order bacon and eggs for us and a nice wedge of cheese for Grunin."

Later, Chip got a call from Tom Hutton of the Collegiate League. "He said they're going to formally withdraw in the best interest of Pittsfield," Chip said. "He thinks they're being used by Fleisig. He said he didn't want their bid to help or hurt anyone else."

"How about that?" I said. "A show of integrity. So rare these days. It's almost shocking when you actually see it, isn't it?"

Then it was evening and I was finally ready to face it.

Today was the fourth anniversary of Laurie's death, and I need to be with Paula when I think about that. The idea that Laurie has missed out on four years now is profoundly heartbreaking. How can we just go on without her like this? It doesn't seem possible. But we do it.

I actually did things today. I ran errands. I hung out with Chip. I got angry at stuff that hardly matters. I was able to feel good about recent triumphs. And I laughed. It doesn't seem right.

"I didn't know whether to remind you of the approaching date or not," said Paula, "because I knew that you had the presentations on Monday and Tuesday."

Am I being disrespectful to Laurie? I don't think she crossed my mind when Chip and I were involved with the Pittsfield nonsense. Or maybe she *had* crossed my mind—sometimes something will remind me of her, and I'll have a flash thought, and then it will disappear. Then I'll recall it later, when I'm home and it's safe to remember.

I try to follow a friend's advice about not marking the death, only the birthday.

"Consciously marking is one thing," said Paula. "But the body always remembers the anniversary. So I absorbed it for you. Last night I was back and forth to the bathroom and my heart was pounding, just like that night when we drove down to the hospital."

Paula said couples who are close can do that. She says things like this to ease my mind.

"Laurie would want you to be excited, Babe," said Paula, putting her arms around me. "She would have had the most fun with this, cheering you on. I can hear her now—'Go for it, Dad.'"

AUGUST 16
THURSDAY

"I would never do anything just to get a vote," said Gary Grunin. He said this to Chip and me over breakfast at Carol's restaurant. "If I feel strongly enough about something, I'll come out with it."

The three of us continued eating as if we actually believed what had just been said. In fact, we all knew that this meeting was nothing more than a charade—a political move one makes before changing horses. "I personally inspected their gums," Grunin could say, "and they look healthy."

We didn't make it easy on him.

"As vice president of the City Council, why didn't you ask Fleisig any questions at the presentation on Monday night?" I said. "Stand up and ask why a guy who's been looking for a new stadium suddenly wants Wahconah Park."

"We can't say anything at those meetings," said Grunin. "The Council can't do anything. What can the Council do?"

"You can refuse to approve a lease when it's offered," said Chip. "Send it back."

"But it would be too late by then," said Grunin.

"You could use the Council as a bully pulpit," said Chip.

"That's why I want to be mayor," said Grunin, "because I think I have the leadership ability."

"Can the Council act between meetings?" I asked.

"Not as a Council body," said Grunin, "but individually we can. I'm going to have an off-the-record meeting with Nilan."

"Why off the record?" I said. "That's what these guys want. They like off the record. That's how they hide."

"We've been hearing that the fix is in," said Chip.

"I've heard the fix is in, too," said Grunin. "Gerry Doyle can do whatever he wants. He doesn't care. The Parks Department doesn't care what happens to Pittsfield."

"But they have to live here," I said. "They shop in town. They've got kids in school."

"They don't care," said Grunin. "People in Pittsfield have short memories. Besides, the stadium vote was against the government, budgets, streetlights, the firehouse."

"And the vote *for*," said Chip, "was people afraid of losing baseball or just happy to have something positive happen in Pittsfield."

"We've got to get the public involved," said Grunin.

"Then why don't you call for a public meeting," I said, "where people can ask questions?"

"I'm going to try and put something together," said Grunin. "You know a lot of people think I'm on the inside, but I'm not. This is a bold move on my part. Most of the other candidates are sitting on the fence waiting until after the Parks Department makes a decision and then jumping on board."

And that's how it went, until Grunin boldly looked at his watch and realized it was time to go back up to Pittsfield.

"So what did you think?" I asked Chip on the way home.

"Unsatisfying," he said. "His heart is still not in the right place, and the only reason he's going to talk to Cliff Nilan is because he's running for mayor, plain and simple."

"And it's going to be off the record anyway," I said, "so no one will even know what was said, if anything."

"Grunin accepts how things are," said Chip, "and then says there's nothing he can do. He's not outraged about it."

I decided to call Dan Bianchi. Bianchi, who wears wire rimmed glasses, has the look and manner of a high school math teacher.

"I spoke to Bob Smith today," said Bianchi, "and he said, 'We got three good proposals here.' I said, 'No, Bob, you got *one* proposal. You're a Parks Department guy.'"

Bianchi was reminding Smith that his first obligation is to Wahconah Park, and not some other agenda like a new stadium.

"Bob is a guy who will only do something if there's something in it for him," said Bianchi.

I asked Bianchi what he thought were our chances of convincing the other commissioners.

"Massimiano is an honorable guy," said Bianchi. "He's concerned about his image. Jim Conant's got to be concerned because he's running for the City Council. And I don't know that much about Sue Colker."

Sue Colker is listed as one of the five park commissioners, but we have yet to see her at any of their meetings.

"Cliff Nilan hangs out at DelGallo's bar with the guys who think they're running this town," said Bianchi. "It's a political Mecca. *Great* decisions are made there," he said sarcastically. "But the only thing great is the pasta fagiole made by Mrs. DelGallo."

Then we veered onto the larger subject, the elephant in the room that nobody else wants to talk about: the new stadium.

"I listened to Andy Mick go through their proposal seven times," said Bianchi. "It was so stupid. I thought I was missing something."

I told Bianchi about my toxic waste theory—that a new stadium might be a Band-Aid over a toxic waste dump. Maybe PCBs.

"I don't know if we're ever going to know the truth," said Bianchi. "This is a GE town. Maybe a ballpark can cover a lot of sins."

"In any case," I said, "it's pretty clear that the people of Pittsfield are behind our proposal. And the park commissioners know it."

"That's what it's going to take," said Bianchi. "To make it so embarrassing they have no choice. They're not looking to fine-tune your agreement; they're trying to find reasons to reject you that look acceptable to the public. And I just heard a rumor that they're going to delay the decision."

I felt my chest tighten.

"Mischief," was all I could think of to say.

"I think it's a good sign," said Bianchi. "It means they're feeling the heat and they need some time."

As soon as I hung up with Bianchi, I called Parks Administrator Bob Mellace to see if it was true about the delay.

"It's being pushed back a week," said Mellace. "They're going to look into it a little bit more."

"What are they waiting for?" I said, trying to hide my annoyance.

"One question they're looking into is the lease," said Mellace.

"Just out of curiosity," I said, "how long did it take the commission to negotiate the previous lease with Gladstone?"

"About a month," said Mellace.

"Since time is of the essence on our proposal," I said, "why don't they take the ten days between now and the twenty-seventh and start negotiating a lease?"

"Because they haven't made up their minds yet," said Mellace.

"They don't have to make up their minds," I said. "The lease can be subject to us being approved. Meanwhile, we might be able to work out any problems during the negotiations. The point is, why wait?"

"That's the way they want to do it," said Mellace, with a hint of resignation in his voice.

"What's really going on here, Bob?" I asked. "Are they just going to announce a decision without even sitting down with us?"

There was a long pause.

"I feel awkward," said Mellace, "because I see what's going on. I ask questions myself, but my job is to facilitate."

"Speaking of that," I said, "whatever happened to the public hearings you said they were going to have?"

"I spoke to Cliff," said Mellace, "and he said, 'I don't want to have to talk to everybody and defend what we're doing. Everybody's just going to have to live with it.'"

Sounds like a slogan for Pittsfield. Something you might see on a bumper sticker. Or on one of those signs as you come into town.

"Pittsfield: Everybody's Just Going To Have To Live With It."

Speaking of slogans, Grunin for Mayor headquarters faxed out a press release this afternoon with the headline "Grunin Backs Bouton Wahconah Park Proposal." The one-page release said, among other things, that "public input remains the most important factor in the decision making." It also said that "Grunin gave his assessment following the Bouton partnership's responses to a series of questions raised by Grunin at a subsequent meeting he requested."

No mention was made of Grunin's responses to questions raised by the partnership.

Shortly after Grunin's fax arrived, I got a call from Jonathan Levine, editor of the *Gazette,* who had some thoughts on Grunin's endorsement.

"I thought you should know," said Levine, "that Grunin has been going around town saying that the new stadium isn't dead. He said it to a fellow mayoral candidate just the other day."

"Jeeez," I said.

"Mr. Weasel himself," said Levine. "He's been saying privately—not publicly—'I will get that thing built.'"

"Maybe he changed his mind this morning," I said. "Or he could work behind the scenes to sabotage us."

"He's capable of anything," said Levine. "But he's also a realist. He might be thinking ahead to future budget meetings—with Fleisig, there are going to have to be cash outlays."

"What do *you* think is going to happen?" I asked.

"I don't know," said Levine, "but the Fleisig group was at the mayor's office at 6:30 on Monday night. They were in the hospitality suite for honored guests."

When I finally caught up with Chip, who had spent the afternoon visiting his dad, I filled him in on my conversations with Bianchi, Mellace, and Levine.

"The roller coaster is headed back down again," I said.

"Not really," said Chip. "I don't get that sick feeling in my stomach this time."

"On the plus side," I said, "Grunin is calling for public input. On the downside, Jonathan Levine is calling him a weasel."

"Grunin may be a weasel," said Chip, "but he's *our* weasel."

"Now that he's endorsed us," I said, "he's actually more like a wolf in a Wahconah Park T-shirt."

"That makes three different animals so far," said Chip. "We're going to need a field guide just to keep track of him."

"Whatever happens," I said, "it sounds like the decision is going to be made at DelGallo's."

"We should go to DelGallo's," said Chip. "I love pasta fagiole."

"We can sit with our backs against the wall," I said, "and get somebody to taste our food."

"We can bring a hamster," said Chip. "If he dies, we don't eat."

"Or we can invite Grunin," I said, "and switch plates with him."

AUGUST 17
FRIDAY

I woke up at 6:30 this morning to the sound of the fax. Chip, the machine gunner who refuses to leave his post, was at it again. This time he was firing back at Cliff Nilan, who was hiding in the pages of today's *Eagle*.

In a story headlined PARKS BOARD DELAYS MAKING BASEBALL PICK, Nilan gave two reasons for the delay: "Wahconah Park's floodplain might have to be looked at again," and the board "may have to contact the city building inspector to see if the [Not-So-Luxury Box] idea is possible." Then, out of nowhere, Nilan said, "But I want our youngsters to be able to use the park for football and soccer."

What can you say to such nonsense? The flood plain hasn't changed in eons, our Not-So-Luxury Boxes are not crucial to our plans, and no one is saying youngsters can't use the park.

All of which Chip explained in his faxed letter to the editor, stating once again that "we seek to negotiate an agreement that is fair and acceptable to the city."

It's this sort of non-dialogue between us and Parks Chairman Nilan that may explain why there are no public hearings.

Meanwhile, Jamie Akers's renderings look fantastic. He made a pair of color sketches that are absolutely magical. One features our Taste of the Berkshires food court, and the other shows where our Not-So-Luxury Boxes would go and what they would look like. What's more, the drawings are alive with kids and adults wearing Pittsfield Rocks! T-shirts and Wahconah Park hats, walking under the new (but retro-looking) arched entryway, relaxing on benches in the enlarged plaza area, buying stuff at the concession stands, and otherwise enjoying Wahconah Park as never before.

"Wait until people see these drawings," I said to Chip. "They're going to go nuts."

"We should have thousands printed up," said Chip, "and do a leaflet bombing."

Instead, we settled for printing fifty copies to hand out and twenty posters to put in store windows. Then we emailed electronic copies to our Wahconah Yes! and Wahconah Media group lists.

The only sad note of the day came from the Internet.

"The Tribute to Fleisig has disappeared," said Chip. "No more horse's ass. Someone must have had them take it down."

"Too bad," I said. "I hate to lose one of our animals."

AUGUST 18
SATURDAY

Chip and I are not the only ones on a mission. Paula and Cindy are working hard to make this year's fund-raising gala for Fairview Hospital even more spectacular than last year's. Like buddies in a Thelma and Louise flick, Cindy calls Paula "Chick" (phonetic for CIC, meaning Commander-in-Chief) and Paula calls her "Quindy" ever since a Scrabble game in which one of us was going to get stuck with the Q, and Cindy was taking forever to make a play. "Whose turn is it?" Chip had asked. "It's Quindy's turn," I said.

Tonight Paula asked me to spend a few hours practicing our dancing in the living room, as a tune-up for the gala. It simply would not do to have me stepping on the chairperson's toes. Or, just as bad, getting that blank look on my face when I'm doing a step that doesn't exist. "What are you doing?" Paula will ask with a strained smile, as we move across the floor. "I have no idea," I say, smiling back. "Just hang on until I do something familiar."

AUGUST 19
SUNDAY

With the Parks Commission decision due a week from tomorrow, it is now a public relations battle. Wahconah Park versus a new stadium. The "South County Trio" versus Jonathan Fleisig, Mayor Doyle, and Miles Wolff (or, higher up the ladder, Dean Singleton, Andy Mick, and Larry Bossidy). Democratic process versus "Everybody's just going to have to live with it."

So far, it's a battle we seem to be winning, in spite of the odds. With the *Eagle* out to get us and WAMC out to lunch, Chip and I have had to fight a guerilla PR campaign. We plot strategy in the hills of South County and get out our message via fax, email, web site, and word of mouth. Every few weeks we raid the Council chamber for three-minute bursts of open mike. We're a two-man, low-budget, kick-ass public relations machine, winning hearts and minds with the power of an idea.

The best evidence that we're winning the PR battle comes from Jonathan Lothrop, a candidate for City Council, who sent this email:

```
>  In my travels, knocking on doors and talking
>  to people, every person is in favor of your
>  proposal. The only doubters are in the
>  political class, so to speak. There are
>  rumblings that if a Fleisig lease were to come
>  before the Council and actually get approved
>  a new petition drive could be mounted. Of
>  course that does not get you a lease, but it
>  is a strong signal.
```

Meanwhile, our opponents are drawing boos. Sandra Herkowitz, ear-to-the-ground political activist, had this to say in an email:

```
>  As a resident of this city, I am becoming
>  embarrassed and angered by the treatment
>  your group has experienced here by the
>  political network. It disgusts me. I had
>  no idea it was this bad.
```

Unfortunately, it's not enough to merely have the support of the vast majority of Pittsfield citizens, which we believe we have. We need to prove it. And how do we do that? Back to our phone poll idea.

"We'll invite our competition to a public hearing," said Chip, "and have it televised. At the end of the evening, we'll take the poll and announce the results."

The phone poll makes me nervous. I'm not so in love with the new technology. It never lives up to its hype and it's always more complicated than it needs to be. When the instructions say "easy installation" or "three simple steps," that's the tip-off it's going to be nearly impossible. Then they won't let you call in for help because they can't afford the customer service reps it takes to guide you through the "three simple steps."

Computer programmers with far too much time on their hands are always sitting around saying, "Let's see if we can make it do this." That's why everything is all geeked up. Machines are so complicated today that they can't do the simple things they were intended to do.

My television set, for example, lies in wait for me to insert a video, after which I'm unable to watch TV without a channel's call letters, in green no less, blocking the screen. And don't try to remove those green letters unless you're not interested in watching television for about a month. Once, before a World Series game, I looked funny at the remote and all I could get after that was snow and a hissing sound. When I pushed a button to see if I could retrieve the picture, our toaster went on. I had to call Mark at Tune Street—whose home number I had from a previous emergency—and he talked me down.

Same thing with my car. For no good reason, the horn goes off if I do certain things, like close the passenger door while the glove compartment is open—or not open, I forget which. And then the lights don't go off right away after I park the car. This causes people to say, "You left your lights on," to which I have to explain that it's designed that way. "It's a special feature of the 'nuisance package' I bought for an extra $275," I say.

I don't even want to discuss my computer. Suffice it to say, I do not need a rocket ship to go to the grocery store. I told Paula the only solution was to have electrodes attached to the beach chairs of technology company CEOs vacationing in the Bahamas, which could be activated just by pushing a button on whatever device was causing the problem.

"That would put an end to it," I said.

"It would probably backfire," said Paula, "like your father's squirrel zapper."

Years ago, my dad had gotten tired of having squirrels raid his bird feeder. He had tried everything, including suspending the bird feeder from a wire strung across the backyard. The more ingenious his plan, the smarter the squirrels got. What he was doing, I explained, was training squirrels.

Finally, he rigged up an electric shock device with a transformer and a plunger that he could operate from his living room. The idea was to watch out the window and push the plunger whenever he saw a squirrel climbing on the bird feeder. The first time he tried it he burned a perfectly round circle, about the size of a Frisbee, in the living room rug.

I expressed my reservations to Chip.

"What if there's a technical glitch and we lose our own poll?"

"It's all computerized," said Chip. "These guys have assured me they can handle thousands of calls in a matter of minutes. They do this all the time."

"But why risk losing what everyone believes we already have?"

"It's a chance we have to take," said Chip. "We need something that even our opponents will have to acknowledge. And we'll bend over backwards to make it fair. Maybe we can even get someone like Tom Hickey to be the moderator."

Having the president of the City Council as a moderator would certainly lend credibility to the proceedings. Chip was thinking smart and fast, forcing me into the unaccustomed role of doubting skeptic.

"And what if our competition doesn't show up?" I said.

"We could have Hickey present their proposals in the most positive terms imaginable," said Chip. "That'd be okay. We'd still win, hands down."

"Hickey would actually do a better job than Fleisig," I said. "Maybe we should just play the tape of Fleisig's presentation."

"Now *that* would be unfair," said Chip, flashing a wicked grin.

I took a chance and called Hickey at his home. He was very cordial. And surprisingly candid.

"You know, I recommended your proposal on my television show last week," said Hickey. "I said it was the best by far. I called Grunin after your presentation and I told him, 'You need to get out front on this because if you come out afterward you're going to look bad.' That's why he came out for you guys the next day."

"Now we won't be able to present you as a neutral moderator," I joked.

"I don't even know if I can do it," said Hickey. "I'll have to check my schedule." Then he paused. "You know, I've been taking an unbelievable amount of shit on this."

"From the public?" I asked.

"No," said Hickey. "From my friends on the City Council and others."

"The new-stadium people."

"That's it," said Hickey.

"Are we correct in assuming that the opposition to our proposal comes from the guys who still want a new stadium?"

"You got *that* right," said Hickey.

Webster's definition of conspiracy: a secret between two or more people to do something wrong, treacherous, or illegal.

It would seem that "friends on the City Council and others," secretly supporting a new stadium contrary to the wishes of the people of Pittsfield as expressed in every referendum on the subject over the past four years, certainly qualifies as wrong. The jury's still out on treacherous and illegal.

It's the damnedest thing. A conspiracy, in plain view of anyone paying the slightest attention, remains a "secret" because no one is covering the story—no newspaper reporter, no enterprising radio or television journalist. How hard could this be to expose? Evidently, a lot of high-profile people are dishing out "an unbelievable amount of shit."

I got the information just by asking. A reporter would have to be blind not to see it. Or overly enamored of being employed. I wonder, for example, what the future might hold for an *Eagle* reporter who would pursue such a story? Meanwhile, we're stuck with Ever-Scrib knocking, as he did on July 26, "Mr. Elitzer's stance that any competing idea is a conspiracy to reactivate the defunct downtown stadium project."

In the final analysis, I agreed with Chip—that risky as it is, we needed to try the phone poll. We have to prove beyond any doubt, in a public hearing—which so far everyone refuses to have—that the overwhelming majority of Pittsfield citizens prefer our plan for Wahconah Park.

As Dan Bianchi said, we "have to make it so embarrassing [the park commissioners] have no choice."

o o o

CHAPTER 9

"The fix is in"

AUGUST 20
MONDAY

By 10:00 a.m. today, Chip had put together the phone poll with 7 West Communications, and had arranged for Joe Guzzo to be the producer. And I had talked Dan Bianchi into being the moderator, because Tom Hickey said he had a scheduling problem. Our press release read as follows:

WAHCONAH PARK
PHONE POLL TO BE TAKEN
AT PUBLIC MEETING

At Wednesday night's televised open meeting in the City Council chamber, viewers will be given the opportunity to call a toll-free number to register their preference for one of three proposals for baseball at Wahconah Park.

The 7 p.m. meeting, at which the public is invited to ask questions and make comments, will be broadcast live on Channel 18.

The trio of Bouton, Elitzer, and Margenau, who scheduled the meeting, have invited their "competition," Jonathan Fleisig of the Northern League and representatives of the Collegiate League, to join them on stage.

The meeting will be moderated by Dan Bianchi and produced by Joe Guzzo as a special edition of *Perspectives.*

We emailed it to our Wahconah Yes! and Wahconah Media lists, and faxed it to our competitors, the city councilors, and the parks commissioners.

A few hours later, Chip got a call from the *Eagle*'s Bill Carey.

"I tried to get him to do a story about the newsworthiness of the phone poll," said Chip, "and the fact that this is the first time the public has been asked to participate. But he said the gist of the story would be whether Fleisig will come."

The answer to that question came to me in a call from Fleisig.

"I'm not going to be at your meeting," he said. "You're just trying to get the public all riled up to influence the commissioners."

"You'll have the same chance 'to get the public all riled up' in favor of *your* proposal," I said.

"It's a slap in the face of the commissioners," said Fleisig. "If they want to hear from the public, *they* should call a meeting."

"The public has never been asked to be involved," I said. "That's one of the problems."

"I'm all for the public being involved," said Fleisig. "I'll answer any questions. All they have to do is call me."

Just leave a message on his answering machine.

"There's never going to be a public hearing on this," I said to Chip. "Especially with us involved. They do not want their flunkies and patsies—the park commissioners and Fleisig—exposed to any kind of scrutiny."

"The last thing these guys want," said Chip, "is to have everybody on a stage, with the cameras rolling, and engage in a free and open discussion."

"Can you imagine Nilan and Fleisig being grilled?" I said.

"We'd have to be careful not to make them look too bad," said Chip. "They'd get the sympathy vote."

"I'd like to challenge all the new-stadium guys to a debate," I said. "Either one of us against any six of them."

"That seems fair," said Chip.

AUGUST 21
TUESDAY

I'm nervous about our phone poll tomorrow night. My newest fear is that not many people will watch the program, and that Cain Hibbard and BS&E will find someone with a speed dialer and we'll lose our own poll 300 to 100—thereby giving the Parks Commission the break they're looking for.

We're not getting the publicity I expected, considering this is the first public hearing ever held on the subject. The *Eagle* buried it in the Community Notes section as if it were a store opening or a Kiwanis meeting. And we have yet to hear anything from WAMC.

So why don't I pick up the phone and ask my friend Alan Chartock to cover the story as it should be covered? Holler at him as a friend might do. "Hey, Alan, what the hell's going on? You're missing the boat here!"

I could talk like that to Alan because we *are* friends. We joke that he once saved my life. Actually, I was just passing a kidney stone, but it felt like I was dying. It started while I was a guest on his *Vox Pop* program and I was in so much pain I couldn't continue. This was in the dead of winter, and Alan drove me to the hospital, slowing down every few miles so I could open the door on the passenger side and throw up. Once you've thrown up from a guy's car, you're usually friends for life. And Alan knows I would let him throw up from my car.

Then why don't I call him? For one thing, I don't want to pressure him. Whatever Alan feels he owes the *Eagle* or David Scribner is his business. The story goes that the *Eagle's* previous owners, the Millers, had hated Alan, but when they sold the paper to MediaNews Group, Scribner befriended Alan and he's been grateful ever since. Alan probably sees it as loyalty.

But the main reason I don't call Alan, or any other friends in the media, is that I want to win this without any outside help. Just Chip and Eric and me against the big boys—three against thirty. It's more fun that way. I don't want it to look like I sicced the media on them—even though it is legitimate news. So, while it's partly true that I'm saving that play for after we get Wahconah Park, it also has to do with fighting fair.

The good news is that we're getting rave reviews on Jamie Akers's renderings. Here's what Eric Lincoln had to say in an email:

```
> The latticed gateway is awesome. Walk through
> the gates, ladies and gentlemen and step back
> in time, to a place where things were simpler
> and a real community existed—where baseball
> had not yet been affected by the dollar bill.
> It was the Old Towne Game and this is what you
> have magically re-created. It's glorious. I'm
> a cynic, always have been, but I've always
> rooted for the good guy in the movie and the
> underdog on the playing field. Under your
> stewardship, Wahconah will indeed be the
> finest place in America to watch our beloved
> game of baseball.
```

Eric is trying to get his editors at the *Record* to print the drawings on the front page of the paper.

"So far, they won't do it," said Eric. "They said, 'It's a Pittsfield story' and the *Record* is mainly a South County paper."

This has not kept Chip and me from putting up a few posters around Great Barrington. Shige Tanabe has one on the wall inside Gon San. Shige thinks he's going to be taking batting practice at Wahconah Park when the team is on the road. Okay, I might have mentioned it in passing.

Our man Gary Grunin called to say he hasn't been able to download our color renderings on his computer. I promised to resend them. Then he had this to say:

"We've really never had issues as big as this. The last one was the PCBs. Now the stadium thing. A lot of this stuff has been going on behind closed doors. I told them from day one they rolled this thing out wrong. A combination of BS&E and the mayor's office. I wasn't involved in any of those meetings. They did one PowerPoint out at the GE site."

"Why GE?" I asked.

"They wanted a neutral site," said Grunin.

Taste of the Berkshires Food Court

Not-So-Luxury Boxes

Peter Arlos called today. He thought I might like to know that Fleisig's attorney, Mike MacDonald, was the same guy who had drafted the language for the Civic Authority—the entity that would have managed the new stadium. This is further evidence that Fleisig is just a place holder for the new-stadium guys.

Arlos also said there was a rumor out of the mayor's office that I had once demanded $3,000 to speak to the Boy Scouts. And this is further evidence that our opponents are scumbags.

Curiously, the story is based on a true incident. I recently declined to speak to the Boy Scouts, but for a different reason—namely their reprehensible exclusion of gay scouts. It isn't fair to the boys, of course; it's the leaders who are imposing their warped sense of morality on others. One day they'll wise up, but until then you can't accept it. That's what I told Cheryl Raifstanger at Kwik Print, who had asked me on behalf of a friend if I would speak to the Scouts.

But I had originally said yes—until I thought about it for a few hours—because that's my first impulse when anyone asks me to do something for the community. It's part of giving back, part of the privilege of living in such a wonderful place. Paula thinks people sometimes take advantage of me, but I don't see it that way. Taking advantage of someone is turning the truth upside down and leaking it anonymously for political purposes.

This has nothing to do with Cheryl, who has a heart of gold. I believe Arlos when he says he got it from the mayor's office. But where did *they* get it from? And why didn't someone like Tom Murphy or Curt Preisser call me first to see if it was true?

As I said, scumbags.

The New England Collegiate Baseball League has officially withdrawn its application for Wahconah Park and will not be at the public hearing tomorrow night. This means it's just going to be Chip and me versus two empty chairs.

I have to remember to make name plates for those empty chairs.

Paula is getting into the swing of things. When I mentioned that I had to resend the color renderings to Grunin because he hadn't received the first transmission, she said, "Did you put a piece of cheese on it?"

AUGUST 22
WEDNESDAY

At 3:30 this morning, Chip went on the Internet and downloaded Bill Carey's story from today's *Eagle*. Under the headline BASEBALL RIVALS WILL SIT OUT INFO MEETING, Carey wrote about tonight's meeting and quoted Chip, among others.

> Only one of the three groups proposing new baseball clubs for Wahconah Park will be represented at a public meeting tonight—the group that arranged the meeting.
>
> "We're ready to put ourselves up on the stage in the City Council chambers, in full public view and on live television, to let the public take its best shot," Elitzer said yesterday. "We are warmly welcoming our competition to share the podium. We have not tried to make this a pep rally for the Bouton proposal.
>
> "We don't claim [the phone poll] is a stratified, scientific sample. It is what it is, hopefully a comprehensive way for people to register their preference. . . . It could go against us."

At 3:40 this morning, Chip emailed Carey's story to Jonathan Fleisig, along with the following note:

```
> Jonathan,
> Here is today's article which you may have seen
> already. Won't you reconsider your plans for
> tonight and join us on stage? (Or alternatively,
> designate a representative?) We don't intend to
> re-present our proposal. Tonight is the public's
> turn at bat. They'll make whatever comments
> they want, for or against any proposal, and ask
> whatever pointed questions they have for any
> one of us. Please join us. We'll treat each other
> with respect, and hopefully the public will too,
> regardless of personal differences.
> Regards, Chip.
```

At this point, I hope Chip went to bed.

And that he actually slept—for Cindy's sake. She hasn't been sleeping well lately and she thinks she knows why.

"If Chip's awake, I'm awake," she said recently. "Even if he's just lying there, I can hear him thinking."

Paula, on the other hand, has made a beautiful adjustment.

"I've learned to incorporate the sound of the fax machine into my dreams," she said.

Chip and I arrived at City Hall about an hour before our public meeting. We put up a poster with Jamie Akers's renderings, placed color copies on each chair, went over the phone poll scenario with the TV guys (we held back on the phone numbers until just before show time to avoid any chicanery), and linked up with 7 West Communications. Since Chip never heard from Fleisig today, we figured he'd be a no-show.

As we bustled about, we noticed that the room was not exactly filling up. Fifteen minutes before the meeting was set to begin, there were fewer than twenty people in the room. Where the hell was everybody?

Sandy Herkowitz, who was planning to say a few words on our behalf tonight, had an encouraging theory.

"I couldn't get anybody to come tonight," she said. "They all wanted to stay home and vote."

Dusty Bahlman of the *Eagle* was standing near the empty dais.

"Hi, Dusty," said Chip, as we approached. "What's new?"

"As long as you asked," said Dusty, with a very slow grin, "Larry Bossidy has an option for a New York–Penn League team. He wants to play in Wahconah Park for a year or two until a new stadium can be built."

I knew it was coming and I still felt a jolt.

Even when you know the bad guy is in the closet, it's still a little scary when he finally jumps out.

This was the August surprise that Chip and I had predicted and that Murphy had confirmed with his phony announcement that there weren't going to be any more proposals. Of course, Murphy knew what Bossidy was up to. Can you imagine Bossidy shopping for a franchise without telling anyone in the mayor's office? Call Murphy the Oracle of Deceit.

"Okay, what's your reaction?" asked Dusty, flipping open his notebook.

"No surprise to us," I said, like nothing bad had happened. "We always believed that Fleisig was a stand-in, a place holder, for a new stadium. Fleisig was just being used by the mayor to block us from getting a Northern League franchise."

"It explains the postponements and delays over the past few months," said Chip. "As a new-stadium wannabe, Fleisig now becomes irrelevant."

As Dusty scribbled in his notebook, a guy from WBRK radio held out a microphone and asked us the same questions about Bossidy's return.

He's baaaack!

Bianchi hadn't even heard the news. We filled him in as he took his seat on the dais, about to assume his duties as moderator. Bianchi didn't seem surprised either. He smirked and slowly shook his head.

Without mentioning Bossidy, Bianchi addressed the audience, explained Fleisig's absence "due to scheduling problems," and described the phone poll as "something unusual." He said the audience could ask questions, and he gave out the Council chamber phone number, in case viewers at home wanted to ask questions. Spotting Commissioner Jim Conant in the audience, Bianchi invited him to sit on the dais to field questions, but Conant declined.

Bianchi then invited us to make a brief opening statement, and I jumped in, leaning into the microphone perched in front of me. I began by breaking the news that Bossidy was now back in the game. I explained that it did not surprise us, nor did it change anything. In fact, it only sharpened the issue—give us Wahconah Park for the long term, or give it to Fleisig or Bossidy for the short term until a new stadium can be built.

A handful of people stepped to the open mike to ask questions, none of which was difficult to handle. Conant himself asked the toughest questions, which we relished, of course, because it gave us one more chance to highlight the unique aspects of our proposal.

While Conant was at the podium, I took the opportunity to ask *him* a question: "What is the risk to the city if we live up to the commitments we've outlined?"

Conant's answer: "I think it is just the process that we are in now is a due diligence process."

While Conant was demonstrating why the commissioners don't want to field questions, Chip and I passed notes back and forth about how to handle the Bossidy situation, since we did not have a separate phone number for him. Our solution? Have one phone number stand for our two competitors—Fleisig and Bossidy. Total their scores and we'd still win decisively. Two against one.

"That's fair," I said, my jock confidence trumping my tech fears.

By nine o'clock, the public had been heard and it was time for our phone poll. The plan called for a guy named Jay at 7 West Communications to give me the running totals on my cell phone as the calls came in. I'd tell Chip and he'd announce it to the audience in the Council chamber.

"We've decided to use two toll-free numbers tonight," Chip explained to the audience. "Fleisig and Bouton. There are *three* reasons to dial the Fleisig number: (1) if you're in favor of the Fleisig proposal, (2) if you're in favor of the Bossidy proposal, or (3) if you're not sure of either of those but you would like a new stadium. And there is only *one* reason to dial the Bouton number, and that's if you're in favor of the Bouton proposal."

On his own, Chip had added the new stadium as a *third* reason to dial the Fleisig number, but that was okay with me. At this point, I would have given Fleisig "people who like puppies."

"We're going to leave the lines open for one minute," said Chip. "Then we're going to cut them off and give you the results."

Now we were ready to proceed.

The TV guys signaled that the phone numbers were on the screen, and the clock started ticking. With me holding my cell phone and Chip ready at the microphone, we looked like precinct captains waiting to announce the downstate election results.

"We're going to have instant gratification," Chip announced, while the people at home were dialing, "because a minute after the polls close, we're going to know the result."

I studied my watch. Twenty seconds went by—but it seemed like two minutes because Jay at 7 West wasn't saying anything.

"What's happening?" I said into the phone.

"Nothing yet," said Jay.

"Nothing so far," I said to Chip.

A mildly quizzical look came over Chip's face.

"What's happening now," Chip explained to the audience, "is that my partner is waiting to get the results."

I checked my watch. A minute had passed. With the phone still pressed to my ear, I smiled as if nothing were wrong.

"It's more than a minute," I said to Chip, "and still no calls."

"Can that be possible?" said Chip, anxiety in his eyes.

"No calls?" I said into the phone, uncomprehending.

"No calls," said Jay.

Seeking instant gratification myself, I pictured beach chairs jumping with voltage, electrifying their CEO occupants.

"We seem to be having some technical difficulties," Chip said very calmly, in the manner of a British Airways pilot announcing a small fire on the wing. "This is somewhat embarrassing, I must say," he added.

Embarrassing? We were having a meltdown in the City Council chamber!

On live television.

"What the hell's going on?" I said to Jay. My face felt flushed and I was sweating.

Jay left the phone to see what the problem might be. Meanwhile, the audience in the Council chamber had been sitting there quietly. Very quietly, since they were mostly our supporters. Suddenly, a phone rang in the room next door to the Council chamber. Dan Bianchi got up to answer it. Then it rang again. And again. Dan answered the calls and returned to his seat.

"Calls are coming in next door," said Bianchi, "from people who are all getting busy signals."

Chip announced that the lines would remain open because people were getting busy signals. Five minutes had gone by since they were first opened. I called 7 West again. Jay had some numbers. Bouton 151, Fleisig 122. He said that was all he had.

We were crushed.

Chip couldn't even bring himself to announce the results. He wrote the numbers on a piece of paper and handed it to Dan Bianchi. Bianchi read the results to the audience. Then Dan closed the meeting.

Within five minutes the Council chamber was empty.

In the car on the way home, Chip and I were too devastated to stop for ice cream. We had planned to celebrate at Ben & Jerry's. I called Paula on my cell phone to give her the bad news about Bossidy and our phone poll.

"I'm so sorry for you, Babe," she said.

"But we're still not going away," I said, defiantly. That's what you say right after you get your ass kicked.

"I'm so pissed off at 7 West," said Chip, spitting out his words. "They assured me they could handle this. They guaranteed it."

"Fucking assholes," I said.

Back at Chip's house, we went up to his office to holler at 7 West Communications. Chip got Jay on the phone and let him know how embarrassed we'd been. How much we'd been damaged. Jay said they didn't understand what happened and that they're still trying to figure it out. He said he'd call us back.

"We're going to get killed tomorrow," I said. "The *Eagle* is going to have a field day."

Chip and I just sat there, exhausted. Too angry to think straight. Too distracted to come up with solutions.

Ten minutes later the phone rang.

It was Jay. Chip put him on the speaker phone.

"The problem was," said Jay, "that there were so many calls it jammed the system."

"But you said that couldn't happen," said Chip.

"We've never had this many calls," said Jay.

"Do you have any idea how many people may have called?" asked Chip.

"Sure," said Jay. "We record the busys as well as the connects."

"So how many were there?" asked Chip.

"I'll check," said Jay. Then he hung up again.

With our hearts beating a tad more rapidly, Chip and I speculated on what the results might be.

"The same ratio will probably prevail," said Chip, sadly. "55/45 in our favor."

"But what if the two phone lines are like two doors into a room," I said. "There could be a thousand people lined up behind one door and a hundred behind the other. Both doors would yield approximately the same number of people at first. But the ultimate total could be much different."

The phone rang again. It was Jay.

"The computer is still counting them," he said. "The number is in the thousands. I'll have to call you back."

Thousands!

What the hell does that mean? It could be good, or bad, or anything in between.

"Maybe I was right about the two doors," I said. "Or maybe Andy Mick and the boys used a speed dialer."

It was eleven-thirty. I called Paula to tell her I'd be a while. She said that was fine, she was watching a movie on TV.

"Do they record the phone numbers of the individual callers?" I asked Chip. "So it can be checked and audited?"

"Yes," said Chip. "And you can eliminate the repeats."

"That means any speed dialers will be exposed." I said.

"That's right," said Chip.

Fifteen minutes went by. What was the problem? Was 7 West still counting? We couldn't stand it any more. So Chip called Jay.

That's when we heard the magic words.

"Your man Bouton won in a fucking landslide," said Jay. "And we don't usually use that word around here. So far, the numbers are 3,209 to 437."

So far.

Hallelujah!

The people have spoken. And evidently they're still speaking.

Chip immediately called Dusty Bahlman to tell him about the new poll numbers and promised to email him tomorrow with the final results.

Chip and I shook hands and hugged each other. Then he walked me to my car. As I pulled away, I could see that he was hollering something. I rolled down my window to hear what it was.

"Drive carefully," he said. "An accident now would be a real bummer."

We laughed into the cool Berkshire night.

AUGUST 23

THURSDAY

I must have been sleeping lightly because at about 4:00 a.m. I heard the fax machine. Slipping quietly out of bed so as not to disturb Paula, I tiptoed in the dark to my office, took the papers off the fax, and carried them into the bathroom. Seated appropriately enough on the toilet lid, I read the online version of today's *Eagle*. Under a full-page headline STADIUM II: IT'S BACK IN PLAY, Bill Carey had written:

> Lawrence Bossidy Jr. said yesterday that he has signed an agreement to purchase a New York–Penn League franchise and will renew the effort to build a downtown stadium. . . . The team would use city-owned Wahconah Park until a downtown stadium is built.
>
> Bossidy said he has discussed reviving the stadium with MediaNews Group CEO William Dean Singleton, Berkshire Bank, Mayor Gerald S. Doyle Jr. and City Council President Thomas E. Hickey Jr.

Aside from the thought that one of my problems could be that I'm not a Junior, I suddenly understood the "scheduling problem" that Hickey said had prevented him from moderating our public hearing.

In a smaller story, under the headline: BOUTON, ELITZER 'NOT GOING AWAY,' Dusty Bahlman covered our public meeting "attended by about 20 people, a half dozen of whom rose to ask questions or make comments." At the end, Bahlman mentioned our phone poll, and quoted me saying that the 151 to 122 result was "unofficial."

It could have been worse. But not much.

Our extremely slim victory, and the sparse number of attendees and callers, suggested precisely the level of apathy over Wahconah Park that the *Eagle* has been trying to peddle. Left unexplained, the numbers destroy our most important claim—namely that we are the people's choice. How the hell are we going to get this straightened out? I went back to bed, sleeping even more lightly than before.

At 5:30 a.m. I heard the fax again. Chip must be an insomniac. That's in addition to maniac.

I slid out of bed in the dark and made the now familiar trip from the bedroom to the office to the bathroom. The papers in my hands were proof positive that you do not want to challenge Chip Elitzer at any time, on any matter, that has anything to do with anything.

Ready for faxing and emailing—to a list that included every media outlet, politician, committee chairman, and green grocer within a hundred-mile radius of Pittsfield—was the following letter:

Ladies and Gentlemen:

In conjunction with the live telecast from the Pittsfield City Council chamber last night, the following attempts (completed calls or "busy" calls) were tallied between approximately 9:00 p.m. EDT and 9:15 p.m. EDT to two separate toll-free numbers:

3,209 (88%) in favor of the "Bouton proposal"

437 (12%) in favor of the "Fleisig proposal" (which included, according to televised instructions at the start of the call-in period, supporters of the new Larry Bossidy proposal or anyone interested in keeping alive the possibility of a new baseball stadium for Pittsfield).

These results can be confirmed by calling 7 West Communications in Minnetonka, MN (888-XXX-XXXX) and speaking with Adam Boroughs, Director of Operations, or Jay Aupperle, Assistant Director of Operations and Programming.

For Pittsfield's elected and appointed officials to ignore this clear indication of public sentiment would be highly corrosive to public trust. My partners and I commend Mr. Bossidy for his abiding interest in the welfare of Pittsfield, but ask that he follow the sportsmanlike example set by the New England Collegiate Baseball League Commissioner yesterday in leaving the pitcher's mound. The call has gone in to "Bulldog" Bouton to close out this game and win it for Pittsfield.

Sincerely,
Chip Elitzer

I almost got a tear in my eye.

After going back to sleep again for a few hours, I awoke in time to listen to the *Dan Valenti Show.* This is not so easy because the Pittsfield station wasn't designed to reach South County. I have to stick the radio in an open window in our kitchen and crank up the volume. Even then there's a lot of static, but Paula is pretty good about it. She just sighs and reads her book while eating her yogurt with granola and strawberries.

Today's question by Valenti was this: "Imagine the best incarnation of a new stadium and a restored Wahconah Park. What side are you on?"

Almost every caller was in favor of our plan for Wahconah Park. One complained about the deceptive slogan, "no stadium, no baseball," that BS&E had used to scare people. Another caller said he had heard a rumor that the team Bossidy has optioned is the Utica Blue Sox, a minor league affiliate of the Florida Marlins.

Then I heard a familiar voice.

"Hi, Dan, this is Chip Elitzer. I thought your listeners might want to hear the latest results of our phone poll last night."

I turned up the volume on the radio, which squawked like a World War II battle update from the BBC. Paula winced.

"The latest figures," said Chip, "are 4,665 for Bouton and 488 for Fleisig—which also includes those who preferred the Collegiate League, Larry Bossidy, *or* a new stadium. That makes 91% in favor of our proposal for Wahconah Park, and just 9% for everyone else—combined." (Correction: Fleisig got 388 calls, giving us 92%.)

Hooray! The Germans were being routed on the northern front.

Then Chip got a call inviting us to be studio guests on the Larry Kratka radio program at eleven. Since we have no other life at this point, I threw on a T-shirt and jeans, picked up Chip, and we headed for Pittsfield. On the way we talked about the phone poll.

"Fleisig actually had 606 calls," said Chip. "11 were one-time repeats, but *144* came from one number and *63* from a second number. That means there were two speed dialers at work."

"We should have somebody call those numbers," I said, "and find out who they were. Wouldn't it be great if they belonged to someone at Cain Hibbard or the *Eagle*?"

"I gave them to Dan Valenti," said Chip. "He's on the case."

"Does that qualify as fraud?" I said.

"No. Dirty tricks."

"The roller coaster is back up again," I said.

"I predict Bossidy will bow out," said Chip.

"No way."

"He didn't get that far in the business world without knowing when to cut his losses," said Chip.

After the Kratka show, which went very well, we decided to visit a guy named Ray Parrott, whom we'd heard wanted to be one of our investors. Parrott owns the A-Mart near Wahconah Park. We called him, and he invited us over.

With our color posters in hand, Chip and I were led to a spartan office in the back, crowded with boxes, a metal desk, and some steel beer kegs. Parrott is a beefy guy, about forty, friendly and direct, an outdoors type, definitely not a suit-and-tie guy.

"I watched the three proposals and I liked yours," said Parrott. "I want to invest."

"We're not ready for investors just yet," said Chip. "But we wanted to meet you and enlist your support."

"I know Gerry Doyle and all those guys," said Parrott, laying our posters on his desk. "He and Conant and Smitty are all tight."

"Did you happen to see the meeting last night?" asked Chip.

"I already talked to Conant about it," said Parrott. "I said, Jim, you're up there asking questions to try to stump these guys, and they crushed you."

"The only reason Conant showed up," I said, "is because he's running for City Council."

"Whatever Jim does, Smitty is going to do," said Parrott. "Jim's got a political future to live up to."

"We've heard the decision has already been made," said Chip.

"I talked to Gerry right after the City Council meeting," said Parrott. "He said, 'They're not going to get it.' I asked him why, and he said, 'The fix is in.'"

"Doyle actually *said* that?" I asked.

"Those were his exact words," said Parrott. "Sometimes he'll let things out without actually saying so. Then when something happens you say, Oh, *that's* what Gerry meant."

"What *is* it with these guys?" I asked.

"All my life I've watched them," said Parrott, "and every time someone comes in and tries to help Pittsfield, they won't let them. They want to say, 'I came up with the solution.' Doyle wants to get credit for the new stadium. 'This is what *I* did. *I* did the GE deal.'"

"But if there's a new stadium one day," I said, "Gerry Doyle is going to be long gone by that time. There's got to be something else in it for him."

"The town has a history," said Parrott. "We had a mayor, Charles Smith, who put in the Krofta water filtration system. It made millions for Krofta. Then he became the vice president of Krofta."

"You think Doyle's going to end up at GE?" I asked.

"Knowing Gerry, he's probably already got something lined up," said Parrott. "I know he's looked at some houses down the Cape. He's done a lot of favors for a lot of people. Something will come up."

At the end of the meeting, we thanked Parrott for his time and he promised to put our posters in the window of his A-Mart.

Back in the car, Chip and I drove to the Lantern for some lunch and planned our next move.

"It's pretty obvious that Fleisig was being used," I said. "Here he is being wined and dined by the mayor, at the same time that the mayor knows Bossidy is shopping for a franchise."

"Fleisig has always been the back-up to Bossidy," said Chip, "just like during the Civic Authority vote. If it had passed, and Bossidy hadn't been able to get a team, Fleisig was in there. The same holds true now."

"Miles Wolff should cut Fleisig loose and cast his lot with us," I said. "Now that Bossidy is back, we're clearly the best bet for the Northern League."

After lunch, Chip had an idea.

"Let's stop by the *Eagle* and give them the latest poll numbers."

"But I'm just wearing jeans and a T-shirt," I said.

"I think you're showing the proper amount of disrespect for those fuckers," said Chip.

In a room across the hall from where we had met last month, Chip and I spent an hour with reporter Jack Dew and editor David

Scribner. Dew is a five-foot-eleven, blond-haired guy, in his late twenties, who already looks like an old newspaper man—overweight, baggy pants, shirttail sticking out, permanent slouch, hangdog face. You can see exactly what he's going to look like in thirty years.

Chip gave them the latest figures—4,665 to 488 in our favor—and explained about the computer not having been able to "answer" the volume of calls, but that the busys had been recorded.

"You didn't get the results you wanted," said Dew, suddenly playing the role of hard-nosed reporter, "so you changed the rules."

"No!" said Chip. "We didn't change the rules. We announced that the lines would stay open because we knew people were getting busy signals, but that didn't change the results. Ninety percent of the calls came within the first five minutes, anyway. We can show you the printouts."

"In any case, both sides had the benefit of the extended time," I said. "The only possible cheating came from the other side, with two speed dialers accounting for 207 calls!"

"It's not a scientific sample," said Dew, with a dismissive curl of his upper lip.

"A total of 5,153 people called, with verifiable phone numbers," I said. "That's more than a third of the number of people who voted in the June 5th referendum!"

Dew, looking unconvinced, had stopped writing by this time and sat slumped in his chair like a giant bean bag.

Scribner, who had alternated between standing and wandering around, just as he had the last time we met with him, finally spoke.

"I really believed the stadium was dead," he said, raising both hands skyward. "That BS&E didn't exist anymore."

"How can you say that?" I said, incredulous. "Chip and I weren't surprised by Bossidy's return. We knew it was coming. And we're not even in the news business."

Chip had a peeved look on his face.

"You guys don't challenge city leaders to involve the public, or make any move to sponsor a public hearing yourselves," he said, "yet you criticize our phone poll as unscientific."

Scribner squinted at Chip.

"Your sample is limited to people who care," he said, with professorial hauteur.

"Any election is confined to the minority who care," said Chip, getting more agitated. "Fifty percent is rare. Most people get elected to important government jobs with far less than a majority of the population."

Dew sat slouched with his elbow on the table and his head in his hand, like a kid who didn't want to do his homework.

"Whenever I ask people on the street," said Scribner, waving his hand airily, "most never go to a ballgame. And at the games, half are from out of town."

"Most New Yorkers have never been to the Statue of Liberty," said Chip, thinking way too fast for Scribner, "but they don't want it torn down."

Scribner smirked, by way of reply.

"The point is," I said, jumping in, "no team owner in America has ever made this kind of proposal to a city."

There was a long pause as Scribner tousled his hair with his hand. He was working hard on this one.

"Cal Ripken is building a stadium in Aberdeen, Maryland," he said, grinning, as if he'd just come up with a blockbuster.

I felt like punching him in the nose.

"You would never get away with comments like that in front of other people," I snarled. "Why don't you and I discuss the matter on *Vox Pop?*"

"That's up to Alan Chartock," said Scribner.

On the way out of the building, Chip and I marveled at what had just transpired.

"Scribner just will not give in on any point," said Chip. "And what are the chances of his going on *Vox Pop* with you?"

"Two chances," I said. "Slim and none."

"How about Jack Dew," said Chip. "Can you imagine him challenging the mayor like that? Or a councilman? Or Andy Mick?"

"Exactly," I said. "Where was he when his own newspaper was lying to the people about why there had to be a new stadium?"

Then we spotted a copy of today's *Eagle* in the lobby.

Under the front page headline announcing Bossidy's return, there were two pictures. One was Bossidy leaving the Stadium Yes! headquarters after the Civic Authority vote back in June. The other one, entitled "The Wahconah Alternative," was a dark and foreboding sketch that looked like a street scene from Dickens.

What the hell was that?

Lo and behold, it was Jamie Akers's color drawing of our Taste of the Berkshires food court that we had sent to the *Eagle* last week—only it had been printed in *black and white!* And poorly printed at that: the green ballpark was now black, the blue sky was now threatening rain, and the open plaza looked like the midway at a low-rent carnival. Not the kind of place you'd want to watch a ballgame. How could something so beautiful be made to look so bad? And why would they print a *color* picture in black and white?

Maybe they used up all the color on the Bossidy picture.

Chip and I were so jangled we needed to burn off a little energy. And where better to do that than at a ballpark?

It was about four in the afternoon when we arrived at Wahconah. The staff for Gladstone's Pittsfield Astros was doing what a stadium staff does—watching out for dangerous characters. Inside the gate, Chip approached an old guy wearing a gray T-shirt that said, appropriately enough, STAFF. When Chip offered a friendly greeting, the guy ignored him and walked away.

"He's in charge of customer relations," I said.

Instead of going into the stands or onto the field, where we could have been ignored by upper-level management, we decided to circumnavigate the ballpark.

Tramping through the underbrush, and stepping over puddles, we made our way around the back of the outfield fence. There we noticed the small drainage canals that had been hacked out to channel water on rainy nights from the far reaches of the outfield to the river, fifty or so feet behind the fence.

In dead center field, we arrived at the back of the football press box, which is supported by rusty steel beams. Of course we had to climb them.

"Hey, there's a light on in the press box," I hollered down to Chip, who was still navigating the cross-hatched beams in his loafers.

"How can there be a light on?" asked Chip.

"They just turned on the electricity," I said, "hoping we would grab a live wire."

And the day was still not over.

Back at the house, I got a call from Peter Arlos, who gave me the latest from the Pittsfield courthouse.

"I spoke to Cliffy today," said Arlos, using his pet name for Cliff Nilan, "and he says, 'They're *out*, just forget about it.' I said why? And he said, 'Environmentally it can't be done. They got these plans. They can't do it.'"

"Nilan's just making up reasons," I said. "He's referring to the parking lot, but there are plenty of other things we can do."

"He was looking very stressful," said Arlos.

"He's looking stressful," I said, "because Chip and I are making headway."

"If you lived in Pittsfield," said Arlos, "you'd replace me as the most popular guy in town, you know that? You could run for mayor."

"I'd make you my PR guy," I said.

"Aw shit, you don't need PR," said Arlos. "You got 'em in the palm of your hand. All except Cliffy."

But Cliffy is calling the shots.

The day ended with Chip getting the agenda for the next scheduled Parks Commission meeting on August 27th. There was no mention of the promised decision on Wahconah Park.

Another delay. These people are unbelievable.

Angry, I called Andy Nuciforo, a state senator from Berkshire County. Andy was once a new-stadium supporter who now says he's neutral. I don't really know why I called him, except to vent my frustration at the sorry state of politics in Pittsfield. Maybe Nuciforo could make a few calls, write a letter, launch an investigation.

"It's up to the people," said Andy. "I can't take sides."

"But the *people* have indicated that they're behind us," I said. "We just got 91% of the vote in a phone poll with over 5,000 callers. The *people* are being ignored by their city officials. Not taking sides is like staying neutral during a mugging."

"It's not over yet," said Nuciforo, evenly.

"Did you know," I said, "that the decisions in Pittsfield are being made at a bar called DelGallo's?"

"I know that," said Nuciforo.

So much for representative government.

AUGUST 24
FRIDAY

Today we learned the proper way to conduct a preference poll: send Jack Dew down the street to a Big Y supermarket and have him interview six people.

This was the method that produced a large headline in today's *Eagle:* NEW STADIUM DRAWS APPLAUSE. Dew's story was accompanied by photos of four of the six people he interviewed. Candi Eichesler, owner of Oasis Hair Design, was quoted as saying, "I guess I'm for the stadium, but not for the Civic Authority." An older gentleman named Edward Carroll said a new stadium is "going to help." Frederick A. Dillard said, "We need some refurbishing in Pittsfield." And Tom Spratlin said, "I think it's exciting."

As if to provide balance for this effusive praise, David Spiess, 12, was quoted as saying that "the city shouldn't build a stadium if it means taking people's property and raising taxes."

I nominate David Spiess for mayor.

Then it was time to dance. The Fairview Gala was held in the spacious dining hall of the Berkshire School, a private prep school with a college-like campus at the foot of a mountain in nearby Sheffield. By the time Paula and her crackerjack committee were finished decorating and lighting the place, it looked like some kind of Starlight Ballroom.

Paula and Cindy looked equally spectacular. Cindy wore this navy blue sheath with no back at all, and Paula wore a long, swishy skirt with what I call her "Daisy Mae" top—with the tantalizingly precarious straps.

It was a great night.

Three hundred fifty people—including both transplants and locals, as Paula is proud to say—danced to the big band sounds of Vince Giordano's Nighthawks, thrilled to the down-home blues of singer Ruby Wilson, and bopped spasmodically to guitar hipster Albert Cummings.

When Paula introduced Cummings and happened to mention that he would be playing next week at Wahconah Park, someone hollered, "Wahconah Park!" Whereupon Paula came back with,

"Wahconah Yes!" and the audience—aware of our adventure up in Pittsfield—responded with a chorus of "Yay, Wahconah!"

After I danced a few numbers with Paula, a lot of women came over to ask me to dance, thinking I could do the same thing for them. Unfortunately, they did not know when to exert pressure on my shoulder or squeeze my left hand and twist it back.

And of course, all the men wanted to dance with Paula—and a lot of them did—because she's such a great dancer. It had nothing to do with the precarious straps. Sure.

The evening netted a big chunk of change for the hospital, and half a dozen business cards for Wahconah Park.

And I got to go home with Daisy Mae.

o o o

CHAPTER 10

"Go take a shower"

AUGUST 25
SATURDAY

Saturday. A good day for playing tennis. Swimming in a lake. Reading a book. Sleeping on the porch.

Unless, of course, you're certifiably nuts.

Then you write letters—to people you don't particularly like, who will probably not respond.

Chip, who leads the league in letters unanswered or unpublished, sent one to Larry Bossidy, if you can believe that. He described our phone poll results that showed that only 9% of callers supported a new stadium under any circumstances. Chip also enclosed our original letters to BS&E, which argued that Pittsfield should use the new-stadium money for a new civic center or an indoor arena instead.

"Make the civic center/arena your idea and we will back you to the hilt, and you'll have 90% of the citizens behind you!" Chip wrote. "Jim Bouton and I would like to speak with you at your earliest convenience."

As if to cinch it, Chip enclosed a copy of *Ball Four*, which I signed and inscribed as follows: "Help us with Wahconah Park and we'll help you with Bossidy Arena."

There is no brick wall we will not run into.

Repeatedly.

Chip also wrote a letter to the *Eagle*, contrasting Jack Dew's survey of six people that he interviewed on the street, with our "much more relevant indicator of public opinion: the televised phone-in." Chip then provided the most recent results from 7 West Communications, showing that in the first minute—from 9:07 to 9:08—there were a total of 1,269 calls, of which 1,149 were in our favor, giving us 91% of the vote (corrected net first-minute results: Bouton 1,128 [94%], Fleisig, Bossidy, new stadium 75 [6%]).

When Chip's letter was rejected by Bill Everhart on the grounds that it violated the paper's "thirty-day rule" against anyone appearing in the letters section more than once within that period—the paper's equivalent of the "three-minute open mike rule"—Chip emailed Everhart suggesting that the letter could just as easily carry my byline.

Everhart's reply? No. Eric Margenau's byline? Another no.

But Chip still wasn't finished. Calmly and politely, he wrote again to Everhart, saying, "I would like to suggest that you adopt a small exception to your thirty-day policy to allow people to respond in their own words when they are cited in a material way in one of your news articles. Otherwise, someone could find himself, his words, or his actions subject to thirty consecutive days of reporting by the *Eagle* and only have one chance to set the record straight."

Everhart's response to that? "You might want to contact Jack [Dew] or Dusty [Bahlman] to see if there is a news hook here."

Of course, Chip then forwarded everything to Dusty—forget Jack Dew—with a note that said, "So, is there a news hook here?"

When Bahlman didn't respond, I had two thoughts: (1) Documented proof of overwhelming support for our proposal will never get printed in the *Eagle*. (2) Chip Elitzer should be required to register with the police as a serial letter writer.

My contribution in the letter-writing department was a one-pager to Miles Wolff, in which I said that Bossidy's return effectively ends Fleisig's bid, "since Fleisig's only support came from the new-stadium proponents who will now back Bossidy." I said his best shot at the Pittsfield market now rested with us, and that he should back our proposal in the best interest of his league and the city.

I wonder if Miles Wolff has the same filing system as Everhart.

AUGUST 27
MONDAY

On the drive up to Pittsfield for tonight's Parks Commission meeting, Chip and I went over the presentation we would make, opposing any delay in a decision on Wahconah Park. The latest rumor had it that the mayor would ask for a postponement until October to allow Bossidy to craft a proposal.

October!

The bastards.

It's obvious what they're doing, but they have no shame. They're not even slightly embarassed about it. And why should they be? Who's going to call them on it? Chip and I decided that should be my job tonight, since I'm so popular I could be mayor.

This reminded Chip about the most difficult speech he ever had to give.

"I was working for Eugene McCarthy," said Chip. "And I had to tell an all-male college crowd that I would be speaking instead of Jill St. John. Two-thirds got up and walked out."

"Why only two-thirds?" I said.

Waiting for us at Springside House was Eric Lincoln, sitting on the front steps in his basic dress slacks, sneakers, and baseball cap. As always, Eric was slightly disgruntled and definitely beleaguered, but still ready to laugh at the slightest bit of humor, even if it came at his expense.

"How long have you been sitting there?" I asked, as we walked up. "You look like you've been here all day, waiting for the other kids to show up for a game of stoop ball."

Eric smiled. "It's a sad commentary on my life," he said, "that I have nothing better to do than sit out here and wait for you guys."

The three of us filed inside, to the room with the two fat columns and the beat-up linoleum floors. There were only about a dozen people scattered in the forty or so chairs—a few media folks, and a handful of city officials, including Peter Arlos and Dan Bianchi. The Wahconah Yes! team doesn't bother to suit up for ordinary Parks Commission meetings.

A few commissioners were already seated at their laminated, wood-grained table. I took the opportunity to pass out our color copies of Jamie Akers's beautiful drawings.

Whenever Chip and I are in the company of city officials, we adopt an attitude of confident jocularity—as if we've got the winning bid, and it's only a matter of time before that's acknowledged, and let's get along because we'll all be working together one day. It was in that spirit that I introduced myself to Sue Colker—who had missed earlier meetings we attended—and joked with Jim Conant.

"You should frame these, Jim," I said, as I handed Conant the color copies. "You can tell your grandchildren, 'You see these pictures? I turned that down.' And when they say, 'Why did you do that, Grandpa?' you can say, 'I'll tell you when you get a little older.'"

Conant, a heavy-set guy with glasses, thinning hair, and a bushy mustache, sort of laughed. Nilan, who was sitting nearby, did not. All Nilan did was take them from me, give them a cursory glance without expression, and lay them on the table.

On the matter of Wahconah Park, the first ones to be called on by Nilan were Chip and me. This was a bit startling because it seemed out of order, and Chip stood up to respond.

"We understand there's going to be a request for a postponement," said Chip. "Since we're here to address that, we'd like to wait until the request has been made so we can know the particulars."

Nilan could barely contain his anger. He tapped his pencil on the table and tugged at his collar. Then he exploded.

"When you're the chairman, you can set the agenda," he said loudly and rudely, pointing at Chip. "Go now or not at all."

It's getting more like Alice in Wonderland every day. "Sentence now, trial later," says the Red Queen.

The room got very quiet. All you could hear were some birds chirping outside and people shifting uncomfortably in their chairs.

I couldn't believe this was happening. Who the hell was Cliff Nilan to holler at Chip Elitzer? Chip is the most courteous guy I've ever met, thanking these guys every time he stands before them. Nilan couldn't carry Chip's jock as a human being. I was pissed.

But I didn't say anything.

Instead, I looked at Chip, who was thinking cool. He signaled that we should just go ahead, and so I rose to speak.

224

Still shaking with anger, I made the following points:

1. Bossidy and Fleisig both want a new stadium, but a new stadium is not the Parks Commission's responsibility.
2. We are the only group with a long-term commitment to Wahconah Park, both financial and emotional.
3. Who, besides us, is going to maintain Wahconah Park for all the uses the Commission feels are important, including high school sports?
4. We're the only group ever to present a marketing or facilities plan for Wahconah Park.
5. Our partnership has owned and operated seven successful minor league baseball franchises. Neither Fleisig nor Bossidy can claim even one.
6. We're offering 100% private funds to restore a public ballpark to house a 100% locally owned baseball team that can't be moved out of town.

"This will be a first in America," I said, "and a great distinction for Pittsfield. And the decision is in your hands."

Then I sat down to a creepy silence. The only response was Conant's muttered comment as I returned to my seat that our proposal was "clever." I missed the sustained applause we always got at the City Council meetings.

It felt like I had just delivered some bad news to city officials. And I guess, on some level, I had.

The next person to be called on was Peter Arlos, who shuffled to the front of the room with his folder of papers. As a local fixture with a certain amount of comedic value, Arlos always gets a respectful hearing. At least until he's finished speaking.

"The problem with Bossidy's option to buy the Blue Sox," said Arlos, who always does his homework, "is that the lease they have with the city of Utica gives local investors ninety days to match outside offers. That means the town still has all the cards to keep the team in Utica."

Now this was an important piece of information.

It meant that even if Bossidy could put everything together by October—$20 million for a new stadium and someone to run and manage a team—and the Parks Commission selected him and he exercised his option, the city of Utica could still snatch it back as late as December 31, 2001. Much too late for anyone to field a team for the 2002 season.

Then Arlos made another important point. He said the Commission should make its decision shortly after the September 25th primary, at which time the two surviving mayoral candidates "should be asked their opinions."

"Look," said Arlos, waving his papers in the air. "We have a new mayor and seven new councilors coming in, with a new mandate. To have such an important matter decided by a lame-duck mayor and a lame-duck city council is wrong." He paused for emphasis. "And if you wait until October 5th, you won't have a team."

The commissioners nodded without comment, and the Aging Greek God shuffled back to his seat, his body language conveying little or no confidence that his words of wisdom would ever be heeded.

Finally, the subject at hand was formally introduced. In the time it takes to say 'phony baloney' five times, Tom Murphy read a letter from Mayor Doyle, asking that a decision "be postponed until October 5th to allow Lawrence A. Bossidy time to craft a detailed proposal for the use of Wahconah Park."

As soon as Murphy sat down, Chip stood up.

"What is it?" snapped Nilan.

"I'd just like to add one more thing," said Chip.

Nilan yanked on his tie and glared at Chip. "Oh, all right, go ahead," he said, angrily. "You always have to have the last word."

Damn! I wanted to knock Nilan on his ass.

But Chip just brushed it off.

"I want to remind the Parks Commission," said Chip, "that we first introduced our proposal back on June 11, and it is unfair to have to hurry up and wait until October 5, and then be given what could be twenty-four hours' notice to begin to implement it."

While I was standing there next to Chip, I figured I'd give them one more thing to consider.

"You may want to wait for the Bossidy proposal," I said, "but you can at least make one decision *now*—between us and Fleisig. You've seen both our proposals and his doesn't compare. By eliminating Fleisig tonight you give Pittsfield its two best options—us, with an independent league team in a refurbished Wahconah Park, and Larry Bossidy with a New York–Penn League team, ultimately in a new stadium. We can spend the time between now and October 5th bidding against each other, for the benefit of Pittsfield."

Then we sat down.

There was no discussion regarding the pros or cons of any points made by us or Peter Arlos. Instead, the Parks Commission voted unanimously to postpone a decision on Wahconah Park until October 5th.

In the car on the way home, neither of us said anything for about ten minutes. I was feeling bad about not standing up for Chip. But I hadn't been able to think fast enough at the time. Also, I didn't want to do anything I'd regret the next day. Still, I should have said something.

"Has Cliff Nilan ever returned any of your phone calls or responded to any of your emails?" I asked, breaking the silence.

"Never," said Chip.

"Where do these guys get the nerve to treat us like this?" I said. "We offer to invest private money in a Parks facility and we have to take shit from the Parks chairman?"

"It's more than that," said Chip, sadly. "For public officials to act with such naked disregard for the public good is disheartening, and it's not just an isolated instance of one or two officials."

Back at the house, I told Paula what had happened.

"It's not worth it," said Paula. "There are better things you could be doing with your time."

"I know," I said, as I turned on my computer.

"It's midnight," said Paula, agitated. "What are you doing?"

"Writing a letter," I said. "An open letter."

"To whom?" asked Paula, incredulous.

"Cliff Nilan."

And I began pecking away.

AUGUST 28
TUESDAY

I woke up at six o'clock this morning to put the finishing touches on my letter to Nilan. Here's what I ended up with:

> To: Cliff Nilan
>
> Your behavior last night toward my partner Chip Elitzer was shamefully rude and unwarranted. You had no right to shout at him early on, and your angrily sarcastic comment later that he always has to have the last word is simply false. The only time Chip asked for (and initially received) permission for our partnership to speak last was before the August 13 presentation, which you then revoked when Jonathan Fleisig asked for the same. Rather than flip a coin, we ceded the last position to Fleisig, with your explicit agreement that we could have three minutes of rebuttal (followed by a final rebuttal by Fleisig). Instead of honoring that agreement, you simply terminated the meeting after Fleisig's presentation.
>
> This continues a pattern of rudeness on your part that goes all the way back to the introduction of our proposal on June 11. It includes your refusal to return any of our phone calls or respond to any of our letters, your ignoring our requests for a public hearing on the matter, and your thinly veiled hostility whenever either one of us is speaking before the board.
>
> You would think we had committed a crime instead of having made a proposal that might benefit the parks and the citizens of Pittsfield. You seem to have some kind of personal agenda. What else is one to think of your behavior in light of comments from the people of Pittsfield that "the fix is in," and "the government doesn't listen to us?" We know exactly how they feel. And we just got here.
>
> We understand that you are a volunteer, performing a frequently thankless task, and we have always tried to be respectful and appreciative of that fact. Chip Elitzer, with his excellent manners, deserves nothing less than the same respect that he has shown you and the committee each time we have appeared before you.

Unfortunately, you have not responded in kind, which makes your adverse rulings against us appear to be biased. Your last-minute decision on August 13 to forbid public comment because you understand the public supports us is one example. Your frequent delays and postponements that you know negatively impact us more than our competitors is another. If you were a judge, you'd be taken off the case.

You have dirtied yourself and the process. Go take a shower.

Jim Bouton

As soon as I was finished, I attached it to an email addressed to our Wahconah lists and hit the button. I was in such a hurry to get it off I didn't even pass it by Chip or our top advisors—Paula and Cindy. I guess I'll do that tonight over dinner at the Elitzers'.

Meanwhile, the Parks Commission notwithstanding, we seem to be making headway in what is now a full-blown public relations battle. Even my friend Alan Chartock is finally getting involved.

Almost.

In his column in today's *Eagle,* entitled INFLUENCING THE MEDIA, Chartock gives Chip and me credit for "knowing how to get the word out." He even acknowledges that we've had problems.

> To put it mildly, they have been met with a less than friendly reception from some quarters of the community, including the *Berkshire Eagle.* What they have done could be a primer for how to do—and not do, depending on your point of view—public relations when you're unhappy with the media.
>
> I'm not going to debate the merits of their case. In fact, I don't understand it. But these guys have tried to do it right. They've gone out into the community and talked where they were asked to talk.

And even where we weren't asked to talk, I might add.

But why should we have to do that? Why should we have to constantly pound the pavement and write letters and draft position papers? What would have happened if we had just made our proposal and sat back and waited for a decision, like everyone else? Like Fleisig and Bossidy, for example. Forget about it. Our plan would have simply disappeared, which, according to local folks, is what happens to a lot of good ideas in this town.

The truth is, the media has *not* done its job on this story. Our proposal remains a possibility only because we've dedicated a good piece of our lives to it—a lot of that time spent correcting misinformation spread by the media. Influencing the media, my ass. Exactly what media have we influenced? Influencing in *spite* of the media is more like it.

It upsets Paula to hear me talk like that about Alan Chartock. Hell, it upsets me.

"Alan wants to do the right thing," said Paula. "But he's suffering from cognitive dissonance. He can't bring himself to understand the merits of your case because if he does he'll have to take another look at Scribner. And he doesn't want to have to do that."

"He's been great on most issues," I said. "Especially the environment. Tim Gray told me he's been a guest on WAMC about a hundred and fifty times."

"Alan's usually on the right side of the ethical questions," said Paula. "And I don't believe he's part of that Pittsfield machinery. But he has a vested interest in keeping Scribner as an ally."

I'm liking Peter Arlos more and more every day. He's not only smart, he's funny. Today he gave me his thoughts on the mayoral race. When the Oracle of Delphi speaks, I listen.

"It's going to be between [Jimmy] Ruberto and [Sara] Hathaway," said Arlos. "Ruberto stands for nothing. Talks out of two sides of his mouth. If you played 'The Star Spangled Banner' he wouldn't stand up—afraid to commit himself. Hathaway is strong for you. She's got more guts than Ruberto. She's a nice person. Educated."

"What about Grunin?" I asked.

"Grunin can't get elected," said Arlos, derisively. "If he was running unopposed, he would get beaten by the blanks."

I laughed, and asked him where he got his sense of humor.

"My wife," said Arlos. "Compared to her I'm a dud. I married an orthodox Jew. Alma. Summa cum laude law degree. Modest. No makeup. Great mother. That's all I ask. We've been married forty-eight years. Never had an argument. I do exactly as she tells me."

The secret to a happy marriage. I can understand that.

Just how strong is Sara Hathaway for our proposal? Chip called the "Sara Hathaway for Mayor" office to find out. And got Sara.

"You've created a situation where the political heat is on them," said Sara, speaking of our opponents. "We were all just at a forum at GE and the first question was, 'Where are you on the stadium?' I was in your corner and Grunin and Ruberto were on the fence."

Chip asked how the people at the forum felt about Bossidy, who is a former GE executive.

"The GE employees are not crazy about Larry Bossidy," said Hathaway. "They just don't trust him."

Then it was time for dinner. We met, as usual, in the Elitzers' kitchen. Cindy was putting marinated chicken breasts onto a plate so Chip and I could grill them outside. Paula was trying to keep the Elitzers' overly friendly golden retriever, Serra, from sticking her nose where it didn't belong.

Cindy was not in favor of the Nilan letter.

"I don't think it's a good idea to personalize things," she said. "Nilan has been a city official for many years. I'm sure he's got his supporters."

"On the other hand," said Paula, "it's a genuinely felt response to something that happened."

"But you don't want to turn the community against you," said Cindy, trying to interest Serra in an old rag.

"I'm usually on the side of caution," said Paula, "but this feels right. I think it *needed* to be sent. You guys have been too polite."

"I'm never good at these things," said Chip. "But if Paula says it's a good idea, I think it's fine."

"Well okay," said Cindy, "as long as you're ready to face the consequences."

Having heard from our top advisers, Chip and I went outside to grill the chicken—and a few hot dogs in case we got really hungry. And we took Serra out with us to guard against squirrels.

Before going to bed, I checked my email and saw a note from Chip, who is now fully behind what he called "your new offensive of telling it like it is." He wrote, "You should be the bad cop (the wild-man author of *Ball Four* who once again is showing no respect for the unspoken clubhouse rules) and I should be the good cop (still trying to be restrained and respectful)."

Chip's right. No more Mr. Nice Guy. From now on we'll be Dr. Jekyll and Mr. Hyde. Except I can never remember which one is waxing and which one is waning.

AUGUST 29
WEDNESDAY

As part of our plan to get endorsements from mayoral candidates, I picked up the phone and called Ed Reilly, who also happens to be a former mayor of Pittsfield. Reilly was both friendly and honest.

"Given a choice between a new stadium and Wahconah Park, I'd choose a new stadium," said Reilly. "But if I was mayor I would have treated you fairly."

"Do you think the Parks Commission will have the nerve to go against the mayor?"

"They're not likely to go against him," said Reilly. "They've been told to wait. They're sitting on their hands, trying to stall. Stalling you in the process. The first thing to stall was the college thing."

"They're probably waiting for Bossidy to come up with the money," I said.

"I'm not sure the last one [new stadium] was going to be built without city money," said Reilly. "The city lied about it. The city knew it was going to be required to invest money. They never told anybody they were going to have to put up money. The state wouldn't give money to a private entity, only to the city—but only if the city participated."

"How much of the $18.5 million would the city have to pay?"

"I don't know," said Reilly. "But somebody from the state told me that the city was lying about not having to put up some money."

"Why doesn't the state step forward and say something?"

"The state is a political organization," said Reilly. "They want to wait and cross that bridge when you come to it."

"Who told you that?"

"A state official," said Reilly. "He said to me, 'I can't believe they never told the people this.'"

"Well, I can," I said.

Meanwhile, Chip and I have to cross our bridges *before* we come to them. At a strategy session, we agreed on the following: We can't sit back and wait. We're the people's choice, and we need to try and prove that, any way we can. Pittsfield is clearly not a democracy, but officials may still be embarrassed to make an obviously bad decision. Call it an embarrasstocracy.

Here are some things we can do:

1. **Debate and phone poll.** This time, invite Fleisig and Bossidy to pick a date for a televised debate. One that would end with a phone poll they could help organize and authenticate.
2. **Ballot question.** Ask the City Council to put the question of who should get Wahconah Park onto the November ballot. The Parks Commission may be reluctant to decide against us in October if they know "the people" will be choosing us in November.
3. **Unofficial ballot box.** Have the Wahconah Yes! team man ballot boxes near voting locations during the September 25th primary. "Voters" would check one of three options: Bouton, Fleisig, or Bossidy and a "winner" could be announced along with the primary results.
4. **Petition drive.** Have the Wahconah Yes! team gather signatures on a petition that could be used to put Wahconah Park on the November ballot, and/or encourage candidates to endorse us or risk losing the election.
5. **State Oversight Board.** Make a presentation to the board that now controls Pittsfield's finances. Show them the savings that can be achieved with our plan, and conversely, the likely costs to the city of a new stadium.

We chose to go with options 1, 2, 3, and 4.
For now.

Within an hour, Chip had drafted a one-page press release entitled **Debate Challenge Issued to Wahconah Park Petitioners**, explaining, among other things, how it would work.

"The suggested format for the debate would be to answer questions posed by the public, and to allow each of the three parties to comment, subject to judicious intervention by a moderator. The suggested format for the new telephone vote will be to count only calls received in the first minute of voting, originating from identifiable residential numbers listed in the June 2001 Verizon phone book, and eliminating calls made from numbers outside the Pittsfield Community Television viewing area."

The release also included this quote from me:

"We will leave the field if we lose the vote, and we challenge our competitors to make the same promise, not just for Pittsfield, but for all of Berkshire County. For the good of Pittsfield and its proud heritage, we need to close ranks soon behind a single plan."

Then we sent it off to our fax and email lists. The one Chip faxed to Bossidy had a note attached that said, "Jim and I look forward to speaking with you."

Poor Bossidy. He's probably so absorbed in the book I sent, he hasn't had time to get back to us on the last letter.

While Chip was taking care of the debate and phone poll, I was following up on the ballot question with Peter Arlos. And while I was on the phone with him, he asked me to hold on for a minute. "A very charming woman just walked into my office," said Arlos, "and she has a question for me." So I held on while Arlos spoke to the woman.

When he came back on the line he was laughing. "Listen to the question she asked," said Arlos. "She wants to know how to put Wahconah Park on the ballot in November. Whether to make it Wahconah Park versus a new stadium, or your proposal versus Bossidy and Fleisig."

The woman's name was Katy Roucher—an esteemed member of the Wahconah Yes! team—acting, it turns out, on behalf of a group that includes Dave Potts, Jonathan Lothrop, and others. You know you've got a good ball club when the players are working out on their own.

"But it may be too late to get on the ballot," said Arlos. "I'll have to research it."

Whatever happens with the ballot question, better it should come from someone in Pittsfield than two maniacs from South County.

Before going to bed, my fellow maniac faxed me the online version of tomorrow's *Eagle* that pertained to us. Above the masthead, where they promote special stories, was a picture of me and the headline BOUTON LASHES OUT AT PARKS BOARD: SOUTH COUNTY PARTNERS UPSET BY DELAY IN BASEBALL DECISION.

The story, by reporter Bill Carey, quoted a few lines from my letter to Nilan, including the words "shamefully rude and unwarranted" and "Go take a shower." Unfortunately, Nilan—sounding polite, warranted, and clean—was quoted as saying that he had no comment on my letter and that he hoped we would keep our "proposal on the table."

The story also announced our new "debate challenge," which is already being met with gales of indifference. Carey quotes Fleisig saying he is "not in favor of a polling system that is neither scientific nor accurate and does not appear to work based on [their] last failed attempt," and that our debate format "may, in fact, hurt the Berkshires' chances of securing a team in any league with this continued divisive mentality."

And whose fault might that be?

The mayor says "the fix is in." The City Council president says he's getting "an unbelievable amount of shit" from new-stadium councilors "and others." A mayoral candidate says state officials told him "the city was lying about not having to put up money." A state senator says he "knows" decisions are being made at a bar. And the Parks chairman is going around telling people we're "out" before the Commission has voted.

And Chip and I are somehow responsible for "this continued divisive mentality"?

Well, too bad.

Everybody's just going to have to live with it.

AUGUST 30
THURSDAY

I woke up depressed this morning.

I'm thinking the debate is not going to happen. We're probably too late for the ballot question. And my letter to Nilan went too far.

Whenever I get depressed, which isn't very often, I need to be doing something that seems to address the problem. Even if it turns out to be a colossal waste of time, while I'm doing it, I feel better. If I were in the middle of the ocean in a rowboat, with no hope of being rescued, I'd feel better if I were rowing.

That's why I couldn't wait to make the mechanicals for our sign-up sheets, and posters, and wall banners, which is what we're going to need for our ballot box and petition drive ideas. As I worked, I listened to the Larry Kratka show, with the entire radio hanging out my office window. Kratka's guest was mayoral candidate Jimmy Ruberto, who asked this question: "What is the Bouton group going to do for jobs?"

Now we're responsible for the economic revival of Pittsfield. I called Chip and told him we needed to open a factory, too.

Chip and I hammered out the language that would appear on the petition people would be asked to sign:

I support the Bouton, Elitzer, and Margenau long-term commitment to Wahconah Park, and I oppose a new stadium built in Pittsfield at any location with any type of financing. I also support the above statement, or its equivalent, being placed on the November 2001 ballot as a yes or no choice.

"I think we should go to Jonathan's thing tonight," I told Chip, referring to the fund-raiser for City Council candidate Jonathan Lothrop at the Italian-American Club up in Pittsfield. Lothrop had said that a lot of our supporters would be there, including some other candidates.

"It might be a good opportunity to put together a team to run the petition drive," I said.

"Good idea," said Chip, "and I'd love to go, but I'm going to be with my dad tonight. It only takes one of us. And you should be the one to go since you're so popular you could be mayor."

"Thanks."

At about five o'clock, I stuck our proposed petition sheet and some color posters—which I still carry everywhere—into my saddle bag and rode up to Pittsfield. The Italian-American Club is located on Newell Street, in the heart of GE country. Driving on East Street, before I got to Newell, I passed abandoned GE buildings—giant, brick hulks that looked like the set from a gangland movie.

Making a right onto Newell—next to a field enclosed with barbed wire and a sign saying Keep Out—I saw a truck container sitting in the weeds. Spray painted on the side of the container, in large black letters, were the words "GE poisoned my land with PCBs. Under the backroom deal, GE and EPA will leave this land contaminated. Newell Street will never be clean." Underneath that was a skull and crossbones.

A few yards down Newell, on the left, just before Gina's Beauty Studio, I passed the seat of government in Pittsfield—DelGallo's. It was surprisingly small, considering its importance. Just a one-room box stuck onto the front of what looked like a two-family house. Even though the door was wide open, I avoided the urge to go in. Maybe because I was alone. Where would the cops even *begin* to search for my body? Assuming they wanted to find it.

A half-mile down on the right was the Italian-American Club, a one-story, wood, brick, and cinderblock building that looks like it's been added onto over the years. An American flag flies proudly in front. To the left and right are abandoned buildings. One has signs that read Moldmaster, Berkshire Business Ventures, No Trespassing, Property of General Electric, and Violators Will Be Prosecuted. The other has signs saying Ravin Auto Body and Closed. Just behind these buildings flows the Housatonic River.

After parking my car, I ran into Dan Bianchi who was being earnestly lobbied by an older woman, on some matter or another. Dan smiled and said he'd see me later.

Inside, the Italian-American Club turned out to be a low-ceilinged catering hall, with a large main room and a bar in the back. A multicultural catering hall. Against the wall to my left, as I entered, were several long tables of food—guacamole, Polish sausage, Swedish meatballs, lasagna, something with rice, brownies, cookies—obviously all home cooked, and arranged potluck style in an assortment of platters and bowls.

Not wanting to call attention to myself, I made a beeline for the food and mingled with some people near the coffee machine. There I scanned the room for familiar faces, spotting Dave Potts, Anne Leaf, Gene Nadeau, Katy Roucher, Councilman Rick Scapin, mayoral candidates Henry Hebert and Peter McHugh, and State Senator Andy Nuciforo. There looked to be about sixty people, either seated at tables or standing around.

With a paper plate full of lasagna, I headed for Nuciforo, a handsome little guy with black wavy hair and glasses. I knew he wasn't going to have much time, so I got right to the point.

"Hey, Andy," I said. "We're being nibbled to death by so-called experts and city officials who say we can't do this or that because of environmental reasons. We need someone like you to say maybe we can—if that's true."

"I can't do that," said Andy. "I have to be neutral."

"If the others wanted information, you'd give it to them," I said.

"I can only answer questions," said Nuciforo.

"Okay, I'm *asking* you," I said. "Are there any exceptions to EPA regulations that might allow us to deal with things like the parking lot?"

Nuciforo smiled, displaying the charm that gets him elected.

"Okay," he said. "I'll get that information for you."

"And while I'm at it," I said, "are state funds available for historical landmark improvements?"

"I'll check on it," said Nuciforo. "Bossidy is already asking about state funding."

Then someone started tapping their knife against a glass to get people's attention, as Jonathan Lothrop picked up a hand-held microphone. Jonathan thanked everyone for coming and introduced his wife and daughters as the reasons why he wants a better Pittsfield. Among notables in attendance, I was introduced as "a special guest who wants to save Wahconah Park" and received a nice round of applause.

I waved humbly, with a mouthful of cookies.

Toward the end of the evening, a dozen or so people, including Potsy, Nadeau, Leaf, and Roucher, along with Elaine Soldato, Thelma Barzottini, and City Council candidate Rick Jones, gathered around a large table to talk about the petition drive. I handed out copies of the sign-up sheet that Chip and I had drafted.

"Here's what you and Chip should do," people started saying to me as soon as I sat down.

I looked around and smiled.

"No," I said, gently. "Here's what *you* should do. This is *your* battle. Chip and I are suggesting a strategy—and we'll give you the materials and advice—but it's your ball game."

I explained that Chip and I did not want to get too involved in Pittsfield politics—beyond trying to sell our plan to the people and the politicians. It's why we decided not to come out for or against any particular candidate. We wanted to be advocates for a plan, not political operatives. Besides, if we had to get our own signatures, what would that say about our support?

"We've already done this so many times," someone said, wearily.

"I know," I said. "And you have to decide if you want to do it again. But if it's something you care about, you can either march now or you can march later. This time you'd be marching *for* something, not against."

This appeared to register, and the focus shifted to the details. There was some concern about the language on the sign-up sheet, which a few of them felt would not be allowed on a ballot.

"They will attack anything that's not explicitly worded," said Anne Leaf, the seventy-year-old artist who, along with Potts and Nadeau, had led the petition drive that sank the Civic Authority.

"They'll challenge whatever language we use," I said. "But this is a political battle, not a legal one. Chip and I wanted to draft something that would be clear and unambiguous to everyone—from a county judge to a city councilor. The final ballot language can be legally crafted."

Katy Roucher, a pretty woman with reddish brown hair, had a different problem with the language.

"I don't like the words, 'I oppose a new stadium built at any location with any type of financing,'" said Katy. "It should just be what you're *for* and not against."

I thought about that for a minute. This was a document these people needed to believe in, if they were going to go out and sell it. On the other hand, I didn't want to take the guts out of it.

"If we get 10,000 signatures on something that just says 'I support Wahconah Park,'" I said, "our opponents will say they could have gotten the same 10,000 signatures on a petition that said 'I support a new stadium.'"

A few nodded in agreement.

"The June 5th referendum didn't mention a new stadium," I said, "only the Civic Authority. So when it was defeated, the new-stadium people were able to claim that it wasn't against a new stadium. This time we have to kill the new stadium in order to save Wahconah. The two are incompatible."

This they all seemed to understand.

"But Katy makes a good point about the rest of it," I said. "So let's take out the words 'built at any location with any type of financing.'" And I crossed out that part with my pen.

After a little more tinkering, everyone felt comfortable with the wording.

"Now we need some team captains and a leader," I said. "The captains will organize their own teams to go out and get signatures, and the leader will distribute the numbered sign-up sheets to the captains, keeping track of who has what, and collecting the completed sheets."

Within a few minutes, we had a dozen captains. But no leader— the result of work schedules, family obligations, and what Anne Leaf described as "petition fatigue."

"I can't go through that again," said Anne, who speaks with a husky, Tallulah Bankhead voice. "Too many threatening phone calls."

Threatening calls?

But I didn't have time to focus on it just then. For some reason, I zeroed in on City Council candidate Rick Jones. Rick is a guy in his thirties who comes across as half-man, half-boy, with thinning black hair and a deer-in-the-headlights air of uncertainty about him.

"What about you, Rick?" I asked, catching him off guard.

"I'll do it with someone else," said Rick, looking anxiously round the table.

But no one else volunteered.

"Rick," I said, "it looks like you're it. But you'll have plenty of help. Chip and I will make sure you have all the materials you need, and your team captains here will all pitch in. They'll actually be doing most of the work. You'll be the executive in charge of the in and out box."

The group promised to help, and a few of them made sure that Rick had their phone numbers.

"Well," said Rick, smiling with a mixture of resignation and pride. "I always seem to end up running things at work."

"This will be the defining issue of your campaign," I said to him. "What got Dave Potts a shot at being mayor could put you on the City Council."

Rick's brown eyes brightened. "Yeah, maybe you're right," he said, smiling.

With that, the meeting was over. We said our goodbyes, and I headed for the door, grabbing a brownie on the way out.

Only to bump into Rick Jones in the parking lot.

"I just talked it over with my girlfriend," he said. "And she agrees with you that this could be what gets me elected."

"Good," I said. "I'm sure you'll do fine."

What I meant was, I *hope* you'll do fine.

In the car on the way home, I called Chip and filled him in on what was happening—and how I sort of appointed Rick Jones.

"You think he can handle it?" asked Chip.

"Rick's young, and he's enthusiastic," I said. "If he wants to be a city councilor, it'll be good experience. Sometimes people are ready to step up and all they need is a chance."

AUGUST 31
FRIDAY

Today we received a response to our debate challenge *and* my letter to Cliff Nilan. In an *Eagle* editorial headlined GIMMICKRY, INSULTS OFF THE PLATE, Ever-Scrib wrote:

The future of professional baseball in Pittsfield is too important to be determined through reality-show style debates and gimmicky, unscientific polls, as is the apparent strategy of the partnership of Jim Bouton, Chip Elitzer and Eric Margenau. Mr. Bouton's promise that the group will abandon its plan if it is in essence "voted off the island" calls into question the seriousness of their bid.

Equally troubling is the contrariness of a group that is insulted by legitimate comment and sees challenges to its plan as part of a massive conspiracy. City officials must also ask, in light of Mr. Bouton's insulting open letter to Parks Commission Chairman Clifford J. Nilan in which he instructed Mr. Nilan to "go take a shower," if they want to assure themselves of a long, contentious relationship by allowing the group to bring an independent team to Wahconah Park.

Here is a newspaper that for years has steadfastly refused to either sponsor or promote a public forum on the "too important" matter of "the future of professional baseball in Pittsfield." Of course, a public forum or debate is the last thing the *Eagle* wants because they know what the result would be—the defeat of their new-stadium agenda.

And in furtherance of that agenda—as far as the *Eagle* is concerned—any act is fair game for distortion. So, just as our phone-in results are less newsworthy than Jack Dew's questioning of six people at a Big Y, and there is no conspiracy because the mayor said there wasn't, so Cliff Nilan's rudeness to us becomes our rudeness to him.

The *Berkshire Eagle* is nothing if not consistent.

Having used up our quota of letters to the editor, what can we do? Go to a competing purveyor of news and information?

o o o

CHAPTER 11

"You've got to fight the madness"

SEPTEMBER 1
SATURDAY

It was winter when Chip and I first brought our plan to Berkshire Sports & Events. It was spring when we introduced it to the public, and summer when we won them over. Now it's almost fall, with a month to go, and still we wait. It's a good thing we had said "time is of the essence." Otherwise there's no telling how long it would take.

Most normal people, with families and jobs and hobbies, would have dropped out long ago. But Chip and I are not normal—at least not when we're together. Then we become something else. Like a science experiment gone bad. Two ordinary elements—hydrogen and sulfur—mixed accidently to make sulfuric acid.

"Both my mother and my wife think we feed off each other's worst tendencies," said Chip.

"And what might those be?" I asked.

"Something about relentlessness," said Chip, "and stubbornness, and cowboys and Indians."

"But those are our *best* tendencies," I said.

This morning we took our relentless selves out to get some bows and arrows for the petition drive. We drove up to Staples, in Pittsfield, to get a dozen clipboards and pens, and some string to tie the pens to the clipboards. Then we went to Kwik Print, in Great Barrington, to pick up 1,000 signature sheets and 100 window banners that say "Wahconah Yes!—Petition—Sign up here," which we had ordered yesterday.

Some key dates are coming up, when a growing stack of signature sheets will be hard to ignore:

September 11: City Council meeting. The last chance to put Wahconah Park on the November ballot. The number of signatures needed to force a ballot question is approximately 4,000, which is a near impossibility since we have only ten more days. But anything approaching that number could pressure the City Council into putting it on the ballot.

September 25: Primary day. Candidates will need to declare where they stand on the various proposals for Wahconah Park. This is also the day we plan to make our big push to gather signatures at polling stations.

October 5: Parks Commission makes decision on Wahconah Park—maybe.

November 6: Election day. Candidates may need to declare whether they agree with—or will seek to overturn—the Parks Commission decision.

This afternoon, while Chip visited his dad, I dropped off the petition materials to Rick Jones, who met me in the parking lot at a Friendly's in Pittsfield. In what I took to be a good sign, Rick arrived on time, pulling up in his truck. When he's not running for City Council, Rick works for a small plumbing contractor.

So as not to overwhelm him, I gave him only about a third of the materials. As I went over the plan again, Rick listened and nodded. Then he said something that made me nervous.

"Has anybody ever called you pushy before?" He was half smiling when he said it.

"I've been known to be a little overbearing," I said. "If I am, just tell me and I'll back off."

"You seem to be in a hurry," said Rick, his smile receding slightly. "It's a little fast for some people."

I flinched a bit when Rick said this, because it's not the first time I've heard something like that. It reminded me of when my mother used to say, "The trouble with you is, you refuse to take 'no' for an answer."

She didn't mean it as a compliment.

I know I can be pushy. But sometimes it's hard to know the difference between pushy and persistent. Persistent is what got me most of the good things in my life, including the big leagues, *Ball Four,* and Paula. I give that up and I might as well sit and read somewhere—somewhere other than the house in which we're currently living.

Hell, companies pay me to teach them how to be persistent. I tell them to focus on the process rather than the goal. Do the work for its own sake. Forget the salary and the bonus. Do it for the fun, the satisfaction, the challenge. The irony is that by focusing on the process, you increase your chances of achieving the goal.

It can also drive your opponents nuts. When the *Eagle* asks if the commissioners want "to assure themselves of a long, contentious relationship by allowing the [Bouton] group to bring an independent team to Wahconah Park," the paper is expressing its own fears. When the bully feels bullied, you know you're onto something.

But Rick is not a bully, and I had been pushy when I put him on the spot at the Italian-American Club, maybe even sensing he didn't have the strength to say no. On the other hand, he did have the backbone to call me on it today. So, maybe he's going to be okay after all. And I'll try to ease up a bit.

A bulldog with a few missing teeth.

Conference call today with our partner, Eric Margenau, updating him on what's happening:

"Short of overwhelming public pressure," said Chip, "they will give it to Bossidy or Fleisig. They are prepared to defy all logic."

"We need to have a team," said Margenau. "What's happening with the Atlantic League?"

"Frank Boulton has agreed to 'lease' us a team for 2002," I said, "but he hasn't given us an option to buy for 2003 and beyond."

"Maybe if we commit to the Atlantic League now for 2002," said Chip, thinking out loud, "instead of waiting for the Northern League, Frank will give us the option."

"That's a good idea," I said. "We're probably not going to get the Northern League for next year anyway. And if we have a good season in the Atlantic, we can still pick and choose between the two leagues after 2002."

There was a pause while we digested this shift in strategy.

"There's one move that would nullify everything," said Margenau, an excellent strategic thinker. "Give Fleisig a minority stake."

But this is precisely the offer Fleisig had spurned back in July, saying he didn't need us because he had the "first position" with both the Northern League and Pittsfield. That was also before we knew much about him.

"No!" Chip and I said simultaneously.

"Fleisig would be a pain in the ass," said Chip. "We don't want him in. End of story."

Defying all logic ourselves, we continue to behave as if we have a chance. Tonight, Chip went to Wahconah Park to write down the names of all the advertisers on the billboards in the outfield. That's so we don't have to buy the "advertiser list" from Rick Murphy, the guy who had offered to sell us the "season ticket holder list."

SEPTEMBER 2
SUNDAY

No news on those 1994 test borings that Potsy said were taken on the *Eagle* property. "Nothing so far at the DEP," said Tim Gray.

I asked Tim what he did when he's not running the Housatonic River Initiative.

"I have a greenhouse business," he said. "And I play in three different musical groups. As far as environmental work is concerned, I don't get paid for that. One day, Gerry Doyle said on the radio, 'That Tim Gray is making a big living off this PCB issue.' So I took my IRS forms down to the station. I said, Look at them. Four thousand dollars. Two thousand dollars salary."

"You sound like a '60s guy," I said. "I met people like you when I was speaking against the war."

"I just do what my dad taught me to do," said Gray. "Stand up for my rights. I saw people marching in the '60s, so I learned about marching. We had people marching on City Hall with signs. 'We want a total cleanup.'"

"How did you get to City Hall from the Housatonic?"

"The river led me to GE, then to people's property," said Gray.

"That's sort of how I found you," I said.

"I would go door-to-door," said Gray. "I know families where all the kids are sick. Mr. Haynes has six kids with cancer. Right now, HRI is doing a small survey of the Lakewood section—that's ground zero for pollution."

I told Tim I had been to Newell Street, which is near Lakewood.

"You should speak to Vinnie Curro," said Gray. "He owned a body shop there—Ravin Auto Body. He made a cancer map of the area. He's known as the Mayor of Lakewood."

I said I would give Curro a call.

"The people who took the brunt were the employees who died," said Gray. "We're still trying to do a study of GE workers. We've got videos of employees looking straight into the camera and saying, 'They're just waiting for us all to die.'"

How polluted is Pittsfield?

"The city is marinating in PCBs," said Gray. "State law says two parts per million is safe. The EPA found plumes, which are chemical lakes, measuring 300,000 parts per million. Unheard of levels. Pure product flowing underground."

"What can be done about it?" I asked.

"Instead of trying to hide it," said Gray, "let's get it fixed."

Tim said he would check further on those test borings.

And I was in the mood to test the business philosophy of my investment banking partner.

"If this is a market economy," I said to Chip, "there should be a market solution. Make GE give Pittsfield the money it saved by dumping. No penalties. Just pay what they would have paid otherwise."

"Plus interest," said Chip, getting into it. He keyed in a spreadsheet program with various scenarios. "Assuming $2 million a year in savings for forty years—from 1936 to 1976, which is when the EPA made it illegal—and a 4% cost of capital, GE would owe Pittsfield almost $554 million. Using $4 million annual savings—which is much more likely—and a 5.25% cost of capital, GE would owe Pittsfield a little over $2 billion."

"Either one would put a dent in the city's $9 million debt," I said.

"They probably had some guy with a green eyeshade do exactly that kind of calculation," said Chip.

"And it's fair," I said, "because even if the dumping was not yet illegal, GE knew back then that PCBs caused illness. Their chemists knew. In 1936, two GE vice presidents talked about workers with terrible rashes. They said without PCBs they'd lose the bottom line of their business."

"Their calculation was that they'd never have to pay that much if they ever got caught," said Chip.

"They figured correctly," I said. "And that explains why Pittsfield has to turn out its street lights and Jack Welch has a net worth of $900 million."

SEPTEMBER 3
MONDAY

In celebration of Labor Day, a fax came in from Northern League Commissioner Miles Wolff.

> Thanks for your letter of August 25, and please excuse the delay in replying. While I certainly recognize the logic of your argument, I must continue to support Jonathan Fleisig's efforts. . . . He has worked hard to be in Pittsfield and wants to continue his efforts.

What "efforts"? Fleisig tossed a proposal on the table and went home. His only role is to keep us out of Wahconah Park until a new stadium can be built—either for him or for Bossidy, with Bossidy having first shot.

I bet here's the deal: If a new stadium is built or committed to, and Bossidy gets a team, Fleisig will be told, or maybe paid, to take a hike. If Bossidy can't get a team, Fleisig will get the new stadium he's been looking for. In fact, I wouldn't be surprised to see this: If Bossidy is able to buy the Utica Blue Sox, Fleisig will fill the vacated spot in Utica.

It's a win-win-win for Bossidy, Fleisig, and the new-stadium die-hards. The only losers will be the people of Pittsfield. It's the same strong-arm tactic that teams and leagues have been using against cities all over the country. The difference here—as in New York City—is that the *city* is actually helping them do it.

In a letter to the editor in yesterday's *New York Times Magazine*, a woman named Laura Kaminker wrote in response to a recent article on the stadium follies in New York City:

> Mayor Giuliani may dismiss Andrew Zimbalist, who has made exhaustive studies of the impact of professional sports on cities, as "Castro's economist." But it's Giuliani who sounds more like the dictator when he explains why New Yorkers weren't asked whether their taxes should build ballparks for the multimillion-aires Fred Wilpon and George Steinbrenner: "Because they would have voted it down." The last time I checked, that was the way a democracy worked.

As Pittsfield goes, so goes the Big Apple.

SEPTEMBER 4
TUESDAY

Today Chip got a call from a fellow named Larry Bossidy.

"I'm going to decline your invitation to debate," said Bossidy, "I don't see any purpose to it."

Chip said he asked Bossidy how a new stadium was better than an arena, but Bossidy had waffled. Chip said he offered Bossidy the vision of being the majority owner of a professional hockey team.

"Nah," said Bossidy. "That's not for me. Affiliated baseball is the right way to go."

When Chip mentioned Wahconah Park, Bossidy said, "If you were making the kind of investment I'm making in a team, would you want to play in an old ballpark?"

Chip told him that's exactly what we wanted to do, and that a historic Wahconah Park could outdraw a new stadium.

It was a brief conversation. Chip said he and Bossidy agreed to go their separate ways and that it ended on a cordial note.

"If I get into town," Bossidy said, "maybe we can have a drink." And that was it.

What's a petition drive without campaign buttons? It's like a glove without a ball. A ballpark without a team.

This afternoon, I called New England Ad Specialties and ordered 500 green "Wahconah Yes!" buttons. I told them to ship the buttons directly to Rick Jones.

What's five hundred bucks—more or less—for a good cause?

SEPTEMBER 5
WEDNESDAY

Today we committed ourselves to playing in the Atlantic League for 2002. In a Letter of Agreement, Chip wrote, "We are ready to join your league with great enthusiasm!"

Now all we need is Frank Boulton's signature.

By Tuesday night's City Council meeting, if possible.

And just because he already had his computer turned on, Chip wrote *another* letter—this one to James R. Johnson, head of the oversight board that now controls the financial decisions made by the City of Pittsfield. Chip attached documents showing how much our proposal would save the city, and how much our competitors' proposals would cost it.

We are not expecting an answer by Tuesday night.

Meanwhile, I'm involved in much headier pursuits.

"What do you think of the idea for a radio show called 'Live from Wahconah Park'?" I asked Paula as we dozed off to sleep. "With the game as background noise for discussions about sports, history, life, et cetera."

"I'm too tired to think right now," said Paula, sinking deeper into her pillow.

"I'm just trying to think of creative ideas," I said.

"I think you're going to be surprised at how creative they can be in turning you down," she said.

I should really save my best ideas for the morning.

SEPTEMBER 6
THURSDAY

I drove up to Pittsfield today to get my scruffy old saddle bag fixed. This is a bag I bought about twenty years ago, and the longer I keep it the better it looks. "Where'd you get that bag?" people ask me. "Gabby Hayes gave it to me just before he died," I say, joking. And they nod their heads and say, "Really?"

While I was in town, I figured I'd stop at some stores and see if they'd take a few sign-up sheets and a window banner. Most were happy to do it—like the Lantern, Ray Parrott's A-Mart, Tahiti Take-Out (a sponsor of the *Dan Valenti Show*), and Tim's Sports Zone, a sports collectibles store located right next to Wahconah Park.

But as I walked around town, I noticed a decided lack of window banners in other stores. In fact, there were none, as far as I could see. This was supposed to have been one of the first things Rick Jones would do, along with handing out materials to the captains.

When I got back home, I gave Rick a call.

"When I was in town today," I said, in my least pushy voice, "I didn't notice any window banners. How's that coming along?"

"I gotta eat!" said Rick, sounding pressured. "And I gotta work! If I don't get paid, I don't eat!"

Whoa! What brought that on? A simple question? I tried to calm him down.

"Nobody expects you to take time away from work," I said. "The thought was that whatever time you had planned to spend campaigning would be spent on the petition drive. Your name and address are on all the sign-up sheets. It's a great way to meet people. It's an issue everyone cares about. Look what it did for Dave Potts."

"Well, I gotta work now," said Rick, by way of explanation.

I said goodbye and hung up, deeply regretting that I had pushed him that night at the Italian-American Club.

No sooner had I called Chip to tell him I had chosen the wrong guy, than the phone rang. It was Rick Jones.

"I got a message that Tom Murphy called," said Rick. "He wants to talk to me."

This got my heart beating a little bit. Why would the mayor's water boy want to talk with Rick Jones?

"That should be an interesting conversation," I said.

"Maybe he wants to pay me some money," said Rick.

This was too fast for me. Pay him some money? For what? I tried to collect my thoughts.

"I'm sure he's not just calling to say hi," I said. "Do you know Tom Murphy?"

"I never spoke to him before," said Rick. "I might have said hi to him once." Then he paused. "But he can't threaten me. He can make things difficult for my friends—business-wise. Doyle is very vindictive."

I thought it was interesting that he saw Murphy and Doyle as one person.

"What do you mean?" I asked.

"I was working on this house once," said Rick, "and Gerry Doyle's kid was working with the carpenter. And I was giving him a hard time about the new stadium—I used to drive around with a 'No Civic Authority' sign on my truck—and he went home and told his mother. Then Gerry Doyle wants to check the lettering on my boss's truck, check our license to be a plumber. He's going to call the board of examiners."

"What did you do?"

"It was a tough scene between my boss and me," said Rick. "My boss and I are friends—we go skiing together."

"It's good you've got a boss who can stand up to these people," I said.

"They don't know who they're dealing with," said Rick. "They can't push me anywhere near what I grew up with."

"Who was that?" I asked.

"My father," said Rick.

When I told Paula about my conversation with Rick Jones, she wasn't too happy.

"You see why I'm worried," she said. "That's a very vindictive group up there. They'll hire some goons to do something bad—maybe to our house."

"They wouldn't do that," I said. "They'd be blackmailed by whoever they hire. They'd spend a lot of time in jail."

"As soon as we can," said Paula, "we're putting in a really good security system."

Later, when I was hiding my notes in the closet, Paula happened to notice my Yankee uniform, which I now keep around for Old Timers' Days.

"They could take your Yankee uniform, too," she said.

"Gerry Doyle's too fat to get into my uniform," I said.

SEPTEMBER 7
FRIDAY

Chip and I aren't the only ones in the petition business.

City Council candidate Jonathan Lothrop has a petition—already signed by half the mayoral and council candidates—asking the current City Council to place a non-binding referendum on the November ballot with the following language:

"In order to determine the future of baseball in Pittsfield, we ask that you choose one of the following options: (A) Bossidy, (B) Bouton, (C) Fleisig."

Lothrop is planning to present his petition to the Council on Tuesday night.

A story about the petition in today's *Eagle* quotes Parks Commissioner and Council candidate Jim Conant as saying, "I certainly want to get citizens' input. But very clearly, if we wait for this [ballot] initiative to take place in November, the Bouton Group will be out; they have indicated to me that they just can't wait."

This, of course, is bullshit.

Which is exactly what Chip said to Atlantic League Commissioner Frank Boulton, in a follow-up letter to him today:

Dear Frank:

For your information, here is a headline story in today's Eagle. *Parks Commissioner Conant, one of lame-duck (no offense to your mascot!) Mayor Doyle's appointees, misrepresents our position. We explicitly declined to identify a "drop dead" date for a decision, because that would ratify the Commission's "wait-them-out-until-they-go-away" strategy.*

Clearly, it would be very useful if we could go into the City Council meeting on Tuesday night and announce a deal with the Atlantic League during the televised "open mike" session. We could then ask the council to support this ballot initiative (which we know we will win in a landslide on November 6).

Otherwise, our opponents on the council will oppose placing the referendum on the ballot by using the insincere excuse that doing so would "unfairly" run out the clock on the Bouton proposal. They would much rather have the mayor's handpicked Parks Commission make the decision on October 5th, rather than let the voters pick us on November 6th.

With regards, Chip Elitzer

I asked Chip whether he thought we would have a deal with the Atlantic League in time for the council meeting on Tuesday night. And what would happen if we didn't find out until the last minute?

"Sometimes you put your hand in your pocket to draw out your gun and it isn't there," said Chip. "You find that you're holding something else."

SEPTEMBER 8
SATURDAY

Exciting news from the western front. Brought to you by the *Utica Observer-Dispatch.*

> County and city officials are presenting a united front in
> announcing a committee to study another way to keep the Utica

Blue Sox in town. The committee will examine the feasibility of making the Blue Sox a community-owned team.

A provision in the lease agreement with the Blue Sox states that should they seek to sell the franchise—a 30-day purchase option has been given to Lawrence A. Bossidy—the community will be offered the right to match the offer within a 90-day period.

Well, waddaya know?

Hello, community-owned baseball. Goodbye, Larry Bossidy.

The Oracle of Delphi was right again.

And just to put things in further perspective, the *Observer-Dispatch* cited examples of successful community owned baseball teams in other cities like Syracuse, Auburn, and Rochester.

In Rochester, a successful effort to create community ownership decades ago resulted in the Red Wings becoming one of the most successful teams in minor league baseball.

Of course, those cities don't have the leadership that Pittsfield has. Which includes the kind of newspaper that completely ignored the story of Utica's plans to keep the Blue Sox in Utica.

Pittsfield's business leaders are responsible, too—not just its political leaders. Here's what mayoral candidate Peter McHugh said to me just this morning: "The thing I still don't get," he said, "is how the business community doesn't see that you have the best plan."

This reminded me of a conversation I had the other day in Pittsfield with two guys on their way to a Rotary luncheon.

"How's it going?" they asked, because they had recognized me.

"It's not easy," I said.

"That's Pittsfield," said one guy.

"The people don't know what they want," said the other one.

Coming from these Rotarians—leaders of the community—this irritated me.

"It's not the people," I said. "They know what they want. It's the business community—guys like you—who should be speaking out. It's a lack of leadership on your part, too."

They just smiled and wished me luck.

In an increasingly ominous development, Rick Jones has not called since we spoke two days ago. He had said he would call me yesterday—after the buttons arrived.

I wonder if he's had that talk with Tom Murphy.

SEPTEMBER 9
SUNDAY

The number of candidates who have signed Jonathan Lothrop's ballot petition is growing. There are now twenty-one (out of a possible thirty-two) who will ask the current City Council—Tuesday night—to place the question of who should get Wahconah Park onto the November ballot.

SEPTEMBER 10
MONDAY

I spent the day in Montclair, New Jersey, playing in the Jackie Robinson Charity Golf Tournament, hosted by Yogi Berra. Whenever I see Yogi I remember the 1964 World Series, when the Yankees' traveling secretary handed me an extra ticket in a brown envelope and said, "You're lucky, this is the last one." And Yogi, sitting next to me, said in all seriousness, "Are they all out of them brown envelopes?"

I recently gave a speech in St. Louis, and afterward one of Yogi's relatives came up to tell me the latest family Yogism. He said Yogi walked into the den where his son Dale, visiting for the weekend, was watching a John Wayne movie. "That's John Wayne, isn't it?" asked Yogi. "Yeah, Dad," said Dale. "It's the movie *True Grit*." And Yogi said, "He made that movie before he died."

When someone mentioned to Yogi that I was going to be there today, Yogi said, "He's a character."

SEPTEMBER 11
TUESDAY

Tonight, six of eleven city councilors can put the question of who should get to play at Wahconah Park onto the November ballot. Five are hard-core new stadium guys who will do anything to keep it off—Hickey, Lee, Massery, Kerwood, and Dowd. Of the remaining six, three are guaranteed to vote for putting it on—Bianchi, Guzzo, and Scapin. And James Brassard, a new-stadium guy, has indicated he might vote in favor of the ballot question.

That leaves Bill Barry and Gary Grunin.

And we're pretty sure about Grunin—even though we know he's a new-stadium wolf in a Wahconah Park T-shirt—because if *Councilor* Grunin were to vote against a ballot question, then *mayoral candidate* Grunin would lose in a landslide. Now all we have to do is convince Barry.

Which is why Chip and I happened to be at Kelly's Diner, in Pittsfield, at 7:30, having breakfast with Bill Barry. We brought Lothrop's petition, which has now been signed by twenty-three of the thirty-two candidates for office. We knew Barry had been a new-stadium supporter, but we also knew that Dan Bianchi has been trying to win him over.

"I spoke to him the other day," said Bianchi, "and he said he was a 'lame duck.' I said fine, but don't be a Daffy Duck."

Our meeting with Barry went well. He's a reasonable guy who thinks a new stadium still makes sense, but he saw value in letting the people decide. Most important, he understood how a ballot question would require the Park Commissioners to be responsive in October to voters whose wishes would be made clear in November.

"That makes five," said Chip, "if Brassard stays on the ranch."

"And Grunin will make six," I said. "Only because he'll have no choice."

Feeling pretty good after our meeting with Barry, we got into my car and turned on the radio to catch the last forty minutes of the *Dan Valenti Show*. We always like to hear the latest on Wahconah Park from Dan's callers, who sound like we paid them to call in.

When we found the station, someone was talking about the budget. Then a woman called and asked Dan if he knew about what was happening in New York. Dan said he hadn't heard anything, but he would check it out. And a few moments later we heard this:

"This may be what that last caller was referring to," said Dan Valenti. "Evidently, a plane has crashed into the World Trade Center. . . . We don't know what kind of plane. . . . We'll see if we can get that for you."

On any given morning, Valenti goes back and forth between talk show host and authoritative journalist. Now he was in journalist mode. Chip and I speculated that a private plane must have flown off course. With three major airports in the area, it's a wonder it hadn't happened before.

"It now appears," said Valenti, coming back after a break, "that the plane was a commercial airliner."

This was disturbing news. If the plane was full, it would mean hundreds of people have been killed.

Then it got worse.

"Now we're hearing . . . if this is correct," said Dan, "that a *second* plane has just hit the World Trade Center. And . . . it's also reported that this plane, too, is a commercial airliner. Hard to believe . . . but that's what they're saying."

"Terrorists," said Chip, leaning forward, eyes fixed, listening.

We switched the station to WAMC so we could get the news from National Public Radio.

Both towers of the World Trade Center were now in flames.
Jesus Christ!

I ran through a mental checklist. Three of our kids live in New York City. Two work in the financial district. Paula's brother Alan and his wife, and their two kids work in the city. My brother Bob and his wife live a few blocks from the World Trade Center. The list kept getting longer. My heart was pounding.

I needed to be with Paula. She was supposed to be taking a ballet class at ten-thirty this morning at Fitness Express in Great Barrington. I could go right there after I left Chip's house.

We drove in silence, the reports on the radio completely at odds with the meadows and farms just outside the car window. I studied the horizon, fearing a flash or a mushroom cloud in the distance. It was as if we were in a science fiction movie, only it was real, with real terror. I had an awful feeling in my stomach similar to the one I had the night Laurie died.

I dropped Chip off with the understanding that we'd all get together later. Chip looked like he was about to cry. Me too.

I raced to Fitness Express and jumped out of my car. A few of Paula's ballet buddies were standing outside the building, milling about in confusion.

But there was no Paula.

"Where's Paula?" I asked, in a panic, fearing that she might be off somewhere, dealing with bad news.

"I don't know," said a woman named Ava. "She didn't come yet."

Just then the ballet teacher, Sharon McDonald, arrived.

"It's twenty after ten," said Sharon, looking worried. "Paula's usually here by now."

"She's probably at home," I said to the group. "But if she shows up, tell her that's where I am." And I ran to my car.

Finally at home, Paula met me as I came through the door, expecting the worst. She looked distraught and relieved at the same time, patting the air reassuringly, as she gave me the news.

"Everybody's okay," she said, which I knew meant family and friends. I was temporarily relieved.

"I reached Lee," said Paula, "and he and Elaine and Georgia are okay. Lee said he had spoken to our David, and he's okay. Michael called and he's fine. And I called my brother, and his David and Ronnie are both safe."

In times of crisis, Paula becomes Command Central, wielding her phone like a crazed stockbroker.

"Then our David called me back from his cell phone," said Paula—all the land lines were jammed—"and he said he had been running uptown from his office and had seen the tower collapse and people jumping. My God, I can't think about it."

"What kind of nightmares will that cause," I said, trying to gauge the potential damage of such an experience.

"But I don't know about your brother," said Paula. "How close is he to the World Trade Center?"

"About six blocks away," I said, "but he works in White Plains. I'll try to reach him."

"Oh, and listen to this," said Paula, the fear coming back in her eyes. "You know Liz Thompson works on the top floor of the World Trade Center."

But I knew immediately that she was okay or Paula would have said something right away. Liz—who I call "Shlibeth" because that's what I called my aunt Elizabeth when I was little—is the executive director of the Lower Manhattan Council for the Arts, and part of our Berkshire family.

"I was able to get through to her son Chris, the one who lives in Brooklyn," said Paula. "And he said Liz was one of the last ones to make it out alive! She had had an early breakfast meeting with some guy, and he had to get to another meeting, so she went down with him in the elevator and she had just gotten off in the lobby as the first plane hit."

"Thirty seconds later and she would have been trapped," I said.

The temporary shiver of relief only emphasized the agony of what was unfolding on television. Paula and I stood and held each other as we watched the unbelievable scenes. People hanging out of windows, and looking down. For what? A net? A lower ledge? My God, what must that be like? The few times I'd been to the World Trade Center, I couldn't go near those windows, and now people were hanging outside them!

We saw people jumping, the only alternative to burning or suffocating. We cringed at the heart-stopping sight of a couple holding hands on the way down. I thought I saw a man pretending to relax in the air, with one knee bent and his hand behind his head, as if he were lying in a hammock. I thought that took tremendous courage and cockiness, and I wanted to know his name.

Paula and I asked ourselves what we would have done.

"I think I would jump, too," said Paula, who is so afraid of heights she gets nervous when I go near a ledge of any kind. "For the sense of some kind of final choice."

"If we had been together we would have held hands, Babe," I said. "And if I were alone, I like to think I would have had the nerve to do a swan dive, as a joyful 'goodbye' to my friends, and final 'fuck you' to the terrorists."

My heart ached for those poor people. I couldn't bear to watch, and yet I felt I somehow owed it to them—to bear witness to their final moments.

Later, we sought comfort with the Elitzer family.

"At least you have your boys with you," said Paula. "We wish our kids would come up and stay with us for a while. That's why we built the house with all that extra space. Jim and I had actually talked about having a place they could all come and live if there was ever a disaster."

"It's funny that we still call them kids, isn't it?" I said, "even though they're all grown up. And they'll never know how much we love them and worry about them, until they have kids of their own."

Cindy and Chip nodded in agreement and smiled lovingly at their boys. Daniel, Sam, and Jacob, three hip, former New York City kids who would normally have rolled their eyes at such sentiments, nodded thankfully, too frightened to do anything but snuggle close.

Tonight's Pittsfield City Council meeting was canceled, of course, as was a mayoral candidates' debate at Berkshire Community College. No new dates were scheduled.

It seemed as if the world as we knew it had been canceled. Everything was on hold.

SEPTEMBER 12
WEDNESDAY

I woke up this morning with that awful, surprised jolt I used to get in the weeks after Laurie had died. Yes, it was true. It *did* happen.

I couldn't erase the terrible images. The sight of those people jumping. The thought of all those firemen running into that building, knowing it might collapse. All the families who've lost their own Lauries. Today, in bed, in the safety of Paula's arms, I broke down and cried.

I was also afraid. Afraid that it could happen again, the next time with nuclear weapons. All those Russian missiles, the dismantled ones stripped for plutonium, being offered for sale around the world. People hating us for no good reason. People hating us for plenty of good reasons.

God knows we've made enough enemies. Supporting dictators around the world whenever it's to our economic advantage. Buying Arab oil with dollars that are used to subdue the Arab people. Polluting the world in the name of progress. Refusing to sign any treaty that holds us to account or restricts us in any way. Paying less than our fair share.

Who knows when or where the next attack will be? And what do we tell the children—the little ones?

I remember when I was about eleven, I followed the Korean War in the newspapers. Every day they printed a map of Korea, showing the shifting battle line between the GIs and the North Koreans. The American space got smaller and smaller, until it was just a bubble at the tip of the peninsula.

One night, before I went to sleep, I asked my dad if the North Koreans were going to push the GIs into the Pacific Ocean and then come over here and get us.

"You don't have to worry about that," said my dad, a Navy veteran who had been a PT instructor during World War II. "That won't ever happen."

"Why not?" I asked.

"Because the American fighting man is the best fighter in the world," he said. "Nobody else comes close. In fact, Americans are such good fighters we can defeat armies in their own countries."

"And we have the oceans, too, right, Dad?" I said. "They could never cross the oceans."

"They could try," he said, "but we would bomb them before they even got to the docks. And we have a country that can make anything it needs."

Then my dad would tell me the true stories about my uncles who flew bombing missions over Germany during World War II. And about my grandfather, Edgar Bouton, the Westinghouse engineer, who had helped invent the top-secret "deck-edge" elevator that turned the tide against Japan.

Kamikaze pilots were disabling our aircraft carriers by flying down the elevator shafts located in the middle of the ships. Prior attempts at making deck-edge elevators—which could move laterally along both sides of the ship to bring up planes from multiple bays—had always failed because the ocean waves would sweep them into the water. That's when Grandpa, and some others, came up with the idea for an elevator made out of tubes, which allowed the water to flow *through* the elevator.

"It was so top-secret," my dad had said, "that even today you can't find any photographs of aircraft carriers showing the deck-edge elevators."

The American fighting man, the oceans, my uncles, Grandpa. It was all so reassuring. Especially when, a few weeks later, a new bubble appeared on the map of Korea. This one was way up north, above the bubble down south, cutting the North Koreans off.

Dad was right! I had nothing to worry about.

But what certainties can we offer children today when war can be waged with a bomb in a suitcase? And the enemy lives right down the street?

How could this happen? I've heard people say. But how could it not, if you think about it. We're sitting ducks.

So what is one to do?

As the comedian Mort Sahl once said, back in the '60s, "You've got to fight the madness."

I thought that's what Chip and I were doing, on a much smaller scale. But now there is a new and *bigger* madness in the land. How can we go back to Pittsfield and talk about ballparks, when real madmen are blowing up buildings with people in them? Would it be disrespectful?

It's the same thing I asked myself after Laurie died. How can we go on without Laurie? *Without* Laurie. It didn't seem possible. It didn't seem fair.

Yet we did it.

And as Chip said, "What else can we do?"

What else indeed? I'm too old to reenlist in the army. The last thing they need is a sixty-two-year-old private first class, the highest rank I had achieved, fighting the battle of the New Jersey Turnpike down in Fort Dix, in 1963. No, my job now is to finish our minor skirmish here in Pittsfield. Fight the madness in my own backyard.

Consistent with that charge—and while still glued to the TV—I decided to write another letter to the park commissioners. This is just a few notches down the futility scale from rowing a boat in the middle of the ocean.

Dear Commissioners:

You could perform a great service with two simple actions:

1. *Take the ball away from Jonathan Fleisig, whose continued presence in the game blocks our ability to get a Northern League team and thereby improve our already superior offer for the benefit of Pittsfield.*
2. *Recommend that a decision between the two remaining groups, Bossidy and Bouton, be left to the voters as a ballot choice in November.*

The benefits would be substantial:

A. *Mr. Bossidy would have extra time to refine his proposal.*
B. *Our strengthened offer would raise the bar for Mr. Bossidy, maybe moving him to bring some serious jobs to Pittsfield. The Bossidy/new-stadium group would have to continually sweeten its offer to beat us out.*
C. *Unfair pressure would be removed from your shoulders, and no one could complain about the result.*
D. *The baseball matter would finally be over in November.*
E. *The losing group could happily support the winning group, knowing it was their competition that generated the best deal for Pittsfield.*
F. *Cliff Nilan and I could shake hands at home plate.*

Sincerely,
Jim Bouton

Then I attached a separate sheet that matched our proposal against Fleisig's, in a "Tale-of-the-Tape" comparison—the way they do with boxers before a big fight. But instead of Height, Weight, and Reach, I used categories like Immediate Capital Investment, Percent of Maintenance Costs to be Assumed, and Percent of Local Ownership. It looked like an upcoming bout between Mohammed Ali and Mister Rogers.

Tonight we had Cindy and Chip over to our house for dinner, the Elitzer boys having decided to be with their friends. Paula told the boys that if they had any inkling that they might not be safe, they should call and we would come get them.

Chip said he thought Frank Boulton might have lost some friends yesterday. Frank used to work for Cantor Fitzgerald, whose offices were on the top floors of the World Trade Center.

SEPTEMBER 13
THURSDAY

Amazingly, life moves on. The mundane ordinariness grabs our attention and we turn to it with guilty relief.

And so it becomes somewhat noteworthy that yet another candidate has signed Jonathan Lothrop's petition, asking the City Council to put the Wahconah Park question onto the November ballot. It is now clear, from the candidates who have signed, that no matter which way the November election goes, there will be at least a 6-5 majority on the new council in favor of our proposal. What good this will do if the Parks Commission has decided in October in favor of Bossidy or Fleisig is anyone's guess.

Chip and I decided not to attend tonight's memorial service for the World Trade Center victims at Wahconah Park, scheduled by Mayor Doyle. We thought it would look like grandstanding. We're not citizens of Pittsfield and we didn't want to assume a relationship beyond what already exists, whatever that is. We did find it interesting, however, that the mayor chose Wahconah Park as the city's most appropriate gathering place.

SEPTEMBER 14
FRIDAY

Chip called Frank Boulton today and learned that he had indeed lost a lot of his friends and a family member at the World Trade Center. His wife's youngest brother was killed, leaving three children and a pregnant wife. Frank was at his office in the ballpark, though, even with no games being played right now.

"The ballpark is my refuge," Frank said.

Chip dodged a bullet with Frank about our ballpark—he avoided getting bad news from the Atlantic League. We need to keep the Atlantic League option alive going into the next City Council meeting, now scheduled for the 20th. Otherwise, if asked, we'd have to say we have no team and no options at the moment, allowing our opponents to freeze us out for what they would say are our own shortcomings. But we're still in the game.

And Wahconah Park is our refuge.

o o o

CHAPTER 12

"Somebody get Mr. Bossidy a chair"

SEPTEMBER 15

SATURDAY

Chip and I decided to pay a surprise visit to Rick Jones this morning. It was pretty obvious he was no longer running the petition drive—he had not made or returned any calls, there were no banners in the store windows, and the team captains were saying they hadn't heard from him after sending him their signed petition sheets. In fact, they were now holding on to them.

For the hell of it, I called UPS to see if the Wahconah Yes! buttons had been delivered. The answer was yes. "Saturday, September 8, at 10:47 a.m. Package left on rear porch." That was a week ago.

We felt pretty certain that we knew what had happened—Tom Murphy had scared him off. The trick was going to be getting Rick Jones to admit it. Since I had been the one to recruit Rick in the first place, I told Chip I should carry the ball, and he agreed.

When we arrived at Rick's house, we understood why the buttons had been left on the rear porch. The front porch was under construction, with a gaping hole in the ground and two-by-four supports holding up a small overhang. It was a small house in a neighborhood that seemed to be under, or in need of, repair. A "Rick Jones for City Council" sign was stuck in the ground next to a mailbox by the street. Rick's truck was in the driveway.

We rang the doorbell, but nobody answered.

"When I look at this house," I said to Chip, "the word vulnerable comes to mind."

"I don't think anyone's home," said a woman in the next yard, who was repairing a wall that had collapsed.

Thinking Rick might be at his girlfriend's house, I called him on my cell phone. He answered.

"Hi Rick," I said. "This is Jim. I'm over at your house with Chip. We were in town and thought we might pick up some petition sheets and get an update on what's happening." Rick said he would put on some clothes and be right over.

About twenty minutes later, a pickup truck pulled into the driveway. Rick got out, looking very wary. We invited him to breakfast at a local diner. He agreed to come. We sat in a booth, Rick on one side, Chip and I on the other. It was 8:45 a.m.

"So what's happening?" I said, very friendly.

"Nothing," said Rick, looking nervous. "I've been busy."

I let his words sit there without saying anything, a neutral expression on my face. Rick's brown eyes shifted back and forth between Chip and me. Except for the thinning hair, he could have passed for a high school kid who had just been called into the principal's office.

I smiled at Rick, who got a quizzical look on his face.

"I want to apologize to you, Rick," I said sincerely, because I meant it. "I take full responsibility for putting you in this position. I did not take into consideration the pressures you might have to face."

"We're sorry for pushing you into heavy traffic," said Chip.

"What are you getting at?" said Rick.

"Here's the chain of events," I said, gently. "Tom Murphy leaves a message on your answering machine and suddenly there are no window banners, no buttons, only a few petitions, and no returned phone calls. If you were watching a detective movie and saw that, what would you think?"

Rick's eyes got a little watery.

I reached across the table and touched his arm.

"I admit I backed off," said Rick, embarrassed.

"What did Murphy say to you?" I asked.

"Nothing," said Rick, a little too quickly.

"Nothing?" I asked, incredulous, looking directly at him. He knew he couldn't get away with that.

"He just asked me why I was against a new stadium."

"That's it?" I said. "I thought he wanted to meet with you."

"We never met," said Rick. "He never called back."

"That doesn't make sense," I said, calmly. "You had never spoken to Murphy before in your life and all of a sudden he calls up and asks why you're against a new stadium? What was he doing, taking a belated poll?"

Rick fell into that state known as "a loss for words." He smiled as a holding action, thinking hard with his eyes.

"When did Murphy say that?" asked Chip.

Rick swallowed hard.

"Here's something that did happen," he said, in a sudden burst.

"What's that?" I asked.

"Stanley called . . . and chewed my ear off for an hour," said Rick. "He said, 'The mayor is out to get you.'"

"Who's Stanley?" I asked.

"The plumbing inspector," said Rick. "The mayor called Stanley and said, 'Who the fuck is this guy? I want to pull all his permits, all his boss's permits. I want to see if he's been moonlighting.'"

"In other words," said Chip, "the mayor said he was going to fuck you."

"That's exactly what he said," said Rick.

There was a moment of silence while Chip and I digested this.

"You know that's against the law," I said, evenly.

"It's a violation of the Bill of Rights," said Chip. "Freedom of speech and freedom of assembly. A mayor and an incumbent city councilor making antidemocratic common cause."

"You should take this to the newspapers," I said.

"I've already done something about it," said Rick. "Stanley is writing a letter to the mayor saying, 'Here's the information you requested on Rick Jones.' And he's going to give me a copy."

"If you make it public before the City Council meeting on Thursday," said Chip, "you could have a positive impact on good government."

"That's the thing about Gerry Doyle," said Rick, now getting fired up. "Nobody ever stands up to him."

"It's your civic duty and your boss's civic duty to tell the story," said Chip.

"You'd need to get it to the *Eagle* by Tuesday," I said.

"I'll get the letter on Monday," said Rick.

The three of us finished breakfast and Chip and I paid the bill.

"How do you feel about being a whistleblower?" I asked.

"If it's just me, no problem," said Rick, almost defiantly. "I can stand up to anybody. But I have other people to look out for, including my boss and his business."

"This could *make* your boss's company," I said. "The citizens would respond to that kind of courage and patronize his business."

"I can see that," said Rick. "But I don't do house work. I do industrial work. That means contracts."

"They will do the right thing, too," said Chip.

We got up from the table and headed for the door. On the way, two men recognized Chip and me and told us to "keep going" on Wahconah Park.

Outside the diner, I had a final thought for Rick.

"This is going to be public, one way or another," I said. "The only question is the role you'll be playing. The guy who got intimidated? Or the guy who played the hero."

Rick took a deep breath and nodded. We shook hands and I patted him on the shoulder.

"You're a good man, Rick," said Chip.

Rick climbed into his truck and drove away.

In the car on the way home, we couldn't wait to discuss what had just transpired. We almost couldn't believe it. Except, of course, we could.

"Did you see how badly he wanted to get off the subject of Tom Murphy's phone call?" I said. "First he said Murphy had asked why he was against a new stadium, and then he said Murphy had never even called back."

"There was a sudden shift to Stanley," said Chip. "He was looking for anything to change the subject and, as it turned out, he grabbed the wrong thing to tell us."

"Doesn't that line about the new stadium sound coached?" I said. "As in, 'If anyone wants to know, just say I asked why you were against a new stadium.'"

We thought about that for a while.

"He's not going to give up Murphy," I said. "That's his ace in the hole to keep Doyle from retaliating."

"I hope Rick has a remote control starter on his car," said Chip.

SEPTEMBER 16
SUNDAY

Paula and I settled into our Sunday routines. She with a good book, me with Chip Elitzer and Rick Jones.

We still needed to nail down a few things. The buttons, for example. We had forgotten to ask him yesterday where they were. Also, we thought Rick would need a little support if he was going to tell his story to the *Eagle*, and we wanted to talk to him about that.

Looking ahead, Chip called the *Eagle* from the car, on our drive up to Pittsfield. He told Dusty Bahlman that we might have an important story for him and, if so, we'd like to meet with him tomorrow. Dusty explained that he would have to check with his editor. When Chip said we would prefer that he come alone, Dusty got offended. So without mentioning names, Chip outlined the story for him, and said we would call back in a few hours.

We met Rick Jones in the backyard of his girlfriend's house and began by asking about the buttons.

"I never saw them," said Rick.

"According to UPS," I said, "they were left on your back porch a week ago yesterday. What could have happened to them?"

"I have no idea," said Rick, looking uncomfortable. "I swear to you, I don't have them."

"Did Tom Murphy tell you to get rid of them, by any chance?" I asked.

Rick glared at me.

"If I had those buttons right now, I'd shove them up your ass," he said, spitting out his words.

I deserved that. If Rick was innocent, that is.

"A button enema would probably be uncomfortable," said Chip, trying to lighten things up a bit.

"Maybe some kids in the neighborhood took them," said Rick, calming down. "They're always taking things."

"Maybe Tom Murphy took them without you knowing about it," I said. "Did he know some buttons were going to be delivered?"

"No," said Rick. "I told you we never talked."

Whatever the story was, we weren't going to get it from Rick Jones. Not today, anyway. So we did the next best thing.

"Okay, I'm sorry," I said. "We believe you." But I didn't really mean it. Certainly not the part about his not talking to Tom Murphy.

"Let's talk about the *Eagle*," said Chip. "Jim and I would like to be there with you so they don't brush you off. How do you feel about that?"

"It's okay with me," said Rick. "But I might not have the letter from Stanley."

"Why not?" asked Chip.

"Because when I asked Stanley for a copy this morning," said Rick, "he said he didn't want to get involved."

"He won't deny he sent it, will he?" I asked.

"He already hand-delivered it to the Mayor," said Rick.

"What's Stanley's last name?" asked Chip.

"Greenleaf," said Rick. "But don't use his name."

"He's the plumbing inspector," I said. "They know his name."

"Yeah, but the *Eagle* doesn't have to know who it was that the mayor called," said Rick.

"Just out of curiosity," said Chip, "does your boss know anything about this?"

"Sure," said Rick. "Stanley called *him* before he called me."

"The story gets worse as it goes along," I said.

We agreed to meet at the Lantern at one-thirty tomorrow afternoon. We would call Dusty and ask him to join us at two.

"You're doing a good thing, Rick," said Chip.

"You ever see the movie *On the Waterfront*, with Marlon Brando?" I asked Rick. "It's about a regular guy who stands up to corruption."

"I didn't see it," said Rick.

"Rent it tonight," I said. "You'll enjoy it."

In the car on the way home, Chip said maybe it wasn't such a good idea to mention *On the Waterfront*.

"Isn't that where Marlon Brando gets beat up," said Chip, "and his brother gets killed?"

"I forgot about that part," I said.

SEPTEMBER 17
MONDAY

This morning, Chip accidentally discovered a cute little maneuver by the Parks Commission. He was on the phone, trying to convince Smitty that he and his fellow commissioners should eliminate Fleisig so we could go head-to-head with Bossidy, and Smitty suddenly said, "I understand they're trying to get a meeting together tonight."

Tonight?

"He just blurted it out," said Chip, who knew that last-minute meetings were against the Massachusetts "open meetings" law.

Not that Parks Commission meetings are "open" in any sense of the word—what with the public forbidden to ask questions, little or no discussion among the Commissioners, and no indication of how decisions are arrived at. The few meetings that Chip and I have attended seemed largely designed to either receive proposals or announce decisions, with the deliberations going on somewhere else. Tonight's unannounced "open meeting" appears to be a creative extension of that form.

After hanging up with Smitty, Chip immediately called the Parks Administrator, Bob Mellace, to see if it was true about a meeting. Mellace may do the commissioners' bidding, but he's not the kind of guy who'd lie.

"Yes," said Mellace, "there is a meeting."

Chip asked Mellace to read the agenda to him, which included an item called "Bossidy proposal."

"Will Bossidy be there?" asked Chip, incredulous.

"Probably," said Mellace.

Think about it. The $70-million-dollar man is coming to town—his first public visit since the Civic Authority went down to defeat on June 5, this time with an option to buy a team—and it's not front-page news?

Being the good citizens that we are, Chip and I took it upon ourselves to alert the media to this important development which somehow had slipped through the cracks. Unfortunately, we had to do it from the car, on my cell phone, on our way to Pittsfield for our meeting with Rick Jones and Dusty Bahlman at the Lantern.

While we were at it, we also alerted about a dozen of our most ardent supporters—witnesses you might say—in case the commissioners tried to do something sneaky, like approve Bossidy's proposal *tonight!* Because the clandestine nature of the meeting, plus the arrival of the big man himself, had all the earmarks of a done deal—about to be did.

Are these guys fun, or what?

No sooner had we sat down at our favorite table at the Lantern—the one in the back with the red vinyl banquette—than Rick Jones arrived, with a harried look on his face and a tape recorder he had just purchased.

"Mind if I record this?" he asked, setting his recorder on the table. "A guy I know who's a lawyer said this is what I should do. I just picked it up at Sears. It's brand new."

"No problem," I said. "Nothing secret going on here."

We began by talking about the importance of what he was about to do. Chip explained that Dusty Bahlman would want to corroborate his story with the plumbing inspector and the mayor, and to get a copy of the letter.

"Well, I don't have the letter," said Rick. "Stanley wouldn't give me a copy."

"If it doesn't exist anymore," I said, "that would be a whole different level—destroying evidence. That's a *federal* crime."

"I certainly don't want to be involved in that," said Rick.

"The guys who destroyed the letter would have the problem," I said. "*You* haven't done anything wrong."

"Then why do I still feel nervous?" said Rick.

"Because you're going up against guys who aren't used to being challenged," said Chip. "We've been going up against them all summer long."

"Somebody has to challenge them," I said. "Because if you don't do that, then it continues."

"I agree," said Rick. "But that doesn't make it any easier."

A few minutes later, Dusty Bahlman ambled in. Dusty is a beefy guy with a friendly face, and the demeanor of a world-weary bear.

"No tape recorders," said Dusty, and Rick immediately turned his off and put it away.

"We have enough witnesses here," said Chip.

Then Rick told his story: about having been chewed out for an hour by the plumbing inspector after the inspector had received a threatening phone call from the mayor, and about Tom Murphy's phone call and Rick's understanding of what that meant. Rick did a good job, too, not backing off from what he had told Chip and me.

The only problem was that Dusty did not seem to be too disturbed by what Rick was saying. In fact, most of the time he didn't even take notes. Dusty said it was a mayor's job to check permits, and that Murphy's call to Rick sounded normal, in spite of the fact that it had an intimidating effect.

"Okay, I think I got it," said Dusty, closing his notebook. "But I'm not sure when it's going to run."

This was very discouraging. Dusty Bahlman is one of the few *Eagle* reporters, besides Bill Carey, in whom we have any confidence. Chip and I had expected Dusty to be more receptive to what we believed was a major story. Either Dusty didn't see it or he didn't want to see it. A mayor's job to check permits? Murphy's call to Rick sounded normal? I pushed for something more from Dusty.

"Can I suggest that you try and run it prior to the City Council meeting on Thursday night?" I said. "To help counter the negative effect this has had on our petition drive."

"I'll have to see," said Dusty.

Before we got up to leave, Chip and I asked Dusty if he was going to the Parks Commission meeting tonight.

"There's a meeting?" said Dusty, looking confused.

We explained how Chip had accidentally found out, and how nobody else seemed to know about it either, including the city councilors whom we had spoken to.

Dusty rolled his eyes and slowly shook his head.

"I hate it when they pull crap like that," he said.

That was a good sign. At least something bothered him.

Maybe if Dusty thinks about it, he'll see a connection between the way Rick Jones was bullied by city officials and the way the Parks Commission has been dealing with Chip and me.

It was 6:45 when Paula and I arrived at Springside House. This being the first night of Rosh Hashanah, Chip was at the synagogue with his family. Waiting for us on the front steps, as if he had still been sitting there since the last meeting three weeks ago, was Eric Lincoln, wearing his usual outfit, plus a Yankee cap.

"When did you get here?" I asked him.

"Six o'clock," said Eric, "which is when you told me to be here."

"Sorry about that," I said.

"That's okay," said Eric. "What else have I got to do?"

Inside, I was disappointed to discover a mostly empty room. One of the few people standing around was Cliff Nilan. I went over to talk to him.

"Can I ask why we're not on the agenda," I said politely, "since we've requested that the Commission take an action?"

"You're not on the agenda because we're not going to ask anyone to withdraw," said Nilan, looking right past me. Evidently that particular decision had been made at a meeting we missed.

"Did you understand the logic of my letter?" I asked. "How Fleisig's blocking us prevents Pittsfield from getting the best deal?"

"We want as many proposals as we can get," said Nilan, tersely. "If somebody has a new proposal, we'll look at that."

I knew I wasn't going to get anywhere. I just wanted to hear what he would say.

At 6:50, when Paula and I sat down, there were only about ten people scattered in forty seats. Where was everybody? Then, as the clock ticked toward 6:55, they began entering in groups of twos and threes, and pretty soon the room was packed with Wahconah Park supporters, the few we had called, plus friends, relatives, and neighbors. Plus Dan Bianchi, mayoral candidate Peter McHugh, and some Council candidates I didn't recognize, and by 7:00 it was standing room only.

Rick Scapin, who is an athletic-looking guy with a white brush cut, walked in, grinning, eyes wide with delight. He maneuvered through the crowd, and reached over to shake my hand. "They're shocked," he said. "I can see it in their faces. They're shocked!" When a pissed-off Tom Murphy squeezed past me, I was tempted to ask him where his Wahconah Yes! button was, but I didn't.

Then there was a general stirring as Larry Bossidy entered the room. Bossidy, a big man with jug ears and a stoney face, walked directly to the table where the commissioners were sitting.

"Hi," he said in his CEO voice. "Where do you want me to sit?"

I half expected Smitty or Conant to give up their chairs and sit on the floor.

"Somebody get Mr. Bossidy a chair," ordered Cliff Nilan. An executive-type chair with wheels was rolled in from the next room.

The meeting began with "old business" that was immediately disposed of.

"Proposal from Mr. Bossidy," announced Nilan, reading off his agenda sheet. His very short agenda sheet.

The $70-million-man stood up and handed each commissioner two pieces of paper that had been stapled together. The room got so quiet you could hear a done deal drop. The commissioners silently read what Bossidy had handed them, which took a minute and forty-five seconds. Then it was time for Bossidy to be grilled.

Commissioner Conant, exhibiting the leadership qualities he hopes will get him elected to the City Council, started it off.

"Regarding maintenance," said Conant, "who would pay if the ejector pump went out?"

"I'd take a look at it," said Bossidy, presumably after driving up to Pittsfield from his headquarters in New Jersey. "If it's small, I'll take care of it. If it's significant, the city should participate."

An honest answer that seemed to throw everyone for a moment. No one asked Bossidy's definition of "significant" or "participate."

"What kind of a lease are you looking for?" asked Conant.

"Two years," said Bossidy. "If it looks like the money to build a new stadium is there, I'll take the risk and buy the team."

No one asked Bossidy what would happen if the City of Utica exercised its option to match his offer and keep the team there. Or who would pay to maintain Wahconah Park once a new stadium was built.

"Is there a significant difference in the cost of purchasing an affiliated league team versus a Northern League team?" asked Conant, getting back to the more important questions.

"Four times," said Bossidy.

"That's significant," said Commissioner Massimiano, attempting to help define that term for the benefit of the audience.

"How are you coming on funding for a new stadium?" asked Smitty, just out of curiosity, since his responsibility is Wahconah Park.

"Eleven million has been committed," said Bossidy. "We need to find $7 million in the next few weeks."

No one asked why a new stadium was even being discussed, since one had just been voted down in June. Or how the commissioners' interest in a new stadium might conflict with their sworn obligation to the city's parks. Presumably those questions would be left for another meeting.

The whole thing took ten minutes. But the importance of the meeting was in what *didn't* happen. A Larry Bossidy deal did *not* get done—at least not tonight.

That didn't mean, however, that the audience was done with the commissioners.

As the meeting concluded, there was a surge of bodies toward the table in the front of the room. The commissioners, clutching papers and snapping briefcases, looked for an exit. A few made it out, but not before a lady named Betty Quadrozzi gave Cliff Nilan a piece of her mind.

"What is going on here?" asked Betty, annoyed but polite, as if she were questioning a wrong color choice by the painter. Betty is about sixty, very pretty, with salt and pepper hair. "Why wasn't the public given anything to look at?" she said. "Why couldn't we ask questions?"

Nilan, looking to defuse the situation, responded warmly.

"We'll take a look at it carefully and then make a decision," he said, as if he were talking to his favorite aunt.

But the favorite aunt wasn't having any.

"Is that any way to do it?" asked Betty, still courteous. "This was a public meeting and I didn't learn anything. Shame on you."

Nilan, not looking ashamed, smiled and nodded and turned away.

Moving through the crowd, I timed it so that Bossidy and I would cross paths, in case he wanted to say something like, "Thanks for the book." But he walked right past me. And I understood his eagerness to leave—he had come a long way just to hand two pieces of paper to some parks commissioners.

I made one final request of Cliff Nilan. After Betty had finished trying to register on him, I asked if I could have a copy of the Bossidy proposal.

"I only have one copy," Nilan said brusquely, "and I'm not giving it to *you.*"

Whereupon he adjourned to the parking lot for what someone described later as "an ad hoc meeting" with Bossidy and the other commissioners. The real meeting where the real discussion would take place.

While we were still milling around inside, I was approached by *Eagle* reporter Tony Dobrowolski.

"Do you think you're getting a cold shoulder from the administration," asked Dobrowolski, "because you've alienated them?"

This was particularly annoying, considering the source.

"Besides my letter to Nilan," I asked, trying not to show my irritation, "what have we said about city officials?"

"I can't think of anything specific," said Dobrowolski. "But things I've read."

"Things you probably read in your own newspaper," I said. "You may be confusing what Chip and I have actually said and done with the *Eagle's* interpretation. It's your own paper that's alienating people."

Dobrowolski just shrugged his shoulders, smiled enigmatically and shuffled away.

Outside Springside House, Paula and I said goodbye to some Wahconah Yes! teammates who were still hanging around. They were enjoying a done-deal-undoing, cool-of-the-evening moment.

"See you at the City Council meeting on Thursday," we all reminded each other about the rescheduled September meeting. That's when it will be decided whether or not to put proposals for Wahconah Park onto the November ballot.

"What a scene!" said Paula, on the drive home. "Fifty angry and frustrated people—but all polite to the core. They should have been shouting. 'What's on that paper? What's public about this meeting?' And when it was over they got up quietly and left. No fuss. Nothing."

"Did you hear what Betty Quadrozzi told Nilan?" I said.

"Yes, but it was surprisingly subdued," said Paula. "Maybe they're exhausted from all the battles they've fought. Like Mickey Mouse against the endless brooms in Fantasia."

We gave that some thought.

"I'm glad I'm doing this," I said, a surge of good feelings rising up. "I feel like I'm making a contribution. In some small way, being a good citizen in Pittsfield substitutes for being a good citizen in New York City, where they already have enough good citizens right now."

SEPTEMBER 18
TUESDAY

Susan Gordon has agreed to replace Rick Jones as the leader of the petition drive. Susan is the owner of Bagels Too, a breakfast and lunch restaurant on the main drag in Pittsfield. New signature sheets have been printed, with Bagels Too as the address where completed sheets can be mailed or dropped off.

"And I'll keep separate copies," said Susan, "in case somebody comes in and tries to steal them."

Her fears are well founded.

Anne Leaf and Dave Potts said their Anti-Civic Authority petition sheets were always being stolen or destroyed.

"They were tearing them up all over town," said Anne. "I was afraid they were going to break into my house and take them. All the meetings were held here and I had the Xerox."

"She wouldn't even tell *me* where she was keeping them," said Potsy. "I told her that somebody had to know. So she finally told me."

"I slept with them," said Anne, finally able to laugh about it.

But most of it wasn't so funny.

"I got threatening phone calls all the time," said Anne. "One time I got a call from a man whose voice I didn't recognize. He said, 'You better back off or you'll be sorry.' Then he hung up the phone. I also got a call from the wife of a top city official, who threatened me. Honestly, I thought my house would be set on fire."

Over a baseball stadium?

SEPTEMBER 19
WEDNESDAY

The Rick Jones story appeared in the *Eagle* today. A small piece of it, anyway. Just as I had feared, it ended up looking like a diligent Mayor Doyle just doing his job. And Tom Murphy wasn't even mentioned at all.

What's fascinating, however, is how Doyle handled it. Especially the "smoking letter" the plumbing inspector sent to Doyle, documenting the mayor's demand to see Rick's and his boss's work permits.

Here are the key paragraphs in Dusty Bahlman's story, beginning with a quote from Doyle:

> "On September 13, my office received an anonymous call reporting that a local plumber was breaking the law by using a vehicle for plumbing work that did not have a visible certified logo," Doyle said. "We probably get two or three of these types of calls a week from people who have complaints and we investigate them all."
>
> The Mayor said he requested the information about the permits from Stanley Greenleaf, the city's plumbing inspector. Doyle also said that he directed Greenleaf to submit a written report of his findings.
>
> "Knowing that Richard Jones is a candidate for office, I requested Mr. Greenleaf's report in writing to avoid any appearance of impropriety and to verify that I did indeed have the allegation investigated," Doyle wrote in a memo that accompanied a copy of Greenleaf's report. "The allegation turned out to be false and therefore no other action was required."

Look how clever Doyle is.

He needs a reason for having called the plumbing inspector and demanding that Rick Jones's permits be checked. An anonymous tip about a violation would do, but it can't be a violation related to a particular plumbing job because that could be checked through work orders. But a lettering problem on a truck could be spotted anywhere, at any time, so we get a violation of the "visible certified logo" rule.

It's perfect—as long as no one asks any annoying questions, like how the anonymous caller knew who to blame if there was no lettering on the truck in the first place. Or why Greenleaf felt it necessary to chew Rick Jones's ear for an hour just to save Pittsfield from a lettering problem.

Then there's the letter from Greenleaf. And this is the genius part. Since Doyle is stuck with the letter that Rick had requested Greenleaf send, he makes the most of it. Suddenly it is *Doyle* who requested the letter—*demanded* it, even—because Rick is "a candidate for office" and Doyle wanted to "avoid any appearance of impropriety."

In Pittsfield, you can spray the roads with PCB oil, but you better not go without lettering on your plumbing truck.

Today I met with a guy named Ed McCormick, a lawyer from Great Barrington, who, according to several reliable sources, started that rumor about me demanding $3,000 to speak to the Boy Scouts.

McCormick is a heavy-set, ruddy-faced man. When I called him last week to make an appointment, his secretary had asked what it was about, and I said it was personal. I walked into his office and sat down.

"What can I do for you?" he said, as if I were looking for legal help of some kind.

"Do you know anything at all about a rumor that I demanded $3,000 to speak to the Boy Scouts?" I said.

"Don't know anything about it," said McCormick, in a very convincing manner.

"Why would someone in Pittsfield tell me otherwise?"

"I have no idea," he said, shrugging.

I was about to apologize. There had probably been a misunderstanding. I tried to figure it out.

"Do you have *anything at all* to do with the Boy Scouts?" I asked, about to get up and leave.

"I'm the Scoutmaster for Berkshire County," said McCormick. Oh.

"Then let me ask you another question," I said, back on the scent. "Do you have any connection to Pittsfield politics?"

McCormick's face got redder.

"I got a call from some people," he said, "asking me about you and your partner, Chip. I said Chip is a good guy. I know him. He's my neighbor. I was less than stellar about you."

"Why was that?" I asked.

"Because you canceled out on a Boy Scout meeting and I didn't like the way you handled it."

"How did I handle it?" I asked, more curious than ever because I couldn't remember having met him.

"You should have sat down with me and talked about it."

"I don't recall speaking with you about it in the first place," I said, a bit testy. "I only spoke with Cheryl Raifstanger, but I didn't commit to anything. Then I told her I wouldn't do it because of the Scouts' policy against gays."

McCormick launched into a speech about his Boy Scout troop not discriminating against gays.

"What does that have to do with $3,000?" I asked.

"I don't know anything about that," said McCormick.

That's when I got up and left.

SEPTEMBER 20
THURSDAY

Tonight may be our last chance to get Wahconah Park. If the City Council votes to put the question onto the November ballot, we're in. The Parks Commission, knowing the election was coming up, would have a hard time choosing anyone but us. They might even decline to make a decision and leave it up to the voters.

Since everyone also understands that our plan for Wahconah Park dooms a new stadium, tonight's City Council vote to put the question on the ballot is really a vote for or against a new stadium. On the ballot means no new stadium.

Five of the eleven councilors are probably against us—Hickey, Lee, Massery, Kerwood, and Dowd, the new-stadium die-hards. We need all the rest. The good news is that Gary Grunin stated publicly last night that he'll vote yes tonight on the ballot question—otherwise he has no chance to be mayor. With Bianchi, Guzzo, and Scapin, that makes four. The only question marks are Bill Barry and James Brassard. We feel pretty good about Barry after our breakfast meeting last week, and Brassard recently told Chip on the phone that he would vote in favor. But who knows how solid they'll be?

It's always possible that one of the new-stadium guys will break ranks for some reason. Maybe Massery or Kerwood, who are both running for reelection, will feel the heat that Grunin is feeling. Maybe Hickey will risk taking "an unbelievable amount of shit" and adopt a more even-handed course. Or maybe the fix really *is* in and our defeat, no matter how narrow, was always in the cards.

We'll find out tonight.

At least there's one honest newspaper in town.

This week's *Gazette* contained an editorial by publisher Jonathan Levine entitled SAD TALE CONTINUES. A few highlights:

> The Parks Commission's latest actions have further tainted the board's once-strong reputation and added to Pittsfield's festering baseball sores.
>
> The Commission held a hastily scheduled meeting on Monday to hear Larry Bossidy's vague proposal . . . . While the commission did meet legal requirements for posting this session, the board added further fuel to the fire of public distrust by seeming to do so stealthfully.
>
> Despite the intense public interest in this issue—with many residents especially interested in learning what Bossidy might offer—the meeting was not announced in advance.
>
> Had the grapevine not buzzed Monday among citizens tuned into the issue, no members of the public would likely have been present. The proponents of competing plans were not invited. The community access television station that aired earlier presentations on the topic was not in the loop. And candidates for public office—an astounding two dozen of whom have requested a public referendum on the stadium issue—also weren't informed.
>
> In a related vein, it's unclear why a public session needed to be scheduled at the last minute on the night of a major Jewish holiday.
>
> The Commission's process has disappointed throughout recent months—from the dubiously created "questions" that are supposedly guiding the decision to haughty treatment of the public.

To make a good impression at tonight's Council meeting, Chip and I brought the finest testimonials to our good judgment—Cindy and Paula. Cindy in a fire-engine red jacket and a silk scarf. Paula in a gray herringbone jacket with black lapels. They could sway the vote just by sitting there. And it sure was fun walking in with them.

The Wahconah Yes! team was there, of course, with their game faces on. And we had Bianchi, Guzzo, and Scapin up on the dais.

Everybody was there for one reason—Wahconah Park. Depending on what happens tonight, this could be the fourth time in the last four years that the old ballpark, directly or indirectly, had its own place on the ballot. Not that this had ever settled anything.

At 7:30, City Council President Tom Hickey tapped his gavel and called the meeting to order. He asked for a moment of silence for "the victims and families, and rescue people who are down there working so hard."

Everyone knew where "down there" was.

Then the councilors, all wearing American flag ties and/or lapel pins, recited the Pledge of Allegiance.

Hickey announced that Councilman Brassard would be late because he was attending a neighborhood meeting. Brassard is the vote Chip and I are least sure of. Maybe the tie-breaking vote.

"He's getting his final instructions," I said to Chip.

"He's getting an unbelievable amount of shit," said Chip.

First on the agenda was the open mike period. "We have over twenty speakers," said Hickey, "so keep your comments to three minutes please."

Then began a parade of twenty-two speakers, all but one in favor of putting Wahconah Park on the November ballot. And they did more than simply state their preference. They made a plea for democracy.

Here's a sampling:

"You gentlemen were elected to represent the citizens of Pittsfield, and I do not believe you are listening to them or representing them."

"The voice of the people is something we hold dear and something that we are ready to fight for."

"Here's an opportunity to clean up what has been a very manipulative and closed process."

"You know what the people want from you—a chance to be heard. Why is it they have to resort to referendum petitions?"

"Larry Bossidy is asking for three things that we just voted down—a new stadium, millions of dollars in public funding, and an executive authority to run it. I am personally insulted that nobody said to him, 'We just voted that down, sir!' Now I am offended that we have to go before you and ask for a referendum to consider this thing that we don't want."

Chip and I added our voices, too, but it was really a night for the citizens of Pittsfield.

Then it was time to call the question.

"Madam Clerk," said Tom Hickey, "if we could have item number twenty-six, please."

The clerk advised the council that the three-part question—to vote for the Fleisig, Bossidy, or Bouton proposal—could not go on the ballot as is. The only solution was to turn it into it three separate yes or no questions—with the winner being the proposal that gets the most yeses—as other communities have done.

But Pittsfield is not other communities.

To understand what it's like in Pittsfield, a verbatim transcript of the first five minutes of council deliberations tells you everything you need to know. Keep in mind that the ballot question was non-binding and had the support of two thirds of the candidates running for office.

Brassard: (*who just arrived*) Is there any way that an individual can pull one lever and the rest of the levers be shut?

Clerk: No.

Brassard: Okay, so a person could go in and pull one *yes* lever and two *no* levers, is that correct?

Clerk: Yes.

Brassard: Could they vote three yeses?

Clerk: They could vote yes or no for all three questions.

Brassard: What I want to know is that a person could go behind the curtain and pull more than one lever. Is that correct? (*The clerk nodded.*) They can pull a yes for each question. So they could pull a total of three levers. They could vote for all three plans. They could vote yes for each? Yes, yes, and yes, in any combination? Any combination. You can't lock out . . . That scares me.

A few members of the audience groaned.

Hickey: Let me just try to clear this up. I'll make an attempt at clearing that up for the audience. What the city clerk has said, the type of machines we have, the questions would be set up as three individual questions and you could vote yes or no, or any combination thereof, on each one without being able to lock out the others. So if you wanted to vote for the Bouton plan and the Bossidy plan and the Fleisig plan you could vote yes on all three, or yes, no, no. There's no way to lock out, am I correct?

Clerk: Yes.

The audience grew impatient with Hickey's explanation. They already understood that multiple yes votes would simply cancel each other out, having no impact one way or another.

Hickey: The Chair recognizes Councilor Rick Scapin.

Scapin: I don't think we're going to have to worry about them voting for yes on all three. They're going to vote for one yes and two nos. They're very educated, and a lot of councilors thought they were stupid out there—and I think they showed that at the last Civic Authority vote—and don't underestimate the voters out there. They know what they want and who they want.

Hickey: The Chair recognizes Councilor Kerwood. (*The guy Peter Arlos calls "Little Eddie Munster."*)

Kerwood: I agree with Councilor Scapin that the voters aren't stupid, but I think it's important that we make it as foolproof as possible and whether we like it or not, the system that was just outlined can lend itself to manipulation, and you could have somebody go in and vote three yeses, three no's or whatnot.

This was too much for the audience. Amid the laughter, a number of people hollered out "So what?"

Kerwood: So what? The answer to the question 'so what?' from my perspective is that now if someone goes in and

votes three yeses, are they truly giving you a repre-
sentation of what they feel or are they going in just to
vote three yeses across the board? You could say well,
the greatest number of yeses wins, but that's going to
be dictated by voter turnout.

People were laughing derisively—maybe because they expected more from the Western Massachusetts Director of Economic
Development. (I'm not making that up.) Kerwood became even more
agitated.

> **Kerwood:** Excuse me, I have the floor. We listened to you guys.
> I am stating my opinion, and what I believe, and
> whether you like it or not, the system as outlined, can
> be subject to manipulation . . . . You know, people
> can disagree with me but that's my opinion and if
> we're talking about the democratic system and a pro-
> cess of fairness, we know that whether you like it or
> not there are people out there that are going to try to
> manipulate the system, be dishonest, not play by the
> rules, I mean that is just a fact of life, and I think last
> Tuesday probably was a good demonstration of the
> fact that not everybody plays by the rules.

The audience groaned loudly at the reference to 9/11. But there
was no stopping an idiot on a roll.

> **Kerwood:** We've got to make sure that the system is as foolproof
> as possible . . . but again, that's my opinion, and until
> we can resolve this issue I don't feel comfortable vot-
> ing on the amendment."

The dialogue went on in this vein, but for all intents and purposes, it was over. Without Brassard, it was clear that the ballot question
would be defeated 6–5. The only thing that remained was a further
glimpse into the minds of some Pittsfield city councilors.

Massery: This country has gone through too much, this city has gone through too much. . . . There's no way I'm going to support this. And none of us should. Let's just forget about it.

Guzzo: It's non-binding. It's advisory. I mean, come on. Look what this issue has put this community through. I'm still trying to get over it and I'm a pretty strong individual.

Bianchi: Maybe baseball is not a top-ten issue, but the principle of allowing people to have a voice in what happens in this community is. And I believe we are on the verge of making a change in how things are run.

But not tonight.

After voting 6-to-5 against putting the question of who should get Wahconah Park onto the November ballot, the Pittsfield city councilors moved on to new business—their American flag ties and lapel pins firmly in place.

SEPTEMBER 21
FRIDAY

Peter Arlos called this morning. He said we didn't have to worry about last night.

"You guys are in," he said, in his all-knowing guru voice. "You just gotta wait. You'll be a lot stronger by Tuesday."

By that he meant the primary election. Arlos believes the two mayoral candidates will be Sara Hathaway and Jimmy Ruberto.

"Ruberto is a new-stadium guy," said Arlos. "He would have voted for the Civic Authority. Sara is for you guys. She's got a little class about her."

Arlos also made a prediction about Bossidy.

"The state isn't going to give Bossidy any money," said Arlos, scoffing at the notion. "The economy is collapsing. Hotels are empty."

The Oracle of Delphi has spoken.

SEPTEMBER 22
SATURDAY

"It's not about saving Wahconah Park anymore," said Chip. "It's about beating the evil empire."

Chip and I spent the morning running back and forth in his driveway, spraying day-glo orange paint through hand-made stencils onto three-by-four-foot poster boards, then quickly setting them out to dry ahead of threatening clouds. The posters said "Wahconah Yes!—Petitions—Sign Up Here." The reason for the day-glo was so that people could see them at night if they came directly from work to vote in Tuesday's primary election.

This would be our last stand—a balls-to-the-wall effort to get as many signatures as possible between now and October 5, the date of the Parks Commission decision. The signed sheets would have no legal authority; it was too late to force a ballot question. But they could have a psychological impact, especially if we got something like 8,000 signatures—more than the number of votes that defeated the Civic Authority—and plopped them on somebody's desk.

Whose desk, we'd worry about later.

We had spent most of yesterday on the phone with our supporters, putting together teams to man the polling stations. Or rather stand in the vicinity and corral people before or after they voted. Tomorrow we'd be meeting with the Wahconah Yes! team at Bagels Too, to hand out materials and go over strategy. As if it were a perfectly normal way to spend a weekend.

"We are now over the edge," I said to Chip, surveying a lawn filled with large day-glo spray-painted cardboard squares. "We are crazed warriors. All or nothing. Do or die. Ahabs chasing the whale."

Tonight in the car, on the way to dinner. Paula and I talked about the "crusade."

"Chip and I are those rare individuals who could pull off something like this," I said. "Who else could do such a thing?"

"Single people, mostly," said Paula.

SEPTEMBER 23
SUNDAY

Big day today.

I picked up Chip at eleven o'clock for the drive to Pittsfield and our noon meeting at Bagels Too. We had wanted to make it earlier but too many people said they wouldn't be back from church yet.

The trunk and back seat of my car were piled high with supplies—thirty posters, ninety-six clipboards and pens, a ball of string to tie the pens to the clipboards, scissors to cut the string, 5,000 proposal summary handouts, and 1,500 petition sheets. And we already have about 500 signatures from Rick Jones's aborted petition drive.

We were loaded for bear. Not to mention wolves, weasels, and horse's asses.

As we drove through Pittsfield in our jam-packed car, we joked about getting stopped by the police. In my best Slim Pickens voice I tried to imagine what that might be like.

"Well, well, well, loookie here. Ah do declare. If it ain't Mr. Jiiim Booo-ton and Mr. Eee-litzer. I'll just have ta call down ta the Mayor's office and see what he wants ta do with you boys. Heh, heh, heh."

A half-dozen supporters were already waiting when Chip and I arrived at Bagels Too. They helped us unload the stuff from the car and began tying the pens to the clipboards. Others moved tables around to make room for the stacks of materials that would go to the teams manning the polling stations. By noon, the room was filled with people tying, sorting, and stacking. And asking questions.

What happens if it rains? Bring umbrellas. Are we allowed to set up tables? No. What if somebody tries to stop us? Tell them you have the right to be there. And get the names of anyone who hassles you!

When it seemed that everyone was there, and before people started leaving with their materials, Chip stood up to explain the mechanics of the plan, review the handouts, and try to solve any problems.

There were fourteen polling stations. We still needed captains and workers for some of them. Maybe we could move people from stations where we had a surplus. Polling station 6B had workers but no captain. Katy Roucher knew some people who could help out. Morris Bennett had an extra worker. The room was buzzing.

Then Dave Potts, who had been standing quietly on the periphery with his wife, Grace, just observing, raised his hand. To tell us, basically, that we were overplaying ours.

"I think you're making a mistake," said the firebrand-turned-mayoral candidate. "The people are pretty worn out on this issue from back before you came along. And you got them on your side now, but you don't want to go too far, be too pushy. You don't want to alienate them."

The room got quiet. Suddenly the air had been sucked out. Here we were with all these people, and everything spread out on the tables. Several team members had already left with their materials. What was Potsy suggesting? That we just scrap the whole thing?

There was that word again. Pushy. And while we needed to be pushy with the opposition, we certainly didn't want to do it with our supporters. What Potsy was saying made me uncomfortable, but it felt right. Maybe we *were* about to cross a line. Chip looked like he was ready to say something. I wanted to head him off.

"I think we should listen to what Dave is saying," I said, jumping in quickly, before Chip could defend our plan—if that's what he was thinking of doing.

"The other thing is this," said Jim Moran, a tall, slim man with thinning hair and wire-rimmed glasses. "If you don't happen to get a majority, on a rainy day when people are in a hurry, they'll say we lost our own vote."

That one really hit home—rekindling my fears about the phone poll. I looked over at Chip, who was looking back at me. We smiled reluctantly. We knew they were right, without having to talk it over.

"Let's have a show of hands," said Chip, as a nod to democracy—or a last-ditch effort to salvage the day. "How many agree with what Potsy and Jim Moran are saying?"

Just about every hand in the room went up. There were even a few sighs of relief—including my own. The petition drive was dead.

"But what are we going to do with all these clipboards?" I said, trying to be funny.

"We can save them for the 44A petition drive," said Potsy, and everyone laughed.

The 44A charter provision is vital to what I refer to as Pittsfield's "marching veto" form of government.

"We've done it before," said Potsy, "and we'll do it again."

Then they all helped load the stuff back into my car.

"Dave Potts should be the mayor of Pittsfield," I said to Chip, on the way home. "If he can stop us with a few words, he can stop a freight train with his bare hands."

We talked about what a shame it was that Potts probably wouldn't survive the primary vote on Tuesday.

"He's a little *too* plain spoken," I said.

"A Jimmy Stewart type," said Chip.

What was interesting was that Potsy had tapped into an unspoken feeling among the group that our petition plan was too much. Why hadn't anyone else said anything? Probably because they didn't want to hurt our feelings. They know how hard we've worked on this, and they didn't want to disappoint us.

Sweet people.

SEPTEMBER 24
MONDAY

There was *one* good thing that came out of last week's City Council meeting. The last item of business was a Peter Arlos petition recommending that the Parks Commission hold a public hearing *before* they make a decision. It passed unanimously. When something important looks like it's going to pass, they vote unanimously.

Finally there will be a public hearing—the first ever on this issue—at a time to be announced by the Parks Commission.

I'm figuring it'll be on a Sunday at about 4:00 a.m.

SEPTEMBER 25
TUESDAY

Today I drove Paula to Newark for her flight to Amsterdam. She'll be spending a week with her daughter Hollis and Hollis's Dutch husband, Gert Jan, who are expecting a baby.

This was our first time in the New York area since 9/11.

Our first glimpse was from a distance—across the Hudson River. I never thought I'd be so shocked to see *nothing*. Nothing but a gaping hole in the skyline. And I never liked the World Trade Center, to be honest. I had always thought it was unimaginative and out of scale. And yes, arrogant. But now I missed it dearly. Missed it as a place where people lived and worked, and that now symbolically represented our entire country.

Looking at the empty space, with the smoke still drifting up, was disorienting. I wondered what new horrors might be in store for us. What would happen next? But I kept these thoughts to myself because they were not airplane flying thoughts.

"I can't even look," said Paula, and she focused her attention out the other window.

Before 9/11, Paula liked to get to the airport three hours early. Now she had to be five hours early. I went into the airport lounge and held her hand until she had to go through the machines.

Then I kissed her goodbye, trying hard not to wonder if I would ever kiss her again.

When I returned to the empty house, I called Chip to see what had happened with the primary. He said it had rained most of the day. Our petition drive would have been a soggy mess.

SEPTEMBER 26
WEDNESDAY

I woke up this morning with a simple idea: do nothing.

Don't follow up with Frank Boulton on an option beyond 2002. Don't meet with Sara Hathaway or Jimmy Ruberto. Don't write letters to the editor or op-ed pieces.

Don't push, but don't go away.

Sometimes I think our persistence lulls people into thinking we're going to somehow make it happen. So they're letting us carry the ball—with their invaluable help, of course. But they need to take over. It's their game, their city. We've done all we can do.

Leave it to the people now. Let the Parks Commission choose Bossidy. Let the City Council ratify the lease. Let the people organize a 44A against the ratification. Or, if the mayor signs a lease, let the new administration overturn it—if that's what they want to do.

That might extend things beyond the point where we could still field a team in 2002, but it would give us the whole summer to prepare properly for 2003. And while we were fixing up Wahconah, we could stage some baseball events there. Maybe an Old Timers' Game. Weekly clinics. I could call up my friend, Bill Lee, the "Spaceman," and schedule a game of local players versus his Gray Sox, touring ex-major leaguers. I could pitch for either team. I'm certainly local enough. And gray enough.

I called Chip to tell him what I was thinking, about us doing nothing at this point and leaving it up to the people.

"It wasn't what I had in mind," said Chip, "but I think you're right. It feels right. That's the way to go."

It felt even more right when the primary results were announced. These were the people who should be leading the way.

Just as Peter Arlos had predicted, it will be Sara Hathaway (39.2%) versus Jimmy Ruberto (31.9%) for mayor. Their closest competitors were former Mayor Reilly (8.4%), Gary Grunin (6.1%), and Dave Potts (4.2%). Five other candidates split the remaining 10.1%. According to Katy Roucher, the reason Potsy scored so low was that a lot of his supporters voted for Hathaway because they didn't think he had a chance. I still think Potts would be a good mayor. A Harry Truman type.

The top vote-getter among the at-large candidates for City Council was none other than Arlos himself. I figure it was only modesty that prevented him from making that prediction. Unfortunately, Rick Jones was eliminated and Kerwood, Lee, and Massery are still in contention. Jonathan Lothrop, who is also still in the running, finished just behind Massery.

But no matter what happens with the four at-large spots, Chip and I calculate that the *combined* new City Council—which includes the seven ward councilors, with Bianchi, Guzzo, and Scapin running unopposed—will be at least 7–4 and possibly 8–3 against a new stadium and in favor of our proposal for Wahconah Park.

I called Arlos to congratulate him on his first-place finish and his prognostication skills.

"Nice going," I said. "You're batting a thousand."

"You know what my strength is?" said Arlos. "Keep out of view."

"That's what Chip and I are going to do," I said.

"The *Eagle* is calling the candidates about baseball," said Arlos. "Jack Dew called me. I had to weave it in carefully. I told him the fact is that the $8 million isn't there [for Bossidy]. And the council meeting last week was really about the abdication of democracy, not the ballpark."

"He doesn't want to hear that," I said.

"Then he's talking about you guys," said Arlos. "And the quarter of a million dollars you're going to put in. He says, 'How do you know those guys are serious, that they're not fakes?' I said, 'They'll get a bond.' He found everything wrong, the park doesn't qualify. He gave me every reason."

"He's only twenty-eight," I said, "and he's already a hack."

"Bossidy can't do this," said Arlos. "He's overwhelmed. He's laying off people. He can't put this together. The point is, everything is going your way. You just gotta be patient."

"We're not going anywhere," I said.

"I saw Cliffy today," said Arlos, still savoring his big win. "I said, 'Cliffy, I came in first without your endorsement.' And he said, 'I never want to speak with you again.' There's a lot of people who can't handle criticism. You know what the key is? To be immune to criticism."

"I was surprised to see Kerwood do so well," I said, "after his performance the other night."

"He was the only Republican," said Arlos. "He did a mailing. And I told you what was going to happen to Grunin. He spent $40,000. That's a hundred dollars a vote." [Grunin actually got 807 votes at $49.56 each.]

"How much did *you* spend?" I asked, because I knew the answer.

"Nothing," he said. "You know, I've been around a long time. I've been a shoe-shine boy, a paper boy. I was a three-sport guy— football, basketball, baseball. I even tried out for the Red Sox."

"What was that like?" I asked.

"I've entertained you enough for the day," said Arlos.

So I let him go. I knew he had to return to his duties as county treasurer, councilor-to-be, Oracle of Delphi, and *noodge*-at-arms.

SEPTEMBER 28
FRIDAY

As Tim Gray had suggested, I spoke with Vinnie Curro, the "mayor" of Lakewood, who now lives down in Florida. Among other things, I asked him about his cancer map.

"I know hundreds that died of cancer," he said. "Bladder cancer, lung cancer, pancreatic cancer. My younger brother has cancer. His son passed away at thirty-two. He played in the yard with forty-five parts per million [PCBs]. It's hard to believe, but if you've been involved you know what it's like."

I gave Curro some background about our far less important struggle for Wahconah Park. He was familiar with the characters.

"Tom and Gerry sold us down the river with General Electric," said Curro, referring to Hickey and Doyle. "They have their local group that has their hands in it somehow and it's always been that way. They're all in cahoots together. You sound like a wacko when you tell somebody this."

I asked Curro if he knew anything about the property that the *Eagle* wanted to donate as the site for a new stadium.

"That area is all contaminated," said Curro. "Tons of automobile oil. They would have filled it in and gotten away with it."

"What would it cost to clean it up," I asked.

"A hundred and fifty to two hundred million," said Curro. "There are other chemicals, too—benzene, lead, resins—that are just as dangerous."

Still no word from Gray on those test borings.

"By law, the owner has to report contamination," said Gray. "But if they don't do it voluntarily, the DEP has no way of knowing."

What are the odds that the *Eagle* would report contamination on its own property? Especially when it lobbied against cleaning up the Housatonic.

"The *Eagle* ran editorials and free ads," said Gray. "'Don't clean the river,' and 'Don't go Superfund'—that's the hammer that allows the EPA to go for triple damages. Then they printed a letter, signed by Doyle and some CEOs, saying they didn't want to go Superfund. Jeffrey Cook was one of the big signers. He and the guys at Cain Hibbard all take work from GE. Those are some of the saddest people I know."

Sad and conflicted. One of the signers of the letter was Jim Wall, who preceded Andy Mick at the *Eagle*. Wall even traveled to Washington to lobby Ted Kennedy to urge the EPA not to put Pittsfield on the Superfund list. The city never got on the list, and the story of Wall's trip to Washington never got into the *Eagle*.

"The good-old-boy network has been entrenched for thirty-five years," said Gray. "Doyle and Hickey are the front men. They need to get those people out of office and wipe the slate clean."

"What about Andy Nuciforo?" I asked. "Has he been any help?"

"On the surface he seems supportive," said Gray. "Privately he says, 'You've done a wonderful job for Pittsfield.' But he hasn't spoken out on the matter. He's a good fence sitter."

"That's what we discovered," I said.

"The truth is," said Gray, "what success we've had is only because GE employees came forward to tell me their stories. That brought the national press—the *Boston Globe,* the *Wall Street Journal,* the *New York Times.*"

I asked Gray if he ever feared for his life.

"I've had a lot of people telling me they were afraid for my life," he said. "The good old boys hate my guts in the same fashion that they're against you."

"That's how you know you're on the right track," I said.

"I'm just a small guy who wanted to clean up the river," said Gray, "and I ran into politics. All those guys, the mayor and GE and the staff at the *Berkshire Eagle*—I've never run into a bunch of scoundrels like this before."

SEPTEMBER 29
SATURDAY

With Paula still in Amsterdam, I've been sleeping at odd hours. Which is how I happened to be on the computer at seven in the morning to receive the following email from Jonathan Lothrop:

> The Berkshire Eagle was a stunner this a.m. You
> appear to be back in the ballgame, with a much
> stronger hand, although you know that the Parks
> Commission still will not give you guys a break!
> We need to plan for the public meeting on Monday.

I wondered what the hell "back in the ballgame" meant. Because I don't know how to initiate an Instant Message without accidently downloading half of Venezuela, and I didn't want to call the Lothrops in case they were still asleep, I went to the online version of the *Eagle*.

And there it was.

Big front-page headline: BOSSIDY WON'T BUY A TEAM. Under that was a subhead: INSTEAD HE'LL GIVE $1 MILLION FOR PARKS.

The story, by Bill Carey, said Bossidy was abandoning his effort "after being informed that state funding needed to build a new stadium cannot be assured." The story quoted Mayor Doyle as saying that he was "stunned" by Bossidy's generosity.

I must admit the news got my heart beating a little faster than usual at that hour in the morning. But I had mixed emotions. Half of me was glad to see Bossidy out of the picture. The other half thought his million dollar "gift" looked an awful lot like a deposit.

The story went on to say that the Parks Commission, at the request of the City Council, will hold a "public hearing" Monday at 7:00 p.m. at Reid Middle School on the future of Wahconah Park, and that they are expected to recommend one of the two remaining proposals on October 2th or 4th.

Finally, as if for comic relief, the story quoted Mayor Doyle as saying that while he favored the Fleisig proposal, he would nevertheless "abide by the Parks Commission decision."

I can just see Doyle, lying awake at night, wondering what his hand-picked commissioners might do.

I immediately scribbled a fax to Chip: "Are you up? Bossidy is bowing out! State $ not available. It's us vs Fleisig and the P.C."

Then I checked to see what Ever-Scrib might have to say. As usual, he did not disappoint. Under the headline BOSSIDY GIVES UP THE GOOD FIGHT, Ever-Scrib had written:

> Larry Bossidy's decision to abandon his plans to bring a New York–Penn League team to Pittsfield is another blow for the struggling city, and not just because it means an end to the city's long history of affiliated minor league baseball and the probable end of any hope of building a much-needed stadium in the community.
>
> The decision of Mr. Bossidy, a Pittsfield native and internationally renowned businessman, to walk away from a city that treated his attempted generosity with characteristic suspicion sends a clear message to the business community far and wide that they are not welcome in Pittsfield. And that is very bad for a city that needs all the help it can get . . .
>
> But state money or no state money, the poisonous political climate was working against the Bossidy proposal. The insistence of many civic leaders that crumbling Wahconah Park can somehow be "renovated" and played in indefinitely is an example of the city's inability to come to grips with reality. It would cost millions of dollars to bring Wahconah Park to any presentable standard, money better spent on a new stadium that can offer the wide variety of activities that Wahconah Park cannot.
>
> Beyond the city's paralyzing Wahconah Park fixation is the even more disgraceful suspicion that greeted Mr. Bossidy's efforts . . . . The City Council's Three Amigos—Daniel Bianchi, Joe Guzzo, and Richard Scapin, the latter of whom appears to regard himself as council president material—David Potts, Anne Leaf, and the rest of the modern day Minutemen, the paranoiacs who dominate council open mike sessions, all treated Mr. Bossidy over the past year as if he were a corporate raider here to rip off Pittsfield. Many of these same people clamor continually that Pittsfield needs "jobs," and they can be assured that the businessmen who provide jobs noticed how the city treated the CEO of Honeywell.
>
> Mr. Bossidy's parting gift to Pittsfield is $1 million to help it deal with its budget deficit. Given the way Mr. Bossidy was treated the gift is remarkable, and given the way he was treated the city should have the grace to decline the money. But it will take it, undoubtedly checking suspiciously for attached strings.

The most peculiar thing about Ever-Scrib is his apparent lack of awareness as to the source of his continuing pain.

His problem stems from his refusal to accept that the people of Pittsfield simply *do not want* a new stadium, no matter who builds it with what money. Rightly or wrongly—forget for a moment that they happen to be right about the economic limitations and liabilities of new stadiums—they prefer to watch baseball at Wahconah Park. That is their right, in a democracy.

But Pittsfield is *not* a democracy, in large part because its only daily paper is not a free press. And so we get Ever-Scrib's ridiculous notion that the city is being "paralyzed" by three city councilors and a handful of open mike "paranoiacs." As if that underfunded band could defeat a majority of citizens, backed by the city's only daily paper, its largest bank, and its most powerful law firm.

The truth, of course, is that it's the bank, and the law firm, and the daily paper who are *against* the majority of citizens—whose only voices are the three councilors and some open mike "paranoiacs." *That's* the only alignment that could produce paralysis.

It is Ever-Scrib's "inability to come to grips with [this] reality" that causes him to project that failing onto others, leading ultimately to a world in which a vote against a new stadium is characterized as disrespect toward Mr. Bossidy and a "not-welcome message" to the business community, while *true* disrespect toward three local businessmen supposedly sends no such message.

If the *Eagle* believes Pittsfield "needs all the help it can get," the best thing it can do is stop pushing for a "much-needed stadium" and begin seeking a much-needed change of ownership.

SEPTEMBER 30
SUNDAY

Today Chip and I got tired of doing nothing.

Chip woke up in one of his open-letter moods and drafted a three-page **Update to Our Proposal**. It's addressed to the Parks Commission, but the real target is the public, who, the commissioners know, will be watching. Our best hope is to make our position crystal clear and thereby reduce the wiggle room for the commissioners. To that end, we wanted to address the two issues most likely to be cited as

reasons for choosing Fleisig over us—our long-term contract requirement and our team situation.

We've decided to go with my idea for a two-year contract, "renewable annually thereafter at our option as long as we are in compliance
with the performance terms," wrote Chip.

Then he listed the performance terms:

1. Provide season-long professional baseball every year.
2. Spend a minimum of $100,000 annually—on a cumulative
   basis—for maintenance, repairs, and capital improvements.
3. Make Wahconah Park available for all reasonable uses, including current uses, such as high school sports.

"By way of comparison," Chip wrote, "this arrangement would be
four times more favorable to Pittsfield than the lease that the Spinners
[New York–Penn League team] have with Lowell [Massachusetts]
for the use of their new stadium."

Next, Chip reviewed our team opportunities. Namely, that "the
Atlantic League has asked us to play the 2002 season as their eighth
team," and that "we are negotiating the terms of an option to buy
a permanent membership in the league in the event that (A) a short-
season division currently under consideration is created, or (B) we
have not purchased a franchise in the Northern League."

Finally, Chip reminded everyone what is so special and revolutionary about our proposal:

"Pittsfield has an unprecedented opportunity to do what no
other community has done before—*take control of its baseball destiny*. Instead of having a league or team owner dictate to the city who
will play there or what terms must be met for them to stay, Pittsfield
can—by granting us the Wahconah Park contract—ensure that an
all-Berkshire group will negotiate with both leagues to secure the best
possible deal for the city."

Then he closed with our boiler plate: "As always, we remain available to answer your questions or address your concerns."

Maybe the park commissioners will ask their questions and state
their concerns at tomorrow night's open hearing.

Arlos called this morning.

He said that Curt Preisser had called him. Preisser, whose over-sized head and skinny body puts one in mind of an extraterrestrial, is the mayor's man in charge of spreading false rumors.

"He said, 'They have no money,'" said Arlos. Preisser meant Chip and me. "Then he tells me you wanted $3,000 to speak to the Boy Scouts."

"That's bullshit," I said.

"That's what I figured," said Arlos.

This pissed me off. I've never spoken with Curt Preisser. He's never called to check a fact or ask a question. He just skulks around. These people don't have the guts to confront you face to face.

"What's the payoff for these guys?" I asked, still annoyed.

"Nothing," said Arlos. "They hate the people who were against the Civic Authority and those are the people who are 100 percent behind you. That's the whole thing."

Revenge. The big boys sit back and let the peons like Preisser fight a grudge match.

"People won't go to games if Fleisig owns the team," said Arlos.

"You should say that publicly," I said.

Arlos seemed to give that some thought.

"You should call Sara Hathaway," he said finally.

I paused for a few seconds.

"No Peter," I said politely. "It's not our job to lead Pittsfield. That's your job. The new leaders have to start leading *now*. If I were Sara Hathaway, I'd be rounding up council candidates to help make our case on Monday night. Because you're going to have to live with whatever the Parks Commission decides. And, frankly, if the new leaders can't lead, why should Chip and I even want to be in Pittsfield in the first place?"

There was a long pause on the other end.

"You're right," said Arlos, with a sigh in his voice.

"And I told Katy Roucher the same thing," I said, "when she asked what we were planning to do tomorrow night. I said we're just going to show up."

o o o

CHAPTER 13

"We're gonna give ya a fair trial, and then we're gonna hang ya"

OCTOBER 1
MONDAY

Paula flew in from Amsterdam this afternoon, but I sent a car to pick her up at the airport. I didn't want to miss tonight—the only public hearing on the future of baseball at Wahconah Park in the history of Pittsfield.

Reid Middle School is an old brick building that doubles as a town hall and voting place. Its auditorium, with two aisles sloping down to an elevated stage, seats about three hundred. Tonight the overhead stage lights illuminated a long utility table, behind which the five commissioners and Bob Mellace sat facing the audience.

It wasn't the packed house we had been hoping for. In fact, there weren't more than about seventy people, scattered randomly in groups of two and three. Why only seventy? Could have been any number of reasons: Lack of publicity. Short notice. Ballpark fatigue. Lost cause-itis. The good news was that they were all Wahconah supporters, the only strangers being the new faces that are regularly added to the club.

The meeting was called to order by Chairman Cliff Nilan, who quickly set the tone for the evening. "This will be a public meeting," he began, "and the Commission, after some discussion, has set up somewhat of a format and we would hope everyone would adhere to that format."

Nilan hadn't even warmed up yet, and the public *hearing* had suddenly become a public *meeting*. But it didn't really matter; in Pittsfield, these are interchangeable terms that can mean whatever city officials want them to mean. Under no circumstances, however, does either of them mean that the public will be allowed to engage the officials in a dialogue or be privy to the thinking that goes into a decision.

"Everybody will have three minutes to speak," Nilan went on. "You will state your name and your address and then you speak on the proposal you are in favor of. This is not going to be a dialogue or a debate. If you have any questions that you want the Commission to answer, or you have to ask of the Commission, please submit them in writing before you leave, and give that to Mr. Mellace. I'm sure the commission will consider them in their discussion and their deliberations, whenever that may be."

The public *meeting* had now been downgraded to an open mike session. This raised the question of why anyone, the audience included, needed to be there in the first place. If questions could be submitted in writing, why not the same with comments, and save everyone the trouble of coming? The Commission's actual "discussions and deliberations, whenever that might be," would presumably take place out of state so as not to be in violation of the Massachusetts open meetings law.

Lest the open mike session drift out of control, Nilan had a few more rules.

"This is not going to be a political rally," he cautioned. "We are going to try and keep it polite. There will be no getting up and saying who's in favor of this proposal, who's in favor of that proposal, please raise your hand. We would like to just to discuss the Commission [sic] and try to stay with the format. We thank everyone for coming, we appreciate your input. We would hope to get out of here at a reasonable hour."

Nilan was more in control than I'd ever seen him, almost tic free. His usual collar tugs, ear digs, and nose wipes seemed to have been retired in favor of the tie pull, which itself had been scaled down to the gesture of merely reaching for the tie—as if his wife had told him not to do that anymore, and he'd catch himself in time.

Nilan then stated that Chip and I could have three minutes apiece, but that since Jonathan Fleisig had to rush back to New York, he would go first. Fleisig, wearing a sportcoat, a blue dress shirt over a T-shirt, and an wry smile, strolled down to the podium.

"In August, I presented you with a plan as you had requested, to bring a professional baseball team to Wahconah Park," he began. "You asked me for everything, from proof of the team to articles of incorporation, a litany of items. Each and every one of them I gave you and I stand by them today.

"While the majority of the things you asked for, I gave you, I just want to reemphasize one thing that you didn't ask for, and that's my heart. I love baseball. I love independent baseball and I once again would love to be part of your community."

This was a blatant copyright infringement of my marriage proposal to Wahconah Park at that City Council meeting last month. In the interest of keeping things polite, I decided to let it go.

"The only other thing that I would really like to mention today," Fleisig went on, as only he can, "to take a three-hour drive, is simply that what's gone on in the last couple of weeks, I am kind of in awe of. I've spent my time in New York City dealing with some of the worst things that anyone could ever imagine. I read *my* newspaper for the last couple of weeks and it talks about death, and I read about things in the *Eagle* and it talks about baseball. And what community is supposed to be is about getting things together, so Mr. Bouton"—at this point, Fleisig turned to face me as I sat in the audience—"let's just stop all of this, let's stop the fighting, the politics."

"Jonathan," Nilan interjected, "address the Commission."

"I'm sorry," Fleisig said. "I just publicly want to say let's just *get along*. Let's not fight or bicker. I've never written any nasty letters. I've never done anything, and if it ends up that you choose Jim and the Atlantic League, I'll do everything I can to try to help the City of Pittsfield and to try to make it successful for you, OK, in whatever way that I can. And if I'm lucky enough that you choose me, I hope that the other parties will do the same."

The message was clear: *He* hadn't written any nasty letters because he's dealing with life and death in New York City.

"You know, next year when baseball season rolls around, it's hopefully going to be the Atlantic League or the Northern League, but the community has got to get together," Fleisig continued. "That's the only way anything ever works, and I found that out from Bakersfield to Topeka to Lynn. It only works if everyone here, from the commissioners to the public, does things together as a team. And we may think that the team in between the lines is important, but it's really not. It's the community and the fans and you people up there, so whatever way you go I'll respect it and to me that's the most important nowadays. So, thank you and I appreciate the opportunity to talk. Thank you very much."

Nilan then called my name. The question was, should I stand up and say that this is all bullshit, that they're missing a golden opportunity for a genuine airing of views? Why have Fleisig drive three hours to make a three-minute speech? Don't waste his time. He's here, we're here, let's get it on! Or should I just go along with the nonsense? Afraid of giving them a reason to reject us, I'm sorry to say I just went along.

Standing at my seat in the third row, I said, "We're here tonight just to answer questions."

"The Commission's not going to have any dialogue tonight," Nilan said. "If you want to stay after and answer any questions, you can do that."

"We've already made our case," I said, feigning confidence.

Nilan asked Chip if he wanted to say anything.

"No, I don't," Chip said.

Nilan then introduced people from the audience who walked down to the podium to have their say. They included Peter Arlos, Rick Scapin, Joe Guzzo, Dan Bianchi, Dave Potts, Jonathan Lothrop, and a parade of private citizens, all of whom spoke in favor of our proposal for Wahconah Park.

But the speaker everyone liked best was the last one—a stocky, white-haired lady who limped down to the podium, using a cane. Clarissa Boos, stern and clipped, spoke slowly and forcefully into the microphone.

"Wahconah Park," Boos began. "I went there when there was just a plank from home plate to first base and home plate to third base—to watch baseball games." Pausing for effect, she shook her fist at the commissioners and shouted, "Now, you have a chance to *do* something for the City of Pittsfield. And you better start doing it!"

The audience roared its approval, whooping and hollering—the pep rally that Nilan had said he didn't want. The funny thing was that Boos had not even mentioned which proposal she supported. But nobody had to ask.

Because the shocking thing was that no one had stood up for Fleisig, who sat through the whole meeting. I wondered what he was thinking. Exactly what "community" did he expect would "get together" for him? He couldn't even count on his pals. Where were Mayor Doyle, Andy Mick, Mike MacDonald, the new-stadium councilors?

No doubt, behind a closed door somewhere.

Nilan then asked for "a motion to close the public hearing."

This was the topper. What had been announced as a public hearing—before it became a public meeting that morphed into an open mike session—miraculously *closed* as a public hearing.

It was like a public hearing sandwich—with no meat.

Or a game of three-card monte.

As we left the building, Chip remembered a line from Quick Draw McGraw, the 1960s television cartoon show. Spoofing frontier justice, Quick Draw explains the town's judicial system to a captured suspect.

"We're gonna give ya a fair trial," says Quick Draw, "and then we're gonna hang ya!"

OCTOBER 2
TUESDAY

I woke up feeling great this morning, and not just because Paula was home. The Parks Commission, I believed, has got to give it to us. How can they ignore the overwhelming sentiment at last night's meeting? They had invited the people to speak. As Chip said, "What are they going to say, 'Thank you very much, fuck you?'"

"It would lead to massive anger and cynicism," I said. "They can't possibly give it to Fleisig."

"Don't be so sure," said Paula. "If a toad came hopping along with a team, they'd give it to *him*."

But Peter Arlos thinks we have a good chance.

The Oracle of Delphi called me this morning to say that Curt Preisser is "grasping at straws."

"He said you refused to present your income tax returns for three years," said Arlos.

"Nobody submitted tax returns," I said, laughing. "We're not applying for a loan. That was just a way for them to pry into our personal lives."

"On his way out of the meeting last night," said Arlos. "Preisser said, 'you're backing fakers, they don't have a dime.'"

"That's funny," I said, "because we don't need a dime. We've already got people lining up to invest. And Eric Margenau owns five teams himself."

"I'm just telling you what he said," Arlos explained, before shifting gears. "Some good people spoke up for you last night. Lou Costi and Sue Gordon. Their support was *big*. Two business people, well respected. They took a risk, putting their businesses on the line."

Evidently, Preisser is grasping at straws in neighboring states. Frank Boulton told Chip that Preisser had called him yesterday to ask if it was true that we're welcome to play in the Atlantic League next year. Of course, Frank said yes. Which is not necessarily what the people of Pittsfield are going to hear.

OCTOBER 3
WEDNESDAY

Today is the fiftieth anniversary of "the Shot Heard Round the World," one of the most memorable events of my childhood.

I can still hear announcer Russ Hodges:

"Branca throws . . . THERE'S A LONG FLY . . . IT'S GONNA BE, I BELIEVE . . . THE GIANTS WIN THE PENNANT! THE GIANTS WIN THE PENNANT! . . . BOBBY THOMSON HITS INTO THE LOWER DECK OF THE LEFT FIELD STANDS . . . AND THEY'RE GOIN' CRAZY."

As a twelve-year-old Giants fan this meant only one thing. I had to get to Iriana's house as fast as I could. Robert Iriana was a Dodger fan and we used to argue all the time about which team was better.

Or which player was better, Duke Snider or Willie Mays? Pee Wee Reese or Alvin Dark?

Iriana lived on the opposite side of town, which in Rochelle Park is about a mile away. Running non-stop, I arrived to find what seemed to be an empty house. Nobody answered when I rang the doorbell and the shades were pulled down. Finally, after about ten minutes of ringing and knocking, Mrs. Iriana came to the door.

"Robert's not feeling well," she said.

I told that story to Bobby Thomson the first time I met him, at a sports dinner in New York. He laughed and said he had heard a lot of stories like that over the years. But I never told it to Ralph Branca. Like Robert, he may still not be feeling well.

The Parks Commission will announce its decision tomorrow night at City Hall in Pittsfield. Unfortunately, it's one of the few nights I'll be out of town. I'm giving a speech in Cooperstown to the Life Insurance Council of New York. Instead of coming with me, Paula will go to Pittsfield with Cindy and Chip, to be my eyes and ears and take notes.

Proving once again that truth is stranger than fiction, Chip and I got an Instant Message today from Jim Goldsmith, our first contact with him since the Bob Wirz deal fell through. This time, Goldsmith was offering to represent *us* in trying to get a Northern League franchise.

Which franchise? Any franchise, evidently, including Wirz's! Goldsmith said he could act as an intermediary with Miles Wolff to possibly get us an expansion franchise. We told him no thanks.

"I guess Goldsmith thinks we're desperate," I said, "with the decision coming tomorrow night."

"I don't trust him any farther than I can throw him," said Chip. "He's offering investment banking services. *I'm* an investment banker. You can't kid a kidder."

"How can he represent both us and Wirz?" I asked.

"He can't," said Chip. "Working through Goldsmith would be like trying to do fine needlework wearing heavy mittens."

Email from Gene Nadeau:

> Good luck tomorrow night. I'll be there.
> Wouldn't miss it for the world. My opinion is
> if there is security, it won't bode well for
> your proposal. Having security will indicate
> an unpopular decision is forthcoming.

OCTOBER 4
THURSDAY

D-Day. As in Decision Day.

I left the house this morning for Cooperstown, having absolutely no idea what might happen tonight in Pittsfield. On the drive through the Catskills, past the rolling farms and the fruit stands and the cavern signs, I got to thinking about what a great adventure this has been for Chip and me. It's been a little less so for our wives. Okay, a lot less so.

But the two of us have had a marvelous time. We started out with a small dream and a big idea and ended up in a morality play. And no matter how it turned out, I was glad we had done it. Not just for ourselves but for the people of Pittsfield. Our experience confirms something they've always known—that the deck is stacked against them. Chip and I have provided an independent corroboration, and what's more, we've made it public.

Imagine George Steinbrenner insisting that New York City *not* build him a new stadium, but rather *allow* him to invest private funds to renovate the existing Yankee Stadium in exchange for a long-term commitment from the city. Dozens would be hurt in the stampede to get his signature on a lease before he changed his mind.

But not in Pittsfield. There, it's one postponement after another. And who knows what they'll decide?

Tonight's plan called for Paula or Chip to leave a message on my answering machine at home, so I could call in and get it as soon as I was finished with my presentation in Cooperstown.

And so it was that at 9:46 on the evening of October 4, 2001, I dialed my number, punched in the code, and heard the following:

"Hey Jim, it's Chip," he said in a tired voice. "It's about about 8:35. Paula just dropped us off. The meeting was over rather quickly. And it was a five to zip vote. Against us, I probably don't need to say. And boy, as soon as it was over, I just wanted to get out of there. Dusty Bahlman was there and he asked if I had any comment and I said no. So I think we just retire to South County and get on with our lives. It's up to Pittsfield now."

In spite of having anticipated this, my first reaction was anger. How could they do this, not to Chip and me, but to their fellow citizens? How will they face their neighbors? What do they tell their co-workers?

Then I calmed down. I felt sorry for them in a way. The parks commissioners were just pawns. It was never between us and Fleisig. It was between us and a new stadium. Us and the newspaper and the bank and the law firm. If Tom Hickey, the president of the City Council, had been taking "an unbelievable amount of shit," imagine what the commissioners faced.

It was a decision driven by fear. They were afraid of the big boys and they were afraid of us. Afraid to engage us on the issues. Afraid to field questions. Afraid to sit down and try to work something out. But most of all, they were afraid to have their beliefs challenged. To believe in what they were doing—and they *wanted* to believe—they had to avoid us at all costs. Even if that meant twisting themselves into pretzels.

It's no surprise that they voted unanimously. They needed to protect one another. Safety in numbers, even if it's only five. If you rang doorbells in Pittsfield, you wouldn't find one person who preferred Fleisig over us.

That's why I didn't take it as a personal loss. I didn't feel defeated. I felt as if I had pitched a helluva ballgame and just hadn't gotten the calls.

The umps were in the bag.

By the time I finally got home, it was about two o'clock in the morning. Paula, who had been sleeping with the light on, gave me a groggy kiss and pointed to her notes which she had placed on my side of the bed:

In the car on the way up, I'm tense and so is Cindy.

"I will never ever *buy, own or carry a firearm," she says emphatically. "I'm much too volatile." Obviously, Cindy's expectations are as gloomy as mine.*

At a quarter to seven, all the seats are filled and people are standing in the hallway. A police officer in the back, next to Curt Preisser. Complaints, and nervous humor.

A nearby church bell begins to toll, loudly. Rick Scapin cocks his head in the direction of the sound and says, "That's for us!" Cindy laughs. "Ask not for whom . . . ," she agrees.

Tony Massimiano reads a prepared statement. A line about Wahconah Park "not being available for high school football" jumps out. Even I know that's not true.

Conant is next. He says he never saw a license agreement so how can he "vote on an agreement when I cannot read it?"

The guy called Smitty says the Bouton group has "some good marketing idears" [sic] but are in over their heads. All "sizzle and no steak."

Jim and Chip are described as people who "fail to grasp the enormous responsibility" of caring for "this jewel in the system's crown," and who, unlike the charitable Mr. Fleisig, would keep revenues earned by the local high school for their own benefit. Derisive snorts and laughter erupt periodically from the otherwise well-behaved audience.

Wahconah is described as "a historic landmark" and "a national treasure" that must be protected from "private groups" who want to wrest control of this beloved park.

Cliff Nilan winds up by going clearly over the top. Handing over Wahconah Park to a "private group" would be "like a parent signing away the rights to his children's future." And then his "children's children" would no longer be able to enjoy "the glow of Wahconah Park's lights."

I kid you not. Pukesville.

One by one they vote for "the Fleisig proposal." And then it's over. The audience files out quickly and quietly. There is bitter disappointment in the air, embarrassment.

Cindy, Chip, and I walk to the car without a word. Once inside, doors closed, Cindy turns to Chip and sums things up:

"That's it, Chip Elitzer." Whenever she calls him by his full name, you know an important statement of policy is about to issue forth. "I don't care what happens in January (meaning with the new administration). This has taken too much toll on our family. Pittsfield doesn't deserve you."

Amen to that. Let's put it down and move on.

What I want to do now more than anything is give Jim a big, long hug.

And so she did.

○ ○ ○

A YEAR LATER

FALL 2002–SPRING 2003

It's been a year since the Pittsfield Parks Commission—acting of its own free will, independent of Mayor Doyle, the City Council, Berkshire Bank, the *Berkshire Eagle,* Cain Hibbard Myers & Cook, and General Electric—said, "Thank you very much, fuck you," to its fellow citizens.

Meanwhile, a lot of things have happened.

Chip and I are in a different place. It's called home. Chip is back in the investment banking business, trying to make up for last year's lost income. And I'm trying to write the final chapter of a story that never ends. We still get together socially—Paula and Cindy allow us a two-minute Wahconah Park update—but we sort of miss each other. You can see it in the eyes, the pat on the shoulder. We're like army buddies who fought the business equivalent of a small war.

"It was an honor to have served with you," I said to him the other day, only half joking.

And it was an honor to introduce him when he received his Citizen-of-the-Year award from the Great Barrington Rotary. Chip was selected for having created the Tech Fund, which makes sure every student in the Berkshire Hills Regional School District has a home computer—in some cases personally installed and guaranteed by Chip! As Chip approached the podium to enthusiastic applause, I couldn't help thinking what jerks those park commissioners were for denying their city this man's talent and generosity.

Chip and I try to laugh about what happened. We tell people that we achieved our goal without spending a dime. We turned what

Berkshire Sports & Events had said was "a crumbling, decrepit dump, not worth saving" into what the Parks Commission said was "a national treasure, and a jewel, which must be protected from private groups."

Mostly we try to forget about Wahconah Park because it just makes us sad. But it continues to tug at us. The other day, Chip faxed me a story that said the new park commissioners had agreed to let Fleisig replace the right field bleachers with picnic tables! Can you imagine? What are they thinking? What will that do to the symmetry of the ballpark? And how will it affect Joe Guzzo's campaign to include Wahconah Park in the National Register of Historic Places?

"Jeeez," I said to Paula, "they're taking it down stick by stick."

The only thing standing in the way is Dave Potts, who has become the unofficial, self-appointed historian of Wahconah Park. When he's not tooling around on his motorcycle, or trying to keep the government honest via the open mike, Potsy is down at the library digging through the microfiche. It was Potsy who just discovered that professional baseball has been played at the Wahconah Park site since 1892, not 1919, as most people had thought.

In another interesting discovery, rumor has it that the new-stadium site—property the *Eagle* had portrayed as a "donation" to the city of Pittsfield—has a slight problem.

It's polluted.

Apparently, evidence of contamination comes not from the 1994 test borings—which are still being investigated—but from recent soil samples commissioned by the CVS Pharmacy Corporation, which had an option to buy the property. The story goes that after the samples were taken, CVS declined to exercise its option.

Environmental law states that when a property is sold, the seller must guarantee that it's not polluted, unless the buyer is willing to sign a waiver and assume the responsibility. It's a waiver the *Eagle* very likely signed when it bought an extra 2½ acres (formerly a car dealership) to complete the stadium parcel, in anticipation of a yes vote in the June 5th referendum. More significantly for Pittsfield, it's a waiver the *Eagle's* lawyers had written into the Civic Authority Act, absolving itself of any responsibility for a cleanup. By law, whenever contamination is discovered, perimeter testing is required to determine the extent of any migration, which now includes the entire property. So, instead of sitting on nine acres of polluted land, the *Eagle* may now be sitting on 11½. It's enough to cause panic in the hearts of a newspaper owner and his editorial staff.

Or have they known about the pollution all along? A look back at an old newspaper clipping offers a clue. During the Civic Authority campaign, Andy Mick was quoted as saying, "There is no hidden agenda here." Sounds pretty Murphyesque to me.

So is it true about pollution on the *Eagle* property? And could that be why they wanted to give it away? When someone asked Jack Dew if he planned to investigate the matter, he said, "If there's contamination, it's not news."

If that isn't news, what is?

How about the way in which decisions are arrived at in Pittsfield? The story possibilities are endless. I just learned, for example, that two months before Chip and I first met with Berkshire Sports & Events at the North End restaurant, there had been an important meeting—referred to by insiders as "the secret meeting"—in the boardroom at Berkshire Bank.

According to witnesses, it was "a full house." Mike Daly and Gerry Denmark from the bank, Mike MacDonald of Cain Hibbard, Mayor Doyle and Tom Murphy, and Larry Bossidy and some of his friends had invited the city councilors to a meeting. Actually it was three meetings, one after another, with different sets of councilors so as not to be in violation of the open meetings law.

The law is important to these fellows.

The leader, or "drill instructor" as some described him, was Mike Daly, who underlined the need for secrecy. "And I don't want to hear about this on the *Dan Valenti Show* tomorrow," he warned. Then he went to work on the councilors. "Are you with us or not?" Daly challenged them. "You better get on board." According to one source, "Bill Barry was shaking in his boots." Another said he had heard that "Brassard looked like he might wet himself." Evidently Bossidy just sat there, his mere presence making the point.

Where "the secret meeting" ranks with "an unbelievable amount of shit" is difficult to know. In fairness to Daly, who was then the bank's chief lending officer, it should be said that at no time was the bank's ability to deny loans and/or generally wreak havoc on the business and personal lives of the councilors ever discussed.

Why Andy Mick was absent from the meeting is not known. Maybe he felt he'd have to report it in the *Eagle;* as it was, only the *Gazette* carried the story. Or maybe Mick conducted his own meetings, which could explain Councilor Massery's comment to Chip, early on, that "I can't just walk away from this, unless Andy Mick releases us."

It's hard to keep track of which politicians are beholden to whom.

This is democracy in action, advise and consent, Pittsfield style: The power structure *advises* the council what it wants to see happen, and asks them to play ball or else. Once the council *consents,* which can take all of fifteen minutes, the matter goes to the lower chamber—DelGallo's or the Brewery—for enactment by people like the mayor and his commissioners.

At that point you have a system of checks and balances, with each check balanced by a cost. For example, a few years ago Mayor Doyle hired a company to administer the city's health insurance program, which for some reason was not licensed to certify claims. This led to millions of dollars in losses for the city through overpayments to Berkshire Medical Center, whose president happens to be a pal of the mayor.

In a separate transaction, Mayor Doyle awarded a $30,000 severance package to the city treasurer—which some cynics have called hush money—even though an agent hired by that treasurer had neglected to pay the premiums on city insurance policies. That particular oversight contributed to either $5 or $9 million of city debt, depending on the outcome of a lawsuit filed by city employees.

Nothing illegal, you understand. The mayor was just following a long tradition in Pittsfield.

Then there's the story of EV Worldwide.

Back when Tim Gray was challenging the GE settlement, a company called EV Worldwide came forward and promised to build buses on the old GE site—if and when a GE deal was signed. Also pending was a $3 million state grant—of taxpayer dollars—to help seed EV Worldwide, which promised to employ a thousand people.

"I was accused of standing in the way of a thousand jobs," said Gray. "The *Eagle* kept writing, 'These jobs are in jeopardy.'"

But two years after the GE deal was signed, EV Worldwide announced that it wasn't going to build any buses after all. Unfortunately, Mayor Doyle, with city council approval, had already given $250,000 of the GE settlement funds to EV Worldwide, on top of the $3 million state grant. Then it was discovered that the EV Worldwide CEO had mafia connections.

Whatever happened to EV Worldwide?

"They're still sitting over there," said Gray, "pretending they're a company."

Meanwhile, Massachusetts Secretary of State William F. Galvin is pretending that the unindicted former mayor Doyle is the best possible choice to be his liaison for Berkshire County. Doyle's responsibilities in the paid, no-show job include—hold on to your baseball caps—helping assess potential uses of grant funding from the state Historical Commission. If I could think up stuff like this, I'd make a fortune in Hollywood.

The November 2001 election offered a ray of hope.

The good news came in a call from Peter Arlos on the morning after. "Congratulations!" he said. "You won the mayor and six new council members."

Naturally, he had predicted the outcome. "Sara Hathaway will defeat Jimmy Ruberto," he had said. "The guy's got everything—prominent family, Italian—made every stupid move in the books."

He had also predicted the City Council winners and losers, including the defeat of Jim Conant.

Right after the Commission had handed down its decision, Conant had written a letter to the editor of the *Eagle*, which repeated the lies that Chip and I wanted to confiscate "high school game revenue" and prevent events "such as the candlelight vigil that was recently held at the park."

"Conant can't win," Arlos had said. "He doesn't have the brains God gave a billy goat. Callers have been giving him hell on the radio station. Here's what I'm telling ya. People don't like controversy. They don't like noise. They got Peter Arlos. That's enough."

And they also had the *Eagle*, which provided a valuable guide for voters—in reverse. With few exceptions, whomever the *Eagle* endorsed, the people voted against, and whomever the *Eagle* ignored, they voted for. As a result, Ruberto, Conant, and Massery lost, and Arlos, Tuttle, Vincelette, and Arpante all won.

The only new-stadium guys who survived were Kerwood and Lee. Jonathan Lothrop, who just missed getting elected, was not helped by the *Eagle's* refusal to give him credit—or even mention his name—for having sponsored the candidate's petition that nearly forced a ballot question on Wahconah Park.

"It was satisfying to see Lothrop get more votes than Massery," said Chip.

"Too bad people can't vote the newspaper out of office," said I.

Mayor Doyle delivered a memorable farewell address before leaving office. He called the *Dan Valenti Show* and blamed Dan and his listeners for having disrupted "the administration, my life, and my family's life." On an ominous note, Doyle warned that he planned to "hold people accountable."

"Will there be trials?" I wondered aloud to Chip.

"Usually it's the politicians who have to be accountable," said Chip, still trying to grasp how things work in Pittsfield.

Another way things work is evidenced by what happened to Gary Grunin. Apparently, during the 2001 primary campaign for mayor, candidate Grunin had asked the DelGallo camp for its support in exchange for the going rate for that service. The only problem was that the DelGallo crowd decided to secretly support Jimmy Ruberto instead. Reports say that when Grunin found out what happened, he stopped by DelGallo's and "shot his mouth off." Fortunately, those were the only shots fired.

A word here about Remo DelGallo. By all accounts he is *not* the Godfather, his politically connected restaurant notwithstanding. According to reliable sources, he's a decent guy who was one of the first to uncover PCB pollution on Newell Street, and who may or may not be able to deliver a certain number of votes on election day. In any case, everyone seems to agree that Remo and his wife serve a great pasta fagiole.

Then there is Matt Kerwood—"Little Eddie Munster." With the changing of the guard on the City Council, Kerwood was removed from the finance committee by new council president Rick Scapin, causing Kerwood to whine and act out. As retaliation against Rob

Tuttle for having backed Scapin over Gerry Lee for council president, Kerwood tried to ruin Tuttle's job prospects with the state Republican party. Tuttle then filed a complaint with the State Ethics Commission.

Speaking of ethics, or the lack thereof, it's hard to top the goings on of Jim Conant, who is now Fleisig's groundskeeper, which by itself is a smile. What's not so funny is learning that Conant had been hired by Fleisig *before* the Parks Commission had announced its decision.

Apparently, in late September, prior to a high school football game, a local sports fan was standing on the field at Wahconah Park with maintenance man Tony Stracuzzi. A guy came over and told Stracuzzi that the outfield would need to be seeded. "Who was that?" asked the fan. "Oh, that's Conant," replied Stracuzzi. "He's got the contract to maintain the field."

Our public servants at work.

It's not all disappointing. Some of it is amusing. Like the minor detail that Boy Scout leader Ed McCormick failed to mention in our meeting about the $3,000 speaking fee rumor: He and Nilan were college roommates! Scout's honor.

"What surprises me is that Cliff went to college," said Chip.

And you'll never guess who owns the speed-dialer that made 144 calls in favor of the Fleisig/Bossidy proposal during our infamous phone poll. By sheer coincidence, it's the same company that did phone polling for Berkshire Sports & Events during the Civic Authority campaign.

I even discovered how Jamie Akers's color renderings of our proposed changes to Wahconah Park ended up looking so dark and foreboding on the front page of the *Eagle*: Printing experts tell me instructions had to be given to *not* separate the colors, as is customarily done on a color page. It comes as no surprise to this reporter.

Mystery lovers will be disappointed to learn, however, that the trail of the missing Wahconah Yes! buttons has grown cold. Alert citizens are invited to post promising leads at www.foulball.com.

In the loose-ends department, the Seattle Mariners declined to host a Pilots Old Timers' Day in 2002. They said they liked the idea, but they wanted to do it "during an anniversary of the Pilots or at another meaningful time." Maybe they'll do something on the thirty-fifth anniversary, in 2004.

I called my old roomie, Gary Bell, to give him the news. Gary was a star in *Ball Four*, my book about the Pilots. I asked if he thought the guys would show up for an Old Timers' Day. "Put a fifty-dollar bill on the floor, with a string attached," he said. "They'll come."

Then we got to talking about Wahconah Park. Gary reminded me that that was where he gave up the longest home run of his life. It was during an exhibition game, after his career was over. "Was that the one where . . ." I started to say. "Right," said Gary. "Some asshole in bib overalls got out of a milk truck and hit one over the trees."

On a related subject, ESPN Classic had created a half-hour special on *Ball Four* as part of its *SportsCentury* series. Scheduled to air September 20, 2002, it was suddenly canceled, even though ESPN had already started airing promos for it. A producer told me he didn't think the cancellation had anything to do with my *New York Times* op-ed piece, a week before, which blamed baseball's labor strife on the owners. I could go either way on this one.

Meanwhile, the *Pittsfield Gazette* won a New England Press Association award for "Fairness in Journalism." That weekly's coverage of the stadium issue was judged "down the middle" by NEPA. It was so fair, in fact, that two of the *Gazette's* major advertisers, Berkshire Bank and Berkshire Medical Center, pulled their advertising. Publisher Jonathan Levine, who would like to stay in business, declined to comment on the matter.

In the same vein, Dan Valenti is not saying that his coverage of the stadium issue led to the *Berkshire Eagle's* dropping his column. "Scribner told me they wanted to make a change," said Valenti, "so they could have other voices."

The funny thing is, Dan hadn't even told his best story. Right after the Parks Commission ruled in favor of Fleisig, Conant told Valenti, "We gave it to Fleisig, knowing full well he'd fail." When Valenti asked him why they would do such a thing, Valenti said Conant "sort of laughed and shrugged it off."

Fortunately, the *Dan Valenti Show* is still on the air. Dan is still the adjunct professor of English at Berkshire Community College, and his column now appears in the *Gazette*. Until further notice.

Some of the best reading I had all summer appeared in the *Eagle's* sports section, which Chip would clip for me. It was Jonathan Fleisig's first season at Wahconah Park—with his renamed Berkshire Black Bears. Here are the highlights:

- Finished last in league standings with twenty-four wins and sixty-five losses.
- Finished second to last in league attendance.
- Set new league record for player turnover with fifty-eight, breaking old record of forty-nine held by his own Mad Dogs.
- Several players were dismissed for off-the-field behavioral problems.
- The director of player personnel was arrested on charges of stealing from his former team.
- Manager George "Boomer" Scott was fired.
- Fleisig announced he'd be coming back in 2003.

The good news is that an ejector pump didn't blow.

Fleisig admitted making a few mistakes. "At some point in time," he said, "I should have said, 'We'll come in 2003 instead of 2002.'"

Of course. But that's not what his *backers* had wanted him to say. Trying to run the clock out on us, they ran it out on Fleisig.

What Fleisig didn't say was that the main reason he did so poorly was because nobody in Pittsfield was rooting for him, a distinct possibility made painfully clear at the Parks Commission's so-called open hearing when no one stood up for his proposal.

"Watching Fleisig that night," someone commented later, "was like watching a man at his own funeral."

Instead, Fleisig plowed ahead as if nothing were amiss.

The morning after the Commission's decision, he called Phil Massery, the radio talk show host and brother of city councilor James Massery, to say that he was "proud of the people of Pittsfield" for having chosen him. He said he was "all about togetherness" and that he'd "love to get a call from Mr. Bouton and Mr. Elitzer to say, hey, let's all work together."

"Tell me that's not the most exciting call we ever had," said Massery, who was later hired as Fleisig's director of group sales.

Then Ever-Scrib got into the act. The day after Fleisig's call for togetherness, Ever-Scrib wrote an editorial entitled FLEISIG IS THE RIGHT CHOICE FOR PITTSFIELD:

> We hope the South County partnership will gracefully accept the decision and the city will not be afflicted with paralyzing lawsuits and petition drives . . . .

That was followed by this note in Scribner's own column:

> [We could be] in for 30 years of litigation, so thorough is [the Bouton group's] sense of entitlement to Berkshire baseball bragging rights.

Now there's an idea. Litigation. What kind of case did we have? Restraint of trade? Economic interference? Breach of fiduciary duty? Unfair bidding practice? Fraud? What did the *Eagle* know and when did they know it?

Another reason for Fleisig's tough summer was the local newspaper. The only thing worse than having the fans against him was having the *Eagle* for him. When they weren't propping up Fleisig, they were tearing down Wahconah Park. A relentless stream of negativity is not conducive to ticket sales. A sampling of Ever-Scrib's sniping:

> [The Bouton group] had little comprehension of the many problems any tenant will face at the outdated park.

> Mayor elect Hathaway . . . should not buy the preposterous notion that the Parks Commission [selected] a tenant at decrepit Wahconah Park without adequate public input.

> [Fleisig] had better be prepared to [spend money] to keep the decrepit ballpark in minimally respectable shape.

> [It] has all the ambiance and charm of an old wooden outhouse in the middle of a swamp.

> No amount of renovations and restorations is going to bring it close to the standards set by newly built ballparks.

The Northern League is floundering on the field and with fans . . . [because of] a bush-league setting.

The decaying ruin that is hardly fan friendly, especially in comparison to new ballparks.

Et cetera.

Still another problem was promising the fans a winner.

"I want to win, and I want to win now!" Fleisig had proclaimed on Phil Massery's radio show.

This is the classic mistake of team owners everywhere—promising a result that, for 90% of them, is mathematically impossible. Sports is a zero sum game; you can only win at someone else's expense. Since most fans think *winner* means *first place,* or a close second, you are going to disappoint them most of the time. That's why, especially in the minors, besides family fun, you need to sell community spirit and the ballpark experience—two concepts fatally damaged by Fleisig's own backers.

Without the aforementioned problems, Fleisig's promotional snafus might have been seen as amusing rather than infuriating. Fans might have chuckled when the George Scott bobble-head dolls were not there to bobble on "Bobble-Head Night." Ditto the missing hats on "Disney Hat Night." And when Mia Hamm was a no-show on "Mia Hamm Night," it could have been laughed off and followed up with a "Where Was Mia Hamm? Contest Night."

Of course, there's not much that can be done about a lack of fireworks on "Fireworks Night." Especially if it's the last night game of the season and it's also "Fan Appreciation Night."

"Thank you for coming," the PA announcer was reported to have said, without reference to the missing fireworks. "See you next year."

Fleisig might actually return in 2003, since he has a two-year contract. And what a contract it is, negotiated as it was with his pal, Mayor Doyle. The agreement, which redefines the term "sweetheart deal," even for Pittsfield, contains the same kind of giveaways that are the hallmark of city dealings. Herewith a few items, including my favorite, number four:

1. A piddling $50,000 performance bond that Fleisig gets back as soon as he spends the first $50,000 of the $150,000 promised in his proposal, for improvements, over two years.
2. No timely notice provisions. Once Fleisig has spent his $50,000, he can walk away at any time, without penalty, leaving the city at his mercy on renewals or replacements.
3. Fleisig is responsible only for "nonstructural repairs," and only during the baseball season. If the lights fail or an ejector pump blows, the city is on the hook.
4. All concession operations, year round, for all events, *including high school sports,* are controlled by Fleisig.

The signing of Fleisig's contract was trumpeted with much fanfare by the *Berkshire Eagle,* without apparent embarrassment. In fact, the *Eagle* went so far as to quote Fleisig calling Mayor Doyle a "tough negotiator." Good thing, or Fleisig might have owned the ballpark.

A month after the Fleisig deal was announced, in a development the *Eagle* called "ironic," Curt Preisser was named assistant general manager of Fleisig's Black Bears.

Naturally, the *Eagle* never questioned these goings on. They were too busy beating the new-stadium drums.

"I don't know why they're still doing that," said Chip, "when they know the money's not there."

"Ever-Scrib is a sick man," I said.

Here are the presenting symptoms, which appeared as headlines or items over the last six months:

REVIVE DOWNTOWN STADIUM PLAN

DOWNTOWN STADIUM REMAINS A MUST

A new stadium is necessary for a region so heavily reliant on tourism. . . .

CITY NEEDS STADIUM, AFFILIATED BASEBALL

[A] new stadium the Berkshires so desperately needs . . .

328

Ever-Scrib was even desperate about what the new owners of the Boston Red Sox might do with Fenway Park, clear across the state:

> The prospective new owners appear determined to renovate Fenway Park, a crumbling structure desperately in need of replacement.

Tomorrow on *Oprah*: "People who desperately need new stadiums and the people who love them."

The question Chip and I are still asked, almost daily it seems, is Are we still interested in Wahconah Park? That's hard to answer. On the one hand, we still have a vision of how things could be and we have all these new friends in Pittsfield we'd love to work with. On the other hand, even though most of our political opponents are now out of office—temporarily anyway—we'd still have the power structure against us.

The sad fact is that in Pittsfield, it doesn't really matter who holds office at any given time. The shots are called by Berkshire Bank, the *Eagle*, Cain Hibbard, and General Electric. Whether it's a plan to restore Wahconah Park or a campaign to clean up the Housatonic River, if the Gang of Four doesn't want it, it's not going to happen. No matter what the people want.

And no matter whom they elect.

Sara Hathaway was essentially elected mayor by the Wahconah Yes! voters, who would have gone for Dave Potts if they thought he had a chance. Yet it took Hathaway *nine months* to appoint new park commissioners, one of whom sat in limbo for six additional months, waiting for one commissioner to finally take a hike—you win a case of George Scott bobble-head dolls if you guessed it was Cliff Nilan. Why was he still sitting there? "Political reasons," said Joe Guzzo. "He's part of the old-boy network."

Others have alluded to the Bossidy money, the $1 million check that arrived in a letter from Bossidy, directing that the money be spent in a way that "Cliff Nilan deems appropriate." The theory there was that Nilan was being kept on as a courtesy to Bossidy.

Not everyone is so courteous. A caller to the *Dan Valenti Show* had his own take on Bossidy's $1 million. "Any money Bossidy gives," said the caller, "is coming out of his $120 million in stock options he got for being second in command at GE when they dumped PCBs on our precious city, and second in command when they laid off thousands of workers."

But the possibility of our return to Pittsfield has nothing to do with Sara Hathaway or Cliff Nilan or even Larry Bossidy. There are other forces that need to be dealt with, starting with the Northern League, which currently controls Pittsfield's baseball future.

After the Fleisig contract was signed, Dave Potts and Gene Nadeau, before Nadeau was made a park commissioner, met with Fleisig to see if they could improve the agreement for Pittsfield.

"That contract is a joke and you know it," said Potts. "It's a sweetheart deal."

"I'm not going to give you something if you won't give me something," said Fleisig. "What are you going to give me?"

"What do you want?" asked Nadeau.

"Hypothetically," said Fleisig, "I want to be sure that Bouton and Elitzer are out of the picture, as far as Wahconah Park is concerned, forever."

Then there are the petty officials—both current and former—like Hickey and Massery and Dowd and Lee and Grunin and Kerwood, and even ex-mayor Doyle who, reports say, goes around town telling people he still runs things. Guys who, according to Arlos, hate us simply because they hate our supporters. Like Afghan warlords, they'd rather rule over rubble than share power in paradise.

Behind them all is the Gang of Four—the ones the others have to call to find out what they should think. These are the real obstacles to progress in Pittsfield. Chip and I and Eric Margenau have decided that for us to come back there would have to be nothing short of a regime change.

"We're not coming back to do battle," said Chip. "Everyone's going to have to want us."

"That may not be possible with the *Eagle*—and its weapons of mass distortion," I said. "What about Cain Hibbard?"

"Disband the partnership," said Chip.

"That's a good idea," I said. "What about Berkshire Bank?"

"Let them get behind building the Civic Center or indoor arena that we initially proposed," said Chip. "It would be good for the community and show a change of heart. They could invite us to bring in a hockey team."

Of course, an indoor arena leads back to the *Eagle* property, and the last member of the Gang of Four, General Electric. While there's no direct evidence that GE tried to undermine our plan for Wahconah Park, or that it backed a new stadium to hide a PCB dump site, it's hard not to wonder.

General Electric is the ghost that still haunts Pittsfield. A ghost that walks the streets, carefully watching, keeping the lid on anything that might bubble up, waiting for the last of the witnesses to die. And in spite of what it has done to the community, it walks around in plain view.

This is still "a GE town," as Dan Bianchi said. It's the home of their worldwide plastics division, which employs about five hundred people. Former GE executives run important institutions like the Greylock Federal Credit Union. The board of PEDA (the Pittsfield Economic Development Authority, charged with attracting business to the abandoned, fifty-two acre GE site) has been dominated by former GE executives. Its director Tom Hickey, a GE executive for twenty-three years, is said to be threatening a run for mayor.

"GE has been skilled at involving themselves in the community," said Tim Gray, "so they can keep control."

Control is very important when you are sitting on a toxic time-bomb, with a questionable "settlement," a cleanup of the rest of the Housatonic scheduled for review in 2005, and all of it played out against GE's continual challenges to the EPA order to clean up the nearby Hudson. If you can't control your own hometown, what happens with the rest of the country, not to mention your stock price?

Part of how GE keeps control is spelled out in its own Housatonic River Public Affairs Plan. This is an internal document that Gray said he "found on my doorstep one morning." What it shows, among other things, is how GE keeps tabs on people. "Anyone who is involved in PCBs," said Gray. "Like letter-to-the-editor writers."

GE has lists.

And they have the *Eagle*.

In Berkshire County, it's important to at least *appear* as if you care about the environment. But even when the *Eagle* makes a gesture in that direction, it misleads. A recent Ever-Scrib editorial:

> All across the nation . . . oil and solvents from long-abandoned factories are . . . dribbling into the rivers . . . . On the east side of Pittsfield, where for 70-odd years General Electric made its transformers, filled with a PCB-laden oil. . . . The stuff got everywhere—into the soil, the ground water, the river, people's vegetable gardens.

The key phrases are "dribbling into the rivers" and "the stuff got everywhere," as if the PCBs accidentally leaked out of control. But a much different scenario is described by Vinnie Curro, whose Ravin Auto Body sat next to the abandoned GE buildings on Newell Street. Referring to the tanks of chemical waste that backed up to the Housatonic, Curro said, "The GE bosses would tell their workers to open a valve and take a two-hour lunch."

Based on my experience with Ever-Scrib, I believe Curro.

I also believe Ed Bates.

In 1983, a GE commissioned Stewart Report stated that 40,000 pounds of PCBs had been dumped into the Housatonic River. But Ed Bates, chief of transformers for GE, said his division alone could account for at least two *million* pounds.

And I believe Tim Gray, now a visiting professor at Harvard.

"People would say, 'Tim, you can't fight GE,'" said Gray. "GE employees were always coming to me, 'Tim, take this, I can't do it, GE will stop my pension.' GE told their employees, 'Shut up, you're going to lose your jobs.' Vinnie Curro was dragged through the mud by GE. He had to become an environmentalist."

According to Curro, GE has friends in government.

"I was threatened, you name it," he told me. "I've been checked by every state agency you can imagine. The funniest was the federal. My accountant said [to the investigator they sent], 'Come in the office, would you like a cup of coffee?' I told the guy I've been targeted before. After fifteen minutes checking the books he said, 'This is bullshit, I shouldn't even be here. I got other places to go. What's the way to the Mass Pike?'"

GE has the politicians.

"The city told businesses, 'Stay calm, we'll help you,'" said Gray. "Then the statute of limitations ran out."

And the Chamber of Commerce.

"When the Newell Street property owners came forward to sue GE," said Gray, "the Chamber of Commerce treated them like pariahs. And the banks wouldn't lend them money."

Speaking of banks, the latest news comes from Berkshire Bank, where Mike Daly was just elected president and CEO. And Larry Bossidy was named "nonexecutive" chairman of the board. I'm not sure what *nonexecutive* means, but it can't be good for Wahconah Park. In any case, it looks like Daly will be having more of those meetings with Larry Bossidy just sitting there.

Most ominous of all was Daly's quote in the newspaper, saying that Bossidy would be of great value because "he has good ideas about how to deal with the sharks." This is like saying Godzilla has good ideas about how to deal with the monsters.

What sharks is Daly talking about? Dave Potts, the open-mike fiend? Anne Leaf, the seventy-year-old fax-machine ogre? Gene Nadeau, who can't wait to undermine the bank from his new position as a park commissioner? Any poor devil who might just be *thinking* about poking his head up to ask a few questions?

Or are Chip and I the sharks? And what "good ideas" might Bossidy have in mind for us?

At least we don't have to earn a living in Pittsfield.

Fear of not getting a job, or losing the one you have, is the major instrument of control in high-unemployment cities. It's why people like Jonathan Levine and Dan Valenti are circumspect about how they've been treated. It's why Rick Jones spoke warily about a plumbing inspector's call to his boss. Why GE workers made anonymous calls and why documents are dropped on a doorstep. Folks are afraid of being held "accountable," as Mayor Doyle once put it.

The tragedy in Pittsfield is that the citizens, in order to survive, must rely on the very same people who've harmed them. The best paying jobs are doled out by those in power, leaving the citizens no choice but to help keep the lid on their own grievances.

It's been a strange journey for Chip and me. We started out on a country road and ended up in a back alley—a back alley that's polluted in more ways than one. And our plan for Wahconah Park is the least of the casualties. We're like the old Bowery Boys, who try to help a poor widow recover some lost bonds and discover a dead body in the trunk of a car.

And the story isn't over yet.

In June of 2002, you may have seen a news item about this book: "PublicAffairs to publish new book by Jim Bouton . . . in time for 2003 baseball season." Editor Paul Golob was quoted as saying, "Jim is fearless in opening doors that are closed to others."

I don't know about fearless. Unconscious is more like it.

Submitting the chapters of *Foul Ball* as I wrote them, I got positive feedback from Golob. "I am enjoying the book very much," he emailed me, "and laughing out loud occasionally—a very good sign." Another good sign was that Golob and I agreed on the editing. The only thing we differed on was how much to cut Fleisig's presentation to the Parks Commission. I wanted to keep all sixteen pages, Golob wanted just one, and we compromised at five.

By October, PublicAffairs was pretty hyped up about the book. This would be their big book of the spring, I was told. Catalog copy was written, I had just recorded a promotional audio tape, dinner was planned with the top buyers at Barnes & Noble, and publicity director Gene Taft and I had mapped out a sixteen-city book tour. "Everyone continues to be very excited about your book," Golob wrote, in one of his many effusive emails.

Then, on October 30th, I had lunch with Golob and Peter Osnos, who owns PublicAffairs. Osnos is a sharp-featured man in his late fifties, who favors striped shirts with contrasting white spread collars and cuffs. After a brief discussion about marketing, Osnos talked about the need to document everything in the book, especially what I was saying about GE. "The most important thing in the world to General Electric is how they are perceived as a company," he said. "Any negative references to General Electric have to be balanced by a response from a GE spokesperson."

What the hell was this?

334

"I never asked for a response from the baseball commissioner when I wrote *Ball Four*," I said, annoyed. I couldn't understand Osnos's focus on General Electric, which took up fewer than ten pages of the book. Then it was made a little clearer to me.

"The top lawyer for General Electric happens to be a good friend of mine," said Osnos, as if commenting on the weather. "And he's about to become an investor in PublicAffairs."

What are the odds?

And what should I do? The book was almost ready, a catalogue would soon be printed, names of potential blurb writers were being bandied about. If I jumped ship, how long would it take me to find another publisher? The book could be delayed by months, maybe a year. I wanted to believe the GE thing was just a coincidence.

But I needed to be reassured. A week later I met with Osnos and Golob again. This time I brought Paula, my agent Matt Bialer, and Chip (my partner in all things Wahconah). Osnos, who knew why we were there, walked in shouting angrily. "I don't want any part of this," he roared, jabbing his finger in front of my face. "You're questioning my integrity." At one point, he turned and pointed to pictures of I. F. Stone, Ben Bradlee, and Bob Bernstein, behind him on the wall. "See those pictures? That's my guide, right there."

For twenty minutes Osnos refused to let anyone speak. "And how did you know that Ben Heineman was going to be an investor in PublicAffairs?" he hollered. I told him I hadn't known the lawyer's name until he just said it. "Well, let me tell you something," Osnos continued at the same decibel level. "My friendship with Ben Heineman is more important to me than any book. And Ben Heineman's name WILL NOT GO IN THAT BOOK!"

Let the record show that I never mentioned his name.

After Osnos finally left the room, Golob tried to smooth things over. He talked about the need to back up what I was saying about GE, but he also had some suggestions. "There are ways of rephrasing things so they don't cause legal problems," he said. "And don't worry about Peter. We're going to publish the hell out of this book." Then Golob proceeded to show us some cover designs that the art department had been working on.

In the car on the way back to Massachusetts, Paula and Chip and I tried to figure out what the hell to do. "I've lost that friendly, comfortable feeling about PublicAffairs," said Paula. "But maybe we should stay and try to work things out with them." Chip said, "But if you stay, it might call into question the integrity of the book." And I remembered something Chip had said earlier this summer. Speaking of the James Bond movies, he had said, "The hero would never catch the bad guys if they didn't overreact."

In any case, the decision to go or stay was made for me a few days later. A letter from Golob said, "The subplot about pollution has to be cut, completely," and references to General Electric must be "limited to background" only. "This is strictly an editorial matter," Golob wrote, "and not a business question." It had absolutely nothing to do with GE's top lawyer becoming a partner in PublicAffairs.

Sure. And Jay Pomeroy just loves baseball.

I called Golob to challenge him on his sudden turn-around. "It's a book about saving an old ballpark," he insisted, "it's not about pollution. Pollution is not as salable or marketable."

"The ballpark, yes," I said, "But it's also about the power structure selling its own citizens down the river. The Arundhati Roy quote has been on the opening page from the beginning. What did you think that meant?"

"I never understood the Roy reference," he said.

I felt sorry for Paul Golob. He had done a complete one-eighty on the book after our meeting with Osnos. Before then, he had never had a problem with any of the references to pollution or GE. But Paul is a nice man and I was happy to read in *Publishers Weekly*, a few weeks later, that he had been promoted to the position of vice president at PublicAffairs. It was a promotion that lasted a few months until Golob moved from PublicAffairs to Holt.

One more thing. During his tirade in the office, Peter Osnos had said to me, "If you don't trust me, my integrity, and this publishing house, one hundred percent, then take your book and leave! I won't stop you."

Of course he wouldn't. He'd hire a lawyer to do it. And the first thing the lawyer did was try to buy my silence. During negotiations to get the termination letter that I would need to pitch the book to other publishers, the lawyer told my agent I could keep half the money already paid to me if I promised not to talk or write about why I was leaving PublicAffairs.

"I don't know what my price is for keeping my mouth shut," I told Paula, "but I know it's not $25,000."

I guess I'm lucky that Osnos *didn't* try to stop me. Otherwise it would have taken even longer than three months, plus having had to hire my own attorney, to finally get that termination letter from him.

Why did it take three months? I don't know, but it turned out to be just long enough to make it impossible for another publisher to get the book out by the summer of 2003. Which is one of the reasons I decided to publish *Foul Ball* myself.

Another reason is, I can't be sure the top lawyer for GE won't decide to invest in the entire publishing world, which, sad to say, is down to five companies, or "groups" of imprints, each group under a corporate parent—which itself is part of a conglomerate.

That might also explain today's standard author's contract, which boils down to this offer: "Give us exclusive rights to a piece of your life's work, in all formats and galaxies now and forever, and we may or may not publish your book. If we fail to publish your book within a year and a half after your manuscript has been approved and edited, which itself can take six months or more, you may request a reversion of rights by . . . ."

The editors at the publishing companies even feel obliged to apologize for these contracts. "It's standard in the industry," they say, "there's nothing we can do about it. You just have to trust us."

I'm an old fashioned guy. I believe in hard work and fair play, and let the best man win. That's what I've always loved about sports. You don't make the team because you know somebody—you have to do it on the field. And don't blame it on the umpires if you lose the game—if you were good enough, you could have put it out of reach. Nothing was out of reach. Anything was possible.

When I started out on this adventure, I just wanted to save an old ballpark and have some fun. I knew that building stadiums with taxpayer dollars was fundamentally wrong. What I didn't realize was the extent to which a pathological optimist could be made so suspicious that it is scary.

o o o

SMOKING GUN

As this book went to press, a document called a Release Notification Form—to be completed by property owners who find pollution on their land—was discovered at the office of the Massachusetts Department of Environmental Protection. It shows that the property owned by the *Berkshire Eagle,* which it had offered to Pittsfield as the site for a new baseball stadium, is contaminated with a "release of oil" sufficient to qualify it as a "disposal site," according to a DEP letter acknowledging receipt of the form. The entry for "Date you obtained knowledge of the release" is January 12, 2001.

January 12, 2001, was three weeks before Chip and I first met with Andy Mick and the boys from Berkshire Sports & Events at the North End Restaurant, and nearly five months before Pittsfield would vote for or against a Civic Authority that would build and manage a new stadium on that property. What's more, a special clause—inserted into the Civic Authority Act by BS&E lawyers—would have transferred the liability for any cleanup from BS&E to the Civic Authority and ultimately to the citizens of Pittsfield.

Forget PCBs for a minute. If Vinnie Curro is only 10% right—and his estimate of "tons of automobile oil" now has some documentation—a cleanup could still cost someone fifteen to twenty million. If that's not the case, and the *Eagle* had nothing to hide, why wasn't the Release Notification Form made public at the time? Instead, what the people got was Andy Mick saying, "there's no hidden agenda here."

No agenda. Just a Release Notification Form.

Observant readers will also realize that this particular Release Notification Form is not related to the 2002 soil samples rumored to have been taken by or on behalf of CVS or the 1994 test borings still being investigated by Tim Gray. More likely, it is related to the tests commissioned by BS&E to show that the property could support a baseball stadium.

This raises several questions, besides the whereabouts of the 1994 and 2002 test results. Why would BS&E order the tests whose results are cited above, if testing had already been done in 1994? Could they not find the 1994 results? Or did they not like them? As Tim Gray explains it, the deeper you go, the more stuff you find. And the corollary to that seems to be: the more stuff you find the harder it is to locate the results.

While these pages were at the final blueline stage, I received a call from Clarence Fanto, the managing editor of the *Berkshire Eagle*. Fanto had seen an uncorrected galley and wanted to tell me I had gotten some facts wrong.

"The cleanup is only going to cost $150,000 to $200,000," said Fanto, "and not the one hundred and fifty to two hundred million you have in your book."

I told Fanto that the Release Notification Form described pollution that exceeded the leakage you might find at a car dealership; that Curro's cleanup estimate referred to the entire area, not just the proposed CVS site; and that if it had once been a junkyard, then PCBs are probably involved and a cleanup *could* cost tens of millions.

"Is it just possible," I said, "that the reason people are forced to make guesses is a lack of openness? Or credibility?"

I asked Fanto if he knew why the Release Notification Form had never been made public by the *Eagle*, especially prior to the Civic Authority vote. "I have no idea," he said, "That's the business side of the newspaper. That's completely separate from the news side."

I had this sudden image of Jack Dew, the investigative reporter, grilling Andy Mick, his businessman boss. Then it faded.

Fanto also said he'd heard about the 1994 test borings and the more recent CVS borings, but didn't know the results. I suggested it might be a good story for one of his reporters. Fanto said I could check it out myself by calling the company that had done the testing—Maxymillian Technologies, in Pittsfield. He said they could probably also confirm the cleanup costs.

I remembered the name Maxymillian from a conversation I had once had with Vinnie Curro. So after I hung up with Fanto, I called Curro to get more details about that, and the history of the property.

"Do you know anything about junkyards down there?" I asked.

"It used to be Shapiro's junkyard," said Curro. "All through the '40s, '50s, and '60s, GE was dumping PCBs into junkyards. There was also a brook through there that's been covered up."

I asked him if Maxymillian would have that information.

"Don't trust Maxymillian," he said. "They do all the work for GE. They do their testing *and* their cleanup. They're like twins."

I reminded Curro that he had once told me Maxymillian had been given some land by the city.

"Yeah," said Curro. "On East Street where they have their head-quarters. There was no competitive bidding. A guy named Virgilio bid higher, but he didn't get it. It's terrible to have to say it."

It's terrible to have to write it. I thanked Curro for his time, and placed another call. This one to Peter Arlos, to see what he could remember about a Maxymillian land deal.

"That was back in the '80s," said Arlos, "when Charles Smith was the mayor. We gave it away at a cut-rate price. Cut-rate, you understand? I was the only one that voted against it."

Where do you start with something like this?

How will the people of Pittsfield ever learn the truth? Is some-one going to investigate those test borings? Can the results be believed? Will the DEP require testing for PCBs?

To show you how things work, the DEP's Date Received stamp on the Release Notification Form reads May 10, 2002. Meaning someone at the *Eagle* or Cain Hibbard Myers & Cook, who handled the matter, sat on it for *sixteen months* before sending it to the DEP.

What's more, the letter from the DEP acknowledging receipt of the Release Notification Form, addressed to Andy Mick and head-lined Urgent Legal Matter: Prompt Action Necessary, informs Mick that he has until May 10, 2003—one year from the *receive* date, not the release date—to take some kind of action.

Or not.

By that time, the *Eagle,* in conjunction with CVS, may already have begun to develop it as a strip mall. According to a recent edition of the *Eagle*, plans are underway for a spring 2003 groundbreaking.

I asked Tim Gray if he thought the *Eagle* would get away with it. Gray repeated what a guy at the DEP had told him: "We've got seven hundred sites, and two guys in the office."

"It's a tough battle," said Gray. "The corporations write the laws and the politicians underfund the agencies."

The DEP guy also told Gray that they would not be happy if the *Eagle* property were developed without DEP approval. "Keep your eyes open for bulldozers," he told Gray.

Good advice for us all.

o o o

SPRING–SUMMER 2003

The bulldozers arrived in the spring of 2003 . . .

Nine hundred tons of contaminated soil were removed from a 2.5 acre parcel of land that, along with other property owned by the *Berkshire Eagle*, had been envisioned as the site of a new baseball stadium. The parcel, which the *Eagle* had acquired through Berkshire Sports & Events for $1.23 million, was sold for $1.35 million, plus the cleanup costs, to the CVS Corporation, which plans to build a strip mall.

The cleanup costs, originally estimated at $150,000 to $200,000, ended up being closer to $400,000. Had the new stadium not been defeated in the June 2001 referendum, the cleanup costs would have been passed along to the citizens of Pittsfield.

The contamination—mostly petroleum products—contained traces of PCBs but not enough to trigger a state investigation. Environmentalists, however, questioned the testing supervised by a licensed site professional hired by CVS.

"The entire [stadium] footprint was never tested," said Tim Gray of the Housatonic River Initiative, referring to an additional nine acres still owned by the *Berkshire Eagle*. "And they only went down ten feet."

But as far as the *Eagle* was concerned, the case was closed and the defeat of the stadium was everyone else's fault. In a May 20, 2003, editorial entitled SCRATCH ANOTHER NAYSAYER LIE, Ever-Scrib wrote:

> Scratch another fabrication from the heap of lies used by Pittsfield's naysayer class to frighten a gullible citizenry into rejecting the construction of a downtown [stadium]. The [location] where the stadium would have been built is not the site of major contamination, as at least one environmentalist and one deluded South County author maintained.

Ever-Scrib's "heap of lies" editorial had only two fabrications: (1) My involvement with Pittsfield began *after* the new stadium had been defeated; and (2) the possibility of a polluted site only became an issue *two years later*, when it was revealed in the hardcover edition of this book.

While Ever-Scrib was suffering from a time warp, the *Eagle*'s Bill Carey was reporting that BS&E had been fined $3,750 by the state for reporting—a year late—that its stadium site was polluted. According to BS&E attorney Michael Ostroskey (of Cain Hibbard Myers & Cook), the penalty was reduced from $7,500 because of "mitigating circumstances."

I wondered if a mitigating circumstance might be that BS&E wanted to withhold evidence of pollution until after the vote on a new stadium.

The chances of the *Eagle* property ever being fully tested now seem remote. In August 2003, the Environmental Protection Agency reversed a twenty-five-year-old policy, relaxing restrictions on selling PCB contaminated land.

Meanwhile, shortly after the publication of *Foul Ball*, Jay Pomeroy was let go as Global Communications Manager of GE Plastics, and General Electric instituted a new policy prohibiting its employees from identifying themselves as being connected to GE when involved in non-GE activities.

And there were other developments . . .

END PART I

PART II
FALL 2003–FALL 2004

CITY OF PITTSFIELD
Mayor James M. Ruberto

January 13, 2004

Mr. Jim Bouton
Mr. Chip Elitzer
Mr. Eric Margenau

Gentlemen:

On behalf of the City of Pittsfield, we invite you to bring minor league baseball back to the city.

We strongly feel that Wahconah Park has not only a proud past as a venue for minor league baseball, but also a very promising future. Based on our understanding of your 2001 proposal, we would like to work with you to build that future.

We look forward to your response.

Sincerely,

James M. Ruberto
Mayor

Gerald Lee
President,
City Council

Michael Filipi
Chair,
Parks Commission

James McGrath
Director,
Department of
Community Services

CHAPTER 14

"I promise you it will be different this time"

The letter on the preceding page was not a joke.

At least not right away.

On November 4, 2003, Jimmy Ruberto defeated Sara Hathaway in a re-run for mayor. The next day, Chip and I got an email from Dave Potts that read, in part:

```
>  I've spent a lot of time with Jimmy over the
>  last year or so and I can tell you he's a huge
>  baseball fan . . . and [he's] become a believer
>  in the value of retaining and capitalizing on
>  the historic nature of Wahconah Park. I've
>  been asked by Jimmy to act as a liason of
>  sorts and in the interest of covering all the
>  bases (no pun intended) I'd appreciate it if
>  the two of you would indulge my request for a
>  face-to-face conversation with Mayor Elect
>  Ruberto. The meeting will serve to either, #1,
>  forever close an ugly chapter in the history
>  of Wahconah Park, or #2, give birth to what
>  could become one of the greatest sports
>  stories ever written about.
```

This did not come as a total surprise. Ever since our rejection by the Parks Commission in 2001, Potsy had been emailing us with the latest from the Pittsfield street. He said he was asked "almost on a daily basis, if there is any chance that the Bouton group might return to the picture."

Our response was always the same: No thanks. No way.

The surprise was that Ruberto would accede to Potsy's request for a meeting. Ruberto had been a prominent new-stadium supporter. And *Foul Ball*—which Potsy was calling "The Official Handbook of

Political Chicanery in Pittsfield"—was still a hot topic, with people calling each other to read their favorite descriptions of the local politicians. One of those pols was Jimmy Ruberto, whom Peter Arlos had said was too afraid to stand up for anything, including the National Anthem.

Could the Oracle of Delphi have been wrong?

Or was this a political payoff? Apparently, Ruberto's margin of victory over Hathaway, like her margin over him in the last election, had come from Wahconah Park supporters, and the mayor's request to meet with us might have been his campaign promise to Potsy for delivering those votes.

Out of sheer curiosity, Chip and I agreed to a meeting. Also, I have to admit I liked Potsy's line about "greatest sports stories ever written."

But what were the odds of us actually going back to Pittsfield? Paula didn't even like me going there to promote the book.

"Do me a favor," she would say as I'd be walking out the door. "Don't eat or drink anything up there."

Ruberto probably hadn't even read *Foul Ball*. If he had, he would have known that the people he should really meet with were Paula and Cindy. And Chip's Mom.

"DON'T do Wahconah Park," Maggie Elitzer emailed Chip after hearing that we'd be meeting with Ruberto. "You can't afford the time, the money, or the passion. But I love you in spite of your lack of good judgment."

The meeting took place at 9:00 a.m., on November 12, in the Elitzers' dining room, next to the kitchen where the really big decisions are made. It was just the guys—Ruberto, Potsy, Chip, and me. No sense wasting our wives in a preliminary round.

Ruberto, a Pittsfield native with the enthusiasm of a twelve-year-old boy, appears younger than his fifty-six years. With his square, unlined face and wire-rimmed glasses, the mayor elect looks more like a small town minister than the former CEO of a Texas plastics company, which is what he was before returning to his hometown with his wife Ellen in 2001.

After some small talk about his hopes for Pittsfield and how much he loved Wahconah Park—"it's the centerpiece of what I'm doing"—the mayor elect had two questions: What would it take to get us to bring back our original plan? And could we put a team together for 2004?

Chip and I pretended we hadn't given the matter much thought.

Speaking theoretically, of course—and *assuming* we would even be interested, which we might not be—we said we'd need to get some kind of written invitation from the city, but that in any case, it was too late for us to field a team for 2004, which might not be bad because it would give us a whole year to do it right—*assuming* we even wanted to do it in the first place, that is.

In other words, we could be persuaded.

With one big if: IF Ruberto promised we wouldn't have to fight any more political battles. We said we wouldn't even consider returning without such a guarantee. The mayor elect said he was already working on it.

"You wouldn't believe the people he's talking to," said Potsy, shaking his head in awe. "Some of your biggest opponents from last time."

"I'm telling everybody that having you guys back is in the best interest of Pittsfield," said Ruberto. "And I firmly believe that."

He had us believing it, too.

Almost.

Right after the meeting, Chip and I joked that it might be a trap—they were inviting us back just so they could beat us up again. But, we knew it couldn't be a trap with Potsy involved. And Ruberto seemed so genuine. Unless he was the best actor we ever saw.

"I need to see him up close," said Paula. "I want to look into his face and see if he's for real."

An inspection was planned for December 7 at the Elitzers'.

Meanwhile, Chip and I started to work on a plan. If there was no baseball in 2004, what could we accomplish by Opening Day 2005?

"If we raise enough money," said Chip, "we could do in one year what we had originally planned to do over five years."

Chip began crunching numbers. I sketched bleachers and locker room floor plans. We told Paula and Cindy we were just playing.

But the Parks Commission wasn't just playing. A few days after our meeting with Ruberto, they voted to recommend that lame-duck

Mayor Hathaway break off negotiations with Jonathan Fleisig regarding the 2004 baseball season. Evidently, weeks after his license with Pittsfield had expired—following another disastrous season at Wahconah Park—Fleisig was still using the city as a bargaining chip to get a better deal in New Haven, Connecticut.

By now, you can guess what happened next.

Three days after Fleisig denied he was negotiating with New Haven, he announced that he was moving his team there. And two days after that, in a *Berkshire Eagle* editorial—GOODBYE TO THE BLACK BEARS—our man Ever-Scrib wrote:

> The loss of the Black Bears almost assuredly marks the end of Pittsfield's proud history in professional baseball, a day that became inevitable with the defeat of a proposal for a new stadium . . . and a crumbling Wahconah Park looks forward to a lonely old age.

A stock *Eagle* editorial with a Black Bears insert.

Our second meeting with Mayor Elect Ruberto was a lunch affair featuring Cindy's famous white bean and escarole soup, with turkey sandwich fixings. The new additions to the group included Paula, Cindy, and our other partner, Eric Margenau, who was willing to give Pittsfield another shot.

"Hell yeah," Eric said. "I'm with you guys, all the way."

Now it was up to our wives.

After the raving over the soup had died down, Chip and Eric and I laid out our dream scenario: we would raise money in a limited public offering, mostly from Pittsfield investors if possible, and spend at least $1 million on Wahconah Park by Opening Day 2005. The rest of the deal would essentially match what we had proposed in 2001.

Ruberto's eyes got wide at the mention of a million dollars.

"You think you could really *do* that?" he said, as if he couldn't quite believe what he was hearing.

"We'd probably end up spending closer to $1.5 million," I said, opening my big mouth, "but we couldn't commit to that right now."

Ruberto's cheeks reddened at the possibilities.

And we weren't finished. We said if things went well with the money raising and the permitting, we might be able to break ground as early as July 2004, only eight months away. But we'd need to get a license agreement signed as quickly as possible so we could start meeting with architects and engineers, while Chip got to work on a prospectus.

Now we were into the nuts and bolts. Ruberto questioned Eric about getting a team. Eric explained that the Northeast and Atlantic leagues were in a state of flux, but that they were always looking for strong ownership groups and good places to play. And we had both.

"I have to tell you this makes me very nervous," said Paula, who gets uneasy when things go a little too smoothly. She looked directly at Ruberto. "Our first experience was so unpleasant. How can we be sure that it won't happen again?"

"Paula, I promise you it will be different this time," said Ruberto, who was very courteous to both wives throughout the meeting. "You have my word on that."

"He's got some friends who aren't speaking to him," said Potsy, with an admiring smile and a nod toward Ruberto. Potsy wanted us to know that the mayor elect was spending some political capital.

"There are a few people we're not going to win over," said Ruberto, "and that's just the way it is."

He suggested that it would make his job a little bit easier if I "toned things down a bit" with *Foul Ball*. Suddenly awash in team spirit, I agreed to cut short my promotional tour.

"I'll keep the dates I've already scheduled," I said. "But at least now I can talk about a happy ending. And a gutsy mayor."

Ruberto smiled proudly and promised again that we would have his full support.

"The letter from the city is crucial," I said. "We've always had the people behind us. If we have the government, too, the big boys will have to go along. And we'll eventually win them over, too. If we succeed, what are they going to do, sit on the sidelines and pout?"

"I'll get a letter drafted," said Ruberto.

The conversation was great and so was the soup. By the time the meeting was over, Cindy was pouring leftovers into a plastic container for the mayor elect; he was smiling and shaking our hands, and we were calling him Jimmy.

The postgame analysis went well:

Cindy: Jimmy Ruberto seems like a very decent man.

Paula: I liked him. And I didn't think I was going to.

Me: The book doesn't seem to have hurt us.

Chip: Without *Foul Ball*, we never would have been invited back in the first place. The book made it clear that we really did have a good proposal and that we really were treated badly.

So what should we do?

The tipping point came from Cindy.

"Well, I think they should do it," she said to Paula. "The boys have so much fun together."

"That's true," said Chip.

"Look what's happened here," I said, like a high school civics teacher. "An entire city has turned itself around. Potsy's right, it's a helluva story. It's democracy in action."

"I hope you're right," said Paula.

The new year got off to a fascinating start.

On January 2, 2004, his first day in office, Mayor Ruberto announced that he was interested in bringing an independent minor league baseball team back to Pittsfield, "but only if the owner is interested in making a significant investment, roughly in the neighborhood of $1 million to $1.5 million, to renovate Wahconah Park."

Chip and I laughed out loud. This was quite a request since no owner had ever invested more than $75,000 in Wahconah Park, and the last guy to do that, Fleisig, had just left town because he was losing money. How could the mayor propose such a thing?

It was so hard to absorb that it took Ever-Scrib until January 11th to respond. In an *Eagle* editorial—OUT AT HOME—he wrote:

> It is difficult to imagine why anyone would invest $1 or $1.5 million in an aging ballpark that is beyond hope of reclamation. . . . Pittsfield has gotten itself into a bad situation . . . and there may be no getting out of it.

The mayor's request was pretty bold from our perspective, as well. We had yet to receive the letter inviting us back to Pittsfield that the mayor had promised. A draft finally arrived two days later, for our approval. The only problem was the wording. Specifically, phrases like:

> ...*we invite you to speak with us about your interest*...*there may be areas of shared vision*...*which could form the basis for a broader dialogue*...*we look forward to a possible meeting in the near future.*

Chip and I were on the phone with each other in a flash.

"This is bullshit," I said. "*Our interest? Areas of shared vision? A possible meeting in the near future?* Get me rewrite!"

"I agree," said Chip. "It's not what we talked about."

"The mayor needs to understand that it's not a done deal and that we need to be won over," I said. "I once proposed marriage to Wahconah Park. Now let them propose to us."

"To have any meaning for investors or the leagues, not to mention us," said Chip, "the letter has to clearly demonstrate that we're wanted."

"Exactly."

So, Chip and I edited our own letter of invitation. The mayor then had it copied on city stationery, got it signed by city officials, and released it to the media (see page 345).

Whew. You've got to watch these guys.

Then the real fun began.

After back-to-back front page stories in the *Berkshire Eagle*—NEW MAYOR MAKES PITCH TO BOUTON and OVERTURE TO BOUTON GETS GOOD REVIEWS—poor Ever-Scrib set himself up again. In a January 18 editorial—RUBERTO'S INVITATION TO PLAY BALL—he wrote:

> With the devastating failure of the new stadium initiative... Wahconah Park is of no use to the city rotting away empty... the Bouton group left few bridges unburned three years ago... it failed to land a team... the mayor has given them a chance to put up or shut up. We'll see which option they choose.

It was satisfying to see the *Eagle* trying to guess what might happen for a change, rather than know in advance.

After the city's stunning invitation Chip and I received a flurry of phone calls and emails:

"I nearly fell into my cereal bowl this morning."

"Please consider the mayor's invitation and help keep our beautiful Wahconah Park. It's so necessary, and you're the ones to do it!"

"If you need volunteers, you can count on me."

"Pleeeeese say yes."

And from Steve Picheny, "Congratulations. They had to do it. It's the right thing. Let me know if I can help."

"You're on the team," I told him.

It was a wonderful feeling. Chip and I were back in the dream business again. Of course we said yes a week later. How could we not, with such a warmly worded invitation.

As I traveled around the country, finishing up my abbreviated book tour, I enjoyed telling everyone about the new happy ending in Pittsfield. It always came as a big surprise, and people in the audience would smile and sometimes applaud. It seemed to restore their faith in humanity, which hadn't been having a very good year.

The most rewarding venues are colleges. With *Foul Ball* cutting across several disciplines, I was invited to speak at classes with names like Public Policy (Duke), Urban Studies (University of Illinois), History of Media (Rutgers), Stadiums, Politics, & Media (Villanova), Baseball & Society (NYU), and Journalism (Columbia), among others.

Afterward, I'd sit around with the students and talk about whatever interested them. "What can people do?" they'd ask regarding the lack of democracy. "Get involved and take notes," I'd say. As the philosopher Walter Benjamin said, "Every true story is useful."

I especially liked meeting with the journalism students. Young as they were, they all wanted to have an impact—immediately if not sooner. After I would finish speaking (before the happy ending) I thought a few go-getters were going to march straight to Pittsfield and try to get to the bottom of things. One of them actually did come, just to look around. I have high hopes for that kid.

The problem is, where would he find work? Certainly not at the *Eagle*. And not at WAMC, the local public radio station that venerates the work of investigative journalists but doesn't have one on staff.

What WAMC does have is a news director who at least saw how we'd been treated in Pittsfield.

"What they did to you guys was disgusting," Susan Arbetter told me, during a taping at WAMC on the subject of *Foul Ball*.

Unfortunately, no such sentiment ever made it onto the air. Instead, what listeners heard was an edited two-part piece with balanced quotes, but which omitted any discussion of the media—WAMC or the *Eagle*. Their role in the story, Arbetter explained, would be saved for a guest appearance by me on WAMC's *Media Project*—which she later said would be "better on *Vox Pop* because it's twice as long." But a guest appearance never happened.

What did happen, however, is a good illustration of how WAMC has whitewashed both itself and the *Eagle* on a story that, if it had been properly covered, might not have been so "disgusting." The following is a verbatim transcript of the comments of WAMC's Executive Director Alan Chartock, which aired on the *Media Project* shortly after *Foul Ball* came out.

> *Jim Bouton, the famous* Ball Four *author, wanted to have a baseball stadium in Pittsfield. He wanted the city government to give him a long-term lease on this thing. And he got very angry when he didn't get it—when he and his two business partners, and I emphasize the word* business *partners, didn't get what they wanted. And so now the question is: Did the media let him down? And he wrote a long book about it, and I'm mentioned throughout the book, and called this and that, and he said I'm a courageous guy when I took on GE, but when it came to "my baseball stadium, he wasn't there to help me, and that's probably because he has a column in the* Berkshire Eagle, *and the* Berkshire Eagle *was involved in getting the other kind of stadium, as opposed to the little stadium"—it's a long story, but the point is, people will say whatever they want and Jim Bouton has a lot of power. He had a full page in the* Editor & Publisher *magazine, a full-page story. He's always saying 'poor little me,' but in fact, he's got all these friends, and he manipulates the media shamelessly!*

It was that kind of non-reporting that led me to accept an invitation to speak at the National Conference on Media Reform in Madison, Wisconsin, back in November, 2003. The event, attended by media activists from all over the country and many members of Congress, was organized to challenge (successfully, so far) the FCC's decision to relax the rules against cross ownership of media properties. The sponsors of the conference saw *Foul Ball* as a case study of what can happen when too much power rests in too few hands.

A mini-example of media power is WAMC, which already owns twelve stations in the Northeast. "The problem," said Jeff Cohen, founder of the media watch group FAIR, "is that when WAMC buys a new station it frequently replaces the well respected media program *CounterSpin,* with its own *Media Project,* where the hosts just sit around and laugh."

A far greater problem, of course, exists on the national level, where one of the the leading voices arguing in favor of media monopolies happens to be *Berkshire Eagle* owner Dean Singleton. Can you imagine if Singleton also owned a television station in Pittsfield, which he could have done had the courts not blocked the FCC rule changes?

Two weeks after the Conference on Media Reform, I was a guest on *NOW with Bill Moyers.* Moyers had heard me on a radio show in Wisconsin and had his producer call me. The show aired during a PBS Television fund-raising drive and generated a lot of phone calls.

According to a *NOW* producer, "the show pledged better than it ever has, something like $2,500 per minute. To give you some idea how good this is, the average is $1,000." The next day the Amazon. com sales ranking for *Foul Ball* jumped up from 5,267 to 33.

The show's producers also received letters from lawyers for GE and MediaNews Group, and from publisher Peter Osnos of Public Affairs. They essentially told Moyers their side of the story and demanded that he retract mine. (If you enjoy a good food fight you can read their letters, and Moyers' and my responses, on the web site: www. foulball.com.)

The lawyers' only valid critique was that *Foul Ball* should not have been described as an "investigative report," but rather a diary. Being the good journalist that he is, Moyers apologized, on the air, for presenting my story as truth, rather than "truth as [Bouton] saw it."

"That, of course, is why a man writes a book," said Moyers, "to tell his version of things." Moyers then invited the letter writers "to come on this show and give their version." They declined.

Speaking of truth, an interesting bit of information was inadvertently revealed by the lawyer for MediaNews Group. "The *Eagle* was contributing $2 million in cash," the lawyer said in his letter to Moyers. "It was to receive no benefit in return, other than the right to name the stadium."

I nearly fell off my chair. Naming rights! Who knew that naming rights were part of the deal? Certainly not the readers of the *Berkshire Eagle*, who have yet to be informed as I write this. What are naming rights worth? According to *Street & Smith's Sports Business Journal*, the average naming rights deal for a single A, affiliated team in 2001 was $3.2 million for 13.6 years! Some contribution.

Bill Moyers believes the media monopoly story is the most important one in America today because it determines what all the other stories are and how they are covered. I agree.

March 8, 2004 was a nice day. Besides being my sixty-fifth birthday, it was the day the Pittsfield Parks Commission voted unanimously to approve the license agreement between the city and Wahconah Park, Inc., which was the name of our fledgling corporation.

As always, when Wahconah Park is on the agenda, the little room at Springside House was filled with supporters. Dave Potts, Betty Quadrozzi, Elaine Soldato, Sue Gordon, Jim Moran, Katy Roucher, Thelma Barzottini, Tim Zwingelstein, and the rest of the gang. This time, however, there was a festive air, with people sensing that something good might happen.

As Chip said, "It's just about show time, Jim."

This was a special meeting of the Parks Commission—the opposite of the ad hoc postponements we faced in 2001—and we were the only item on the agenda. We even had an opening act: Mayor Ruberto and City Solicitor Chris Speranzo, who, with Chip's help, had drafted the agreement. Plus our own sexy cheerleaders: Paula and Cindy, all dressed up for the TV cameras and the anticipated dinner celebration afterwards.

The mayor led it off. "We need to look at the level of commitment we are seeing from this group," said Ruberto. "This is a $1.5 million investment made by a private group to improve a publicly owned facility. I strongly urge you to welcome this group to Pittsfield."

City Solicitor Speranzo explained that the agreement was "the same performance based concept they had proposed in 2001," that it was "non-exclusive, allowing for community events and sports groups," and that "the maintenance provisions differ from previous park licenses in relieving the City of all responsibilities."

For some reason, it sounded so much better coming from them than it had from Chip and me.

"It's the best license agreement I've seen in my forty years here," said Commissioner John Marchesi. "It's the first one I could understand."

Then it was time for the Chip and Jim portion of the program. This was the moment we'd been waiting for, and I actually had butterflies as I walked to the front of the room. It was like taking the mound in the World Series, knowing you've got your good stuff.

Chip began with the financial details. He said we were looking to raise $3 million, primarily from local investors, and that our annual expenses would be about $1 million. He also promised that Pittsfield would be featured in the team name, not Berkshire County. This brought murmurs of approval from the audience. "We think this is a tremendous opportunity for Pittsfield," Chip said. "We love this old ballpark; we love baseball."

My contribution was a flip-chart presentation with sketches of planned improvements, including bleachers, locker rooms, restrooms, new dugouts with our Not-So-Luxury Boxes above, twenty-four concession stands for our Shops and Taste of the Berkshires food court, and a Hall of Fame Walkway. Regarding the ladies restrooms, I quoted Chip's line about our plan to "quadruple the pottage."

We explained that we hoped to begin construction that summer and be ready for Opening Day 2005. To achieve that timetable, we needed to move down four tracks simultaneously: architectural, engineering, permitting, and fund-raising. A delay in any one could set us back. Chip reminded everyone that this was a big project and that we couldn't do it all by ourselves.

"Unless we work together it won't succeed," he said. "We can't guarantee success any more than we can guarantee a winning baseball team, but we can promise we'll do the best we can."

After Chip and I sat down, Chairman Mike Filpi praised Mayor Ruberto "for showing a lot of courage" by inviting us back. As the commissioners prepared to vote, the room got quiet. People leaned forward in their seats. Paula reached over and held Cindy's hand.

Then they voted: 5–0 to endorse the license agreement.

A cheer went up. And the Wahconah Park faithful, having saved up two and a half years worth of applause, let it all out.

Then they hung around for a while.

A long while.

"No one wants to go home," someone said.

After we had signed the agreement, and everyone in the room had hugged each other several times, and we had all said our goodbyes, Paula and I and Cindy and Chip celebrated at Trattoria Rustica in Pittsfield. We ate the food and drank the water. Also the wine.

It was a very happy birthday.

We were back in the saddle again.

The next morning, Chip and I headed for Pittsfield, which now seemed like a different place. People who had seen that morning's front page story in the *Eagle* were stopping us on the street to congratulate us and express their affection for Wahconah Park.

"We just love your plans for the ballpark," a couple said to us during breakfast at Adrien's Diner, next to Wahconah Park.

Strangers shouted "Thank you!" from passing cars and trucks. People flashed thumbs up at us through store windows.

Chip and I were feeling so welcome we did something we never thought we'd do. We had lunch at DelGallo's. What would that be like, we wondered? Would Nilan and the boys be there, hunched over their drinks? And what would Remo think? Would he even talk to us?

The answer came the minute we slipped into a booth. Remo marched right over with a scowl on his face. He pointed at Chip.

"You!" he said in a loud voice.

"Don't look at me," said Chip, with wide-eyed innocence, pointing at me across the table. "I didn't write the book."

"You're the one who talked about bringing the hamster," said Remo, referring to Chip's idea for testing food at DelGallo's. The scowl on Remo's face was showing signs of cracking.

"Hi Remo, Jim Bouton," I said, offering my hand.

"I know who you are," he said, smiling now. "I seen your picture in the paper. And I know all about your book, too. I got people sending me copies with the parts about me underlined. Another friend from California just sent me one. People all over are telling me about it."

"You know I had some nice things to say about you," I said. "It was only some of your clientele that we had questions about."

"I know, I read the book," he said, sliding into the booth next to Chip. "You think you could autograph one of my copies?"

Not everyone wanted an autographed copy.

A few days after lunch at DelGallo's, Chip had an unpleasant encounter with former City Councilor James Massery, in a gym at a College Fair in the high school attended by Chip's boys, Sam and Jacob. Chip was manning the Dartmouth booth, answering questions and handing out literature about his alma mater.

"I really didn't appreciate the way I was portrayed in that book," said Massery, confronting Chip in a loud voice. "You said things about me so you could make a profit on his book."

People nearby stopped talking and turned to look.

"You lied," said Massery, in the same tone of voice. By now a small crowd had gathered. The crowd included teachers, classmates, and friends of Sam and Jacob.

"I should tell Dartmouth you're a liar," said Massery, seemingly oblivious of the attention he was attracting. "They shouldn't have a liar representing them."

Chip, the gentleman, said nothing.

"I'm willing to let it go," said Massery, gearing down to a hostile smile. "But maybe I won't let it go."

And that was it, except for the letter Chip sent to Massery the next day. Chip denied he had misquoted Massery in the book, and pointed out that Massery's line in the book about "scores to settle" was reinforced by his words at the College Fair. Then Chip complimented Massery on his candor and his refusal to waffle or pander like so many politicians.

"We now have a chance to do something good for Pittsfield," Chip ended his letter. "I'm willing to leave the past in the past, and I'm sure Jim is, too. Will you join us?"

Massery never responded.

Other book critics included Gerry Doyle, Gary Grunin, Matt Kerwood, and Jonathan Fleisig. They said they hadn't read the book, but that friends had read passages to them. I enjoyed their comments, especially Fleisig's.

> **Doyle:** I wouldn't waste my money buying it.
> **Grunin:** It sounds like a pretty good work of fiction.
> **Kerwood:** Well, I don't like him.
> **Fleisig:** He's a bitter old man who lost, OK?

By the way, Doyle did not deny that he told A-Mart owner Ray Parrott, back in 2001, that "They're not going to get it" because "the fix is in."

Maybe nobody read him that part.

After the book was released Ever-Scrib weighed in with a long editorial, challenging my version of events and countering with his own so-called "truth telling."

As for truth, I offer the unsolicited remarks of Phil Scalise, the guy that Berkshire Sports & Events had said could tell us what was wrong with Wahconah Park. Instead, he told us what was wrong with BS&E.

"Those guys fed the public a whole line of bullshit," said Scalise. "I told them they had problems with [the new stadium site!]. Wahconah Park is a good park. It can be made to work. It won't take much."

Then there were the comments of City Councilor Dan Bianchi.

"The most uncomfortable book I've ever read," he said. "I believe it will be the tough-to-take medicine we need in Pittsfield. It shows all of our flaws and gives us an opportunity to address the way we approach things."

That last part might not be so easy.

Apparently, shortly after the license was signed, Tom Murphy—Gerry Doyle's director of community development—marched into Mayor Ruberto's office and heatedly tried to persuade him to change his mind. In a two-pronged attack Michelle Rivers, Murphy's wife, marched into the city solicitor's office and gave *him* what for. Meanwhile, Cliff "Everybody's just going to have to live with it" Nilan was banned from even calling the mayor's office following a very unpleasant conversation with one of the mayor's secretaries.

But the vast majority of citizens were still on our side, rooting for us harder than ever—although Paula had her own idea why that might be.

"I think they were surprised that someone could write a book like that and still be alive," she said.

o o o

CHAPTER 15

"Baseball's Garden of Eden"

When I wasn't in Pittsfield with Chip, I was hunched over my light table at home, positioning my latest sketches over Clark & Green's most recent architectural drawings.

"Are you having fun?" asked Paula.

"Yes, I am," I said. "I was born to do this."

When I was a kid I had three main hobbies: playing baseball, drawing pictures, and building forts.

"Now you have all three," said Paula, smiling. "I'm so glad."

A few weeks after our license with the city had been signed, Mayor Ruberto was casting about for someone to play a baseball game at Wahconah Park on the Fourth of July. This was traditionally a big weekend in Pittsfield, with its famous parade of marching bands from around the country, followed by a ballgame and fireworks.

Since Chip and I wouldn't have a team until 2005, the mayor asked us how we'd feel about the Dukes—a New England Collegiate League team based in nearby Hinsdale, and named for its owner, former Boston Red Sox General Manager Dan Duquette—playing a game there that day.

The mayor didn't want the game to interfere with our construction plans. Forget construction, we didn't want it interfering with our *marketing* plans. If we were going to invest money in Wahconah Park, we preferred that the city not showcase a future competitor.

So we gave the mayor a better idea: how about a vintage baseball game that would pit a yet-to-be-assembled team of Pittsfield players against the Hartford Senators, an existing vintage team from Connecticut? Vintage baseball is a growing sport that features amateur teams conforming to the rules, uniform styles, and equipment of the 19th century.

Several months prior to our having been invited back to Pittsfield, I'd received an email from Greg Martin, founder of the Senators and owner of a company called the Vintage Base Ball Factory (base ball was two words in the 1800s). Martin had inquired about my possible interest in vintage baseball and, having had no interest at the time, I filed it away.

Now, suddenly, I had interest.

We could resurrect the Hillies, a professional team that represented Pittsfield in the Eastern League from 1919 to 1930. Their arch rivals back then, the Hartford Senators, had that first baseman named Lou Gehrig, who hit a home run at Wahconah Park that landed in the Housatonic River. We could promote the game as the teams' first meeting in seventy-four years.

I envisioned a sepia-toned event—a step back in time—that would begin weeks in advance with the printing of old-fashioned tickets and posters. At the game itself, I imagined kids in newsboy caps hollering "Extra! Extra!" and handing out scorecards, while costumed actors strolled about to the sounds of ragtime playing over the speakers.

The day would combine baseball, history, and theater, which fit nicely with our plans to market the "experience" at Wahconah Park rather than the game. It also would be good for Pittsfield and give us a chance to show what we could do.

But Chip and I had no experience promoting events: we had no staff, we were trying to raise money, we were up to our ears in meetings with architects and engineers, and Paula and Cindy were already into the early stages of eye rolling.

Naturally, we decided to do it.

Mayor Ruberto was skeptical but Potsy thought it might work. Potsy, who had become the mayor's assistant on Wahconah Park, was now showing up at all our meetings. It was Potsy who suggested we start by contacting Chuck Garivaltis, a local baseball legend, who might make a good manager for the Hillies.

Garivaltis is craggy handsome, with a prominent nose and a furrowed brow that cause him to resemble a worried bird. Tall and slim at sixty-nine, he looks like the former star first baseman that he once was at Colgate—where he roomed with high school teammate Larry

Bossidy. Garivaltis liked the vintage idea so much that within a few weeks he had assembled a staff of coaches—all old-time Pittsfield sports heroes—and scheduled the first tryout.

Then, as if guided by vintage ghosts, a baseball legend walked out of a cornfield and spoke to me. Well, not exactly, but close.

The legend was noted baseball historian John Thorn, and the cornfield was a makeshift green room at the courthouse in Hackensack, New Jersey. ESPN was taping a show there called *Yankees on Trial*, and Thorn and I had been asked to appear as witnesses.

Thorn, who knew I was involved with Wahconah Park, walked over to me and said, "I have something that might be of interest to you."

"And what might that be?" I asked.

"The earliest known reference to baseball in North America," he said, "could be sitting in the basement of City Hall in Pittsfield."

Thorn described a 1793 bylaw banning the playing of baseball within eighty yards of a new town hall to protect against the breaking of windows. He said he'd been doing research on the Internet and read about the bylaw in a book called *The History of Pittsfield, (Berkshire County) Massachusetts, from the year 1734 to the year 1800.*

"The original bylaw may still exist," said Thorn.

As soon as the mock trial was over, I drove home and called Potsy to get him started looking for the bylaw. Then I called the mayor to enlist his help. Ruberto, who had done his college thesis on baseball marketing and knew Thorn by reputation, understood immediately what this could mean for Pittsfield. Cooperstown, a sleepy village in upstate New York, had turned itself into a major industry on the now-debunked claim that baseball had been invented there in 1839. The 1793 bylaw, if it could be found, would beat Cooperstown by nearly half a century!

"Pittsfield can call itself 'Baseball's Garden of Eden,'" said Chip. "We can put that on the 'Welcome to Pittsfield' signs."

Two weeks passed and nothing was found. Meanwhile, Chip and I were moving ahead with our vintage baseball game. On Friday, April 23, we met in the mayor's office to discuss the game and how best to use the 1793 document in case it was found. Seated around a coffee table across from the mayor's desk were the mayor, Potsy, Bill Wilson of the Berkshire Visitors Bureau, President of the Chamber of

Commerce David Bassillion, Lisa Wiehl, one of the mayor's secretaries, and me. Chip was on a family vacation in Israel.

In the middle of a discussion about how and whether to connect the vintage baseball game to the 1793 document, the phone rang. It was Ann Marie Miles from the Atheneum, Pittsfield's library. Potsy got up and took the call at the mayor's desk.

"This could be it," I said.

All eyes were on Potsy. Time stopped. Potsy listened. He smiled. A big smile. He paused, just to drive us nuts.

"So, they found it," Potsy said into the phone, for our benefit.

A shout went up from the group as we jumped to our feet and high-fived each other across the table.

"The reason it took so long to find it," said Potsy, "is because it's dated *1791*, not 1793."

"Even better," we shouted. There was a lot of laughing and hollering and slapping of knees. Potsy and I grabbed our coats and headed for the Atheneum to see the document in person.

At the library a folder was carefully opened on a table and Potsy and I gazed at what looked to us like the Magna Carta. A single sheet of obviously hand cut paper had yellowed with age, and the ink of the flowing script had turned brown. I liked the fact that the 1791 date was right on the document itself and that the "s" in baseball was written like an "f"—*bafeball*—just as it was when George Washington was our *Prefident*.

Back in the mayor's office, Potsy handed out color copies of what the group was now calling "The Broken Window Bylaw." We agreed that it should be delivered to the Williamstown Art Conservation Center for authentication, and that no one should say a word until we figured out how to make best use of this amazing gift.

"Baseball's Garden of Eden," said Mayor Ruberto, "I like that." Then, with a big smile on his face and an imaginary drink in his hand, he said, "You know, this job is a lot more fun than I thought it would be."

Of course, everyone laughed.

I couldn't wait to tell Paula—and email Chip.

The baseball gods were smiling upon us.

At a legal Meeting of the Inhabitants of the Town of Pittsfield qualified to vote in Town Meetings, ~~on the Twenty~~ holden on Monday the fifth day of Sept.r 1791 — ~~Voted~~, The following Bye Law, for the Preservation of the Windows in the New Meeting House in said Town — viz,

Be it ordained by the said Inhabitants that no Person an Inhabitant of said Town, shall be permitted to play at any Game called Wicket Cricket, Base ball, Bat ball, Foot ball, Cat, Fives or any other Game or Games with Balls, within the distance of Eighty yards from said Meeting House — And every Person who shall play at any of the said Games or other Games with Ball, within the distance aforesaid, shall for every Instance thereof, forfeit the Sum of five Shilling to be recovered by Action of Debt brought before any Justice of the Peace to the Use of the Person who shall sue and prosecute therefor —

And be it further ordained That in every Instance where any Minor shall be guilty of a Breach of this Law, his Parent, Master, Mistress or Guardian shall forfeit the like Sum to be recovered in Manner and to the Use aforesaid —

But not everyone was smiling.

After Chip got back from Israel, he spoke with Kevin Kinne, a fellow board member at the local community center, who's also a partner at Cain Hibbard Myers & Cook. Chip gave Kinne the background on our story and said it would be nice if we could mend fences with his law firm.

"We should all want to be on the same side," said Chip, "and work together for the good of Pittsfield."

"That sounds like a great idea," said Kinne. "I'll set up a meeting with the partners. What days are good for you?"

Chip and I came up with three or four dates and waited for Kinne's call. It came right away.

"I had no idea there was so much hostility," said Kinne, with genuine surprise. "Some of them hope you fail. And I don't know if they're going to oppose you passively or actively."

Whatever that meant.

The next day, Chip and I met with our friend Steve Picheny at his office in Great Barrington. We wanted to get his thoughts on Chip's prospectus. Picheny wanted to talk about *Foul Ball*.

"I've had a lot of arguments with those guys up there," said Picheny, referring to his lawyer friends at Cain Hibbard Myers & Cook. "They're saying that the book is wrong and that you made unfounded accusations."

"I just described what people said and did," I said.

"That's right," said Picheny, "but according to them, you drew the wrong conclusions. I told them that given the same set of facts, it's just as reasonable to see it your way as it is theirs."

Picheny said his friends at Cain Hibbard weren't too happy with him for defending us. Then we moved on to our prospectus. Where Picheny wasn't too happy with *us*.

"You guys don't have any money in the game," he said. Picheny was referring to the paragraph which said that whatever cash Chip and I had to lay out to get the company started would be reimbursed by the investors.

"It's the first thing I noticed," he said, tossing the prospectus on the table. "And your opponents are going to notice it, too. They're going to say, 'See, they don't have the money.'"

"We're taking the biggest risk," said Chip. "If anything goes wrong before the closing—if we can't get permits, if there are environmental issues, if we can't raise enough money—we're the only ones who lose."

"Plus we're not taking any salary for two years," I said. "And we're both putting our lives on hold. I'm giving up other opportunities and Chip is completely shutting down his business."

"Nobody cares about that," said Picheny. Then he offered some advice regarding his attorney.

"You should call Jeff Cook."

"Somebody already tried that," said Chip. "He wasn't interested."

"You should try again."

We thanked Picheny and said we would keep him informed.

Even before we left Picheny's office we knew he was right about the money. Whatever Chip and I spent up front would have to stay in as stock. How much stock should we commit to? We came up with $125,000 each. Now all we had to do was explain it to our wives.

"I think Steve is right," said Paula, almost causing me to lose my balance. "It's the fair thing to do."

"That's wonderful, Babe," I said, putting my arms around her. "We'll get it all back and more when this thing is successful."

"I hope you're right," she said, looking worried.

Later that afternoon, we called Picheny and told him we were updating the prospectus, based on his advice.

"I knew you were stand-up guys," he said.

And Paula was a stand-up wife. Next morning, she wrote the first check for our share of the Wahconah Park bills to date: $15,000.

A week after our meeting with Picheny, Chip was speaking with David Bassillion of the Chamber of Commerce. As part of our plan to sell stock to local investors, Chip had asked Bassillion if we could make a presentation to the Chamber. Bassillion doubted he could arrange that. Why? Bassillion said he had to be sensitive to who was on the board.

Let's see now, who was on the board? Among others, there were Mike Daly, Andy Mick, and Mike MacDonald.

Then there was Downtown, Inc., a body that shared office space and some of the same goals with the Chamber of Commerce. This organization was headed by Mike MacDonald. But here we had Mayor Ruberto pushing hard for us. And to help clinch the deal, we even offered to have me stay home and just let Chip make the presentation. They finally went for that.

"That's outrageous," said Paula, who would have made a good lioness. "How do you feel about that?"

"It doesn't bother me," I said, matter of factly.

"Well, maybe it should," Paula said.

The most disheartening response may have been the one from a group called WHEN, whose acronym stands for either Women Helping to Empower Neighborhoods, or the far more popular We've Had Enough Nonsense. This was the political action committee that got credit for having three women elected to the City Council.

What happened was that Chip and I had been invited by a WHEN member to make our pitch at a WHEN meeting, only to have the invitation withdrawn by WHEN leader Laurie Tierney. Her email said:

```
> We have decided not to get involved in issues,
> other than to inform the membership that these
> issues are out there. . . . We must inform you
> that it is not possible to have you as speakers
> on behalf of [Wahconah Park] at this time. . .
> these are exciting, and yet precarious times
> in the City of Pittsfield . . . .
```

It sure sounded like nonsense to us. But it didn't matter. We shrugged it off, just as we had shrugged off the reluctance of Downtown, Inc. and the Chamber of Commerce. What did we need them for? After all, we'd been welcomed by the city. We had a signed license agreement. We had the mayor behind us. We had the Parks Commission. The City Council. The citizens of Pittsfield.

And fans from all over the world.

On May 11, in Pittsfield's City Council chambers, the 1791 Broken Window Bylaw was unveiled to the world. It was a sweet press conference, and very well attended. The original document was mounted behind glass and displayed on an easel. Next to it was a pen and ink drawing of the town hall whose windows needed to be protected from flying *bafeballs*.

Mayor Ruberto, a little nervous with all the TV cameras and tape recorders, had fun proclaiming Pittsfield to be "Baseball's Garden of Eden." And John Thorn confirmed that Pittsfield was, in fact, "the birthplace until further notice, let's put it that way."

At the very end, I announced that "in celebration of finding the Broken Window Bylaw," a vintage baseball game between the Pittsfield Hillies and the Hartford Senators would be played at Wahconah Park on the Fourth of July. Displayed on a table was a turn-of-the-century glove (no bigger than a hand), a vintage ball and catcher's gear, and a mocked up Hillies uniform shirt.

The coverage was sweet, too. Not just nationwide but worldwide, with a front page story in the *International Herald Tribune* headlined: BASEBALL DISCOVERS ITS 'GARDEN OF EDEN.'

"I see busloads of Japanese tourists," said Chip.

We were even going to have our own television special.

Twenty-four hours after the 1791 press conference, Mark Durand, a producer at ESPN, called to say that ESPN Classic wanted to broadcast our vintage game—four hours, live, from Wahconah Park! This would be ESPN Classic's first live game broadcast. (It was ESPN Classic that had canceled *Sports Century: Ball Four* back in 2002, before airing it a year later.)

The ESPN call was the big break we needed. Chip and I had always said we could attract a national audience, but we thought that would come later. Four hours on national television would put our marketing program ahead of schedule. Way ahead. Especially combined with the 1791 document, which suddenly put Pittsfield on the world map. And directly or indirectly, we were responsible for both. That's got to win a few people over, we figured.

How about Berkshire Bank?

In a two-page letter to Mike Daly, Chip wrote:

The Wahconah Park project, in conjunction with baseball's newly discovered 18th century heritage right here in Pittsfield, has the potential to make this town a national shrine for baseball pilgrims . . . as a point of civic and personal pride I would like to see most of the investment and most of our 400 investors come from Berkshire County . . . . I know of no one person nor one business better equipped to accomplish that than you and Berkshire Bank.

The July 3rd vintage game [the date was changed from July 4th to accommodate the ESPN program schedule] *will begin with pre-game activities at 4:00 p.m. with a 'Taste of the Berkshires' food extravaganza, whereby the Berkshire's best eating establishments will offer samplings from their menus under a big tent in front of the ballpark. At 6:00 p.m., a parade down North Street will feature local marching bands and the Hillies riding in vintage automobiles. Upon arriving at the Park, the Hillies will disembark and immediately take to the field of play. The game will commence by 7:00 p.m., following introductions, and will end with a fireworks display.*

ESPN expects to have ample time during the game to interview notable people in attendance, including individuals from the worlds of politics, business, entertainment, and sports. We would be pleased to have Berkshire Bank be introduced as the cohost, together with Wahconah Park, Inc., of this great celebration of Pittsfield's baseball history and future.

Chip asked Daly to propose to his board of directors that in addition to co-hosting the event, the bank become a major investor in Wahconah Park, Inc.; that the bank's branches become the sole outlets for walk-in ticket sales; and that the bank be the sole sponsor of our official game program.

Attached to Chip's letter was a Berkshire Bank vintage billboard ad that I had prepared.

After a presentation to the board, which included Larry Bossidy, the vote was unanimous: "They don't want anything to do with you," said Daly.

And that was just *one* bank president. Angelo Stracuzzi of Greylock Federal Credit Union, Berkshire County's *second* largest financial institution, was equally enthusiastic.

"I'd like you to meet Jim Bouton," said a mutual friend, who tried to introduce us at a Chamber of Commerce mixer.

"I know who he is," said Stracuzzi, with a look of disgust. "I don't want to shake his hand."

I wondered if Stracuzzi's greeting had anything to do with the fact that Cliff Nilan was on the Greylock board.

If not the banks, how about Cain Hibbard?

I didn't call Jeff Cook, but I did call his partner Sydney Smithers, who was our attorney when Paula and I first moved to Massachusetts. I thought a good way to break the ice might be to offer Cain Hibbard some business, namely the intellectual property work for a variety of trademarks, including Hillies T-shirts, hats, uniforms, and beer (Hillies Summer Brew), and Pittsfield of Dreams T-shirts and 1791 Ale, all of which would be available for sale at the July 3rd vintage game.

My phone call didn't even scratch the ice.

"This firm has been working for the good of Pittsfield for thirty years," said Smithers, with a touch of anger in his voice, "and that's not how we were portrayed in your book."

"I didn't make anything up," I said. "The quotes are accurate and the actions speak for themselves. It's also the view of my partner Chip Elitzer who was a witness to the same events. We, too, felt we were badly treated, but we were persuaded by the mayor to let bygones be bygones. Let's work together for the good of Pittsfield. I'm calling in that spirit."

"There's something to be said for that," said Smithers. "Give me a few days and I'll call you back."

Two days later Smithers called back.

"If you believe your book is accurate, you don't want to be associated with us," said Smithers, who sounded even angrier than the last time.

"Reasonable people can disagree on the meaning of events," I said. "We're willing to accept that you have a different view, and move forward on that basis. For the good of Pittsfield."

"I spoke with my partners," said Smithers, "and they believe the book is actionable or near actionable. You don't want to do business with us."

Then he hung up.

o o o

CHAPTER 16

"Not in my wildest dreams"

With the vintage game fast approaching—and no end to the work involved with our master plan for the ballpark—it was all Wahconah, all the time for the Bouton and Elitzer teams, which now included eighteen-year-old Sam Elitzer "as a force multiplier," as Chip put it.

To maximize efficiency, we divided the vintage game work. Chip: Food court (vendors, tents, sanitation), game tickets and food coupons (distribution, cash sweeps), parade, and fireworks. Jim: Graphics (logos, tickets, posters, game program, merchandise, hand operated scoreboard, and signs), Hillies uniforms, and equipment. Chip and Jim: Sponsors, ESPN liaison, and TV necessitated ballpark upgrades. Cindy: Bookkeeping. Paula: Music, costumes, and props. Sam: Whatever else was needed, which was plenty.

Chip and Sam and I were practically living in Pittsfield. But now we took separate cars to multiply the mobility of our force multiplier. While Sam was handling special assignments, Chip and I would go to meetings with contractors about improvements to the ballpark for national television, and meetings with engineers and architects regarding estimates or permitting.

We were getting a good response on the environmental front.

"Thank you for being the first in the history of Pittsfield to actually send out the [Environmental Notification Form] to the local groups asking for input," wrote Jane Winn of the Berkshire Environmental Action Team.

My reward for all this, besides the fantasy of our dream coming true, was to try out for the Hillies. This involved asking Chuck Garivaltis what he thought about it, and Chuck saying he believed it would be a great idea, and his decision had nothing to do with the fact that the Hillies were playing with what amounted to my bat and ball. In anticipation of a favorable response, I had begun throwing a ball against the wall in my basement again.

It also helped that ESPN wanted me to pitch to a few batters during the game. Who better for a vintage baseball game than a vintage pitcher? ESPN probably figured a sixty-five-year-old knuckleballer would attract the type of viewers who like to watch people wade through crocodile-infested swamps.

The tryouts reminded me of my sandlot days. Guys wearing all kinds of mismatched outfits—shorts, uniform pants, jeans, hats, no hats, T-shirts, sweatshirts, and all of them with logos and colors representing everything from junior colleges to building supply companies. My kind of players.

And there were a lot of them. More than eighty showed up over a three-week period. The fun part was watching them try to catch a ball with what looked like gardening gloves. At first, it was almost impossible. With no webbing, you had to catch the ball directly in the palm of your hand, which hurt like hell. If the ball didn't land squarely in your palm, it would bend your fingers back, or break them. For the first few weeks, more balls were dropped than caught. A running catch in the outfield was out of the question.

But these were good athletes and they wanted to master the vintage game. They also wanted to play for the Pittsfield Hillies. At Wahconah Park. July 4th weekend. On national television.

Our fund-raising was going well. By mid-June, eighty-four investors had committed nearly $1 million, not counting the combined $250,000 from Chip and me. Our more sophisticated investors included a retired chairman of a large New York law firm, the managing director of a prominent New York investment bank, the chief operating officer of one of the country's most respected venture capital firms, and a financial executive of Boston's largest insurance company.

Chip estimated the total net worth of our investor group at about $300 million. Unfortunately, less than 3% of the money raised was from Pittsfield, whose appeal as an investment locale seemed to be inversely proportional to the proximity of the investor (see the geographical breakdown of investors in the documents section).

Our cost estimating, however, left something to be desired. Based on preliminary drawings it was clear that our wish list was bigger than our wallet and that we were not going to get everything we wanted for $1.5 million. A scaled-back proposal would get us the new third base line bleachers and Hall of Fame Walkway with clubhouse and restrooms underneath, plus a food court with twenty-four concession stands. But the first base line bleachers with clubhouse and restrooms underneath, the outfield fence-top bleachers, and the new dugouts with Not-So-Luxury Boxes above would have to wait.

As the committed dollars were coming in, the real dollars were going out. By that time, Paula had written checks totaling $38,000 to cover our share of the expenses. And there were more bills on the way.

Meanwhile, we were ahead of schedule on a few improvements to Wahconah Park, as a result of the vintage game. Most noticeable was a new paint job on the grandstand exterior, where we covered a hideous electric blue—a Jonathan Fleisig special that looked like a bridge primer—with a soft sage green. We also replaced the illuminated plastic Black Bears sign above the grandstand entrance with a hand-painted wooden sign that read: Historic Wahconah Park, Organized Baseball Since 1892.

Inside the ballpark, fans would be greeted by another handpainted wooden sign reading: No Spitting, Cursing, or Gambling Allowed by Ballplayers. In the outfield, we covered the electronic baseball and football scoreboards with handpainted, hand-operated, wooden scoreboards that featured sage green lettering and white numbers on a dark green background. Like a page from a history book.

Finally, to make room for our concession tents, we removed some rotting sheds and replaced an old chain-link fence with a new construction fence that quintupled the food court area.

We discarded Chip's idea for a statue in the food court.

"We could have you stuffed, like Trigger," he said, "and posed in your pitching motion, with your hat on the ground."

"People could toss their gum wrappers in my hat," I said, "and snuff out their cigarettes on my knee."

We had only one small problem. With a little over two weeks to go, we still had no staff—no ushers, ticket takers, cashiers, or parking attendants. What would we do if two thousand people showed up? An English soccer riot came to mind.

The answer? "Booster clubs," said Chip. "High school sports teams are always looking for ways to raise money."

A hastily arranged meeting with booster club leaders from three local schools—Pittsfield, Taconic and Saint Joseph—proved once again that Chip is a genius. For $2,000, and a rush order of official Hillies Staff T-shirts, we'd have 100 trained volunteers for the game. This would be in addition to the actors and the paperboys.

"If it works," said Chip, "that can be our staff for next year. That's a lot of money for school programs."

"It beats standing in the road with a car wash sign," I said.

In the days leading up to the big game, Pittsfield was abuzz with the Hillies. Using John Thorn's *Treasures of the Baseball Hall of Fame* as a style guide, I had posters made that pictured manager Garivaltis and his coaches, in deadpan poses, wearing period Hillies caps. Under the headline: VINTAGE BASE BALL AT WAHCONAH PARK, it read: Pittsfield's best Amateur Players Coached by its Greatest Legends. The oversized (three-by-eight-inch) tickets looked like they could have gotten you admitted to Comiskey Park in 1918.

The team was looking good, too. With a roster of twenty-seven players, which included a painter, a cop, a lawyer, a civil engineer, a real estate appraiser, a chiropractor (who broke a finger in practice), two carpenters, a lifeguard, a fifty-one-year-old school teacher, and a sixteen-year-old student, the Hillies resembled the town teams of years gone by. And they were learning. No more "sissy gloves" (their new name for regular gloves) for these guys.

What the Hillies needed help with were the rules of vintage baseball: There is only one umpire, positioned ten to fifteen feet behind and at an angle to the batter. The umpire is always addressed as "sir" by the players and may smoke a cigar. In the event the umpire does not have a clear view of a play he can request a "Gentleman's Ruling," in which the players involved tell what transpired and a call can be reversed. And my favorite—the umpire has the option to ask for input from the fans in the stands.

Batters request a "high" or "low" strike zone before their at bat and the pitcher must throw into the area requested to earn a strike. There are seven balls and three strikes, but foul balls are not counted

as strikes. Foul balls into the stands must be returned and baseballs are not replaced unless lost. There are no balks and "quick" pitches are legal—for example, the pitcher can fake two throws to first then quickly pitch to the batter. Also, there is no pitcher's mound or rubber, and the pitcher must remain entirely inside a four-foot by six-foot box, which is only fifty feet from home plate.

As part of the theater, players are expected to incorporate vintage game jargon into their infield chatter, including: *ballist* for player, *hurler* for pitcher, *behind* for catcher, *ginger* for determination, *muff* for error, *daisy cutter* for grounder, *sky ball* for pop up, *hands down* for out, *ace* for run, *frame* for inning, *dish* for home plate, *nine* for team, and *cranks* for fans.

In other words, if it's *two hands* down in the last *frame* with the local *nine* up by an *ace*, and their *hurler*, working well with his *behind*, shows some *ginger* and induces a *daisy cutter* or *sky ball* that doesn't get *muffed*, the *ballists* from both *nines* will gather at the *dish* to shout *Hip Hip Huzzah!* and the *cranks* will go home happy.

Most important were the vintage uniform and behavior codes, which I personally would like to see enforced today: no batting gloves, helmets, wrist bands, elbow pads, shin guards, sunglasses, logo shoes, pajama pants, gold chains, or earrings. No arguing with the umpire, stepping out of the batter's box, calling time out, charging the pitcher, posing at home plate, curtain calling, chest bumping, high-fiving, pointing to the sky, or kissing jewelry.

Just baseball, dammit!

Ticket sales had been going well. With a week to go before the game, all of the 390 box seats (at $20) and most of the 1,110 upper grandstand seats (at $10) had been sold. There were still plenty of bleacher seats (at $5) and standing room (at $3) available. Chip said we could have squeezed in more grandstand and bleachers (bench seats) if we had reduced the "butt width" variable from twenty to eighteen inches.

Chip obviously has very sophisticated software.

Things were coming together. Pete's Motors, a local car dealer, had agreed to be our event sponsor and major ticket outlet. "Doc" Piazza—our broken fingered, chiropractic third baseman—turned out to be a sure-handed parade organizer. Parks foreman Tony Stracuzzi, once a new-stadium guy and brother of Angelo the banker, was now happy to remove the mound and create a pitcher's box. And we had Betty and Elaine and Katy and the gang volunteering to do things like recruit paperboys (and papergirls—with hair to be tucked under their newsboy caps). All and sundry were pitching in.

Except Dave Potts.

Ever since we were invited back, Chip and I had wanted to find a place on our team for Potsy. Because he was the most knowledgeable man in town regarding Wahconah Park, the best position seemed to be facilities manager—which we had promised him, once we closed on our financing. And Potsy seemed appreciative, at first. But then he started getting weird.

It began with the tickets.

"You're not going to get people paying $20 for a box seat," Potsy said, "when the most they ever paid was $8. You're just going to get people mad at you. And you're not going to sell as many tickets as you think."

Then it was the national anthem.

"You got a whole neighborhood mad at you," he said one day, after I'd chosen a group called Quintessential to sing the national anthem before the game, instead of the Sweet Adelines. "They're going to boycott the game. And it's going to have a negative effect on your attendance."

"How can that be?" I said. "I've never even spoken with the Sweet Adelines."

And I explained that even if I had, I still would have chosen Quintessential—a quintet that suddenly breaks into song like the barbershop quartet in *The Music Man*—over a chorus of thirty women. Then Potsy, with a tight face, revealed a possible source of his anger.

"And you rebuffed me on the singer I recommended," he said, speaking about a female vocalist friend.

"I didn't *rebuff* you," I said, annoyed. "We simply made a different choice. Why is that rebuffing you?"

"And Girardi's mad at you, too," said Potsy, referring to a local beer distributor. "He called the mayor yesterday and he's pissed off. You should have used a local guy instead of Berkshire Brewery."

Berkshire Brewery is based in Great Barrington, which must seem like a foreign country to Potsy.

"Why is Girardi calling the mayor?" I said, my voice rising. "Why didn't he just call *us*. I've never heard of Girardi."

"Well, you gotta talk to people," said Potsy.

I had the distinct impression that the "people" we were supposed to talk to was Dave Potts.

The three days prior to the big game were a blur of details. To give you a flavor, here's what I needed to do:

Pick up: 6,000 Wahconah Park Times broadsheets (game program) at Kiwk Print; renderings of planned renovations at Clark & Green to display at game; scoreboard numbers from painter; sample food court paving stones from Empire Monuments.

Drop off: Hillies uniform shirt for Steve Valenti's clothing store window; vintage chest protector to be fixed at shoe store; food vendor signs and season ticket and paver order forms at ballpark; megaphones to painter.

Supervise: Removal of dead tree behind fence (now spoiling shot by ESPN camera); removal of pitcher's mound and outlining of pitcher's box; packaging of 1791 documents in shipping tubes for sale at game; erecting of snow fence in outfield; installation of ESPN portable lighting; arrangement of tents and tables in food court; positioning of advertising banners on outfield fence; attaching signs on vendor tents in food court.

Check on: Greg Martin to bring vintage bases and extra bats; wiring options for sound system; working condition of toilet trailer and Port-a-Pottys. (As it happened, the Port-a-Pottys were the exact same shade as Fleisig's awful paint job, giving a name to the color: Port-a-Potty blue); VIP parking area; delivery of sod to square off pitcher's box.

And Chip was doing twice as much as I was!

Two days before the game, ESPN taped an opening to the program featuring Chip and me at Wahconah Park in a takeoff of a scene from

Field of Dreams. Chip wore a polo shirt and slacks. I was in my Hillies uniform, having just arrived from another era.

Looking slowly around the ballpark, I said, "Is this heaven?"

Chip, using the Stanislavsky method, said, "No, this is Pittsfield."

Next, ESPN taped a segment with former Boston Red Sox pitcher Bill "Spaceman" Lee, who would be providing color commentary for the game and pinch hit against me, if it was okay with the Senators. In his inimitable style, Lee postulated his own theory on the origins of baseball.

"It started with cavemen throwing rocks at ducks," he said. "The guy who killed the most ducks, that's your starting pitcher."

The best part for me was the final Hillies workout—a bunch of guys still wearing their assorted outfits, but now playing with a certain confidence and precision. They had it down. Catch and flip, rather than pump and gun. But still swinging from their asses because they love to hit. The Senators would be in for a shock.

"We're going to cream those guys," I told Chip. "We've got some ballplayers here."

Chip smiled like a greedy owner.

After the workout, I handed out the game day itinerary and the comp tickets for the players' wives and girlfriends. I also reminded the guys that this was a theatrical experience as well as a ballgame, and that they should use the vintage jargon and manners at all times.

The highlight was handing out the new Hillies uniforms and the official Hillies duffle bags. For players, it's always a thrill to put on a new uniform, no matter what team it is. How does it fit? How do I look? Since there were no mirrors in the parking lot, where I had the uniforms in the back of my car, the players had to appraise each other.

"These are cool, man."

Hey, Dude, you look like Ty Cobb."

"No Dudes," I reminded them. "We're ballists."

Our only concern was the weather. It had rained most of June and it looked like we might get more of the same for July. A rainy weekend would be a major setback for us. In view of the importance of the event, I asked for assistance from someone I had not seen in seven years, but think about daily.

"C'mon, Laurie," I said, in one of my private conversations with her. "See what you can do about a nice day. For your Dad."

And she obviously had some influence, because July 3rd was glorious. Not just spectacular, but one of those summer days you remember for the rest of your life.

Thank you, sweetheart.

The only cloud on the horizon was a Bid Protest, filed with the Massachusetts Attorney General by the New England Council of Carpenters, Local 108. The carpenters were claiming that WPI and the city were not following proper procedures with respect to renovating Wahconah Park.

"That doesn't sound good," said Paula.

"Another nuisance," I said. "It can wait until after the game."

I awoke that morning with a feeling you sometimes have, when you know it's going to be a good day and the only question is, How good? I lifted my Hillies drawstring duffle bag—which held my Hillies uniform and my 1964 Yankees logo-free spikes—placed a bowler hat on my head, and gave Paula a goodbye kiss. She'd be coming later with the newsboy caps and the music.

At nine, Wahconah Park was already in motion. People scurrying here and there with clipboards and boxes and all manner of stuff in their arms. I grabbed a bunch of food vendor signs and hustled over to the tents. On the way I ran into Pete Lamb, the food service manager at a local yoga center, who was helping us for the day. He looked at my face and made a patting motion with his hands and said, "Breathe . . . breathe . . ."

I wasn't working very efficiently. My head was already into the game I knew I'd be playing in later. I'm not a multi-tasker. I can do consecutive but not simultaneous. If you want me to fix the sink *and* answer the phone, you're asking for a flooded kitchen.

Especially when it comes to baseball. It's not that I'm actually thinking about pitching; it's more that I'm *not* thinking about *anything*, thus clearing the way for whatever instincts might still be in there. I'd only be pitching to one or two batters, but even that would

384

take some focus, especially with the crowd and the real possibility that if my knuckler refused to show up, I could be out there all night. I did not want to provide the evening's fireworks.

By noon, it looked like the attendance might go beyond 2,500, the advance ticket sale. A number of people had come to the gate, saying they were from places like Virginia and Canada and could they still get tickets? Amazing.

At three o'clock we had to start letting people into the ballpark even though the tickets said: Game at 7:00, Gate opens at 4:00. By four o'clock, there were already several hundred people in the food court, some of them buying Hillies shirts and drinking Hillies Summer Brew. They were buying a fantasy, I thought to myself. From the Thin Air Company.

Then, as if on cue, coming through the gate and into the food court—wearing 1890s Hartford Senators uniforms, and carrying a large wooden water tank and a shiny brass spittoon—were what looked like Roy Hobbs, Ray Kinsella, Henry "Arthur" Wiggen, and their teammates. The enchanted fans surrounded the players—the adults tossing friendly taunts, the kids touching the water tank and the spittoon. The players joked back with the adults and tousled the hair of the kids.

I half-expected a director to shout, "That's a wrap!"

At six o'clock the Hillies assembled in a parking lot, a few blocks from Wahconah Park, for the start of the parade. Lined up were thirteen antique cars, the Berkshire Highlanders Pipe Band, and fifty Little Leaguers holding a banner that read WELCOME HOME HILLIES.

Waiting to get into the lead car, a 1931 Chrysler Roadster supplied by Pete's Motors, were Jimmy and Ellen Ruberto, dressed in period costume. The mayor wore a snazzy old-fashioned tux, and Ellen looked lovely in a wasp-waisted ankle-length dress and a big flowered hat. The mayor, who couldn't stop smiling, shook my hand, and I gave Ellen a peck on the cheek.

"This is unbelievable," Ruberto said, looking at the pageantry about to unfold. "Fantastic."

The best-looking vehicle was a 1934 Ford panel truck, which quickly filled up with players who couldn't wait to play their roles. Standing in the back of the truck, they struck jaunty poses—bats over their shoulders, unlit cigars in their mouths. I got into a 1922

Starr convertible—"the oldest car for the oldest player," said parade organizer Doc Piazza.

At 6:30 the bagpipes sounded, the car horns ooga ooga-ed, and we were on our way. My excitement was balanced by worry. This was a small parade—would we look compact or forlorn? How was Paula doing? It had been a long day. How were things going at Wahconah Park? Were the toilets working? How many fires was Chip having to put out? Most important, what was happening with the attendance?

As we turned a corner I could see Wahconah Park, a few blocks distant. But the vision was disturbing. It looked like there was an arm-flailing brawl in the food court, kicking up a dusty haze over the area, like you see in a cattle stampede. I squinted into the sun, trying to figure it out. Then I realized it *was* a stampede. Of people! Huge masses of them, surging in our direction and waving at us.

Holy smokes!

We had done it. We had pulled it off. Relaxing in the car, I felt a combination of triumph and relief. No matter what else happened, we had already succeeded. The rest would be just fun and games.

In the food court, the parade was stopped in its tracks by hordes of cheering people. They were walking between the cars, shaking hands with the players, and taking pictures. They ignored the car horns, probably thinking they were part of the entertainment, like the newsboys and the actors and the Scott Joplin coming from the speakers. I did interviews with two film crews while sitting in the car.

"This is amazing," people shouted. "Thank you."

I saw Paula working her way through the crowd. She was with her brother Alan and his wife Sally. They were literally jumping up and down. Paula was teary eyed.

"This is so wonderful," she said, squealing with excitement and giving me a sweaty kiss. "It makes everything worthwhile."

And people were still coming in. There were three long lines in front of the ticket tables. Paula said later that they ran out of tickets and were just stamping people's hands for $3, for an opportunity to park a lawn chair or a blanket in the outfield.

When the parade finally entered the ballpark itself, I saw that the stands were as packed as the food court! I figured we must have close to 5,000 in attendance! For the trip to home plate, past the third base stands, the Berkshire Highlanders Pipe Band kicked into *Badge of Scotland,* and the parade took on the air of a procession. People screamed and shouted and the players waved back.

The game hadn't even started yet and it was already one of the greatest nights of my life.

And the game didn't start for another ten minutes, because after the players had disembarked, the cars couldn't leave the field. There were too many people on the warning track. And they couldn't move, trapped as they were between the outfield wall and the snow fence.

Milling around on the field with the players, I looked up into the stands at the ESPN booth, behind home plate, and wondered how they were handling the delays. Fifteen minutes is a lot of air time to fill.

"Well, Bill," I imagined announcer Ron Thulin saying to Bill Lee, "This is probably the first time a game was delayed on account of too many cars on the field."

"They should just leave the cars out there," I pictured Lee saying in response. "The team that dents the most cars wins."

Finally, the cars crossed in *front* of the snow fence and the festivities resumed. Quintessential, wearing striped shirts with suspenders and newsboy caps, sang the national anthem, the mayor lobbed out the first pitch, and the Pittsfield Hillies took the field to a tremendous roar. A roar that continued halfway through the first inning.

I walked back and forth in the dugout, too juiced to sit.

The Senators jumped off to a two run lead in the second inning. In the third inning, an ESPN guy asked me to join Thulin and Lee up in the booth. We kibitzed on the air for a while before Tim Robbins joined us. I had invited him on the condition that he bring his wife, Susan Sarandon, who's as beautiful in person as she is on the screen. Susan sat next to Paula, for what I'm sure was a high-level discussion about what it's like when two very substantial women marry boys.

On my way back to the dugout, I ran into Chip, taking a break from his food court duty. The place was such a madhouse, I hadn't seen him since before the parade. He had a huge grin on his face.

"It's magical," he said, as we hugged. "The whole panorama."

By the fifth inning, the Hillies had pulled ahead 9–2, adopting a daring base-running strategy to take advantage of some Senators' fielding miscues. (I hesitate to call them errors because of the difficulty of catching a ball with those little gloves, especially under the lights. But that's part of the charm of vintage baseball.)

As my brother-in-law said, "Every play is exciting because you never know what's going to happen. It's not like regular baseball where flies and grounders are automatic outs."

No matter what was happening on the field, the fans were stamping and hollering their pleasure in the stands. It was as if they'd been rooting for the Hillies all of their lives. And in some sense, maybe they had been.

The fans were so involved they actually got into the game. With the Hillies flying around the bases, an errant throw had bounced into a crowd of kids sitting in the grass along the left field foul line. Instinctively, a girl of about ten grabbed the ball and, in what looked like a practiced play, flipped it to the just arrived left fielder who picked it out of the air and fired it home, all in one motion, to prevent another Hillies run.

In the spirit of the evening, the crowd roared its approval of this fielding gem by one of its own daughters, and play continued without protest from the umpire or manager Chuck Garivaltis. Whatever its impact on the outcome of the game, the play led to a noticeable increase in the pounding of gloves among the kids along both foul lines.

In the seventh inning, Quintessential sang a song they wrote especially for the occasion: "Take Me Out to Wahconah." You all know the tune:

> Take me out to Wahconah
> Take me out to the park.
> Of all the old parks, well it's still the best
> I don't care if it does face the west.
> And it's right in beautiful Pittsfield
> Where baseball first made its mark.
> So it's root, root for our home team
> At Wahconah Park.

Paula said later that Jimmy Ruberto could hardly contain himself. All night long he kept saying over and over, "I could never have imagined this. Not in my wildest dreams."

In the bottom of the seventh, word came down from the booth that it was time for The Ol' Knuckleballer to toss a few. By then the Senators had dinked and blooped and quick-pitched their way back

390

into the game, and the Hillies' lead had been whittled to 11–7. I had been hoping for a nine-run lead.

Fortunately, the knuckler was moving and it was three up and three down. No hits, no runs, no errors. This brought another roar from the fans, and I trotted off the field as modestly as possible, in the vintage manner.

How much happiness could I stand?

And where was Bill Lee? Evidently, ESPN had decided I should pitch to him leading off the eighth inning. This had the added theatrical advantage of having me bat in the bottom of the seventh. And you wonder why television producers make so much money.

Of course, I knew nothing about this plan, and therefore had not spent the past month also swinging a bat in my basement. In fact, the last time I had even picked up a bat was 1978, when I was with the Atlanta Braves. So I reached into the past and pushed a bunt down the first base line—a lost art today—and ran my ass off.

And I almost beat it out.

I was told later that as I was running to first, Paula was screaming at the top of her lungs, "And that man is sixty-five years old!"

Now, I just had to get Bill Lee out and I could die happy. But I knew that wouldn't be easy because Lee, who is eight years younger than I am, still plays competitive baseball. And he can hit! At the ESPN taping session, the six-foot-three Lee was talking about a home run hitting contest he'd recently won.

I certainly didn't want that to happen.

As I finished my warm ups, here came the Spaceman, swinging three bats and grinning. He was wearing a faded 1903 Red Sox uniform shirt, the one he keeps in the trunk of his car in case a game breaks out. This would be like a shootout between Bat Masterson and Billy the Kid. In front of their nursing home.

Fortunately for me, Lee tried to pull an outside knuckleball and hit an easy roller to first for the unassisted out.

This is the point at which any normal person would have walked off the field, tipped his cap, and treated himself to a cold Hillies Summer Brew. But no, I had to be a big shot and finish the game. Get the save. So I deserved what happened next—a walk, a few muffs, a couple of hits, and before I knew it the score was tied and Garivaltis had come to get me.

"What do you think?" said Chuck, kindly, not having removed a team owner before. "The score is tied. If Tommy [Rizzo] can hold 'em here, we can still win the game."

Translation: Don't make me yank you.

"Good idea, Chuck," I said, and I left the field to sympathetic applause.

I found out later that Chip, in his only Steinbrenner-ish move, had told Garivaltis to take me out. And it was a good thing, too, because one of my problems is, I don't know when to quit. If I had been a boxer, without a good corner man to throw in the towel, I'd be brain damaged by now. More than I already am that is.

Of course, we lost the game 14–12 and I was the losing pitcher. But no one seemed to care. The final out triggered a continuous standing ovation—not just to say thank you, it appeared, but to extend the evening for a few more minutes. I've never had so much fun losing a game in my life.

And they were still applauding when the Hillies and Senators strolled to the dish for the traditional Hip, Hip, Huzzah! This ritual is accompanied by brief remarks from the team captains, addressed to the opposing nine, to the effect that it was an honor to have shared the field of play with such upstanding and determined gentlemen.

I grabbed Chip and walked him onto the field for the ceremony, where we stood near the on-deck circle with our arms over each other's shoulders.

"We're bulletproof now," I said, referring to our off-field opponents. "They can't stop us."

"That's right," said Chip. "They wouldn't dare."

By Sunday morning, emails, articles, and phone calls from around the country confirmed that something special had occurred at Wahconah Park the night before.

"All I can say is WOW!!! Bravo, and way to go," wrote Jamie Dobrowski of Pittsfield. "What a happening."

"It was a picture postcard come to life," wrote Joe Palladino, reporter for a Waterbury, Connecticut, newspaper. "A jittery old black-and-white newsreel that burst into living color, and a stroll through a museum where you were permitted to reach out and touch the history."

"Loved the Hillies on TV," emailed Dick Silc of Tucson, Arizona. "Will be there next summer."

Even the *Berkshire Eagle*—but not the editorial page—paid tribute with a front page photo and a story headlined: IT WAS A FINE PITTSFIELD VINTAGE.

"An unbelievable event," wrote Gary Goldberg-O'Maxfield, of Hartford, who was at the game. "It seems more from a movie than reality."

If this were a movie, the story would end right here. Fade to black over exploding fireworks and triumphal music. But it was not a movie. And this is not Hollywood.

It's Pittsfield.

Where heaven barely lasted the weekend.

o o o

CHAPTER 17

"You guys are starting to rub me the wrong way"

A few days after the game, Potsy asked us if he could "borrow" the Hillies for a benefit game to help a guy named Dave Southard with his medical bills. We told Potsy we'd consider helping Southard in some other way, but we didn't want our new Hillies brand to be used in an event over which we had no control. Also, we were still recovering from the July 3rd game and didn't want to lose focus on our main goal—renovating Wahconah Park.

That's when Potsy began talking about a mutiny on the Hillies, some of whom, according to Potsy, wanted to continue playing. A mutiny! Great. One game and we've got an insurrection already.

To head off a possible half-baked production by Potsy and some Hillies, Chip and I proposed two more games—July 31 in Hartford, and September 4 at Wahconah Park. At a barbecue that we had planned as a thank you to the team and a return of their uniforms, the players voted yes to playing both games. They understood why we didn't want them playing without us. And they did not appear mutinous.

I took the moment to congratulate them on their marvelous play and predicted they would thrash the Senators in the next two games. Especially since the losing pitcher had just retired, and they wouldn't have to put up with any more celebrity-walk-on bullshit.

But Potsy wasn't finished.

On July 19, I got a call from Chuck Garivaltis asking if we'd heard about Potsy's email to the parks commissioners asking them to get us to donate proceeds from the September 4 game to the Dave Southard Fund. As a commissioner, Garivaltis knew that Chip and I would be at the meeting that evening to request a second use of the ballpark. I thanked Chuck for the heads up and said we'd see him later at Springside House.

What the hell was it with Potsy? Now he was sandbagging us—a mere sixteen days after our validation of Wahconah Park! "It's a good thing we didn't draw *ten* thousand fans," I told Chip, "or he would have had us killed." To try to straighten things out, we asked Potsy to meet us at the Lantern, before the Parks meeting.

"Potsy," said Chip, after the burgers arrived. "We told you how we felt about using the Hillies. Why are you going behind our backs?"

"Because you won't listen to reason," he said, thrusting his chin out to underline his reasonableness.

And he wouldn't budge. For Potsy, the July 3 game was now ancient history. He seemed to think that the Hillies were some kind of civic asset he could personally exploit. The more we talked, the angrier Potsy got. Suddenly, he exploded.

"You don't own the Hillies!" he barked, pointing a finger at us.

"As a matter of fact, we do," Chip said, quietly.

"No, you don't," said Potsy, indignant. "It belongs to whoever owned it a long time ago. You didn't *buy* it from them."

I explained that a trademark is owned only through "use" and that an unused mark falls into the public domain where it can then be claimed by a new user, which is what we were.

Potsy just sat there, his jaw clenched, staring straight ahead. He was like a guy off his meds. It was kind of scary.

This was a different Potsy from the one who had always been on our team. The Potsy who loved Wahconah Park. The Potsy who led the charge against a new stadium, who had fought City Hall and won. The Potsy who was going to be our facilities manager!

That Potsy, who Chip and I once likened to Jimmy Stewart, had turned into Lon Chaney, Jr.

At Springside House that evening, with nothing at stake but a routine approval of our September 4 game date (our use of the ballpark would not be automatic until 2005), only a handful of people showed up. Besides the five commissioners—Chuck Garivaltis, Gene Nadeau, Mike Filipi, Elinor Persip, and John Marchesi—there were a few petitioners, Dusty Bahlman of the *Eagle*, Jonathan Levine of the *Gazette*, Sam Elitzer, and a grim and determined-looking Dave Potts.

Last on the agenda, Chip began, as usual, by thanking people—the commissioners, the groundskeepers, the clean-up crew—for a "magnificent performance" on the July 3 game.

mere sixteen days after our validation of Wahconah Park! "It's a good thing we didn't draw *ten* thousand fans," I told Chip, "or he would have had us killed." To try to straighten things out, we asked Potsy to meet us at the Lantern, before the Parks meeting.

"Potsy," said Chip, after the burgers arrived. "We told you how we felt about using the Hillies. Why are you going behind our backs?"

"Because you won't listen to reason," he said, thrusting his chin out to underline his reasonableness.

And he wouldn't budge. For Potsy, the July 3 game was now ancient history. He seemed to think that the Hillies were some kind of civic asset he could personally exploit. The more we talked, the angrier Potsy got. Suddenly, he exploded.

"You don't own the Hillies!" he barked, pointing a finger at us.

"As a matter of fact, we do," Chip said, quietly.

"No, you don't," said Potsy, indignant. "It belongs to whoever owned it a long time ago. You didn't *buy* it from them."

I explained that a trademark is owned only through "use" and that an unused mark falls into the public domain where it can then be claimed by a new user, which is what we were.

Potsy just sat there, his jaw clenched, staring straight ahead. He was like a guy off his meds. It was kind of scary.

This was a different Potsy from the one who had always been on our team. The Potsy who loved Wahconah Park. The Potsy who led the charge against a new stadium, who had fought City Hall and won. The Potsy who was going to be our facilities manager!

That Potsy, who Chip and I once likened to Jimmy Stewart, had turned into Lon Chaney, Jr.

At Springside House that evening, with nothing at stake but a routine approval of our September 4 game date (our use of the ballpark would not be automatic until 2005), only a handful of people showed up. Besides the five commissioners—Chuck Garivaltis, Gene Nadeau, Mike Filpi, Elinor Persip, and John Marchesi—there were a few petitioners, Dusty Bahlman of the *Eagle*, Jonathan Levine of the *Gazette*, Sam Elitzer, and a grim and determined-looking Dave Potts.

Last on the agenda, Chip began, as usual, by thanking people—the commissioners, the groundskeepers, the clean-up crew—for a "magnificent performance" on the July 3 game.

"But the principal purpose of our being here tonight," said Chip, "is to request permission for the availability of Wahconah Park for the Labor Day weekend."

What happened next can best be explained by an edited transcript of the hour-and-thirty-two-minute response to Chip's request. Beginning with the first words from Commissioner Filpi.

> **Filpi:** As you are probably aware, I guess you found out sometime today that one of the longtime parks department employees, David Southard . . . is on long term disability. . . . severe financial constraints on the family. My only request to you would be I hope you would seriously consider donating X amount of ticket revenue to the Southard family . . . I know what you're trying to do down there, but my intent is to help out David along with a lot of other people. . . . Part of building your team is to build community consensus . . . and get it to be a blue collar event. Some of the stuff you did at your [July 3rd game] was a little upscale. Pittsfield is not an upscale community. I don't want to get into specifics . . .
>
> **Marchesi:** You'll get a lot of mileage out of the City of Pittsfield if you donate the money . . .
>
> **Elitzer:** Sounds like a worthy purpose . . . but because we haven't closed on our financing yet, everything is coming from our own checkbooks. We're paying vendors, suppliers, engineers, architects . . . you name it, on a weekly basis. Right now that is all money out and the return will be in a successful 2005 season when we are an established organization. . . . That would be the time when we could show our philanthropic side.
>
> **Filpi:** Who has the naming rights to the Hillies? [Can] the Hillies have their own game at Wahconah Park with our approval as an independent thing, not through Wahconah Park, Inc.?
>
> **Elitzer:** Our belief would be no . . . . If they want to play a game, not as the Hillies, but as a collection of guys, we certainly have no say over that . . . . We have

taken what was essentially an asset with zero value [the Hillies name] and with the July 3rd game begun to build a national brand . . . that will bring value to Wahconah Park.

Bouton: I would like to see a number of different events to help the Southard family, and we would be happy to participate in those events.

Elitzer: We could contribute a tented booth, if some volunteers wanted to staff it and sell raffle tickets.

Filpi: What if the Southard committee set up a booth and sold food? For whatever percentage you get, whatever your split is.

Elitzer: We would do the same deal as everyone else . . . depending on how successful the booth is, you could make a couple thousand.

Filpi: Just to clarify, if we gross $1,000 what do we have to give you?

Elitzer: $250.

Filpi: Okay, that's all I want to know.

Marchesi: I'm all set.

Commissioner Marchesi, conspicuously unhappy with Chip's answer, meant that he was "all set" to vote—*against* our request to use Wahconah Park. The body language of Chairman Gene Nadeau and Filpi was sending the same message.

Nadeau: You said that the plans for next year are to have the Hillies play about fifteen games?

Elitzer: Yes.

Nadeau: I kind of wonder because . . . when we approved the license agreement several months ago, this vintage game wasn't even a pipe dream, so I'm hearing that we need this to make some of the improvements . . . and that was never a thought back then when it was presented to us . . . . I think you're going to hurt yourself, personally. I didn't attend the game, you priced me out, personally. I didn't go.

Bouton: At three dollars?

their cans [just] because it's a good cause. It would devalue the name. And anything less than a first class show would devalue the Hillies.

Marchesi: OK, I've been listening here between you and him regarding this, OK. And I gather by listening to you that the Wahconah Park, Inc. is not interested in running a benefit for David Southard.

Bouton: We *are* interested.

Marchesi: No, I'm not hearing that.

Bouton: We'd like to be involved in any *other* event. We're not interested in using this particular game as a benefit.

Elitzer: We are willing to have a booth operated on behalf of the Southard family. We are personally willing to come to any event that might be organized. We could even [bring] the Hillies players, if they choose.

Marchesi: You know, I've been in favor of you guys but now I'm thinking twice, okay? You're a good talker, but I'm really upset. You guys are starting to rub me the wrong way.

Chip and I were upset, too. And confused. The Boutons and Elitzers write plenty of checks to charities. So why not this one? Were we angry at Potts for having put us in this spot? Were we feeling unappreciated? Was it resentment over being rolled? And what else could you call it? It was clear that the use of the ballpark was dependent upon a donation. Whatever the reason, we went blindly ahead.

Bouton: Can we do something at the September 11 event [a fund-raising clambake for Dave Southard]? Can we help with that?

Marchesi: You two guys sitting out there all you're thinking about is the almighty dollar. . . . We're not asking for all the money, just so much a ticket, that's all.

Elitzer: At a dollar a ticket, that could work out to $5,000. And you're saying that as a start-up enterprise that is not [profitable], that we should give the Southard family $5,000. . . . You're basically saying that Jim Bouton and Chip Elitzer should write a check.

Marchesi: No. I'm saying you should run a benefit. I'm not saying to write a check.

Elitzer: It comes to exactly the same thing. . . . And I do feel a little bit put upon. I'm sure that Dave Southard is a fine gentleman and he is very deserving . . . [but] we have a money losing operation at this point.

Marchesi: The contract said that you were going to spend $1.5 million fixing the field . . . [it] had nothing to do with the Hillies or anyone else going in there and playing a game and making money or losing money. So you're using that money that you made to fix up the park.

There was a long pause while Chip tried to grasp the notion that it was somehow unfair of us to use the object of our affection as a further means of its enhancement.

Elitzer: Let me put it this way. Jim and I are personally out of pocket about $160,000 so far.

Marchesi: That's nowhere near the $1.5 million.

Elitzer: This is before the financing is closed. . . . Jim and I are not taking anything out until 2006 at the earliest. . . . Asking [us] to make what amounts to a personal contribution of thousands of dollars . . . will scare our investors if they think that we can be leaned on.

Marchesi: Well . . . then I'm going to vote against this date and I hope the other parks commissioners vote against it.

This drew a response from commissioner Garivaltis, who had appeared distressed throughout the discussion.

Garivaltis: Here we go again . . . we have a new business that has brought, in a very short period of time, extraordinary good publicity to Pittsfield and has put on an extraordinarily good show. As a Hillies volunteer I had a ringside seat, but that was second fiddle compared to what I saw when I went home and saw the tape on TV, because that showed Pontoosuc and Onota Lake, it showed the mountains, it showed the announcer saying that, "This is a community that has taken a hit when GE left town, but as you can see tonight, flashing the crowd and the smiling kids and the ballplayers and what you are seeing tonight, this is a community that is now on the rebound". . . . It takes new businesses like WPI to do this and look what we're doing. Who would move into here and create jobs for us if they were treated this way by any public body in the City of Pittsfield? It wouldn't happen. They deserve a lot more respect than they've had here tonight.

Marchesi: I think you're out of order!

Garivaltis: I have the floor.

Marchesi: You're part of the organization!

Garivaltis: I didn't interrupt anybody. But as a new business that has done the extraordinarily good things that they have done and probably will continue to do for Pittsfield, I welcome them to the community and will give them all the support they need.

Marchesi: I just want to say one more thing to what Charlie says about community smiling and cheering. I think that what we're saying here tonight is that we've got an individual that we care about and we would like to see something done for him, so that's the kind of community I also live in.

It was about this time that young Sam Elitzer, as part of his ongoing civics education, whispered in my ear. "It's obvious they're going to vote against you," he said, "so you better do something." So Chip and I did what we probably should have done in the first place.

Elitzer: We've been talking . . . and we have a better answer for you. We would be willing to contribute a dollar of every ticket sold . . . [but] I want it to be clearly understood that we are doing this because we are listening to you and it would be devastating to us, in terms of presentations that we still need to make to our investors, for this to be taken as a precedent or to be considered as an expense item.

Bouton: Or as a necessary thing to get [future] approvals.

Filpi: We won't be coming back to you again. . . we're not going to tie your hands on any issues. . . . You can call me any time you want and things will get done. I'm not here to put you out of business.

Marchesi: And I'm sorry if I come on too strong, I'm too close to the kid. Charlie, I'm sorry I jumped on you but you are a part of the organization and that's why I jumped on you, but I'm sorry.

At that moment, in the spirit of forgiveness, and with an eye toward reconciliation, Chip Elitzer set a new Guinness Book record for magnanimity.

Elitzer: For the record, I want to give credit to Dave Potts who first sensitized us to this issue.

Personally, I would have said something else, but Chip is a better man than I am. And a better man than Potts, who left the room without so much as a nod in our direction.

In retrospect, I don't believe the commissioners understood what they were doing. For one simple reason: this was Pittsfield, where the rule is that you're entitled to a piece of the action. If you don't get your piece, like the Girardi beer distributor, you call City Hall.

It's a credit to Mayor Ruberto that he apologized to Chip and me when he heard what happened with the commissioners. Of course, we said that no apology was necessary—and so did Ever-Scrib at the *Eagle*, which may be the only time we ever agreed on anything.

But Jonathan Levine had it right. His opening line in a *Gazette* editorial—BLACKMAIL—summed it all up:

Members of the parks commission moonlighted as extortionists this week—and it was ugly.

o o o

CHAPTER 18

"The Attorney General fucked us"

By the next morning, Chip and I had put the commissioners behind us. We had other things to do. Like meet at a coffee shop in Pittsfield with Tim Craw, regional representative for the New England Council of Carpenters, Local 108.

Craw is a brawny guy with a pot belly, a kewpie-doll mouth, and bulging eyes. He looks like a cross between a child's bathtub frog and a linebacker from a small college. He has stab wound scars on his arms and chest, which he volunteered to show us. Craw explained that getting stabbed was part of his job when he worked undercover for the U.S. Drug Enforcement Agency.

Craw said he filed the Bid Protest because he saw that we had hired Allegrone Construction, a non-union shop, as our contractor. We explained that we hadn't hired a contractor yet and that Allegrone was only providing pre-construction services. In any case, we said we weren't against unions; that I myself belonged to four unions, and that I had walked picket lines, sat in on labor negotiations, and testified at arbitration hearings.

"This is a union town," I said. "We expect that most of the work will be done by union labor."

"We just can't live with the Public Bid Laws," said Chip. "They're too rigid and too cumbersome. Look at the 'Big Dig' in Boston: $12 *billion* over budget—five times the estimate! And it's five years late, and it's still not finished. The local school renovation: millions over budget. All under the Bid Laws. Governments can overspend because they can tax. We can't. No investor will accept being treated as a public entity."

"We need to break ground this fall," I said. "Otherwise we have to wait until spring, and we won't be able to do everything we want by Opening Day."

Craw said that the union Bid Protest was "a matter of principle" and that he would get back to us.

I had one more question. "Since we signed that license in March, can I ask why you waited four months to come forward?"

"We just heard about it," said Craw.

From there, Chip and I went to Carr Hardware, looking to have them sponsor our September 4 game and also become investors in WPI. With the Pittsfield business community basically sitting on its hands, we needed a big local investor to lead the way.

The owners, Bart Raser and his father Marshall, are big baseball fans. They liked our plans for Wahconah Park and were happy to be sponsors, but they didn't have the time or the money to invest.

"Our big concern right now," said Marshall, "is figuring out how we're going to replace our warehouse."

"What happened to it?" asked Chip.

"We had to give it up because the Colonial Theatre needed the space," said Marshall, referring to the renovation and expansion of the long dormant, century-old landmark in downtown Pittsfield.

"How can they do that?" I asked.

"Don't ask," said Marshall, pressing his hand to his forehead and rolling his eyes. "The pressures are unbelievable. We had no choice."

The pressures.

The Colonial Theatre restoration, decades in the works, is Pittsfield's largest welfare recipient. Of the estimated $9 million raised to date by the Colonial Theatre Association (a quasi-public-private venture that some say, unfairly booted out the grassroots Friends of the Colonial), 70% is public money, including: $2.5 million from the Massachusetts Historical Commission; $400,000 from the "Save America's Treasures" program; and a requested $1,000,000 from the same GE settlement fund that gave $250,000 to EV Worldwide for buses that never got built.

Add that to the easements and free parking on city-owned land, the use of eminent domain to oust adjacent property owners, and the removal of commercial property from the tax roles—"all approved without due diligence or public explanation," wrote Jonathan Levine, "or a visible business plan"—and you have a project that is clearly blessed from above.

The Colonial Theatre Association board includes Mr. and Mrs. Jimmy Ruberto, the major private donor is Berkshire Bank, and the attorney is Mike MacDonald of Cain Hibbard Myers & You-Know-Who. Think of the CTA as a Civic Authority for a theater instead of a stadium. Except there was no referendum on the Colonial Theatre Association.

As with the new stadium, the Colonial Theatre was pitched as some kind of economic engine. "Think about this not as a charitable gift but as an investment," said board president Howell Palmer. What kind of investment? Forget the fact that theaters like this need to be subsidized. The Colonial Theatre would draw 100,000 fewer people annually than Wahconah Park. And we were offering stock!

"Can you imagine if people got to *vote* on where to invest the $1 million of GE money?" I said. "The Colonial or Wahconah Park?"

"Wahconah in a landslide," said Chip. "Nobody's going to come all the way from Arizona to visit a theater."

The Colonial Theatre Association is lucky it doesn't need the Parks Commission. Those champagne press conferences and $50 tickets would be "a little too upscale" for the commissioners. Unless of course they were pressured. Then they could be persuaded that *Romeo & Juliet* was "a blue collar event."

Speaking of blue collar events, at a July 21 meeting at Wahconah Park, Tim Craw explained how we could satisfy the carpenters.

"We'll withdraw the Bid Protest," he said, "if you get Allegrone to become a union shop."

So much for "a matter of principle."

Craw also proposed a solution regarding guaranteed work.

"We'll make everything go away," said Craw, "if a certain percentage of the job goes to union contractors."

"We can't be bound by guarantees," I said.

"Our focus is local," said Chip. "We'd choose a non-union contractor from Pittsfield over a union guy from Springfield or Albany."

Craw has his principles, we have ours.

"This will probably be at least a 70% union job, anyway," I said, "given that Pittsfield is a union town."

"But understand, we have deadlines," said Chip. "This needs to be resolved soon, or the project is at risk."

Chip handed Craw a copy of our Working Backwards Timeline:

OCT 1   Drop-dead date for starting construction.
SEPT 17   Close financing. Two weeks notice to contractors.
SEPT 3   Prospectus declared "effective" by SEC. Two weeks notice to investors to close.
AUG 6   Final prospectus filed with SEC to begin four-week review period.
JUL 28   Completion of construction budget.

Craw looked at our timeline.

"I'll talk it over with my people," he said. Then he hopped into his truck and drove off.

Meanwhile, we were ahead of schedule on the field. Suddenly, we had *two* leagues interested in us. In addition to the Atlantic League, which Frank Boulton had said we could join if they began a short season division in 2005, we now had a feeler from the Northeast League. The day after the vintage game, Miles Wolff was quoted as saying that the league "would consider" moving its traveling team to Pittsfield in 2005. How impressed was Wolff with our vintage game? "An expansion team is also a possibility," he said.

If we build it, they will come.

Ahem.

On July 31, a lovely day at Bushnell Park in downtown Hartford, the Pittsfield Hillies blasted three home runs and beat the Senators 9–5. This was perfect, because it evened the series at one game apiece, thereby setting up The Deciding Game at Wahconah Park on Labor Day weekend.

The most interesting part of the game, however, was the attendance. In spite of the free admission, the turnout was estimated at thirty-five to forty fans, not counting the eight from Pittsfield that included Dave and Grace Potts.

Earlier that week Potts had tried to undermine us with the Hillies by showing them a Senators poster, pointing out the free admission.

The idea being that we were taking advantage of our players by selling tickets. The lack of attendance at the Hartford game was a good marketing lesson for Potts: free ain't worth much.

In spite of Potts' behavior, Chip actually walked over to say hello to Dave and Grace during the game. All I could manage was a wave across the field. And I was really just waving at Grace.

On the morning of August 2, Chip and I and City Solicitor Chris Speranzo drove to Boston to attend a Bid Protest hearing at the office of the Massachusetts Attorney General Thomas F. Reilly. Speranzo—thirty-two, friendly and smart—would be a unanimous choice for Mr. Congeniality at a Pillsbury Doughboy look-alike contest. Conveying more niceness than strength, he seems like a guy who still has dinner every Sunday at his mother's house.

"The union is just using the bid laws to get their foot in the door," I said during the ride.

We tried to speculate why the Attorney General didn't just tell the union to take a hike, since the Public Bid Laws were designed to protect taxpayers and don't even mention the *word* union.

"Reilly might run for Governor," said Speranzo, "in which case he won't want to do anything that looks anti-union."

"So he's just going to give them a hearing," I said, looking for an encouraging interpretation.

"That's the sense I got," said Speranzo.

Basically speaking, the Public Bid Laws were designed to prevent a mayor from hiring his brother-in-law to build the new courthouse. To make it fair for all contractors, under the law, architects must draft what are called *biddable specs*, which are detailed to the last nail. These are accompanied by equally detailed invoices from the architect.

Biddable specs are followed by a group *walk through*, which gives all the contractors the same view of the *scope of work*. Any alteration to the *scope of work*, *before* a contractor has been selected, requires new *biddable specs* and a new *walk through*. Also, new invoices.

Alterations *after* a contractor has been selected are called *change orders*. These are accompanied by a shaking of the contractor's head and the uttering of one or more of the following phrases: "Oh boy, I don't know. We probably can, but it won't be easy. Too bad you didn't think of it earlier, 'cuz now it's gonna cost ya. Whew!"

The Public Bid Laws, under the guise of protecting the taxpayers, often end up costing them far more than a project otherwise would. Why is this allowed to continue? You need to ask the politicians, architects, contractors, and unions, who seem to like these laws for some reason.

The hearing was conducted by Assistant Attorney General Joseph E. Ruccio III. Sitting across the table, next to the union lawyer, was Tim Craw, whom we had not heard from since we showed him our timeline and told him that our project was at risk.

During the three-hour hearing, our lawyer (hired and paid by Chip and me) made the argument that a private company using private money was not subject to the Public Bid Laws. The union lawyer argued that while Chip and I were no doubt honorable, our license contained "language" that, if allowed to stand, could be used by future "bad actors" to circumvent the Bid Laws.

How could that happen? You'll enjoy this.

According to the union, an unscrupulous government could grant a short-term license (our eighteen-month initial term) to a "sham corporation," to restore a city asset with a "required amount" of the sham corporation's money (our $1.5 million). Once the project was completed, the government could simply not renew the license, thereby getting an improved public asset without having to go through the Bid Laws. Of course.

That a city would even bother going through such a process tells you something about the Bid Laws, but never mind. When lawyers talk like that, the best thing to do is humor them. So we said we understood the union's position, strained as it was, and that we would make whatever revisions the Attorney General deemed necessary.

In the car on the way back, Chip and Chris talked about how to revise the license to eliminate the offending language. But whatever might happen, it was abundantly clear that the union's power derived not from the strength of its argument but rather from its ability to delay our project.

Or possibly derail it.

"This is like a slasher movie," said Chip, summing things up, "and the vintage game was that moment in the story where everyone is feeling safe, and suddenly . . ."

The whole business with the union was a drain on our time and energy. Especially with the problems we were having with Dave Potts and the parks commissioners. And we were still trying to raise money, complete our permitting, get a better handle on our construction costs, and prepare for the September 4 game.

Paula tried to slow me down whenever she could.

"After dinner and a nice glass of wine," she said one evening, "let's say we do something romantic, like sit on the porch and enjoy each other's company."

"Fine," I said, looking at my watch. "What time would you like to be romantic?"

The most disheartening thing was the money.

In spite of the fact that we had a vastly improved story to tell—our vision for Wahconah Park, our concept of marketing an experience, our plan to put Pittsfield in the national spotlight, and our ability to deliver, all now a matter of record—we weren't getting anywhere with investors.

The uncertainty about the Bid Laws, which we were ethically and legally bound to mention in our presentations, was now a problem. And it didn't help that our prospectus was now invalid, including as it did our yet-to-be-revised-and-approved license agreement. Still, if we could raise $1.2 million (including our $250,0000) *before* the July 3 game, what were the odds that we wouldn't be able to raise anything *after* the game?

Having struck out in Pittsfield, we were now traveling all the way to New York City looking for investors. We made four presentations at Mickey Mantle's restaurant, before large groups of prime candidates assembled by owner Bill Liederman, who was now on our board. These were guys with deep pockets who loved baseball and *wanted* to invest because they knew me or had seen or heard about our vintage game. Nada. Zip. "It looks interesting, Jim, we'll give you a call."

Meanwhile, as Cindy said, "The bills just keep on coming."

An accounting of the July 3 game—which included the ESPN-inspired improvements that we hadn't planned on making until after we closed on our financing—showed we lost $47,000 on a cash flow basis. Which meant that Paula had to write another check, bringing our share of the expenses to $94,000.

"I love you, Babe," she said with a sigh. "We're going to hell in a hand basket, but we're going together."

"We'll get it all back when this thing is a success," I said.

And I still believed that.

On August 13, a decision came down from the Attorney General's office that was just as we had anticipated. Here's the key wording:

> [W]e have identified evidence that the City has retained control over the construction, which raises concerns about whether it is subject to the competitive bidding laws . . . a term of 18 months suggests that a license may have been structured to circumvent the bidding laws, since many similar construction projects take this long to complete . . . by the terms of the license certain construction is required. . . . However, this is a close case. . . we remand this matter to the City for further action in accordance with the foregoing opinion.

By the next day, *"in accordance with the foregoing opinion,"* Chip and Chris had identified two ways in which the license could be revised:

1. The initial term was increased from eighteen months to fifteen years (still cancelable at any time if we failed to meet our performance criteria).

2. The "requirement" to spend $1.5 million was removed (we'd still be responsible for all repairs and maintenance—structural and otherwise—year round).

But the clock was ticking. We were already a week past the date we had set for submitting our final prospectus. Without a license, we had no prospectus. Without a prospectus, there was no point meeting with potential investors. And without new investors we were stalled at $1.2 million.

The question was, How soon could the mayor and the Parks Commission sign the license and get it back to the Attorney General for his approval?

"Right now the mayor is on vacation," said Speranzo. "And I'm leaving this afternoon for my vacation. It will have to wait until we get back."

Did I mention that we didn't have a professional team yet?

To round out the week, on August 20, the always reliable Ever-Scrib surprised no one with his editorial CITY MUST PLAY BY THE RULES.

> The recommendation of the state attorney general's office . . . constitutes a much-needed reminder to City Hall that the ballpark belongs to the city and is not the private plaything of Jim Bouton and Chip Elitzer, even if they behave as if it is.

In an obvious rebuke to Ever-Scrib, that evening a small tornado roared through Wahconah Park and lifted the roof off one of the clubhouses (and set it back down again) that we had planned to remove. The tornado also flattened a section of fence that we had earmarked for demolition.

At least somebody was on our side.

On August 21, Paula and I flew to the Netherlands to visit family for ten days. We hated to leave Chip and Cindy with all the work leading up to the September 4 game, but the plans had been made before the game was scheduled. And we didn't want to disappoint the grandchildren.

I wouldn't be missing any investor presentations because there weren't going to be any without a revised license agreement. For some reason, the mayor still hadn't decided what he wanted to do about the "further action" recommended by the Attorney General's office. How about his signature on the license revised by his own city solicitor?

Our new drop-dead date for construction, which we kept to ourselves, was November 1. Not that it seemed to matter to anyone but the Boutons and the Elitzers.

It was in the front room of my stepdaughter's house in Amsterdam, overlooking a canal, that I received my emails from Chip.

August 24, Speranzo to Chip:

> ```
> I cannot be sure that any action is going to be
> taken because I haven't spoken to the mayor.
> ```

August 27, Chip to Speranzo:

> ```
> Any chance you could send me a revised agreement
> this weekend?
> ```

August 30, Chip to Speranzo:

> ```
> You and I should hammer out the final draft
> of a possible revised agreement today in order
> to have a document to discuss with the mayor.
> ```

It was like watching grass grow. Or, in Amsterdam, watching the rain pelt the cobblestones. I couldn't stand it, and I flew home—by myself—two days earlier than planned. Don't ask.

On September 1, Chip and I met with the mayor in his office. He began by complaining about the Attorney General.

"The AG didn't do us any favors," said Ruberto. "Now we've got a real problem on our hands."

We told Ruberto we weren't worried about the AG, because we believed he would approve the revisions. Our enemy was time. The mayor needed to sign the license and get it to the Parks Commission for their approval.

Ruberto pressed his lips tightly together. He looked distressed.

"Guys, we don't have the votes," he said, meaning the commissioners. "The fifteen years and removing the $1.5 million are a very big problem."

"The problem was created by the union and the Attorney General," said Chip, with some intensity. "Everybody understands that."

"How could we not have the votes?" I said, incredulous. "Even revised, it's still far better than any license the city has ever had."

"The word I'm getting," said Ruberto, "is that they're not there."

"I can't believe they've already decided," said Chip. "We haven't even made our case for why the revisions are necessary."

"By the way," I said, as cautiously as I could, "what's happened to Potsy? He's been acting strange lately."

"I don't know what's happened to David," said Ruberto, shaking his head, as if he'd been wondering the same thing. "But you've got to get him on your side. He's important here."

Potsy was important for the simple reason that people believed him. He had been right about the Civic Authority, hadn't he? That gave him the street cred for whatever came next—against Ruberto, then for Ruberto and against Hathaway, for us and against Fleisig (although Fleisig was his own worst enemy). Potsy was a one-man word-of-mouth campaign, for or against any person or proposition. The question was, who was he for or against at the moment?

From the mayor's office, Chip and I went to Wahconah Park, where the Hillies were having their final practice before The Deciding Game, as we were billing the September 4 contest against the Senators. And who should we see sitting in the stands but Potts and Gene Nadeau. A perfect opportunity to get things back on track.

So we walked over and struck up a conversation that lasted through practice and into the darkness at Wahconah Park. It was not exactly warm and fuzzy. Potts and Nadeau were a matched set—unsmiling, arms-folded prosecutors with a case of particulars. They revisited our past sins—ticket prices, anthem singer, Girardi's, Dave Southard—and we tried to understand how stuff like that could possibly put us on opposite sides of something so important to the community. And to *them*.

The upshot of the conversation?

"You should have hired Potsy as a consultant," said Nadeau.

Say it ain't so, Potsy.

But he didn't.

On September 4, the Pittsfield Hillies secured worldwide bragging rights for vintage baseball by beating the Hartford Senators 12–4 on a beautiful afternoon at Wahconah Park. The paid attendance of 1,503 was less than we had hoped for but still pretty good for a Labor Day weekend, when the tourists have gone home and kids have left for college.

The honor of throwing out the first pitch, which once would have gone to Potsy, went to ninety-three-year-old Christine Ungewitter, a life-long Pittsfield resident who remembered rooting for the Hillies at Wahconah Park when she was a little girl.

"Why do they want me?" Christine asked her son George when he told her we were looking for an original Hillies fan. "A lot of people went to those games."

The *Wahconah Park Times*—our broadsheet game program—updated fans on the Attorney General's ruling and the need for a revised license agreement. "Ironically," we wrote, "the only way that the Company can proceed with its plan to spend over $1.5 million on the ballpark before Opening Day 2005 may be for the City to eliminate the requirement that it do so!"

By game time, however, weeks after the *Wahconah Park Times* had gone to press, we realized we were not going to be able to raise more than our current $1.2 million. So we adjusted our plan as follows: not counting the $250,000 of our own money we would have already spent, we'd put another $500,000 into the ballpark by Opening Day 2005 and keep the remaining $450,000 for working capital. Future improvements would be paid for out of cash flow.

Chip and I were not happy about the prospect of investing only half as much money in Wahconah Park by Opening Day as we had wanted. It would not only cut into our plan to market a fully renovated ballpark, but it might look as if we had reneged on the agreement. Our enemies would be happy to ignore the fact that we'd been well on our way to reaching our goal of $2.8 million until the carpenters filed a Bid Protest, and that $750,000 invested by Opening Day was still ten times what Fleisig or anyone else had ever invested in Wahconah Park in a single year.

On September 9, Chip and I stopped at Clark & Green to pick up the drawings reflecting our scaled-back plan, and headed for Pittsfield to meet with the mayor and Chris Speranzo.

"When we accepted your invitation to come back," Chip began, "we said there was no limit to what we could accomplish if we all worked together. We need to do that here."

"Guys, you gotta work within the Bid Laws," said Ruberto, with obvious frustration. "That's the only way this is going to get done."

But why was *he* frustrated? It had been nearly a month since the AG had invited the city to take action, which now amounted to nothing more than the mayor's signature on a piece of paper. Meanwhile, our time, our money, and a wonderful project were going down the drain.

"Why can't you sign the license?" I said. "Send it to the AG and see what he says? If it was a 'close call' before the revisions, it should be a no-brainer now."

"The AG is not going to help us," said Ruberto. "He never should have ruled on it in the first place. Damn!"

"Chris said he believed the revisions would pass muster," said Chip, recalling his collaboration with Speranzo on the language.

Ruberto looked cornered.

"That was my *initial* response," said Chris Speranzo, the loyal employee.

"We can't circumvent the Bid Laws," Ruberto said firmly, once again ignoring the point we had all made in the AG's office that the Bid Laws didn't apply to us. "I can't sign it and I won't sign it."

Won't is one thing, can't is another. Why *couldn't* he?

Ruberto brought up the financial plight of the city and the difficulties he faced trying to renegotiate the contracts of a large number of municipal unions. He implied that a tough stance against the carpenters could hurt him with the cops, the firemen, and the teachers.

"I have to think of the city," said Ruberto.

In the game of Find A Reason For Not Signing, this was a brilliant move, casting Ruberto as the savior of the city budget and us as bankrupters!

But then it was Chip's turn.

"We can help you with that," he said. "We'll provide the political cover you need. We'll lobby the parks and the council to strongly request that you sign the revised license and send it to the AG."

"The unions will see that your hand is being forced," I added.

"I can't have you do that," said Ruberto.

"We'll do it on our own," said Chip.

"I won't be any part of that," Ruberto said, firmly.

"We understand," said Chip. "Leave it to us."

It was hard to tell what Ruberto was thinking. He looked upset, but why? Was he afraid that our lobbying would be traced to him, making things worse with the unions? Or did he just not want to be pressured into signing the license in the first place, because he *couldn't* sign it?

The whole thing was exasperating. Here we were again, three years later, fighting political battles that Ruberto had promised we wouldn't have to fight. But what choice did we have? We were too far in, financially and emotionally, to just walk away.

Acting on his belief that "transparency brings people along," Chip sent an email to the mayor and each of the parks commissioners and city councilors. In it he listed a dozen *successes*, including: marketing the 1791 bylaw; the Hillies; ESPN; the $1.2 million; the completion of our engineering, zoning, and permitting; and "the diligent work of our families on behalf of Wahconah Park without pay."

He listed three *challenges*: getting a professional team; the lack of Pittsfield investors; and the Bid Protest. He described how the Protest had cost us time and money, and he laid out our scaled-back plan.

Chip wrote that we would "blow our budget and lose our investors" under the Bid Laws, but that the Attorney General "has given us a clear set of guideposts for getting us treated as the private enterprise" that we were. "This is where you come in," he said, inviting the political action that might provide cover for the mayor. "We are requesting a revised license agreement that costs the city nothing."

A few hours later, Chip and I received Ruberto's response—in an angry three-way phone call.

"You've just lost me as your biggest supporter," he said, extremely irate. "And now I am *not* going to change that agreement."

Finally, the mayor had A Reason: he could blame us.

The response of some other recipients wasn't much better. The day after the mayor blew up at us, Chip was in Pittsfield at a Dave Southard fund raiser to present our check from the September 4th game, as promised.

In spite of the fact that Chip had given up his Saturday morning—and had made some very gracious remarks in behalf of Southard and the Parks Commission—he got a noticeable cold shoulder from

Mike Filpi, the commissioner who had said, "You can call me any time and things will get done."

Unless you happen to believe in transparency.

The reactions of Filpi and Ruberto to Chip's email did not make sense. Nor did the ensuing silence of most of the commissioners and city councilors. So, what was going on here?

The clock was now ticking loudly.

September 14: Chip and I met at Wahconah Park with Tim Craw, who brought a guy named John Kelly, organizer for the International Brotherhood of Electrical Workers, Local 7 AFL-CIO.

The more the merrier.

Kelly, who looks to be in his mid-thirties, is a tall guy with brown hair and a mouth that turns down at the corners when he speaks. In spite of his height, there is a certain softness about him, as if he's never actually soldered a fixture. He and Craw made a good pair—the prince and the frog.

Craw, puckering his little lips, said there was another way to fix the problem. "Give the whole job to Dave Tierney," a union contractor.

Obviously, another union "principle."

"In the entire history of Wahconah Park," I said, "nobody ever had to publicly bid the improvements."

"They will from now on," said Craw.

"We don't want to make trouble," said Kelly. "We like this project. I'm getting calls from our members saying, 'don't screw this up.'"

We told Kelly that things were already screwed up, that a $1.5 million project had now been cut in half, and that if the unions didn't back off, even that would be lost.

"This will be a major black eye for unions," I said. "People all over the country are watching. Wahconah Park is now a national story."

"You gotta obey the law," said Craw, his ham hock arms folded over his Buddha belly. He was one large and smug amphibian.

To prove that we weren't anti-union, I had begun getting prices from contractors for our scaled-back plan. There were six categories of work: electrical, plumbing, demolition and excavation, fencing, concessions, and carpentry. I called every union contractor in Pittsfield in each category.

September 15: Chip and I met with Mayor Ruberto at City Hall. Among other things we talked about the carpenters' union.

"I've never seen anyone more anti-union than you guys," Ruberto said at one point.

"We're not anti-union, goddamit!" I said, my voice rising. "Craw is the one hurting unions, with his bullying. It's guys like him who've dragged unions down from 40% of the workforce to 12%. I've been a union man all my life and it hurts to see it."

"Jim is getting prices from local union contractors right now," said Chip.

The mayor returned to his mantra. "I want you guys in Wahconah Park. But you've got to live with the Bid Laws."

"We'll fold our tent before we do that," said Chip.

Ruberto looked off into the distance and slowly shook his head.

"The Attorney General fucked us," he said, using an expression we'd never heard him use before. "There's nothing the city can do. Tim Craw holds the keys."

o o o

CHAPTER 19

"What is the matter with you?"

September 16: Someone on an Internet message board (user name, BerkshireFan) asked how the Bid Protest and "the hoops you have to jump thru" in Pittsfield might affect our chances of getting a team.

Chip (user name, Chip Elitzer) replied that the "ambivalence on the part of the city has not gone unnoticed by the Northeast League, which has a meeting of team owners next Friday, September 24. It is not helping our cause."

Someone, probably Potsy (user name, Wahconah Fan), showed it to Ruberto, who got all upset again. Even though Ruberto refused to sign the license, he maintained a public posture of supporting us.

So the mayor called Chip, who added this note to the message board: "We continue, however, to have the support of Mayor Ruberto, who will be calling Miles Wolff before the owners' meeting to express his strong interest in acquiring a franchise in the Northeast League for Pittsfield."

And, we discovered later, the mayor did call.

But one of the things Ruberto asked Miles Wolff was whether or not Pittsfield could get a franchise *without* Bouton and Elitzer.

September 17: According to a story in the *Berkshire Eagle*, the City Council approved Mayor Ruberto's request for a $1 million allocation of GE funds for the Colonial Theatre. The only dissenters were Dan Bianchi, who argued that the theater was "not an appropriate use of this money," and Chuck Vincelette, who said that the city had "done enough for the Colonial."

"I believe that was the same meeting," said Chip, "where Peter Arlos petitioned the council to require that construction on the Colonial be publicly bid because 70% of it was public money."

"What happened to the petition?" I asked.

"They tabled it," said Chip.

September 19: Chip calculated that so far we've pumped over half a million dollars into Pittsfield's economy.

"It's not just the $250,000 of our own money," said Chip. "There's the $125,000 from the vintage game tickets, concessions, and advertising that went to vendors, booster clubs, fireworks, rental companies, etc. What was left over went into our general kitty for things like architects, engineers, construction, and painters—all local people" (see our cash-flow summary in the documents section).

"That's $375,000," I said. "Where's the other $125,000?"

"ESPN spent about $50,000 locally for things like camera platforms, the additional scoreboard, turf repair, a new announcer's desk," said Chip. "A fairly large crew stayed at the Crowne Plaza."

"You're up to $425,000," I said.

"Then there were the 7,000 people who came to the games, a lot of them from out of town," said Chip. "I spoke to merchants who saw a real spike in their sales. It's not unreasonable to assume that the Pittsfield area received an average of $11 a head from the 7,000 people. There's $77,000. And that comes to over half a million."

September 21: In an attempt to see if we can "work something out" with the union, Mayor Ruberto invited Tim Craw, John Kelly, Dave Potts, Gene Nadeau, and Chip and me to a meeting at City Hall. Not to be outnumbered, we brought Sam Elitzer and Paula, as special advisors.

What we needed were mind readers. Before the meeting began, as we waited for the mayor to join us in a conference room, Tim Craw and John Kelly were conspicuously smirking at us. Craw, sitting diagonally across the table, made a concerted effort to catch my eye, grinning and nodding as if he were trying to send me a message. I couldn't figure out what the hell he was trying to say.

The mayor entered the room looking sweaty and harried. He began with his usual pitch about why Chip and I should live with the Bid Laws, and we repeated the reasons why that was impossible. And that's about how it went until Tim Craw helped make our point. Inadvertently.

I was telling the mayor about the estimates I was getting from local union contractors for our scaled-back plan.

"That's against the law," said Craw, jabbing his finger at me across the table. "You'll have to re-bid it."

"Why?" I asked, irritated by the interruption.

Craw had a sarcastic little smile on his face.

"You didn't use biddable drawings, and you didn't have a walk-through," he said, arrogantly.

"The drawings are good enough for our purposes," I said, addressing the mayor. "None of the contractors seem to mind. In fact, they're even making suggestions for how we can save money."

"You have to re-bid it," said Craw.

Craw and Kelly were clearly enjoying themselves. Kelly even looked down a few times to stifle a smile. The mayor, looking tense and nervous, followed the exchange closely.

"And you broke the law when you hired the architect," said Craw. "Before you do anything more, you have to bid the architect."

What about the work we had already done at the ballpark?

"Against the law."

Our completed engineering?

"Against the law," said Craw. "You have to bid it."

Bid it. Re-bid it. Ribbit.

After delivering his tutorial on union law, Craw leaned over and informed Ruberto that he and Kelly would be leaving, since it was obvious there was nothing more the union could do and it was now up to the city. Whereupon Ruberto, as if on cue, solicitously escorted Craw and Kelly from the room.

When Ruberto returned, about ten minutes later, he looked even more frazzled than he had before.

"Now I'm *begging* you," he said. "Please go along with the Bid Laws."

The mayor sounded desperate. As if he had already made a decision not to sign the revised license, no matter what.

But how could that be? He had just witnessed what our lives would be like under Tim Craw. Didn't the mayor understand what he was risking? I reminded him what we had achieved in just a short period of time.

"The 1791 document, the Hillies, ESPN . . ."

"You just got lucky," said Potts, who had been quiet until then.

There was a brief silence. Then Paula exploded.

"Lucky!" she turned on Potts. "*Lucky!!!* How *dare* you say that!"

I tentatively reached for Paula's knee.

"No," she said, pulling her knee away. "I'm sick and tired of being quiet! I've had *enough* of this."

I withdrew my hand.

"Luck had nothing to do with it!" Paula shouted. "You think *you* could have gotten that story on the front page of the *International Herald Tribune?* You think you could have gotten ESPN to come here and give you four hours of airtime? You think you could have come up with the concept, designed the uniforms, printed the materials? You damn well couldn't have!"

Potts was stone faced. The mayor was bug-eyed, transfixed.

"That wasn't luck!" Paula raged, her voice starting to crack. "That took a helluva lot of work—from all of us, 24/7! And what were *you* doing? Undermining us every step of the way, that's what you were doing."

By now, Paula was crying.

"Don't pay any attention to these tears," she said, wiping her eyes with her fingers, annoyed with herself. "It happens when I get really angry."

I leaned over to comfort Paula, but she shrugged me off. That meant she wasn't finished yet. And I had no desire to stop her.

"What is *wrong* with you people? You get something good happening and you crap all over it with your complaints—the tickets are too expensive, it's the wrong beer, the wrong singers, you're not getting *paid!*"

Paula shifted her focus from Potts to Nadeau.

"And then 5,000 people show up, have the time of their lives, a magic night, and you can't even spring for a $3 ticket?!"

Paula had a look of utter contempt on her face, as she paused to catch her breath. Then she looked at Ruberto.

"You asked Jim to stop promoting his book," she said, "and he did that for you."

"Yes, he did," said Ruberto, relieved to find something soothing to say. "He kept his word."

"But that's how we earn our living!" Paula interrupted harshly. "You stop promoting a book and it dies. Did you give any thought about how we were to earn our living while we were putting money into *your* city? We are now personally $100,000 in the red for the benefit of Pittsfield and you can't even give us the support that you promised when you invited us back? *What is the matter with you?*"

Total silence.

"You think we're made of money? All this talk of how blue collar you are. We didn't grow up rich, either. We worked just as hard for our money as you have for yours. And what do we get for our blood, sweat, and tears? Nothing but backstabbing and extortion and obstacles and complaints. I've had it with Pittsfield and the Parks Commission and the newspaper and with all of you! No more. I want out! Let's go home."

There was an awkward silence in the room. Nobody knew what to do or say. When Paula stood up, the rest of us stood up too. That seemed to be the signal that the meeting was over. Without a word, the group made its way to the door. In the flow of bodies, Ruberto gave Paula a hug.

For me, I felt lucky to be married to her. In five minutes of unscripted fury, Paula had delivered a super nova of truth to a room full of people who needed to see it. Including Chip and me. I wasn't sure what would happen next, but I knew at least the air would be cleaner.

September 22: I sent the following email to Chip, which he forwarded to the mayor, along with his own comments:

```
> It just occurred to me that the carpenters'
> original complaint had to do with the
> 'language' of the license agreement, and that
> none of the cases they cited said a city-
> owned facility must be publicly bid --
> BECAUSE THERE IS NO SUCH CASE. The carpenters
> want Wahconah Park to be that case and they
> believe a vulnerable mayor will give it to
> them. Ruberto has to call this strategy for
> what it is: massive overreaching that will
> retard development across the state. Which
> will not be good for the Attorney General
> when it gets traced back to him.
```

September 23: Chip and I met with the mayor again at City Hall. He said he had a new idea.

"What if we did a Fleisig deal?" said Ruberto, with his old enthusiasm. "Two years at $75,000 a year! That at least gets you into the ballpark. And you can make improvements whenever you want."

"Fleisig lost money on the Fleisig deal," Chip quickly reminded him. "Our business plan calls for upgrading the ballpark. We can't do that with a two-year deal."

The mayor looked deflated.

Then, after some thought, he hinted at his real Reason For Not Signing the revised license agreement.

"The revised license won't get past the AG's office," said Ruberto, suggesting he either knew or believed that the Attorney General would not approve it.

"That doesn't make sense," I said. "The AG *wants* the city to revise the license. He doesn't want to set a precedent that would destroy private investment in all public buildings in Massachusetts!"

"We believe strongly that he *will* approve it," said Chip. "And we'll put our belief to the test. If you'll sign it and send it to the AG, we'll close on our financing, go ahead with construction, and take our chances on a favorable ruling. That's how confident we are."

The mayor looked troubled.

"I can't do it," he said.

September 24: Paula woke up in the middle of the night, feeling anxious.

"I want to move away from here," she said, in the darkness.

"Where would we go?" I mumbled.

"New Zealand."

"We'd be too far away from the kids," I said. "And the little ones [our grandchildren] would have trouble finding us on the globe. They'd think we were going to fall off the bottom."

"That's what it feels like now," said Paula.

Why did Chip and I continue? Because we still had that dream of what it could be like at a renovated Wahconah Park—especially now, with the Hillies. I remembered what Paula had said at the July 3 game. "This makes it all worthwhile." I imagined her saying that again.

And we also wanted to understand what was happening.

September 26: Miles Wolff called and offered Chip and me the "eighth team" slot in the Northeast League for 2005. Unbelievable! Here was the call we'd been waiting for since 2001, and we couldn't really enjoy it.

"Now we have a team and no ballpark," said Chip.

"This is like trying to mate a pair of elephants," said I.

September 27: I continued to get estimates for our scaled-back plan, which was pricing out as follows: demolition and excavation ($182,300); electrical ($103,400); plumbing ($69,600); painting ($35,000); fencing (24,000); concession sheds ($22,000); and carpentry ($17,000).

Except for the painting and the prebuilt concession sheds, almost the entire job (91%) would be done by local union contractors. And all of it put at risk by the carpenters over a mere $17,000, or 3.7% of the total job! But, as Craw had said, "It's a matter of principle."

Or maybe a favor for an old friend.

We had just learned from City Councilor Chuck Vincelette that Tim Craw used to manage the Brewery, the bar owned by ex-Parks Commissioner Bob "Smitty" Smith, drinking buddy of ex-Mayor Gerry Doyle.

"I think this whole thing is motivated by more than a coincidence," Vincelette said.

"Tim Craw could be the instrument for all those guys who hate us," said Chip.

"Okay, so Craw gets the ball rolling with the Bid Protest," I said, playing detective. "But he's not keeping the mayor from signing the license. That's coming from somewhere else."

"Higher up," said Chip. "Craw is just the henchman."

"Who's higher up than the mayor?" I asked. And we both laughed at the possibilities just within walking distance of City Hall.

September 29: Backed by a league invitation and union contractors, Chip and I decided to give democracy one more shot. We would ask the Parks Commission and the City Council—on October 4 and 12 respectively—to recommend that the mayor sign the revised license and send it to the Attorney General. To get a feel for our chances, I asked Parks Commissioner Garivaltis what he thought of our strategy. He wasn't optimistic.

"Minds will be made up before the meeting," he said.

"Before we even make our case?" I said. "Would they vote against public sentiment?"

"They're not alone," Garivaltis said. "They know the banks are against you. Some of the big lawyers in town. The *Eagle*. And the mayor's stand is a major barrier—he gives them cover."

September 30: Our largest Pittsfield investor agreed to speak on our behalf at the October 4 Parks Commission meeting. She also offered some thoughts on the problems we were facing.

"I understand there are a couple of goons involved," she said.

October 1: Chip and I were guests on the *Dan Valenti Show*. We explained our strategy and asked the listeners to make their wishes known to the parks commissioners and city councilors. We said if we struck out with them, the game would be over.

After the program, Valenti told us something strange that his news director Len Bean had told him.

"About a week ago," said Valenti, "Len said that Tim Craw had told him there wasn't going to be any baseball played at Wahconah Park in 2005."

"Did Craw say why?" I asked.

That's all he told me," Valenti said. "And Len's not here right now or you could ask him yourself."

"We'll check it out later," said Chip.

"Jeeez," I said. "Maybe Ruberto meant it when he said 'Tim Craw holds the keys.'"

In the lot behind City Hall, where we had parked for Valenti's show, who do we see going in the back door but Craw's old pal Gerry Doyle, looking dapper in a shiny black suit. Doyle of course is now a lobbyist, taking the standard career path of ex-politicians—experts at currying favor, having been curried themselves.

Was Doyle still lobbying for a waste transfer station (read dump) in a residential neighborhood? Or was he there to help facilitate a proposed strip joint in a residential neighborhood? I swear I'm not making this up. Now, if I said that the strip joint was going to be called the Bada Bing Club, *that* would be making things up.

October 2: Speaking of making things up, how about this quote from Mayor Ruberto in the *Eagle*? Responding to Chip's comment that the mayor was refusing to sign the license because he has to negotiate with municipal unions—which originated with Ruberto in the first place—Ruberto said, "I want every collective bargaining unit to hear that I am going to respect the Attorney General's position because I respect the right to organize."

Now we were against the right to organize!

It's that kind of absurdity that tells you something is going on.

October 3: Paula and I drove down to New York City to celebrate a family birthday. We talked in the car.

"I don't know why you and Chip continue," said Paula.

"Because it'll be a wonderful thing," I said.

"But look what you're dealing with," said Paula. "Doyle and Craw are pals. Craw is smirking because he obviously knows something. Potts wants to get paid. Nadeau doesn't know the meaning of the word extortion. The mayor is dealing behind your back with Miles Wolff, and giving you no support. The banks want nothing to do with you. Jeff Cook and his boys are opposing you. The Chamber of Commerce won't even meet with you. And they're all pressuring the parks commissioners, who don't have the strength to stand up to it. Just who are you doing this wonderful thing for?"

There was a long silence.

"The vast majority in Pittsfield," I said. "Besides, if we bow out now, our opponents will call us quitters."

"Better quitters than fools," said Paula.

o o o

CHAPTER 20

"And if you quote me, I'll deny it"

October 4: The two fools, plus their wives and supporters—who now included Hillies players and coaches, local union contractors, an investor who drove 2½ hours from Boston, and our only significant Pittsfield investor—filed into Springside House for the 7:00 p.m. meeting in a last-ditch effort to save our plan for Wahconah Park. Also in attendance were an unsmiling Dave and Grace Potts, and the perpetually smirking Tim Craw.

Outside on the porch, a few commissioners peered anxiously in the window at the growing crowd, and then at their watches. It struck me that these were not the arrogant, plotting commissioners of 2001, but rather an uncertain and vulnerable bunch.

At the stroke of seven, just as the commissioners had taken their seats, City Solicitor Chris Speranzo burst into the room and, in a routine that looked choreographed, was immediately recognized by Chairman Gene Nadeau. Speranzo said he had a message from Mayor Ruberto regarding our agenda item.

"We are asking that you consider a motion to file," said Speranzo, who looked nervous and out of breath.

A motion to file, like a motion to table, would forestall action on our request to have the commissioners endorse the revised license, copies of which we had sent to them with the revisions clearly marked. Evidently, the mayor wasn't taking any chances that Chip and I just might change a few of the minds that Garivaltis had said "will be made up."

"This is not the proper forum to negotiate a revised license," said Speranzo, misrepresenting our purpose for being there.

Commissioner Elinor Persip, an attractive older woman with a long family history in Pittsfield, quickly sized up the situation.

"I just want to say that I am terribly sorry that all of this has happened," she said, casting her eyes down. "And I feel that the commissioners are being put in the middle of this. But it appears to me, and I hate to have to make this statement, that some group or individual or someone has made a great effort to try to make Wahconah Park, Inc. fail."

Nevertheless, Persip went on to say it was "not our responsibility" and that she would vote for a motion to file.

The amazing thing was that no one—not the commissioners nor Speranzo nor the audience—responded to Ms. Persip's astounding charge that Chip and I were being sabotaged. There was no scoffing in disbelief *or* calls of outrage. It was simply assumed that we were being undermined. This was Pittsfield, after all.

Accordingly, the discussion proceeded as Speranzo had requested—not to the question of how the commissioners felt about the revised license, but whether or not it should be tabled. And what the consequences might be.

"If we go against what you're telling us as our legal counsel," said Mike Filpi, who happens to be the Financial Secretary of the Berkshires Central Labor Council, "shame on us because we can get ourselves in trouble."

What kind of trouble was not explained.

Garivaltis was the only one who seemed to be worried about more than himself. "It is the health of my community that is at stake here," he said.

Then he and Speranzo got into it.

Garivaltis: Why would the Attorney General rule on a matter that involved private money? These are not taxpayer dollars. He has nothing to say on how they spend their money.

Speranzo: I argued that exact position at the AG's office. I argued for the city. I really wish we had won that case. Unfortunately we didn't and we have to play the cards as they are.

Garivaltis: They sent it back to you and the mayor.

Speranzo: That's right.

Garivaltis: To act on it. Why can't you act on it? It's private dollars. They've got a million plus dollars that they're going to put in . . . and they're not asking for one dime from the taxpayers. That's wrong. 100% wrong!

Speranzo: (flustered) I understand where you're coming from.

To explain where *he* was coming from, Speranzo launched a barrage of verbiage so convoluted as to be unintelligible, ending with his own version of the now classic defense of the indefensible: "This is not where I want to be, but we have to do what we have to do with what we have."

With that, Speranzo beat a hasty retreat to where he wanted to be—outside the building—relieved not to have to do anything more than he had to do with what he had.

Undaunted, Chip and I plowed ahead.

Why not? We had a better story than the city solicitor. We had a 91% union project, we had $1.2 million in private money, and we had *two* teams. We even had color pictures.

"Not only do we have access to a professional team," I said, waving a manila folder with the flourish of a magician, "but we now have a name for that team. A name that's been right before our eyes all along at Wahconah Park. Hanging up there in the rafters . . . the Pittsfield Owls!"

During the happy applause, which did not include the commissioners or Tim Craw's group in the back, I distributed copies of our 2005 Pittsfield Owls logo, as it would appear on the uniforms.

"We are looking for the Owls to take their rightful place alongside the Hillies," said Chip, jumping in with the zeal of a missionary. "Leagues will come and go, but with a community-owned Wahconah Park and its ownership of two teams, we're well on our way to establishing Pittsfield as the Santo Domingo of baseball in America."

More applause. And an interruption from the chairman.

"Just a second," said Nadeau, a distinguished-looking fellow with a full salt-and-pepper beard. "This really wasn't part of the agenda. I know it's a promo for the endorsement but I would prefer us to stick to the license agreement. I don't really want to engage the audience."

Let's hear it for candor, at least.

Shifting gears, Chip talked about our "vision of Pittsfield being a year-round sports mecca." He said we were on track to "exceed expectations," allowing us to "go back to our investors" and raise even "more money for an indoor arena," establishing "a virtuous cycle" that would "keep the tourist dollars flowing year round." Chip said he wanted the commissioners to know "what could be possible if we don't derail it tonight."

Chip also pointed out that it was not "highly unusual" for the Parks Commission to make a recommendation to the mayor, as Speranzo had said. In fact, "it is the role of the commissioners to recommend to the mayor," said Chip, as was done "three years ago with the Fleisig proposal," months before it was negotiated by the mayor.

We then asked Nadeau that members of the audience be allowed to address the commissioners.

"This wasn't advertised as a public hearing," said Nadeau.

"But these are not simply members of the public," I explained. "They're part of our organization and are speaking on our behalf."

"Howard Cronson, one of our investors," said Chip, "has driven all the way from Boston and will drive all the way home tonight."

"I guess my decision is that we've heard the pitch," said Nadeau. "My feeling, as far as I'm concerned is, again, I'm not a negotiator."

I wanted to scream at Nadeau: You're not being asked to negotiate, damn it, you're being asked to recommend!

Powered by a surge of anger, I took the floor.

"We came back on a promise," I said loudly, addressing the entire room, "that we were going to get cooperation, we'd get democracy, we'd get openness, we'd get fairness. That we would not run into procedures that prevent people who have come here and given their *time*, and their *energy*, and their *love* for a ballpark to be brushed off with tabling something. *No!*"

I couldn't stop, and besides it felt good.

"This city is sick and tired of people passing the buck," I said, even louder. "You are parks commissioners! I'm sure you're here because you love the parks. It's a simple question. You've seen us in action. You've seen what we've done so far. *Do you think it's a good idea to have us in Wahconah Park?* If you do, vote yes because this is the only way we're going to play—with a modified agreement. If the mayor doesn't want to sign it he doesn't have to, but let him know how *you* feel! Let him know how you feel about *us.*"

All the hours of hard work were pouring out of me.

"Let [Parks Director] Jim McGrath tell you about Chip Elitzer getting down on his hands and knees vacuuming rooms at Wahconah Park that haven't been cleaned in over thirty years! Our wives up until 2, 3, 4 in the morning, bookkeeping, paying bills, emptying our bank accounts, putting it all into Wahconah Park, and we're going to come here and have you tell us you're going to *table it?!* You don't have any *thoughts* on the matter? You don't have any wishes? You're going to *table* it? This is *bullshit!!"*

The room burst into sustained applause.

"We didn't table the Hillies," I sputtered. "We didn't table ESPN. We're not tablers. That's how we get stuff done."

It seemed like a good place to stop.

"I understand that," said Nadeau. "My thing is, once again Jim, and I understand your outburst, but we are not negotiators."

Does the word *oblivious* mean anything?

A man in the audience stood up.

"I don't know these two gentlemen from a hole in the ground," he said, "but I'm for them 100%. And common courtesy is to hear from these other people that have come a great distance to speak. Thank you."

Another burst of applause.

The words of this stranger were so starkly and stunningly true that even Nadeau had to nod his reluctant approval.

And the speakers spoke.

A Hillies player: "It doesn't sound like you're risking much by just telling the mayor, 'Hey we're backing these guys.'" Applause.

An investor: "No competent investor would put money into a minor league baseball team under the Bid Laws." Applause.

A union contractor: "I'm willing to take a chance on them if they're willing to take a chance on Pittsfield." Applause.

But none of it mattered. Not even an attempt by Garivaltis to lighten the mood.

"I'm voting for what I hope will be baseball in Wahconah Park in 2005," he said, standing up to make his point, "and if that happens, the Hillies are prepared to challenge the Owls to a baseball game!"

The audience loved this idea, laughing and applauding.

"The only stipulation," said Garivaltis, now pointing a finger, "is that the Owls have to use the vintage baseball gloves."

The room howled with delight at this thought. Seasoned professionals outplayed by their own local boys.

Then their own local commissioners voted 4 to 1 to table our request for a simple vote of confidence. It had been exactly three years to the day after the Parks Commission had voted 5 to 0 against us, in favor of Fleisig.

We had picked up one vote in three years.

My mind went back to what Commissioner Persip had said about *"some group or individual or someone"* having made *"a great effort to try and make Wahconah Park, Inc. fail."*

The question was, who? Besides the Attorney General. And "a couple of goons."

October 5: But we couldn't focus on that. We were already looking to the upcoming City Council meeting. And we had an encouraging email from councilor Dan Bianchi:

> Keep the faith, the people are with you.

In response to Bianchi, Chip posed a few questions that the councilors should ask the mayor:

1. Why aren't you accepting the AG's offer to revise the license?
2. What changed between the time that Chris and Chip co-authored the revised license in response to the AG's opinion and about a week later?
3. Why does the City no longer support WPI's right to pursue a privately funded project outside the Bid Laws?
4. Who is hijacking unionism's good name to kill baseball in Pittsfield?

That afternoon, I stopped by City Hall on the chance that I could meet with the mayor. Ruberto seemed glad to oblige and invited me into his office. We smiled at each other in anticipation of something positive. He may have thought I was going to tell him that we would accept the Bid Laws. Instead, we chatted about the Red Sox and the Yankees and the playoffs.

It was in that relaxed atmosphere that we talked about "the larger story" in Pittsfield—from the role that Wahconah Park plays in the community to how the mayor would be remembered. I said that if he pulled back the curtain, stood up to our enemies, and signed the license, he would go down as a great mayor, maybe even a great man.

Ruberto smiled, as if he would think about it. And, pathological optimist that I am, I left his office with a good feeling.

But it disappeared that evening. In a phone conversation between Chip and the mayor, Ruberto said it would be futile to send the revised license to the Attorney General.

"There's more to it than what you have in your hand," Ruberto said, in reference to the AG's opinion. "It goes beyond what he wrote in his decision. And if you quote me I'll deny it."

October 6: I woke up at 4:20 a.m. in a cold sweat. I had a terrible sense of dread that we were about to step into a trap. Different from the trap we were already in. Call it stage two: the mayor would *sign* the revised license but not support it—letting it sit in the AG's office without a decision, while our investors' money followed ours down the drain.

Eventually someone would make a phone call and the Attorney General would rule against us, and we'd be stuck with the Bid Laws. I pictured Craw with a bullhorn ordering workers down off their ladders because we had just violated union regulation 412.8c, or some such bullshit.

I wasn't having a bad dream; I was having a bad reality.

I knew if it wasn't Craw or Doyle or the AG, it would be somebody else—our enemies working "passively" and "actively" against us, while Mayor Ruberto stood on the sidelines, begging and wringing his hands.

Trap or no trap, we had to get out. And fast.

Unable to sleep, I tiptoed into my office and faxed a note that read: Chip, If you're up, give me a call. But Chip didn't call back until 6:00 a.m. He had slept late.

I told him why I felt we needed to abandon ship.

"You're right," he said, almost shockingly acquiescent. "If it's not this, it'll be something else."

"Can you imagine down the road," I said, not sure that my partner was really on board, "going back to the parks or the council to ask for something we hadn't thought of?"

"We just saw what that would be like," Chip said.

There was a long pause.

"So, what do you think?" I said.

"I think it's right," he said. "We really don't have any choice, when you stop and look at it."

"It's a big decision," I said. "Should we check to see if it's okay with our wives?"

We both laughed.

When Paula woke up and I told her what Chip and I had decided to do, she said only two words.

"Thank you!"

But she said them four times, loudly, with her arms raised to the ceiling, and her eyes uplifted to the sky.

Now, the trick was to call our partner Eric Margenau and our three other board members before emailing a public announcement, and to do all that before telling anyone else, including Ruberto. Especially Ruberto. My fear was that if we were to tell the mayor what we planned to do, he'd say he had just signed the revised license and was about to go public himself.

Not taking any chances, Paula scribbled a note and handed it to me while I was on the phone with Chip:

Tell Chip not to return any phone calls until this media announcement is a fait accompli—particularly no calls to or from Ruberto, or any other city official. NO NEW "INFORMATION" will alter the scenario we are surely facing. (Chip may still be fighting his own impulses to explain, educate, find a way to forge ahead.)

Paula was right. I may be known as the Bulldog, but Chip is the Energizer Bunny.

At 12:15 p.m., we emailed the following press release to city officials and the local media:

> My partners and I announce regretfully that we have withdrawn our plan to renovate Wahconah Park and bring professional baseball back to Pittsfield, MA. It is clear that we no longer have the necessary support of the City officials who on January 13, 2004, invited us to return with a proposal we had originally made in 2001, a proposal that was substantially improved by our current plan.
>
> We don't want to stand in the way of other opportunities for the city regarding baseball, and we will ask both independent leagues to consider favorably any other Wahconah-based proposals which may come their way.
>
> Sincerely,
> Jim Bouton
> President of Wahconah Park, Inc.

Twenty minutes later, Chris Speranzo called and left a message on Chip's answering machine, wondering if our announcement had been widely released. Then Chip left a message on the mayor's machine, saying that it had been. We heard nothing more from City Hall.

One wonders what the mayor would have done if he thought he'd been the sole recipient of a *draft* press release. More begging, perhaps? A suddenly signed revised license?

It felt as if we had just dodged a bullet.

o o o

CHAPTER 21
"Whodunnit?"

According to the *Berkshire Eagle*, we had done it to ourselves. The day after Chip and I bowed out—October 7, 2004—Everhart's editorial (David Scribner had been asked to resign for reasons that had nothing to do with his lack of journalistic skills)—BOUTON, ELITZER PACK IT IN—contained these gems:

> That Jim Bouton and Chip Elitzer would pick up their ball and go home, blaming Pittsfield officials for their woes, is graceless but hardly surprising . . . the pair were not team players. . . . That they gave up so easily raises questions about the depth of their devotion to the project. . . . It is important to note that at no time during either of their bids for use of Wahconah Park did the partnership actually have a baseball team. . . . Mr. Bouton is now free to write *Foul Ball 2*, with a new cast of characters to flay.

The irony of course is that if the *Eagle* had been doing its job there wouldn't have been a need for *Foul Ball* in the first place. It's not just their biased editorial page. They lack the old-fashioned "nose for news."

After Chip and I bowed out, Tony Dobrowolski called to ask if I thought the timing of the Bid Protest was suspicious.

"What do you think?" I asked.

"I'm just a reporter," he said.

Not being reporters, Chip and I wanted to find out exactly what had happened.

"This is a regular 'Whodunnit,'" I said.

"It was the perfect crime," Chip said. "We were screwed no matter which way we went. It cost us time and money. It was made to look like our fault. And they have deniability."

However, the perfect crime leaves no clues. And we just happened to have a few. But first there were the coincidences.

Beginning with a story in the *Eagle* on the very same day as the above editorial. On the front page of the B section—LOTHROP CLARIFIES STATEMENTS ON TALKS WITH DOYLE—City Councilor Jonathan Lothrop is quoted as saying he inaccurately described the ex-mayor as having "approached" him about a strip club ordinance, when in fact a meeting was arranged by a "third party." Fellow by the name of Tim Craw.

Besides the question of why Doyle felt he needed an intermediary (and whether a fee was involved), the funniest part was Craw's explanation for why he had brokered the meeting. Craw said he was concerned about the ordinance and thought Doyle would "help make it stricter."

"Can you believe these people?" I said to Chip.

"They're just trying to give you some good material for the movie," he said, looking at the big picture.

Then there was the relationship between Doyle and Attorney General Thomas F. Reilly. It turns out they were friends, too.

"That might explain why the AG agreed to a hearing in the first place," I said. "As Dan Valenti pointed out, a union protest normally goes to the Inspector General first, and *he* decides if it's worth taking to the AG."

"I wonder if Reilly circumvented the Inspector General when he cleared Doyle of wrongdoing back in 2002?" said Chip.

"Maybe they both broke the law," I said.

The big question has always been this: why didn't Ruberto sign the revised license that his own city solicitor had co-authored, a remedy the Attorney General invited in his remand back to the city?

I played Watson to Chip's Sherlock Holmes.

"Even if Ruberto is telling the truth about the AG saying he wouldn't approve the revised license," I said, "why didn't he sign it anyway and put the AG on the spot?"

"Maybe someone didn't *want* Ruberto to put the AG on the spot," said Chip, raising an eyebrow. "Someone who got the AG to issue an ambiguous opinion in the first place."

442

Even if the scheme hadn't been orchestrated from the beginning, the Attorney General's opinion offered an excellent opportunity to stop us. Just call the mayor and make a deal. Here's where the clues come into play.

Clue #1. THE PREDICTION

On the morning of September 21, after a press conference at City Hall, Tim Craw told WBRK news director Len Bean, in conspiratorial tones, "I can't give you the details, but there won't be any baseball at Wahconah Park in 2005."

The above quote was confirmed by Bean, after Dan Valenti had brought it to our attention.

"Craw's prediction about there being no baseball at Wahconah Park," said Chip, "was delivered as he was coming out of the press conference that announced the airport compromise. I think the two are connected."

What would a press conference about an airport compromise have to do with Wahconah Park?

The expansion of the Pittsfield Municipal Airport had been a four year battle that pitted local farmers, homeowners, and environmentalists against "an elite group" of businessmen—a group that had threatened to confiscate property under eminent domain, close an important road, and destroy a Wild Acres habitat while removing property from the tax roles and appropriating $1 million of local taxes, all, wrote Jonathan Levine, "with little regard for meaningful public involvement."

"We stand to lose up to 100 acres and our most productive land," said Ed Watroba, speaking of property his family had farmed since 1915. "If they were going to build a hospital or a school I would understand, but this isn't going to benefit the general public."

Pittsfield native Ann Truran said the benefit would go to "those who are already comfortable," while others paid with health and environmental costs just so a few private jets can "swoop in and out."

For some citizens, the airport expansion, supported by the *Berkshire Eagle* and questioned by the *Gazette*, was "another Civic Authority," involving many of the same players, using the same "scare tactics" and the spreading of "false information" in behalf of a "famously flawed project."

In December, 2003, the beleaguered expansion opponents, led by City Councilor Jonathan Lothrop, developed a compromise plan that would give the businessmen "90% of what they want." But the hardliners, led by Jeff Cook, refused to budge and the compromise sat for almost a year. Which is why it came as a big surprise when they suddenly gave in.

Clue #2. THE TIMING

"We're creating a new model of how to do business in Pittsfield," Ruberto had said in announcing the airport compromise, a major goal of his administration. "A model based on sensitivity to individual interests."

The question was, What individual interests led the hardliners to yield—at that particular time?

"I think they agreed to the compromise," said Chip, "in exchange for the mayor's agreement not to sign our revised license."

"In other words," I said, "Ruberto traded the airport for the ballpark."

"That's right," said Chip. "But the mayor figured he wouldn't lose the ballpark because he thought he could convince us to live with the Bid Laws."

"And Craw made sure that wouldn't happen," I said, following Chip's logic, "at the meeting where he threatened to make us re-bid everything."

"That was the same day as the press conference," said Chip. "It was the announcement of the airport compromise that sealed the deal with the mayor. And that freed up Craw to slam the door on the Bid Law option that afternoon by demonstrating how impossible he'd be to work with."

Clue #3. THE SMIRK

"That could explain why Craw was smirking at me before the meeting," I said. "He wanted me to know that *he* knew we were already screwed because he was about to lower the boom."

"I think he blindsided the mayor, too." said Chip.

"I'll bet that's why Ruberto walked out with Craw and didn't come back for ten minutes," I said. "He was giving Craw hell for scaring us off."

"Remember how sweaty and agitated Ruberto was when he did return," said Chip. "That's when he started begging us."

"And that's why he always said 'I *can't* sign it' instead of 'I won't sign it,'" I said, regarding the revised license.

We paused to marvel at the scheme, which we both agreed was way beyond the capabilities of either Doyle or Craw.

"So, in the hours between the press conference and our meeting," I said, "only Craw and a very small group, maybe only one other person, knew there would be no baseball at Wahconah Park in 2005. Can you imagine what a big shot Craw must have felt like, knowing he was personally going to finish us off?"

"He couldn't wait to tell someone like Len Bean," said Chip. "Just like when Doyle told Ray Parrott 'the fix is in.'"

"Guys like Doyle and Craw cannot resist letting people know how close they are to power," I said.

"Beavis and Butthead," said Chip.

To test our theory, Chip sent an email to Jonathan Lothrop, who was also going to be one of our stockholders.

Chip to Lothrop:

> Just out of curiosity, I'd like to ask you a few
> questions about the airport compromise. Please
> call me at your convenience.

Lothrop to Chip:

> What did you want to know?

Chip to Lothrop:

> I know that you started as a strong opponent of
> the original "maximalist" airport expansion plan,
> and that one of the strongest proponents of that
> plan was Jeff Cook. Some months ago, you began to
> champion a compromise plan. From accounts I read,
> the "maximalists" held firm for a while. At what
> point in time did they agree to compromise, and
> how did that come about?

Clue #4. THE STONEWALL

Lothrop never responded. In our various communications since we met him in 2001, it was the first time he had failed to do so.

"In the game of *Clue*," I said, "you would postulate that, 'Someone did it, with an airport compromise, in the mayor's office.'"

The mayor would deny it, of course. He would say we walked out because, "They didn't have the money"—as he later insisted on the *Dan Valenti Show*. That charge, which became the mantra of many city officials, added to the smokescreen that included, "They didn't have a team" and "They didn't want to play by the rules."

But what else could they say?

Would the mayor say: "I was afraid to stand up to the Attorney General?" Or, "I traded 950 feet of runway for Wahconah Park?"

Would the councilors say: "We can hand over $1 million to the Colonial Theatre and protect them from the Bid Laws, but we can't get the mayor to sign a piece of paper that wouldn't have cost the city a dime?"

Would the commissioners say: "We had the last shot at saving the best deal anyone ever offered for Wahconah Park and we tabled it?"

Not likely.

And what might the Attorney General say? Had he really told Ruberto, or someone else, that he wouldn't approve the revised license if it were sent to him?

"That would be a good question to ask him on the campaign trail," said Chip. "The man who supposedly 'fucked' Pittsfield is running for governor of Massachusetts."

Months after we had bowed out, Chip had a long conversation with Steve Picheny, whose tough love and good advice had gotten us to revise our prospectus and avoid some early criticism. As always, Steve was in our corner.

"Your motives were pure," he told Chip. "You weren't greedy like they're saying."

But Picheny's prescription for success was still the same.

"You should have called Jeff Cook," he said.

"We tried," said Chip.

"You should have tried harder," said Picheny.

"He's an asshole," said Chip.

"In sales," said Picheny, "if the guy is an asshole, well, then you better learn how to sell to assholes."

"We could have sold this anywhere," said Chip.

"In any other city you could have got it done," said Picheny. "But not in Pittsfield."

When something like this happens in a democracy, somebody usually pays on election day. And there is a big turnover of politicians in Pittsfield, but nothing ever changes. For a very simple reason: the people running the city aren't running for office.

But how do you vote a law firm, two banks, and a newspaper out of town? Pittsfield needs a U.S. Marshal to come riding in. Or an Attorney General.

Oops.

"A day doesn't go by that I don't think about it," said Chip.

This was six months after we had called it quits.

"It was real for me," he said, the passion coming back into his voice. "It was tangible. It was going to be such an unalloyed benefit for Pittsfield. It was going to be fun. And it could have been something even bigger. Meaningful economic development—240,000 visitors, exceeding our investors' expectations, tapping them for more money to build an arena, hockey, concerts, trade shows, and no taxpayer dollars needed . . ."

My partner's voice trailed off, and I thought he might cry. This had been Chip's dream—the dream of the idealistic investment banker with a graduate degree in economic development who could have lifted Pittsfield off the canvas by himself if they had let him.

"Look what we did with just two games!" said Chip. "Out of our back pocket. Without an organization. That was just a flavor of what we could have done with sixty games."

"Our project would have done more for Pittsfield than the airport expansion and the Colonial Theatre combined," I said.

"More than government handouts to the politically connected," said Chip, "Pittsfield needs to attract private capital."

"The city is used as a dumping ground and a piggy bank," I said. "We represented a different way of doing things. And we were succeeding. That's what frightened them."

"They rejected us as a foreign body," said Chip.

"The *Eagle* always talks about how rudely Bossidy was treated," I said. "Here they kicked $300 million of net worth in the teeth."

"And look at their motives," said Chip. "Fear, revenge, greed, envy. Base motives. Nothing high-minded. Nobody seemed to have any concept of the public good. That just got my goat."

"'The few spoiling it for the many,'" I said, repeating a line from a condolence card we had received from Betty Quadrozzi.

"And they can blame the book," said Chip, "but you know what? They did the same thing to us the first time around."

"All they did was prove that the book was accurate," I said. "If not for them, we'd be renovating Wahconah Park right now."

"And they can still have that," said Chip. "It's within their power. The whole city would have to get together. But it wouldn't cost them anything."

"What about our investors?" I said.

"They'd be with us in a heartbeat," said Chip. "Right now, they'd follow us anywhere."

There was a long silence.

"How is Cindy feeling these days?" I asked.

"She's still disappointed for me," said Chip. "She knew how alive I was for it."

"And what are *you* feeling?" said Paula, who is always asking me questions like that.

"I think I'm feeling resigned," I said. "But it's hard to tell because I'm concentrating on the book. Chip says it's like a death in the family, where you're so busy with the funeral arrangements you don't feel the full loss until later."

"The reader needs to know how you feel at the end," said Paula. "And that there *is* an end. Or else Paula will move out, you can tell them."

Paula turned to look out the dining room window.

"Sometimes I wonder if we'll ever be rid of Wahconah Park," she said wistfully.

"As soon as I'm finished with the book," I said, "I'm going to get to work on that patio."

"No you won't," said Paula. "You'll be out promoting the book and that's what I'm worried about next. That Tim Craw is going to rough you up, or worse."

"*He's* not going to do anything," I said, scoffing at the notion. "He'll get a guy from Toledo."

What I have are pangs. Pangs of sadness, whenever I go down to our basement. Against the far wall, I see Hillies uniforms, cleaned and hanging on a coat rack. A dozen Hillies bats stand in a corner. Against another wall is a massive tower of boxes containing thousands of 1791 documents packed in mailing tubes. Next to that are plastic bins of Hillies T-shirts, Hillies hats, and Hillies tote bags, plus boxes of Hillies autographed balls and posters we had planned to sell at future Hillies games.

If I really want to feel bad, I visit the sample paving stones near the furnace. The ones that showed how, for $200, people could "Own a Piece of Wahconah Park" by putting any name and message on an eight-by-fourteen-inch stone implanted in the plaza "at one of America's most beloved ballparks."

Stones with sample engravings like: JIMMY RUBERTO, MAYOR OF PITTSFIELD, which I had imagined by the main gate. Or the one marked IN MEMORY OF LAURIE BOUTON, which I had planned to put near a tree in the plaza.

But I choose not to feel bad, so I steer clear of the furnace. I choose to remember the good times. Like the vintage game. I see the fans with the big grins on their faces. I see Coach Zavatarro with tears in his eyes as we roll past the stands in the antique cars. I see Chuck Garivaltis shaking his head in wonder. I see the players in their jaunty poses, equipment bags over their shoulders. I see the look on Chip's face as he surveys the happy crowd.

I even see a beaming Jimmy Ruberto, in period tux, tossing out the first ball. And I can hear Quintessential singing the national anthem.

But I can't recall whether Ruberto stood up for it or not.

THE END

Fox and Scorpion came to a brook. Wide was the water. Scorpion asked Fox for a ride on his back. Fox said, "Scorpion, will you not sting me?" Scorpion said, "If I did, it would mean the death of us both."

Fox agreed, and Scorpion climbed onto his back. Fox swam, but halfway over, Scorpion struck with a deadly sting. Fox gasped, "Fool, you have doomed us both. Why?"

"I am a scorpion," said Scorpion. "It is my nature."

Indian Proverb

POSTSCRIPT

NEWS ITEMS
FALL 2004–SPRING 2005

OCT 27, 2004 – PITTSFIELD BUSINESS DAY FORUM HELD
The Jobs for Pittsfield Task Force hosted an all-day business forum at the Crowne Plaza Hotel. The purpose of the event, which featured presentations by Mayor Ruberto, Larry Bossidy, and Mike Daly, was "to attract companies and celebrate success stories in Pittsfield."

NOV 10, 2004 – PITTSFIELD TO GIVE $750,000 TO START-UP FIRM
WorkshopLive—a Connecticut-based company of six executives with plans to offer music lessons over the Internet—will begin receiving the money when they relocate to Pittsfield. WorkshopLive's Vice President Bob Hoeffner said the money was "fantastic" but that the company was coming to Pittsfield "with or without the incentives."

JAN 18, 2005 – NATIONAL SEARCH FOR WAHCONAH PARK TEAM
Parks Commissioner Mike Filpi called for "a national bid search" to find a baseball team to play at Wahconah Park. Filpi seemed not to understand that a team needs other teams to play against.

JAN 24, 2005 – CAN-AM LEAGUE FRANCHISE TO WORCESTER
Commissioner Miles Wolff recently announced that the Can-Am League—formerly the Northeast League—will place its 8th team (once earmarked for Pittsfield) in Worcester, Massachusetts, beginning in 2005.

JAN 28, 2005 – WAHCONAH PARK UP FOR NATIONAL REGISTER
The Massachusetts Historical Commission will meet in June, 2005, to decide whether to recommend that Wahconah Park be included on the National Register of Historic Places. A recommendation generally leads to approval about forty-five days later.

FEB 8, 2005 – PITTSFIELD GIVES SECOND TAX BREAK TO COUPLE
Joyce Bernstein and Larry Rosenthal received an eleven-year tax abatement worth an estimated $300,000 to build a restaurant/art gallery/noodle bar three blocks from the Lantern, which gets no subsidy. The millionaire duo had also received an eighteen-year tax break from the Doyle administration for their Link to Life emergency response business, which employs the ex-mayor's community development director, Tom Murphy. Bernstein and Rosenthal, generous campaign contributors—sometimes to opposing candidates—are represented by Mike MacDonald of Cain Hibbard Myers & Cook.

FEB 9, 2005 – COLONIAL THEATRE COSTS RISE AGAIN
Unplanned construction costs may add another $1.5 million to the current price tag of $20.6 million. This is up from earlier projections of $3 million, $8.2 million, $11 million, and $16 million since 1983. To date, the Colonial has received more than $8 million of public dollars—including $1.3 million of city funds—and is seeking another $6 million of historic tax credits.

FEB 14, 2005 – DUKES TO PLAY AT WAHCONAH PARK
The Parks Commission voted 5–0 to approve a one-year license that will bring Dan Duquette's New England Collegiate League baseball team to Pittsfield for the 2005 season.

MAR 1, 2005 – STRIP CLUB FILES FOR PERMIT
Residents blamed ex-Mayor Doyle, who said he has "no connection" to the club's management but is "acquainted with" its president. When asked if Doyle was the "paid agent" who had spoken to him about the strip club, councilor Matt Kerwood declined to comment.

Mayor Ruberto was quoted as saying, "This mayor does not welcome [the strip club] in Pittsfield, and I would hope and wish and pray that they will reconsider."

454

MAR 3, 2005 – Cinema Gets $900,000 Tax Credit
Secretary of State William F. Galvin (ex-Mayor Doyle's boss) announced the gift from the Massachusetts Historical Commission, worth $765,000 in cash to developer Richard Stanley. Stanley, whose investment of $500,000 "of his own money" represents 5.6% of the $8.9 million project, has already received a $500,000 loan from the city, and is seeking an additional $1 million in state grants and another $3.2 million in tax credits. Stanley is represented by Ed McCormick, the lawyer, scoutmaster, and college roommate of Cliff Nilan.

MAR 19, 2005 – Bouton Files for Hillies Trademark
"Anyone interested in reviving the Pittsfield Hillies or using the baseball team's name for any other purpose may soon need to receive permission from former Yankees' pitcher Jim Bouton."

(Note: This story, by Tony Dobrowolski of the *Eagle*, appeared more than five months after we filed a trademark application for use of the Hillies name on uniforms and T-shirts. During that time no one has asked to license the name. And it's not out of the question that we would resurrect the Hillies. On January 18, 2005, Chip and I and television sportscaster Bob Costas met with the head of programming for NBC Sports to discuss the possibility of staging a vintage baseball game—with Costas doing play-by-play—at Doubleday Field in Cooperstown. But the economics of a single event did not work out and we declined to accept a prime July, 2005, Saturday-afternoon slot.)

MAR 23, 2005 – GE Recontaminating Housatonic
Local environmentalists blasted an EPA permit that would allow General Electric to continue discharging PCBs into the Housatonic River. The EPA data shows that for at least the past three years, PCBs—"at levels hundreds of times higher than federal water quality standards for aquatic life"—have been leaking into the river from no fewer than ten pipes on the GE property in Pittsfield.

This was "our worst fear," said Tim Gray, whose Housatonic River Initiative had raised the issue of recontamination when the GE settlement was being drafted in 1998/99 (without HRI's participation). "We worked for fifteen years of our lives, coming to meetings, unpaid, to get this cleanup. And now we find that there is still pollution coming into the river."

455

APR 6, 2005 – Vɪɴᴛᴀɢᴇ Bᴀsᴇʙᴀʟʟ Rᴇᴛᴜʀɴs ᴛᴏ Pɪᴛᴛsꜰɪᴇʟᴅ
The Parks Commission voted to allow Dave Potts to stage two vintage baseball games at Wahconah Park in 2005. The team will be called the Elms, after a team that played in Pittsfield between 1862 and 1882. Former Hillies coach Paul Procopio will manage the team, consisting mostly of Hillies players.

(Note: Procopio had been added to the Hillies staff at the insistence of Jimmy Ruberto. Manager Chuck Garivaltis, who had honored the mayor's request to add Procopio, has refused to have anything to do with the Elms.)

APR 12, 2005 – Sᴘᴇʀᴀɴᴢᴏ Wɪɴs Sᴘᴇᴄɪᴀʟ Eʟᴇᴄᴛɪᴏɴ
Former City Solicitor Chris Speranzo received 70% of 4,941 votes cast, to win the 3rd Berkshire seat in the state House of Representatives. Speranzo succeeds Peter Larkin—now a lobbyist—who announced his resignation in January, a few days after he was sworn in.

Speranzo had received a rare 100% rating from the Berkshire Central Labor Council, a division of the state AFL-CIO. The union endorsement, and contributions, were believed crucial to winning the hastily called election. Tim Craw, a member of Speranzo's campaign team, said communication with union members was essential.

"It's constant phone-banking," said Craw. "It's a busy time of year for our members, but you'll see them at the polls."

Speranzo, a Democrat, also got endorsements from ex-Mayor Gerald S. Doyle and Attorney General Thomas F. Reilly.

During the campaign, Speranzo had said he was most proud of his role in the 1998 PCB settlement negotiations with the EPA and General Electric, when he was an aide to ex-Mayor Doyle. Speranzo was also given credit for having "created a sensible compromise solution" for the airport expansion.

MAY 15, 2005 – Bɪʟʟ Mᴏʏᴇʀs ᴀᴛ Mᴇᴅɪᴀ Rᴇꜰᴏʀᴍ Cᴏɴꜰᴇʀᴇɴᴄᴇ
In a keynote address at the National Conference for Media Reform in St. Louis, MO, Moyers said, among other things: "A free press is one where it's OK to state the conclusion you're led to by the evidence."

o o o

CAST OF CHARACTERS

(Includes only those who are not always identified)

Acton, Jay . . . . Part-time broker of minor league baseball franchises

Akers, Jamie . . . . . . Wahconah Park sketch artist

Arlos, Peter . . . . County treasurer and a former and future city councilor; aka the "Aging Greek God" and the "Oracle of Delphi"

Bahlman, Dusty . . . . *Berkshire Eagle* reporter

Barry, Bill. . . . . City councilor and new stadium supporter during the Doyle administration

Bassillion, David . . . . President of the Chamber of Commerce in 2004

Bean, Len. . . . . WBRK radio news director

Bianchi, Dan . . . . . . City councilor and new stadium opponent; with Guzzo and Scapin, one of the "Three Amigos"

Bonnevie, Frank . . . . Karate school owner and new stadium supporter

Bossidy, Larry . . . . . Pittsfield native son, former CEO of Allied Signal, and chairman of Berkshire Bank

Boulton, Frank . . . . . Founder and CEO of the Atlantic League, and owner of the Long Island Ducks

Brassard, Jim . . . . . . City councilor during the Doyle administration and new stadium supporter

Callahan, Mick . . . . . Owner of outdoor sign business and member of Berkshire Sports & Events

Carey, Bill . . . . *Berkshire Eagle* reporter

Chartock, Alan . . . . . Executive director of WAMC, Northeast Public Radio

Colker, Sue . . . . Parks commissioner during the Doyle administration

Conant, Jim. . . . . . . Parks commissioner during the Doyle administration, new stadium supporter, and groundskeeper

Cook, Jeff. . . . . Senior partner of Cain Hibbard Myers & Cook

Craw, Tim . . . . Carpenters union representative

Curro, Vinnie. . . . . . Made cancer map of PCB "ground zero" neighborhood

Daly, Mike . . . . Vice President of Berkshire Bank; later, bank president, and Berkshire Sports & Events member

DelGallo, Remo . . . . Former mayor, owner of DelGallo's Bar

Denmark, Gerry . . . . Lawyer for Berkshire Sports & Events

Dew, Jack. . . . . *Berkshire Eagle* reporter

Dobrowolski, Tony . . . *Berkshire Eagle* reporter

Dowd, Paul. . . . . . . City councilor during the Doyle administration and new stadium supporter

Doyle, Jr., Gerald S. . . . Mayor of Pittsfield during new stadium campaign, aka "Tony Soprano"

Duquette, Dan . . . . . Owner of the Dukes, a New England Collegiate League team, and former GM of the Boston Red Sox

Everhart, Bill . . . . . . Editorial page editor of the *Berkshire Eagle* and half of Ever-Scrib

Filpi, Mike . . . . Chairman of Parks Commission in early 2004

Fleisig, Jonathan . . . . New York energy trader and owner of the Massachusetts Mad Dogs and Berkshire Black Bears

Garivaltis, Chuck. . . . Manager of the Pittsfield Hillies and Parks Commissioner

Gladstone, Bill . . . . . Owner of Tri-City Valley Cats (formerly Pittsfield Mets)

Goldsmith, Jim . . . . . Jay Acton's partner in baseball franchise brokerage

Gordon, Susan . . . . . Owner of Bagels Too and Wahconah Park supporter

Gray, Tim . . . . Housatonic River Initiative environmentalist

Grunin, Gary . . . . . . City councilor during the Doyle administration and 2001 mayoral candidate

Guzzo, Joe . . . . City councilor and new stadium opponent; with Scapin and Bianchi, one of the "Three Amigos"

Hathaway, Sara. . . . . Mayoral successor to Doyle

Herkowitz, Sandra . . . Wahconah Park supporter

Hickey, Tom . . . . . . City council president during the Doyle administration

Jones, Rick . . . . City council candidate and Wahconah Yes! petition leader

Kelly, John . . . . Electrical workers' union organizer

Kerwood, Matt. . . . . City councilor and new stadium supporter; aka "Little Eddie Munster"

Leaf, Anne . . . . Pittsfield artist and new stadium opponent

Lee, Gerald . . . . City councilor during the Doyle, Hathaway, and Ruberto administrations, and new-stadium supporter

Levine, Jonathan . . . . Publisher and editor of the weekly Pittsfield *Gazette*

Lincoln, Eric . . . . . . Reporter for the weekly *Berkshire Record*

Lothrop, Jonathan . . . City council candidate in 2001; city councilor in 2004

MacDonald, Mike . . . Senior partner of Cain Hibbard Myers & Cook

Marchesi, John . . . . . Parks commissioner during the Ruberto administration

Margenau, Eric. . . . . Jim and Chip's partner; minor-league sports entrepreneur

Massery, James . . . . . City councilor during Doyle administration, new stadium supporter, and brother of Phil

Massery, Phil . . . . . . Talk-show host, new stadium supporter, brother of city councilor Jim, and father of Hillies player Mike

Massimiano, Anthony . Parks commissioner during the Doyle administration

Mellace, Bob . . . . . . Parks director during the Doyle administration

Mick, Andy. . . . . . . Publisher of the *Berkshire Eagle* and president of Berkshire Sports & Events

Murphy, Tom. . . . . . Director of community development in the Doyle administration, and Mayor Doyle's cousin

Murphy, Rick. . . . . . GM of the Pittsfield Astros (formerly Pittsfield Mets) and the Tri-City Valley Cats. Also a cousin of Mayor Doyle

AUTHOR'S NOTE

There have been two experiences in my life that I felt compelled to write about. One was playing in the big leagues; the other was my adventure in Pittsfield, Massachusetts. In both cases, I was blessed with a marvelous cast of characters and a story that told itself. All I had to do was watch and listen. And take notes—now five cartons full for *Foul Ball*.

Other source materials include letters, emails, instant messages, Internet downloads, videos of televised meetings and presentations, and a variety of newspaper articles, editorials, and letters to the editor. Every event, story, or quote in the book is supported by one or more of the above. I am less certain about events that occurred before Chip and I came on the scene, in June of 2001. From that hotly debated time there seem to be as many versions as participants.

All events took place on the dates shown. Some conversations may be off by a day because they occurred after midnight or I forgot to write a new date on the next day's notes. A few conversations with Tim Gray were augmented by later conversations because I couldn't write fast enough the first time around. A number of meetings had more participants than I quote or identify.

All quotes are attributed, except in cases where I felt individuals might be vulnerable to pressure, or worse. This is an important consideration in a city where people are "held accountable" by ex-mayors who claim to still be "running things," and city councilors who say they have "scores to settle."

Because this is a diary, no story can be fully told in isolation. All incidents, quotes, and thoughts must be considered in the context of the entire book. A complete reading, for example, makes clear that "bribes" or "payoffs" do not mean bags of money.

"Are you afraid of lawsuits?" friends have asked. Not really. The manuscript was reviewed and approved—with minor changes—by Frankfurt Kurnit Klein & Selz, PC, which specializes in First Amendment law. And the best defense is the truth. The most damning events occurred in plain view, especially the first time around. You'd have to be blind, or working for the *Berkshire Eagle*, not to see what was happening.

What's more, the most incriminating comments came from the most unimpeachable sources—mayors, councilors, commissioners, lawyers, and newspaper executives. Who needs Deep Throat when there are so many loose lips?

And I have Chip as my witness.

"Unless you go south on me," I said to him the other day.

"It all depends," Chip said with a grin, "on what kind of an offer I get from the other side."

In any case, I had no choice but to write this book. Like Arundhati Roy, I had stumbled upon a silent war. And I couldn't look away.

For the latest update, go to www.foulball.com

o o o

ACKNOWLEDGMENTS

Without Paula there would be no book. Even though she had her doubts about what she now refers to as "the mid-life crisis known as Wahconah Park," she was the best partner a man could have.

In a good example of the Stockholm Syndrome, Paula was also the perfect in-house editor. I had only to walk into the next room to see how the story was coming. The sound of giggles and penciled check marks meant I'd written something good. Long silences punctuated by pencil scratches across the page meant I had just wasted five hours.

Paula, who writes her own column for *Berkshire Homestyle* magazine, is not your typical hand-holding editor. Instead of margin notes that say "open this up a bit," or "please explain," she's more likely to write, "Boooring," "Out!" And "NO! NO! NO!" Her "YES!" was like getting a gold star.

Next I have to thank my other partner, the one without the curves. The multi-talented Chip is also a great proofreader—a Herculean task with the self-published hardcover book. To give you some idea, when I forgot to show Chip the acknowledgments page, in which I credited his proofreading skills to his mother the English teacher, I spelled English with a small "e." So don't blame Chip or Maggie.

What would we have done without Cindy Elitzer, the cash management whiz who never got credit for spending the entire July 3rd game underneath the stands, juggling coupons and stacks of small bills. And who, like Paula, is now dealing with a shortage of funds. Asked why she had declined to buy the priciest tickets to a recent fundraiser, Cindy explained that "the Boutons and the Elitzers have each made an involuntary six-figure charitable contribution to the city of Pittsfield."

For the hardcover edition I thank Jim Charlton and Marty Goldensohn for their guidance and support. Daniel Elitzer for his important early editorial suggestions. Eric Lincoln, Dave Potts, Tim Gray, Jack Guillet, Tim Wiles, and Andy Zimbalist for help with research. Terry Kinnas, Joe Guzzo, Anne Leaf, Dan Valenti, Jonathan Levine, and Tim Zwingelstein for the local history. The accuracy is theirs. The mistakes are mine.

For the book you have in your hands, I thank Tom McCarthy of The Lyons Press—one of the last of the independent publishers—for the courage to go where others feared to tread. So far, none of our opponents has offered to buy stock in his company.

Tom was also flexible enough to work with my man Glenn LeDoux, who designed the layout for the hard and soft cover editions. Peter Blossom designed the paperback cover. Ray Shaw took the vintage game photos. And the quote on the front cover is from a review by David Kipen.

I'm grateful once again to Cheryl Raifstanger of Kwik Print for those last-minute copies, Maeve O'Dea for transcribing tapes, and Marjorie Wexler for proofreading and research.

Finally, I want to thank Alex Bloomstein, David Kaufman, Michael Martin, and John Thorn, for their widom and generosity.

This was a team effort.

o o o

DOCUMENTS

To reduce the incidence of back strain and hernia, most of the documents connected to this story—our original Proposal for Wahconah Park, the Bid Protest Decision by the Massachusetts Attorney General, our Revised License Agreement, Bill Moyers' and my response to lawyers from General Electric, MediaNews Group, and publisher Peter Osnos, our Op-Ed pieces, and letters to the editor, etc.—can be found at www.foulball.com.

For story continuity and ease of reference, a number of documents have been included on the following pages.

2001

2004

FEBRUARY 11, 2001
Letter to Andy Mick, Publisher of the *Berkshire Eagle* and President of Berkshire Sports and Events

Dear Andy:

Jim Bouton and I appreciated the opportunity to meet with you and your BS&E colleagues last Wednesday. You have obviously been thinking a lot about the objectives of your ambitious undertaking, and we were impressed with the clarity of your statement that the focus is economic development. In effect, baseball is a means, not an end.

We share your primary objective—economic development—and also your secondary one: keeping baseball in Pittsfield. After consulting with our own group, we believe that we can free BS&E to maximize its primary objective by eliminating any uncertainty about the secondary one. We are prepared to state, without qualification, that we can bring a Northern League team to Wahconah Park beginning with the 2002 season, without any cost to the taxpayers. If environmental hurdles can be surmounted, then we will construct improvements to the ballpark; if not, then we will still build a team that fans will enjoy watching, and create a "must-see" entertainment experience at an historic ballpark that will keep them coming back from all over the Berkshires and beyond.

We believe that the logic of building an indoor arena on the new site instead of an outdoor stadium is compelling for several reasons:

1. Bring a second major professional sport to Pittsfield. Our group is prepared to state unequivocally that we will provide a United Hockey League franchise to serve as BS&E's anchor tenant beginning with the 2002-2003 hockey season if the arena is ready in time.

2. Create a year-round facility that will be truly multi-purpose: conventions, trade shows, rock concerts, circuses, ice shows, graduation ceremonies, professional sports (in addition to hockey, other possibilities are arena football, indoor soccer, indoor lacrosse, and wrestling), amateur sports (skating, basketball, track, volleyball), and various regional and statewide tournaments at both the high school and the college level.

3. Many of the uses of an indoor arena, such as conventions and trade shows, would bring visitors to the Berkshires for several days at a time during the "off-seasons," significantly leveraging the assets of hotels, restaurants, and other local businesses that have been overbuilt to meet the capacity demands of the summer season.

4. A $22 million, 6,000 seat, 12-month arena ($3,000/seat plus $4 million land acquisition and site development costs) would be more cost effective than a $18.5 million 3-month stadium. Least feasible would be building a new stadium, subsequently acquiring additional land (a fear of some Civic Authority opponents) and then building an arena, for a total cost of at least $40.5 million ($18.5 + $22).

Assembling the centrally located site that you have is a tremendous accomplishment. It is more than that: it is a public good. For that land to be used for any purpose other than its highest and best public one would represent an irretrievably lost civic opportunity.

In our view, the sole rationale for building a stadium instead of an arena (in effect, "no new stadium, no baseball") is flawed for two reasons: (1) it contradicts the primacy of the economic development objective, which is clearly better served by an arena, and (2) it presumes that the only baseball worth watching is an affiliated minor league team. We, on the other hand, believe that an independent league team offers more advantages:

1. Team continuity from year to year instead of musical chairs.
2. Local ownership with fans of the team owning stock.
3. Superior quality of play (compared to affiliated "single A") with recently released major and high minor league players.
4. Greater possibility of players going straight to the majors.
5. No conflict of allegiance for local fans of particular major league teams (Yankee fans having to root for Red Sox or Astros farm teams).
6. Favorite players returning from year to year.
7. Greater possibility of local players (Great Barrington's John Raifstanger, retired last year from AA ball, for example).
8. Reduced likelihood of future demands on Pittsfield (such as the NY–Penn League standards that threatened to turn Wahconah into a ghost park).

Finally, we want to address the politics of the proposed referendum. We believe that BS&E would not be well advised to wait until after a vote on the Civic Authority before considering and—hopefully—adopting our "Plan B":

1. If the referendum passes before any public announcement is made of BS&E's support for Plan B, then BS&E is virtually locked into the stadium project, which is clearly inferior to the arena as an economic development tool. Any major *ex post facto* change of plans would be viewed by many voters as "bait and switch."

2. If the referendum fails before any announcement is made of the arena, then it will be practically impossible to return to the voters anytime soon with Plan B. That would be a sadly missed opportunity, because the creation of the Civic Authority is a prerequisite for the construction and operation of any large public facility in that space. By announcing Plan B well in advance of the vote, a potentially critical number of opponents (not all, but certainly the "Save Wahconah" crowd and the people who oppose a "white elephant" in the heart of Pittsfield) could be converted into proponents.

Andy, as you know, we're an all-Berkshire group with a strong set of managerial, promotional, and financial skills. With your group's endorsement of Plan B, we're prepared today to begin the process of generating enormous support from baseball and hockey fans (including many who don't know that they're about to become rabid fans) from as far north as Williamstown and North Adams, to as far south as Great Barrington and Sheffield. Pittsfield is the geographic heart of Berkshire County. It can be the emotional and economic heart as well.

Jim and I look forward to meeting with you and your group again at your early convenience.

Sincerely,
Donald B. Elitzer

cc: T. F. Murphy, M. E. Callahan, Jr., J. S. Pomeroy, M. Thiessen

MARCH 21, 2001
Second Letter to Andy Mick

Dear Andy:

Thank you for making the trek south with Mick Callahan to meet with Jim Bouton and me last Wednesday. Although we believe that the arguments in favor of two professional sports teams for the price of one and a year-round arena instead of a 3-4 month stadium are compelling, you clearly do not. We also believe that our plan, if proposed publicly, would bolster rather than threaten a favorable Civic Authority vote, whereas you would prefer us not to "confuse the voters."

After considerable soul-searching—not to mention alternating with each other several times in the role of devil's advocate—Jim and I have decided to respect your wishes and remain silent through the referendum. Your group has invested a lot of time, effort, and money in getting this far, and we cannot be cavalier in taking action that you believe would jeopardize that investment.

We will call you on June 6, either to congratulate you or to suggest serious reconsideration of "Plan B".

Sincerely,
Donald B. Elitzer

cc: M. E. Callahan, Jr., J. A. Cunningham, Jr. [President of Berkshire Bank], T. F. Murphy, J. S. Pomeroy, M. Thiessen

Open Letter to Mayor Doyle and the Pittsfield City Council

Gentlemen:

Following our open proposal of June 11th for keeping professional baseball in Wahconah Park and bringing a minor league ice hockey team to a new arena on the downtown site, we have been asked to describe how we plan to proceed with our primary and immediate interest: baseball at Wahconah.

1. **Acquire a long-term lease (or its equivalent) from the City.** Proposed term: 30 years, subject to cancellation if we fail to provide a professional baseball team to play in Wahconah Park. (An important component of financing later-stage improvements will be long-term debt, which we will only be able to obtain with a long-term lease. As anyone with a home mortgage knows, a 30-year loan is a lot easier to service than a 15- or 20-year loan.)

   Proposed annual rent or fee: $1.00, subject to our maintaining the Park at no cost to the City and making capital improvements exceeding $25,000 annually.

   Other uses: Because the City would remain the owner of the Park, we would welcome its continued use by Pittsfield, Taconic, and St. Joseph's high school football, and by other civic, educational, and recreational groups, consistent with its primary mission of hosting professional baseball.

2. **Negotiate the acquisition of an independent league franchise.** It will be a Northern League or an Atlantic League franchise. There are currently three dormant Northern League franchises and at least one active franchise whose owners might consider selling. With the long-term commitment for a permanent home (Wahconah) in hand, we will take advantage of a "buyer's market" and purchase a franchise on the most favorable terms possible.

3. **Invite the citizens of Pittsfield and Berkshire County to be our partners.** We will sell substantial ownership in the ball club to individuals and businesses, so that fans can truly say that it is their team. Widespread local ownership will also make it difficult if not impossible for anyone to ever move the team to another city. Although it is premature to describe the terms of the actual offering, our preliminary thinking is that we would offer 25% to 50% of the team to investor/fans. The proceeds would be used to help build the team and finance initial improvements to the ballpark.

4. **Improve the ballpark.** Capital improvements would be implemented on a gradual, multi-year basis and would be prioritized according to four sets of considerations: (1) ensuring safety and sanitation, (2) improving comfort and convenience for fans and players, (3) complying with environmental regulations, and (4) economic viability.

   Prior to the 2002 season, after fixing unsafe conditions, if any, we would replace the orange-and-blue color scheme with a fresh coat of paint (probably forest green). Our capital project list would include bigger and better restrooms, food concessions, and locker rooms, and abatement of flooding conditions in the parking lot, to be accomplished in phases over several years. After at least two operating seasons, we would expect to have a clear, prioritized list of other capital improvements that would have a major beneficial impact on the fans' baseball experience. At some point, we would also like to add a walkway museum and Hall of Fame to commemorate and market our historic ballpark.

Our partnership group brings over 15 years of experience in building and running successful minor league sports franchises. Of 14 professional teams currently or previously owned (7 of them baseball), 12 are enduring assets in their original cities. The other two are thriving in new homes after being forced to relocate by affiliated minor league stadium requirements.

Gentlemen, we look to you now for help in achieving the first step: securing a long-term lease on Wahconah Park. Although we could wait until Labor Day and probably still make the 2002 season, we would benefit greatly from a decision while most of the 2001 season still remains to be played.

Sincerely,

Jim Bouton
Chip Elitzer
Eric Margenau, President
United Sports Ventures

Letter to Clifford Nilan, Parks Commission Chairman

Dear Mr. Nilan:

Based on my conversation with Bob Mellace late last week, I'm assuming that the next meeting of the Board of Park Commissioners will be on Monday, July 23, and that the fate of Wahconah Park will have a prominent place on the agenda.

Given the independent league franchise opportunities that must be pursued before the end of the current baseball season, my partners and I respectfully request that the Commissioners come to that meeting prepared to vote on our proposal for a long term lease or license agreement for the stadium and its parking areas.

The principal points of our proposal are:

1. A 30-year agreement for the nominal sum of $1.00 per year, cancelable by the City if we fail to perform under the terms of the lease at any time, including providing professional baseball each summer season.

2. Our ball club would be responsible for the expense of maintaining the stadium, including any major structural repairs that are or become necessary during the term of the lease.

3. Our ball club would agree to make capital improvements of at least $25,000 annually during the term of the lease. In practice, we expect that amount to be easily exceeded.

4. We would make the stadium and grounds available for other community uses, including high school football, but excluding other season-long baseball leagues.

Why such a long lease? We believe that the City and its citizens are best served by granting us a time frame that enables us to plan projects and financial commitments from the prospective of an owner, not a renter. To use an analogy, whom would you expect to take better care of an historic house for future generations, an owner or someone who was just renting it for a few years?

If your Board approves these principal terms, then we would work with you and the City's attorneys to draft a formal agreement by the end of the month, and to have all necessary and authorized officials execute the agreement with us within a few days thereafter.

Given the strong interest that the citizens of Pittsfield have shown in the fate of Wahconah Park, if the July 23rd meeting and its agenda are publicized in advance we would expect the meeting to be very well attended. We are available to meet with you and any of your fellow Park Commissioners individually or collectively at your convenience to answer questions, address concerns, and entertain possible modifications to our proposal prior to the 23rd.

We do not expect that we will be the only ones making a proposal at the meeting. We welcome a full discussion of alternative proposals by other groups, and we acknowledge that your Board may choose to endorse a group other than ours.

We believe, however, that we are the only all-Berkshire group with a commitment to keeping professional baseball permanently in Wahconah Park, and that our partnership represents the financial strength and operating experience necessary to make it happen.

In keeping with our policy of making our goals and actions open to public view and comment, we will be making this letter available to media outlets.

Thank you for your assistance.

Sincerely,
Chip Elitzer

Open Letter to the Parks Commission, Mayor, and City Council

Mr. Clifford J. Nilan, Chairman, Board of Park Commissioners
The Honorable Gerald S. Doyle, Jr., Mayor of Pittsfield
Mr. Thomas Hickey, Jr., City Council President

Gentlemen:

Once again, I am writing on behalf of my partners and, we believe, the strong majority of the citizens of Pittsfield, to ask for your support—or at least your prompt consideration—of our proposal for a long-term lease on Wahconah Park. If action is not taken in the next few weeks, we believe that Pittsfield risks losing professional baseball not just for 2002, but permanently.

We do not believe that we are overstating the risk that Pittsfield runs. Consider:

1. The Berkshire market is not large enough to sustain more than one professional baseball team.

2. Pittsfield has enjoyed a "natural monopoly" on professional baseball in this county for the better part of a century precisely because would-be competitors recognize this fact.

3. If Pittsfield fails to field a team for the 2002 season, that will create a void that North Adams may fill with their existing Wahconah-like ballpark.

4. Once North Adams has professional baseball, it is unlikely to relinquish it, and the economic reality of "natural monopoly" will keep us and probably any other group from trying to re-establish baseball in Pittsfield.

5. The only site in Pittsfield that can host professional baseball in 2002 is Wahconah Park.

6. The only group with a public proposal to bring a professional baseball team to Wahconah Park in 2002 is the partnership of Jim Bouton, Eric Margenau, and myself. We have proposed to maintain and enhance Wahconah at no cost to the taxpayers.

7. By Labor Day, most existing holders (and potential sellers) of existing independent league franchises will have made plans for the 2002 season, and our options for acquiring a franchise will be limited.

Mr. Nilan, we have not received a reply to our July 10th proposal to you, but we have read in the *Eagle* that the Board of Park Commissioners will not meet on July 23 as we originally anticipated, and that you do not see any urgency.

Mayor Doyle, you have told us that you will not support any professional baseball

473

proposal for Wahconah until and unless Berkshire Sports & Events "folds its tent." At the City Council meeting last Tuesday night, you raised your hand (among a 10% minority) when I asked who still supports a new stadium.

Councilors, most of you have told me in one-on-one conversations that you will not entertain seriously any alternative proposals until you hear from Berkshire Sports & Events that they're definitely giving up any thoughts of building a new stadium.

The two principal backers of Berkshire Sports & Events have been MediaNews Group (the parent of the *Berkshire Eagle*) and Berkshire Bank. Yesterday, Jim Bouton and I met with the Editor of the *Eagle*. He denied emphatically that the owner of the *Eagle* is trying to block our proposal, and pointed to the "For Sale" sign on the West & Center property as a clear signal that the "Stadium—Yes!" plan is dead. This morning, Jim Bouton and I met with a senior representative of Berkshire Bank, who carefully stated neither support nor opposition to our plan, but told us that Berkshire Sports & Events was being dissolved.

In a front-page article in the *Eagle* on July 10, MediaNews Group CEO Dean Singleton was quoted as saying that a new stadium "would work just as well in North Adams, and we own newspapers in both places." Although Berkshire Bank is not making such a suggestion, it also has a public-spirited interest in the well being of other towns and cities in Berkshire County.

However, you gentlemen are all either appointed or elected representatives of the citizens of Pittsfield. We know that each of you, regardless of your future plans for public office, is working diligently to fulfill your duties to the best of your abilities. That is why we are pointing out the peril to Pittsfield's baseball future that further delay entails. That is why we are asking each of you to voice your public support for immediate consideration of our proposal, and to ask each of the other Park Commissioners and City Councilors to do the same.

We are not asking for careless action, but we ask that the process of evaluating our proposal and any alternatives proceed expeditiously. Mr. Nilan, we repeat our request that the July 23rd meeting of the Commission take place, and that it be held in a school auditorium, where a large number of citizens can attend and where TV and radio stations that have already expressed interest can broadcast the proceedings. We would be prepared to present our proposal in all reasonable detail and to defend it, and we would welcome the opportunity to share the stage with representatives of any competing proposals in a real give-and-take format. Whether the Commissioners choose to take formal action at that meeting is, of course, up to you, but at least you will be able to voice your questions and concerns to us and to the public, and we will be able to answer you publicly to the best of our abilities.

Sincerely,
Donald B. Elitzer

Proposal for Wahconah Park (Summary)

TO PROVIDE PROFESSIONAL BASEBALL PERMANENTLY TO A RESTORED WAHCONAH PARK AT NO COST TO THE CITY

PRINCIPALS: Jim Bouton, 62, is a former professional baseball player and business-man who lives in North Egremont; Chip Elitzer, 53, is an investment banker who lives in Great Barrington; Eric Margenau, 60, is a professional sports entrepreneur who owns a home in Stockbridge.

MARKETING PLAN: Double 2,000 average attendance by promoting three under appreciated or previously unavailable assets: a 100% locally owned team with 51% offered to businesses and fans, a historic ballpark marketed to a national audience, the high quality (AA) of independent league baseball.

Implement "share of customer" strategy, capturing tourist dollars now spent elsewhere in the Berkshires, via brochures and cross-promotions with local cultural institutions. Create a national identity for Wahconah Park with its own logo and historic site map identification, attracting fans who tour the country visiting legendary ballparks. Enhance fan experience with a "Taste of the Berkshires" food court, "Shops of the Berkshires" merchandise booths, a Walkway Museum & Hall of Fame, and area-specific promotions.

FACILITIES PLAN: Spend $250,000 on capital improvements by opening day 2002, and at least $25,000 each subsequent year. Immediate improvements will include new concession stands, crushed stone resurfacing of parking lot, fourteen "not so luxury boxes" on the grandstand roof, and painting the stadium. Future upgrades will include restrooms, locker rooms and exercise facilities.

LICENSE AGREEMENT: To allow sufficient time for return on investment, we require a long term lease or license which can be revoked for failure to perform any one of the following: provide a professional baseball team, invest at least $250,000 in initial repairs and capital improvements, invest at least $25,000 for upgrades and repairs in each subsequent year, assume responsibility for all necessary maintenance and repairs ordinarily paid by the city ($500,000 over the past 5 years), allow reasonable use of Wahconah for civic, educational, sports and entertainment consistent with its primary function of hosting professional baseball.

OWNERSHIP STRUCTURE: Initially to be owned 100% by Jim Bouton, Chip Elitzer and Eric Margenau. By November 2001, 51% ownership will be offered to local businesses and fans.

FINANCIAL PLAN: Revenue will come from ticket sales, concession profits, advertising, and corporate suites ("not so luxury boxes"). Based on 43 home games at $10 per fan revenue (including concessions), average per game attendance of 2,000, 3,000, and 4,000 would yield pre-tax income of: $58,000, $488,000, and $918,000,

475

before cash outlays for capital improvements.

LEAGUE NEGOTIATIONS: Atlantic League president Frank Boulton has agreed to approve play in his league for 2002 once a lease is obtained for Wahconah Park. An option price has also been agreed upon for play beyond 2002 if a new "short season" division is created. An option price for a full season membership has not yet been agreed upon.

In addition, the representative of a Northern League franchise has told us that the owner is willing to sell at our offer price. However, since Northern League Commissioner Miles Wolff has given Mayor Doyle a letter of support for Jonathan Fleisig's bid for a Pittsfield team and a new stadium, we have told this potential seller and Mr. Wolff that a precondition of our purchase would be a letter from Mr. Wolff stating that our group is acceptable to the league and that Wahconah Park is a suitable permanent home for our team.

By granting our local ownership group a long term lease on Wahconah Park, Pittsfield will have changed the traditional balance of power between cities and team owners in the city's favor.

NEXT STEPS: In order to successfully conclude our negotiations for a franchise in one of the two leagues, we must have a long-term lease or license agreement for Wahconah Park. Our preferred home is the Atlantic League, but if we are unable to negotiate an acceptable option price for a full season membership, then we will purchase one of several Northern League franchises that are potentially available.

With the unconditional support of the citizens of Pittsfield and the officials—both elected and appointed—who act on their behalf, we will succeed in our effort to provide professional baseball permanently to a restored Wahconah Park at no cost to the taxpayers.

Note: A complete version of this proposal can be found at www.foulball.com

Bid Protest Decision (Excerpt) from the Office of
Massachusetts Attorney General Thomas F. Reilly

since the Club's indemnification responsibilities under the license do not begin until May 2005.

The Club contends that the Wahconah Park license is not subject to the competitive bidding statutes, based on its analysis of the factors set forth by this office in Foundation for Fair Contracting of Massachusetts v. Enlace de Familias de Holyoke/Holyoke Community Charter School, Attorney General Bid Protest Decision at p. 9 (July 15, 2002). The Enlace decision addressed a project in which the public agency was the lessee, not the lessor. Here, there is not the commonality of identity between the public agency and the developer as in Enlace, where we found an agency relationship existed. Nevertheless, the City will exercise significant control over the Park, construction will be performed in lieu of license fees, and it will take place on publicly owned land, possibly reverting to the public agency for public use in less than two years. These are all relevant factors under the Enlace "test." Enlace at p. 13 (citing Affiliated Const. Trades Foundation v. University of West Virginia Bd. of Trustees, 210 W. Va. 456, 472 (2001) and the factor test therein).

The City suggests that the license contains what is effectively a 15 year initial term, since the Club must make substantial improvements which it cannot possibly recoup during the initial 18 month term. However, this is not what the language of the license necessarily requires. The license does not contain a 15 year term. We must analyze this matter accordingly.

A term of 18 months suggests that a license may have been structured to circumvent the bidding laws, since many similar construction projects take this long to complete. Under these circumstances, if we were to find that the construction contemplated by the license was not subject to either c. 30 or c.149, some could interpret this as an invitation to circumvent the

12

competitive bidding statutes where the legislature intended them to apply.[5] By the terms of the license, certain construction is *required*. Cf. G.M. Builders, supra. Moreover, the construction is the "responsibility" of the City since the City is not indemnified if a construction accident occurs before May 15, 2005. Id.

That the license gives the City relatively unrestricted authority to approve or reject additions to the concession areas also suggests public control of the project. The City and the Club contend that this provision is for the enforcement of health regulations, but there are provisions for adherence to these regulations elsewhere in the license.

In its current form, the license raises serious concerns about the applicability of the competitive bidding statutes. However, this is a close case. During the hearing of this matter, it became apparent that the City did not consider the reasoning of the G.M. Builders case in entering the license agreement. Further, while both the City and the Club view the license as having a 15 year term, the language of the license provides otherwise. Finally, based on testimony provided at the hearing, the parties to the license did not intend for the City to have the right to withhold approval for concession stand alterations except where there are violations of health, safety and welfare regulations.

Accordingly, we remand this matter to the City for further action in accordance with the foregoing opinion.

---

[5]See Office of the Inspector General v. Massachusetts Water Resources Authority, Department of Labor and Industries Bid Protest Decision at pp. 36-38 (June 29, 1989), for an example of a lease that set forth what was "virtually indistinguishable" from a "turnkey" construction contract.

13

478

Report and Request to the Mayor,
City Councilors, and Parks Commissioners

Ladies and Gentlemen:

On March 8 of this year, less than two months after a gracious invitation signed by the Mayor, the President of the City Council, and the Chairman of the Parks Commission, we signed a license agreement for the use of Wahconah Park.

Our goal then was the same as it is now: to bring professional baseball back to Wahconah Park and to keep it there permanently. We have had some gratifying successes and some unexpected challenges. At the time that we signed the license agreement, we stated that we couldn't guarantee success, but that we could promise that we would work tirelessly to produce the best result possible, and that with the strong support of Pittsfield, we thought we could overcome any obstacles.

We have encountered some obstacles, and we're asking you to help us overcome them. I will be highly specific about the nature of that help. But first, I would like to enumerate what we have achieved in the six months since the license agreement was signed:

1. Jim Bouton took a little-noticed discovery of an 18th century bylaw and helped turn it into an international media event that dubbed Pittsfield as "Baseball's Garden of Eden."

2. We brought back the Hillies after 74 years and staged two well-received home games at Wahconah Park.

3. We brought ESPN Classic to Wahconah Park on July 3 for what amounted to a highly complimentary national "infomercial" for Pittsfield and the Hillies that lasted over four hours, and that has been rebroadcast multiple times.

4. We have cleared virtually all regulatory hurdles necessary to begin construction at Wahconah Park, including environmental.

5. We have completed the architectural and engineering work necessary to get "ballpark" numbers from potential contractors, and we have gotten those numbers.

6. We have made cosmetic but important initial changes to Wahconah Park, including paint, signage, scoreboards, demolition of dilapidated concession shacks and wire link fencing, creation of an expanded courtyard within a temporary construction fence, a new gated entrance to the overflow parking meadow, and an efficient new parking layout that has proven its worth at both Hillies games this summer. And all of the work has been done by local firms and individuals.

7. We have filed a preliminary prospectus with the SEC for a public offering of Wahconah Park, Inc. and have received commitments for over $1.2 million to date, including $250,000 from Jim Bouton and me. (Our commitment has already been mostly funded and spent on the architectural, engineering, permitting, and other pre-construction work described above.)

8. We have engaged both independent leagues in discussions regarding Pittsfield's place in a league schedule for 2005, and we should know where we stand around the end of this month.

9. We paid $2,000 to booster clubs at PHS, Taconic, and St. Joe's for volunteer labor for the July 3 game and hope to establish an ongoing relationship with them and other Berkshire County volunteer organizations to supplement their budgets for most of the 60 home games (45 professional, 15 Hillies) that are being planned for 2005.

10. We paid over $1,600 directly to our local game day staff for the Sept. 4 game, because the booster clubs were fully occupied with a large soccer tournament that weekend.

11. We are contributing over $1,500 to the Dave Southard family to fulfill our pledge of $1.00 for every ticket sold to the Sept. 4 game.

12. Jim Bouton and I (and our families) have worked diligently on behalf of Wahconah Park without pay all this year, and will do so again all next year.

We have also encountered some difficulties:

1. Pittsfield's status in a professional league in 2005 is still uncertain. Frank Boulton, the CEO of the Atlantic League, has promised us a franchise in a to-be-formed short season division, but it is now looking increasingly unlikely that the division will be formed in time for the 2005 season. Miles Wolff, Commissioner of the Northeast League, will probably accept Pittsfield as an eighth team in his league if he needs an eighth team, but he is currently negotiating for the Aces (the league's road team) to settle in Ottawa. If neither league is available for 2005, we are considering forming a new league, but it may not be achievable before 2006.

2. We wanted Pittsfield's own team to be majority-owned by Pittfield residents, but to date, only about 2% of the money subscribed has come from Pittsfield (although most of the individual investors, of whom there are more than 80 signed up, are local). That has hurt us in our quest for large out-of-town investors, who properly expect to see some leadership from local businesses and individuals who stand to gain the most from a revitalized Wahconah Park.

3. The carpenters' union bid protest, which was filed in June, has spooked potential investors, and threatens to cost us investors who have already subscribed. Until then, we had quickly signed up most of the $1.2 million that is circled today (out of $2.8 million that we were seeking). Since then, very little new money has been pledged.

Since the bid protest has also cost us the time we needed to begin (and complete) major construction before Opening Day 2005, we have formulated a plan to go forward with the $1.2 already pledged ($950,000 new money, $250,000 already spent), and then "bootstrap" the rest of the construction from profits over the next several years, if 2005 fan attendance warrants the investment. Tentatively, we would use $500,000 to build the new food court, double the size of the women's restrooms within the existing grandstand, remove the cinderblock "goiters" (home and visitor clubhouses), install a temporary trailer beyond the left outfield fence for the visiting team, rehab a home clubhouse within the existing grandstand, and use the remaining $450,000 for working capital.

However, all of this depends on the City's response to the Attorney General's opinion. In response to the bid protest, the A.G.'s office said, in effect, that if the Wahconah Park license agreement remains unchanged, they would side with the carpenter's union and require any work done at the ballpark to be done in accordance with the public bid law. Notwithstanding the fact that no work done by any previous tenants at the ballpark has been in accordance with that law, notwithstanding the fact that the public bid law was written to protect taxpayer dollars from corrupt practices by public officials and that only private investor dollars are at stake here, the A.G.'s office does not want to set a bad precedent.

No one is claiming that Wahconah Park, Inc. is a sham corporation set up by the City to circumvent the public bid law, but the A.G. is concerned that certain features of our license agreement, if left unchanged, would send the wrong signal to other communities if he decided to let us do the construction as the private entity that we actually are. However, his opinion has given us a clear set of guideposts for getting us treated as a private enterprise, rather than a project subject to the City's direction:

1. The initial term of our license agreement is very short-term, expiring in October 2005. The A.G. strongly suggests a minimum of 15 years.

2. The license agreement *requires* (italics in the original opinion) Wahconah Park, Inc. to make an investment in the City's asset. The A.G. implies that the requirement be eliminated.

We will blow our budget and lose our investors if we are required to go forward as if we were a public entity. Therefore, we see only two options: take our loss and go home, or modify the license agreement. That is where you come in. We are requesting a revised agreement that will cost the City nothing:

1. Instead of being automatically renewable annually based on performance criteria, the agreement will be long-term (and renewable) but cancellable at

any time based on non-performance of the same criteria. We would still be held to our commitment to maintain the ballpark entirely at our expense, to provide professional baseball, and to continue to make the Park available for other community uses.

2. Instead of requiring Wahconah Park, Inc. to make a $1.5 million investment in the ballpark by Opening Day 2005 (or any other amount by any other deadline), the agreement will permit (but not require) WPI to make any investments it chooses, subject only to the same regulatory oversight that would apply to any private entity in the business of serving the public. Ironically, eliminating this investment requirement is the only way to ensure that we will be able to invest anything.

We want to stress that we are pro-union. Jim Bouton belongs to four unions and helped to organize one of them. Weeks before the hearing in the A.G.'s office, we met with the carpenters' union rep and asked him to provide names of recommended firms to have on our bid list. He was not willing to accept assurances that contractors would be chosen from a level playing field and wanted special consideration given to union workers. We would rather use local firms and workers, without regard to whether they are union or not.

Contrary to the carpenters' claim, we did not hire Allegrone as general contractor. They were retained to provide some pre-construction services, and with a view to using them as construction manager. All pieces of the actual work, which had not even been fully defined, were to be subject to competitive bid, with union shops included in all bid lists. The delay caused by the protest has cancelled our major construction for this year, and we have released Allegrone to pursue other clients and projects.

With respect to the scaled-down work that we are now proposing to do before Opening Day 2005, we pledge to review bids from as many union (and non-union) shops as are interested in bidding, and to give preference to union shops where bids are similar.

Even with a revised license agreement, which is an absolute prerequisite for our moving forward, success will not come easily. We must average almost 1,900 fans at 60 home games to break even. Our goal is 4,000. If we can do that, or even 3,000, we will be looking to complete our construction plan at the ballpark, including 1,200 additional seats over a new home team clubhouse and public restrooms. And if Wahconah Park is a success, we will be back to you with even more ambitious proposals for Pittsfield, because we will have proved to the capital markets that "tapping private capital for the public good" can be profitable for private investors while starting a "virtuous cycle" of investment and jobs.

I look forward to responding to your questions and comments. Please feel free to contact me by e-mail, or directly by phone at 413-XXX-XXXX.

Sincerely,
Chip Elitzer

Chip's Email Thanking Investors

Dear Investors-in-Waiting,

Well, it was a good show while it lasted. If you live in the Berkshires, you've already heard the news, and if you don't, this may still be news.

Yesterday, shortly after noon, Jim Bouton, President of Wahconah Park, Inc., issued the following press release:

> My partners and I announce regretfully that we have withdrawn our plan to renovate Wahconah Park and bring professional baseball back to Pittsfield, MA. It is clear that we no longer have the necessary support of the City officials who on January 13, 2004, invited us to return with a proposal we had originally made in 2001, a proposal that was substantially improved by our current plan.
>
> We don't want to stand in the way of other opportunities for the City regarding baseball, and we will ask both independent leagues to consider favorably any other Wahconah-based proposals which may come their way.

Jim and I woke up yesterday morning and realized that notwithstanding a new Parks Commission and a new City Council, and especially in spite of a new Mayor who truly wished the best for our project and who wanted us to succeed, the dysfunctional political culture of Pittsfield that permits the selfish motives of a few to dash the hopes of the many had once again prevailed.

We are grateful, at least, that the only money lost in this venture has been our own. We could not, in good conscience, take yours. We were prepared to execute our ambitious plans for Wahconah Park, Inc. and (with full disclosure, of course) have you bear the business risks alongside of us. After adding in the ongoing political risks as we now understand them, we determined that the total risks this venture faced were unacceptably high.

Thank you for your support. We know that for most and maybe all of you, your decision to invest was not based simply on a financial calculation of private gain, but on a sense of public good. Whether your love was principally for a grand old ballpark, or for Pittsfield, or for baseball, thank you for that love.

Sincerely,

Chip

Cash Flow Summary of Wahconah Park, Inc.

	Beginning to End (March to Oct. 2004)	Related to July 3rd game[2]
CASH IN		
Cash contributed by Bouton, Elitzer, & Margenau	$225,729[1]	$47,065
Ticket Sales for July 3 and Sept. 4 games	44,933	29,590
Concession Coupon Sales	54,643	41,422
Sponsorships & Ad Signage Sales	25,191	13,840
TOTAL CASH IN:	**$350,496**	**$131,917**
CASH OUT		
Payments to food & drink concessionaires (including $4,647 to PHS booster clubs for food for July 3, and $4,278 to UNICO for both games)	34,382	27,075
T-shirt and souvenir inventory, plus sales commissions to Tim's Sports Zone	16,982	13,612
Berkshire Fireworks	5,000	5,000
Booster Clubs (PHS Baseball, PHS Girls Soccer, St. Joe's Baseball, and Taconic Baseball), which supplied 100 volunteers for July 3 game	2,000	2,000
Payroll for September 4 game[3]	1,819	
Classical Tents (tents, tables, and chairs)	4,913	3,026
Yankee Septic Services (toilet facilities)	4,620	2,468
Hillies uniforms and equipment	13,606	11,142
Costume rentals and actors	2,385	2,100
Hartford team bus to both Wahconah Park games	1,500	750
Hillies team bus to Hartford game	625	
Callahan Sign Co. (manufacture & installation of outfield advertising banners)	6,358	2,688
Design fees (posters, tickets, programs, uniform logos, ballpark colors, ad banners)	10,810	5,435
Printing of tickets and Wahconah Park Times	3,124	2,041
City of Pittsfield (Parks Dept. labor, phone, plus electric for month of field lights for youth baseball)	5,309	2,669
Liability insurance	3,975	140
Wiring repair of Wahconah Park sound system	450	
Miscellaneous game day expenses	2,525	1,103

CASH OUT (continued)

Newspaper and radio ads (Berkshire Eagle, Pittsfield Gazette, WBRK, Albany Times-Union)	7,893	2,545
Don Lagueux Painting (grandstand exterior)	9,184	9,184
Berkshire Production Resources (construction, painting and installation of scoreboards and signs)	13,270	12,770
Miscellaneous carpentry	700	550
Allegrone Construction Co. (removal of old concession sheds, installation of expanded perimeter chainlink fence, install new electrical and plumbing outlets for restroom trailer, new gate for overflow parking, fill ruts in parking area, scaffolding for scoreboard operators, dumpsters, snow fence, working with architects, engineers, and prospective subcontractors to refine and price ballpark renovation)	35,019	25,019
S-K Design Group (parking plan for July 3, design plans and get permits and approvals for environmental, zoning, and traffic/parking matters)	55,660	600
Clark & Green, Architects (Great Barrington)	60,222	
Hill Engineers (Dalton)	13,800	
Jonathan Baum, Esq. (Great Barrington) for corporate and SEC filings related to public stock offering	17,446	
Printing costs related to financing	3,296	
Office supplies, phone, travel/meeting expenses	3,548	
Dave Southard benefit	1,537	
Teen Night at Wahconah Park sponsorship	100	
Berkshire Chamber of Commerce membership	235	
Boston attorney in bid protest matters	5,000	
Smith, Watson & Co. (accountants)	1,178	
Resort Maps ("Best of the Berkshires")	445	
Berkshire Anthenaeum (authentication of the 1791 "Broken Window Bylaw")	1,580	
TOTAL CASH OUT:	**$350,496**	**$131,917**

NOTES:

(1) Net cash contributed was reduced from an anticipated amount of $250,000 due to Allegrone's voluntary and generous cancellation of their final $9,400 balance, Jonathan Baum's refusal to bill for any legal work subsequent to the amended prospectus of 8/9/04 (about $10,000 worth) and a partial insurance premium refund of $5,564.

(2) No expenses in this column would have been incurred without the July 3rd televised game. Originally capitalized and then written off (when WPI was forced to withdraw), even the minor construction and painting improvements to Wahconah Park would have been deferred until after the public stock offering.

(3) Game day payroll doesn't include the Hillies players and coaches, who were all talented amateurs. Interestingly, professional minor league ballplayers make barely more than nothing. During the 2004 season, the average player salary in the Northeast League (former home of Jonathan Fleisig's Berkshire Black Bears) worked out to less than $40 per game. Each of the Hillies, during his short three-game series, did better than that, receiving approximately $150 in personal goods and services (cap, vintage ball, glove, drawstring duffel, logo sweatshirt, pre-game breakfast, and a family picnic).

The Hillies did get something, however, that few professional minor league teams ever receive: live national TV coverage.

Geographical Breakdown of Investors

	#	% of #	$	% of $
Pittsfield	16	19.05%	$28,056.05	2.29%
Berkshires	23	27.38%	$427,982.29	34.93%
2nd home	28	33.33%	$473,382.08	38.63%
MA	5	5.95%	$40,298.69	3.29%
NY	8	9.52%	$208,124.88	16.99%
CT	3	3.57%	$32,136.93	2.62%
NJ	1	1.19%	$15,303.30	1.25%
	84	100.00%	$1,225,284.22	100.00%

Pittsfield: Investors who reside or have a principal business in Pittsfield
Berkshires: Investors whose principal residence is in the Berkshires but not in Pittsfield
2nd home: Investors who have a vacation home in the Berkshires
MA: Investors residing in Massachusetts, but not in the Berkshires
NY: Investors residing in New York
CT: Investors residing in Connecticut
NJ: One investor who resides in New Jersey

INDEX

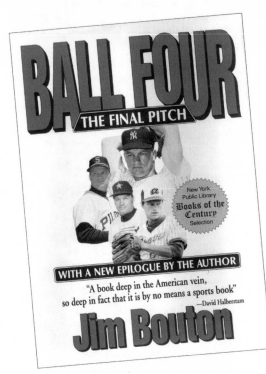